SOVEREIGN OF THE SEAS

THE SEVENTEENTH-CENTURY WARSHIP

JAMES SEPHTON

AMBERLEY

To: Those who go down to the sea in ships and follow their trade on great waters

Psalm 107, line 23

First published 2011

Amberley Publishing
Cirencester Road, Chalford,
Stroud, Gloucestershire GL6 8PE

www.amberleybooks.com

Copyright © James Sephton 2011

The right of James Sephton to be identified as the Author
of this work has been asserted in accordance with the
Copyrights, Designs and Patents Act 1988.

All rights reserved. No part of this book may be reprinted
or reproduced or utilised in any form or by any electronic,
mechanical or other means, now known or hereafter invented,
including photocopying and recording, or in any information
storage or retrieval system, without the permission in writing
from the Publishers.

British Library Cataloguing in Publication Data.
A catalogue record for this book is available from the British Library.

ISBN 978-1-4456-0168-7

Typesetting and Origination by Amberley Publishing.
Printed in Great Britain.

Contents

	List of Appendices	5
	List of Illustrations	7
	Acknowledgements	13
	Preface	14
	Introduction	15
1	Phineas Pett's Early Career	17
2	A Great Ship is Born	27
3	Some Original Drawings, Paintings and Models	45
4	Her Size Calculated in Tonnage	71
5	A Description of her Decorative Carving	85
6	The Nature and Disposition of her Armament	98
7	Her Masting and Rigging	118
8	The English Civil War 1642–49	139
9	The First Anglo-Dutch War 1652–54	143
10	The Second Anglo-Dutch War 1665–67	152
11	The Third Anglo-Dutch War 1672–74	164
12	The War of the English Succession 1689–97	176
	Appendices	187
	Bibliography	245
	Index	252

List of Appendices

1. The Shipbuilding Family of Pett
2. Vessels Built or Rebuilt by Phineas Pett
3. Vessels Built for Charles I
4. Vessels Built for Parliament
5. Main Dimensions of the *Prince Royal* (1632)
6. Main Dimensions of *La Couronne* (1635)
7. Proposed Dimensions of the *Sovereign of the Seas* (1635)
8. Main Dimensions of the *Sovereign of the Seas* (1637)
9. The Charge in Materials and Workmanship in Building and Launching the *Sovereign of the Seas* (9 January 1638)
10. An Abstract of First Rates from a List (1651)
11. An Abstract of First Rates from Dering's List (1660)
12. An Abstract of First Rates from Deane's List (1670)
13. An Abstract from Deane's List of the *Sovereign of the Seas* (1670)
14. An Abstract of First Rates from Teonge's List (1675–79)
15. An Abstract of First Rates from Martin's List (1685)
16. An Abstract of First and Second Rates from Pepys' List (1686)
17. An Abstract of First Rates from a List (1688)
18. An Abstract of First Rates from Thomas' List (1689)
19. Cross Sectional Areas for the Immersed Hull of the *Sovereign of the Seas*
20. Height between Decks of the *Sovereign of the Seas* from the Draughts
21. Main Dimensions of the *Sovereign of the Seas* from the Table on the Draughts
22. Main Dimensions of the *Sovereign of the Seas* from the Draughts
23. Principal Guns of the Sixteenth Century
24. Principal Guns of the Seventeenth Century
25. Dimensions of English Culverins
26. Bore of Piece, Diameter of Round Shot and Windage
27. The Gun Founding Family of Browne
28. Original Armament of the *Sovereign of the Seas* from the Record of Production of John Browne and Thomas Pitt
29. Original Armament of the *Sovereign of the Seas* (1637)
30. Gunners' Stores of the *Sovereign of the Seas* for 1654–55
31. Analysis of Armament of First Rates from a List (1664)

32. Armament of the *Sovereign of the Seas* from the Ordnance Establishments
33. Analysis of Armament of First Rates from Teonge's List (1675–79)
34. Principal Guns on the Establishment of 1677
35. An Abstract of First Rates from James' List on the Establishment of 1677
36. Analysis of Armament of First Rates from a List (1687–88)
37. Armament of the *Sovereign of the Seas* from the Survey of 1696
38. Ground Tackle of the *Sovereign of the Seas*
39. Weight of Stores and Equipment of the *Sovereign of the Seas* (1637)
40. Dimensions of Boats of the *Sovereign of the Seas*
41. Mast and Spar Dimensions of the *Sovereign of the Seas*
42. Standing Rigging of the *Sovereign of the Seas* (1640)
43. Standing Rigging of a First Rate from Hayward's List (1660)
44. Running Rigging of a First Rate from Hayward's List (1660)
45. Tackles of a First Rate from Hayward's List (1660)
46. Sails of the *Sovereign of the Seas*

List of Illustrations

LIST OF PLATES

1. D. Mytens' portrait of King Charles I. (*National Maritime Museum*)
2. J. de Critz's portrait of Phineas Pett (1637) (London painting). (*Henri P. Richard, Maroubra, Australia*)
3. J. de Critz's portrait of Phineas Pett (1637) (Sydney painting). (*The Boucher/Thevenin family*)
4. The arms granted to Peter Pett in 1583, from the portrait of Phineas Pett (Sydney painting) (1637). (*The Boucher/Thevenin family*)
5. J. de Critz's portrait of Phineas Pett (1613). (*National Portrait Gallery*)
6. D. Mytens' portrait of Charles Edward Howard, First Earl of Nottingham. (*National Maritime Museum*)
7. J. de Critz's portrait of King James I (*circa* 1610). (*National Maritime Museum*)
8. A. Willaerts' painting *The Embarkation of Prince Frederick V, the Elector Palatine and his new bride, the Princess Elizabeth, on board the* Prince Royal *at Margate on 25 April 1613 for Flushing* (1622). Port bow view. (*National Maritime Museum*)
9. H. C. Vroom's painting *The Arrival of the Elector Palatine and his bride at Flushing in May 1613 aboard the* Prince Royal (1613). Starboard elevation. (*Franz Hals Museum, Haarlem*)
10. H. C. Vroom's painting *The Arrival of the Elector Palatine and his bride at Flushing in May 1613 aboard the* Prince Royal (1613). Detail of the starboard beak. (*Franz Hals Museum, Haarlem*)
11. H. C. Vroom's painting *The Return of the Prince of Wales from Spain, 1623* (1623?). Starboard elevation. (*National Maritime Museum*)
12. C. de Vries' painting of the *Prince Royal*. Starboard elevation. (*Chancellor Press*)
13. Sir A. van Dyck's portrait of Queen Henrietta Maria. (*National Maritime Museum*)
14. C. de Vries' painting of the *Vasa*. Port bow view. (*Chancellor Press*)
15. R. Spence's etching of Charles I and a model of the *Sovereign of the Seas* (1919). (*National Maritime Museum*)
16. Directions given by Charles I for gilding and painting the *Sovereign of the Seas* (23 March 1636). (*Public Record Office*)
17. J. Payne's engraving of the *Sovereign of the Seas* (1637). Port elevation. (*National Maritime Museum*)

18. T. Jenner's engraving of the *Sovereign of the Seas* (1653). Starboard elevation. (*National Maritime Museum*)
19. L. A. Castro's painting of the *Sovereign of the Seas* on canvas (1650–60). (*Michael Hemsley*)
20. C. de Vries' painting of the *Sovereign of the Seas*. Port bow view. (*Chancellor Press*)
21. The van de Veldes' painting *The Portrait of Peter Pett and the* Sovereign of the Seas (1660). The stern carvings. (*National Maritime Museum*)
22. The van de Veldes' painting *The Portrait of Peter Pett and the* Sovereign of the Seas (1660). (*National Maritime Museum*)
23. Unidentified painting, *The Portrait of Peter Pett and the* Sovereign of the Seas. (*National Portrait Gallery*)
24. I. Sailmaker's painting of the *Royal Prince* (1663). (*Antique Collectors' Club*)
25. I. Sailmaker's painting of the *Sovereign of the Seas* (1665). (*Antique Collectors' Club*)
26. W. van de Velde the Elder's drawing of the port elevation and quarter of the Sovereign *of the Seas* (1673 or 1675). (*Royal Museum & Art Gallery, Canterbury*)
27. W. van de Velde the Younger's unfinished drawing of the *Sovereign of the Seas* (1675). Starboard elevation. (*National Maritime Museum*)
28. Sir R. Seppings' model of the *Sovereign of the Seas* (1827). Starboard quarter. (*National Maritime Museum*)
29. H. B. Culver's model of the *Sovereign of the Seas* (1921). Starboard elevation. (*Dr A. R. Kriegstein*)
30. H. B. Culver's model of the *Sovereign of the Seas* (1921). Starboard view of prow. (*Dr A. R. Kriegstein*)
31. H. B. Culver's model of the *Sovereign of the Seas* (1921). Starboard view of waist and fore chain-wales. (*Dr A. R. Kriegstein*)
32. H. B. Culver's model of the *Sovereign of the Seas* (1921). Starboard quarter. (*Dr A. R. Kriegstein*)
33. H. B. Culver's model of the *Sovereign of the Seas* (1921). Stern carvings. (*Dr A. R. Kriegstein*)
34. C. Chaffin's model of the *Sovereign of the Seas* (1982). Starboard elevation. (*Ship Modellers' Association of Southern California, USA*)
35. Sergal's model of the *Sovereign of the Seas*. Aerial view. (*Mantua Model, Italy*)
36. Sergal's model of the *Sovereign of the Seas*. Various details. (*Mantua Model, Italy*)
37. Sergal's model of the *Sovereign of the Seas*. Various details. (*Mantua Model, Italy*)
38. Dimensions of the *Sovereign of the Seas* (13 June 1637). (*Public Record Office*)
39. W. van de Velde the Younger's painting of the *Royal Sovereign* of 1701 (1703). Starboard quarter view. (*National Maritime Museum*)
40. Jan K. D. van Beecq's painting of the *Royal Prince* of 1670 (1679). Starboard quarter view. (*National Maritime Museum*)
41. Contemporary Navy Board rigged model of the *Royal Prince* of 1670. Port bow view. (*Science Museum*)
42. Small bronze gun, inscribed 'JOHN BROWNE MADE THIS PEECE 1638' (Weight 0–1–21). (*Royal Armouries Museum, Leeds*)
43. Bronze demi-culverin drake of the *Sovereign of the Seas*, inscribed 'JOHN BROWNE MADE THIS PEECE ANO 1638'. Muzzle end. (*Royal Artillery Historical Trust, Woolwich*)
44. Bronze demi-culverin drake of the *Sovereign of the Seas*, inscribed 'JOHN BROWNE MADE THIS PEECE ANO 1638'. Cascable end. (*Royal Artillery Historical Trust, Woolwich*)
45. Bronze demi-culverin drake of the *Sovereign of the Seas* (1638). Detail of inscription on first reinforce. (*Chatham Historic Dockyard Trust*)

List of Illustrations 9

46. Bronze demi-culverin drake of the *Sovereign of the Seas* (1638). Detail of cypher on second reinforce. (*Chatham Historic Dockyard Trust*)
47. Scratched drawing of a spritsail topmast vessel around 1660 at Upnor Castle. (*English Heritage, author's photograph 4 May 2002*)
48. Scratched drawing of a spritsail topmast vessel around 1660 at Upnor Castle. Caption. (*English Heritage, author's photograph 4 May 2002*)
49. Sir A. van Dyck's portrait of Oliver Cromwell. (*National Maritime Museum*)
50. Sir P. Lely's portrait of George Monck, First Duke of Albemarle. (*National Maritime Museum*)
51. Sir G. Kneller's portrait of Samuel Pepys (1689). (*National Maritime Museum*)
52. W. van de Velde the Younger's painting of The Battle of Solebay 28 May 1672 (1687). (*National Maritime Museum*)
53. W. van de Velde the Younger's painting of The Burning of the Royal James at the Battle of Solebay 28 May 1672 (1680). (*National Maritime Museum*)
54. N. de Largilliere's portrait of King James II. (*National Maritime Museum*)

ILLUSTRATIONS

1. G. G. & J. Robinson's etching of the *Prince Royal* of 1610 (1800). (*G. G. & J. Robinson, London*)
2. Henry Hondius' print of *La Couronne* of 1635 (1626). (*The Mariner's Museum, Newport, Virginia, USA*)
3. Model of *La Couronne* of 1635. (*Musée Naval, Paris, France*)
4. Rigged model of the *Vasa*. Port bow view. (*Science Museum*)
5. The remains of the first *Sovereign* of 1487–8 as found at Woolwich in 1912. South end. (*Corporation of London*)
6. Admiralty pattern anchor, around 1790. (*National Maritime Museum, author's photograph 9 October 2001*)
7. Admiralty pattern anchor, around 1750. (*National Maritime Museum, author's photograph 9 October 2001*)
8. Title page of 1637 edition of T. Heywood's book, *A True Description of His Majesties Royall Ship ...*, John Okes (1637). (*British Library*)
9. Title page of 1638 edition of T. Heywood's book, *A true Description of His Majesties royall and ...*, John Okes (1638). (*British Library*)
10. W. Marshall's drawing of the *Sovereign of the Seas* (1637). Port quarter view. (*British Library*)
11. Site of the Old Single Dock, constructed in 1623, Chatham Royal Dockyard. Top of stone. (*Chatham Historic Dockyard Trust, author's photograph 27 September 2001*)
12. Site of the Old Single Dock, constructed in 1623, Chatham Royal Dockyard. Front of stone. (*Chatham Historic Dockyard Trust, author's photograph 27 September 2001*)
13. W. van de Velde the Elder's broadside drawing of the *Sovereign of the Seas* (1660). Port bow view. (*The late Junius S. Morgan, Junior, New York, USA*)
14. W. van de Velde the Elder's unfinished drawing of the *Sovereign of the Seas* (1661). Starboard quarter view. (*National Maritime Museum*)
15. T. Cadell & W. Davies' etching of the *Sovereign of the Seas* (1802). After J. Payne. (*T. Cadell & W. Davies, London*)
16. W. van de Velde the Elder's drawing of a Man-of-War (*Royal Sovereign*) (around 1685). Port bow view. (*National Maritime Museum*)
17. W. van de Velde the Elder's graphite drawing of a royal visit to Chatham 1685, for the launch of the *Royal Sovereign* (1684–85). (*National Maritime Museum*)

18. Reconstruction draught of the *Sovereign of the Seas* (around 1800). Starboard sheer plan, half breadth plan, body plan and stern elevation. (*National Maritime Museum*)
19. W. Edye's draught of the *Sovereign of the Seas* (1817). Starboard sheer plan, half breadth plan, body plan and stern elevation. (*Science Museum*)
20. Contemporary Navy Board rigged model of the *St Michael* of 1669. Starboard bow view. (*National Maritime Museum*)
21. Sir R. Seppings' draught of the *Sovereign of the Seas* (1827). Starboard sheer plan, half breadth plan, body plan and stern elevation. (*National Maritime Museum*)
22. Sir R. Seppings' model of the *Sovereign of the Seas* (1827). Starboard elevation. (*National Maritime Museum*)
23. Sir R. Seppings' model of the *Sovereign of the Seas* (1827). Port bow view. (*National Maritime Museum*)
24. J. Fincham's draught of the *Sovereign of the Seas* (1851). Starboard sheer plan. (*Scolar Press, London*)
25. J. Fincham's draught of the *Sovereign of the Seas* (1851). Body plan, half breadth plan and stern elevation. (*Scolar Press, London*)
26. H. B. Culver's model of the *Sovereign of the Seas* (1921). Starboard view of waist and main chain-wales. (*Dr A. R. Kriegstein*)
27. H. B. Culver's model of the *Sovereign of the Seas* (1921). Port quarter view. (*Halton & Co. Ltd., London*)
28. H. B. Culver's model of the *Sovereign of the Seas* (1921). Port bow view. (*The Studio Ltd., London*)
29. H. B. Culver's model of the *Sovereign of the Seas* (1921). Stern carvings. (*Society for Nautical Research*)
30. V. H. Green's unfinished model of the *Sovereign of the Seas* (1934). (*Hurst & Blackett Ltd., London*)
31. G. Robinson's draught of the *Sovereign of the Seas* (1936). Port sheer plan, body plan and sail plan. (*Peter Davies Ltd., & Lovat Dickson Ltd., London*)
32. A. C. Jackson's model of the *Sovereign of the Seas* (1943). Starboard quarter view. (*Science Museum*)
33. J. Dupray's model of the *Sovereign of the Seas* (1982). Ship's bell. (*Ship Modellers' Association of Southern California, USA*)
34. J. Dupray's model of the *Sovereign of the Seas* (1982). Starboard bow. (*Ship Modellers' Association of Southern California, USA*)
35. Pugh's model of the *Sovereign of the Seas* (1982). Stern galleries. (*Ship Modellers' Guild of San Diego, USA*)
36. T. Pugh's model of the *Sovereign of the Seas* (1982). Great lantern. (*Ship Modellers' Guild of San Diego, USA*)
37. Sergal's model of the *Sovereign of the Seas*. Various details. (*Mantua Model, Italy*)
38. Contemporary Navy Board model of the *Royal Sovereign* of 1701. Starboard elevation. (*Central Naval Museum, Saint Petersburg, Russia*)
39. Contemporary Navy Board model of the *Royal Sovereign* of 1701. Detail of stern. (*Central Naval Museum, Saint Petersburg, Russia*)
40. Contemporary Navy Board model of the *Royal Sovereign* of 1701. Detail of bow. (*Central Naval Museum, Saint Petersburg, Russia*)
41. Contemporary Navy Board model of the *Royal Sovereign* of 1701. Detail of taffrail. (*Central Naval Museum, Saint Petersburg, Russia*)
42. W. van de Velde the Elder's broadside drawing of the *Sovereign of the Seas* (1660). Port bow view. (*The late Junius S. Morgan, Junior, New York, USA, indexed by the author*)
43. The van de Veldes' painting *The Portrait of Peter Pett and the* Sovereign of the Seas (1660). The stern carvings. (*National Maritime Museum, indexed by the author*)

List of Illustrations

44. Small bronze gun, inscribed 'JOHN BROWNE MADE THIS PEECE 1638'. (*Royal Armouries Museum, Leeds*)
45. Small bronze gun and carriage, inscribed 'JOHN BROWNE MADE THIS PEECE 1638'. (*Royal Armouries Museum, Leeds*)
46. R. Roth's drawing of the bronze demi-culverin drake of the *Sovereign of the Seas* inscribed 'JOHN BROWNE MADE THIS PEECE ANO 1638' (1638). (*Jean Boudriot Publications*)
47. Millhall Wharf, Aylesford. (*Author's photograph 28 April 2002*)
48. Millhall Wharf, Aylesford. Detail of early masonry. (*Author's photograph 28 April 2002*)
49. H. B. Culver's model of the *Sovereign of the Seas* (1921). Detail of port bow view. (*Halton, Truscott Smith Ltd., London*)
50. Bronze demi-culverin drake of the *Sovereign of the Seas*, inscribed 'JOHN BROWNE MADE THIS PEECE ANO 1638'. (*Royal Artillery Historical Trust, Woolwich, author's photograph 7 August 2001*)
51. Bronze demi-culverin drake of the *Sovereign of the Seas* (1638). Detail of inscription on base ring. (*Chatham Historic Dockyard Trust*)
52. Bronze four-pounder gun, inscribed 'JOHN BROWNE MADE THIS PEECE 1638'. (*Royal Armouries Museum, Leeds*)
53. Bronze four-pounder gun, inscribed 'JOHN BROWNE MADE THIS PEECE 1638'. Detail of cypher. (*Royal Armouries Museum, Leeds*)
54. T. James' profile of a carriage for a gun for the *Sovereign of the Seas* (1638). (*Jean Boudriot Publications*)
55. Replica powder kegs at Upnor Castle. (*English Heritage, author's photograph 4 April 2002*)
56. Iron demi-culverin of the *Sovereign of the Seas* (1691). Muzzle end (No. 6953). (*Chatham Historic Dockyard Trust, author's photograph May 2002*)
57. Iron demi-culverin of the *Sovereign of the Seas* (1691). Cascable end (No. 6953). (*Chatham Historic Dockyard Trust, author's photograph May 2002*)
58. J. Dupray's model of the *Sovereign of the Seas* (1982). Gammonings. (*Ship Modellers' Association of Southern California, USA*)
59. J. Dupray's model of the *Sovereign of the Seas* (1982). Main top. (*Ship Modellers' Association of Southern California, USA*)
60. J. Dupray's model of the *Sovereign of the Seas* (1982). Sprit topmast top. (*Ship Modellers' Association of Southern California, USA*)
61. J. Dupray's model of the *Sovereign of the Seas* (1982). Sprit topmast top, detail. (*Ship Modellers' Association of Southern California, USA*)
62. B. Landstrom's sail plan of the *Sovereign of the Seas* (1961). (*Olof Landstrom, Stockholm, Sweden*)
63. Sir A. Deane's mast and rigging plans of a First Rate of 1670. Starboard sheer plan and sail plan. (*Pepysian Library, Magdalene College, Cambridge*)
64. Rigged model of the *Naseby* of 1655. Port elevation. Reconstruction model by Robert Spence around 1943. (*National Maritime Museum*)
65. Pieter van den [sic] Velde's painting *The Burning of the English Fleet off Chatham 20 June 1667*. (*Rijksmuseum, Amsterdam*)
66. Dutch map showing the chain below Gillingham Fort (around 1669). (*HM Stationery Office*)
67. Map of the River Medway showing Cockham Wood Fort and Gillingham Fort (around 1685). (*HM Stationery Office*)
68. Plan of Cockham Wood Fort (around 1685). (*HM Stationery Office*)
69. Plan of Gillingham Fort (around 1685). (*HM Stationery Office*)
70. J. Almond's map of Chatham Dockyard (1685). Detail of mooring sites. (*HM Stationery Office*)

71. Contemporary Navy Board model of the *St George* of 1708–14. Port elevation. (*Merseyside Maritime Museum, Ron Davies Photography*)
72. G. Collin's map of the estuary of the River Medway (1688). (*HM Stationery Office*)
73. Plan of HM Dockyard at Chatham (1698). (*HM Stationery Office*)
74. J. Grewl's map of the River Medway from Howness to Upnor Castle (1715). (*HM Stationery Office*)

Acknowledgements

The author wishes to thank the organisations and individuals for permission to reproduce individual photographs and drawings.

The compilation of this work could not have been accomplished without the support and assistance from a number of sources, which are recorded in grateful appreciation. The late George Fran Whybrow of Blundellsands, Lancashire (for introducing me to this project, on the basis that such an in depth study has never been published before); Picton Reference Library, Liverpool; the late Edward W. Paget-Tomlinson (1932–2003), former Curator of the Shipping Gallery in the City of Liverpool Public Museums; William H. Eisele, Ship Models, Cincinnati, USA; the Historic Dockyard Chatham, Kent, including John Chambers, Alyson Marsh & Brian Sanders; Chatham Dockyard Historical Society, including the late Harold R. Bennett, Peter Dawson, Phil Poulter & H. E. Penny CEng, CMarEng, MRINA, FIMarEST; Kent Archaeological Society's Library, Maidstone, Kent; Public Record Office; British Library; National Maritime Museum, including Colin Starkey, Picture Library; David Hepper of the World Ship Society; Ronald White, Pudding Lane, Maidstone (processing author's photographs;) KPS Business Solutions Ltd, 1 Viewpoint, Boxley Road, Penenden Heath, Maidstone, Kent (processing author's drawings); and Christopher H. Wilson of Tonbridge, Kent (verification of Latin translations.)

The author is indebted to the following for background research on the Pett family; Raymon Martin of Sidcup, Kent; Ronald & Janette Petts of Holtspur, Bucks; Dr David Petts of Wickford, Essex; Mr Leslie L. Pett of Park Langley, Beckenham, Kent; and Jeannette Smith of Auckland, New Zealand.

The author is indebted to eMag Solutions Ltd, Waterside Centre, North Street, Lewes, East Sussex; and Vogon International Ltd., Talisman Business Centre, Talisman Road, Bicester, Oxfordshire for their individual and invaluable work recovering data from diskettes produced on an old BBC 128K Master Series Microcomputer to Microsoft Word system.

The author also appreciates the invaluable comments from a number of authorities who have read the typescript: Richard G. Endsor; Peter J. Le Fevre MA, PhD; the late Harold R. Bennett & H. E. Penny CEng, CMarEng, MRINA, FIMarEST, both of Chatham Dockyard Historical Society; and my wife, Gillian Margaret Sephton.

Preface

The *Sovereign of the Seas* was a warship built at Woolwich by Phineas Pett in 1635–7, upon the Royal Command of His Majesty King Charles I of England. Phineas has left us his written autobiography. J. Payne produced an engraving, which became the subject of many imitations. Some relevant documents survive in the Public Record Office. Van de Velde the Elder and the Younger have left us a number of contemporary drawings. Several models have appeared in relatively modern times.

It became a challenge for me to try to reconstruct an image of how she must have appeared during the seventeenth century. I immersed myself in the depths of historical research with the prime intention of providing sufficient data on which to base the construction of a model of this vessel. However, I became so involved with the research that the prime objective was abandoned.

It is embarrassing to admit that this work commenced some forty years ago. Due to a succession of events dominating the course of my career, it was not until early retirement that I was able to gather my research material together. I purchased a computer, and for the first time, I was able to assemble the data like a gigantic jigsaw puzzle.

In attempting standardisation, the dates are recorded according to the Julian calendar, with the New Year commencing on 1 January. The definition of nautical terms is based on W. H. Smyth, *Sailor's Word-Book – An Alphabetical Digest of Nautical Terms*, first publication 1867, re-published 1996.

This present study, therefore, is presented as a record for posterity. Doubtless, future naval historians will make their own evaluation, derive subsequent benefits and perhaps make their own model.

James H. Sephton
July 2010
Aylesford
Kent

Introduction

Kentish dockyards and Kentish craftsmen have made significant contributions in the production of many fine warships for the King's Navy. There was an age, long past, when ships relied upon the inconstant winds of heaven blowing upon a complex network of ropes, spars and canvas. These stout vessels of oak, elm and pine were held together by wooden dowels and iron bolts. Such vessels were armed with finely wrought ordnance, which fired cast-iron shot. With such pieces, hitting a target above a range of 400 yards was virtually impossible. Yet manned by patriots trained in discipline in the finest English heritage, these vessels fought for, and attained, mastery over other maritime nations in the relentless bid for the conquest of the sea.

One singular vessel was the grandest venture hitherto created. She was remarkable for her size, beauty and heavy armament. Even her name, the *Sovereign of the Seas,* suggested pride and pomp. She was designed by Phineas Pett, one of a distinguished descent of Kentish shipwrights. His son, Peter, was the Master Builder.

The levy of Ship Money tax, which contributed towards Charles I's downfall, provided for the considerable building costs. The actual charge for building and launching was £33,846 5*s* 4*d*. Her keel was laid on 21 December 1635 at Woolwich Royal Dockyard. She was safely launched on 14 October 1637.

In size, she surpassed all contemporaries. She was not large in comparison to vessels of later periods, but it must be considered that she was timber built, on a timber frame. Some 2,500 great oaks were felled in the forests of Durham. On being carefully marked out to determine their respective positions in the hull, they were shipped to Woolwich. Here, each timber was built into her frame by hand. All her timbers were massive; each member for the curved sections was cut from grown wood. The breast-hooks and futtocks were large because this was a man-of-war and was required to withstand mauling in battle.

Her graceful contours were a delight to any ship-modeller. The long, low, curved beak and high, square forecastle were reminiscent of the galleys. The pronounced tumble-home of her bulwarks was accentuated by the high stepped quarterdeck and poop. Her embellishments were superb. No vessel before her age carried so much adornment, and very few after attempted to compete in this respect. Any ship-modeller would be enthralled by the exquisite design of the lavish friezes along her bulwarks, with the heavy mass of scrolled panels and the great beautifully carved quarter galleries and stern balconies. She was the epitome of the wood carvers' skill.

She was the first warship in the English navy to carry a heavy armament of more than 100 guns. They were arranged on three full tiers, with a small battery on the forecastle and another on the quarterdeck. All the guns were exquisitely cast from the finest brass procurable. They were muzzle loaders, mounted on wooden carriages.

By comparison with later vessels her rig appeared clumsy and unwieldy. But, in her time, she was in an advanced stage of development. Prince Rupert told Charles II that she was the finest ship he had, 'riding or sailing.' She marked a stage in the evolutionary process of development towards the fully rigged ship of the nineteenth century. With the close of the four-masted period, her rig was arranged on three masts. The foremast and mainmast were each fitted with four square sails: the course, the topsail, the topgallant and the royal. Her royal sails were an outstanding feature. Such sails did not come into general use in the English navy until around 150 years later. Her mizen mast was rigged with a topsail and a topgallant above the fore and aft lateen sail. On the foremost end of her bowsprit she carried a small spritsail topmast. Here was rigged a spritsail topsail. Under her bowsprit was a spritsail course. In height, from the main mast-head to the bottom of the keel, she measured 212 feet.

Throughout her sixty years of service life, she was generally well maintained, except for the period 1679–84. Apart from a number of repairs she was rebuilt in 1651, 1659–60 and again in 1684–5.

Against the Dutch at the Battle of the Kentish Knock on 28 September 1652, she fought for the first time in the role for which she was created. She served in several engagements against the Dutch, and distinguished herself with pride.

She was sent to Chatham Royal Dockyard for repairs and alterations. On 27 January 1696 the temporary keeper negligently left a candle alight in his cabin. She caught fire, and before help could be summoned from nearby yards, the great ship was completely gutted.

It was not until the *Victory* was built that a greater warship emerged to claim fame and overshadow the memory of the *Sovereign of the Seas* in our island's maritime history. Built to the designs of Sir Thomas Slade, the *Victory's* keel was laid down on 23 July 1759 in the 'Old Single Dock', now known as No. 2 Dry Dock, at Chatham. Built under the supervision of the Master Shipwright, Edward Allen, she was launched on 7 May 1765 as a first rate of 104 guns.

The *Sovereign* has always been a puzzle for subsequent historians.

CHAPTER 1

Phineas Pett's Early Career

On 26 June 1634, His Majesty King Charles I was rowed serenely along the placid waters of the River Thames to Woolwich Royal Dockyard. He inspected the frame of the *Leopard,* a new vessel being built for the navy. Finding a suitable opportunity away from the company of his retinue, the introvert, thirty-four-year old Charles I shyly drew aside the arrogant, sixty-four-year-old visiting Master Shipwright, Phineas Pett. Amid the sweet fragrance of freshly hewn timber in the uncompleted hold, the royal personage struggled with his speech impediment. He commissioned the vain Phineas to build a great new ship with the words, 'You have made many requests to me: and now I will make it my request to you – to build this ship.'

When Charles I inherited the crown in 1625, his fleet consisted of four first rates, fourteen second rates, eight third rates and four fourth rates. Of these, one first rate, seven second rates, six third rates and the four fourth rates were all relatively new vessels. In 1625 there were twelve men-of-war and seventy-three hired merchantmen.

By 1627, the fleet had expanded to fourteen warships; three were small pinnaces, and eighty-two were merchantmen.

In 1628 Robert Bertie, First Earl of Lindsey, was Admiral of the second fleet despatched to La Rochelle. He commanded twenty-nine warships and thirty-one merchantmen. Of his warships, ten were pinnaces of fifty tons burden or less. Another ten were of the newly created class known as 'Lions' Whelps' (Appendix 3). These vessels were built in private yards by contract at £3 5s per ton. Two differed slightly in size from the remainder. Whelps had oars for rowing in addition to sails. The length of the mainmast was three times the beam. The original armament consisted of fourteen pieces: two to four iron culverin drakes, four iron demi-culverins, four to six iron demi-culverin drakes and two to four brass sakers. These pieces were all cast by John Browne. The Whelps were unsuccessful. The tubby hull and heavy armament impaired their sailing qualities (Appendix 3).

The *Charles* and *Henrietta Maria* were built for Charles I in 1632. Two ships, the *James* and *Unicorn*, were built in 1633. In 1634 the *Swallow* and the *Leopard* were built (Appendix 3).

No ships were built in 1635, and only three were added in 1636. With his fleet composed of vessels so small as to be inadequate to the demands of the time, Charles I therefore desired to build a great new ship. It was destined to be the largest, not only of his reign, but of several reigns to come. During her early lifetime she was called a great ship. Under Admiral Robert Blake (1599–1657), she was termed a ship-of-the-line, or line-of-battleship. Later, she was called a three-decker, or first rate.

Phineas Pett, the man whom Charles I selected for this task, was a man equal to the demand of the moment. The Pett family had been associated with the Kentish dockyards for nearly a century. Peter Pett, the son of John, made a will in March 1554 bequeathing to his son, also named Peter, a dwelling house and private shipbuilding yard at Harwich. Peter entered the royal service some time before 1544. In 1544, he was sent with James Baker, the father of Matthew Baker, by Henry VIII to survey the ships at Portsmouth Royal Dockyard. Peter was granted a pension or fee of 12d daily in 1558. He was granted his patent of Master Shipwright in 1582.

He was twice married. By his first wife he was blessed with four sons and one daughter. By his second wife, Elizabeth, daughter of George Thornton, the marriage was blessed with three sons and six daughters (Appendix 1).

In 1583, Peter Pett, then Master Shipwright at Deptford, obtained a grant of arms from Herald's College: *'Or, on a fesse gules between 3 roundels sable, a lion passant of the field.'* The crest was: *'Out of a ducal coronet, or, a demi-pelican wings expanded argent.'*

He died in 1589, bequeathing to his family a house and almshouses at Harwich, a house at Deptford, land at Frating near Colchester, the lease of a house at Chatham, and a shipbuilding yard at Wapping. Peter was succeeded as Master Shipwright at Deptford by his second and eldest surviving son, Joseph.

Phineas was born of Peter Pett and Elizabeth Thornton at his father's house in Deptford Strand on 1 November 1570. He was the fifth in direct descent, with innumerable close relatives, all of whom practised the art and craft of shipwright. As an infant, Phineas played with his brothers and sisters among the shavings at Deptford shipyard while his father built the *Revenge*, a 471/589-ton ship of forty guns launched in 1577, and the *Rainbow*, a 384/480-ton galleon of thirty-six guns launched in 1586.

In 1579 Phineas was sent to the King's School at Rochester. He boarded with a Mr Webb for a year then resided for three years at his father's lodging in the Queen's House, also called Hill House, Chatham. This was built before 1567. It occupied a position at the top of what was once known as Chatham Hill. The house stood across the road on the east side of St Mary's church, and fifty yards to the north. The rear of the property looked north-west across the old dockyard and over the river.

The site was formerly the freehold property of the Dean and Chapter of Rochester, who owned other land in the vicinity. During almost the entire period of Hill House's existence, the Navy Board, and subsequently the Admiralty, had no more than a lease-hold interest. By 1579 it was rented by the navy from Adam Keeler, who leased it from the Dean and Chapter of Rochester. It was the local 'Admiralty House' from 1567 to 1720. In the early days of Chatham Royal Dockyard, this house was used by the Master Shipwrights. One of the earliest senior officers who lodged here was Peter Pett. It was furnished for use by the Lord High Admiral and naval officers. It was subsequently used as lodgings for senior naval officers and other important officers visiting the dockyard.

North and south gables supported a steeply sloping roof. This two-storey building had seven first-storey windows and three dormer windows, which overlooked the road that later became Dock Road.

In about 1583, Phineas attended a private school at Greenwich managed by Mr Adams. Phineas entered Emmanuel College, Cambridge, in 1586. He was nearly eighteen years of age when, in 1588, the English defeated the might of the Spanish Armada. Phineas may not have understood the revolution in tactics of naval warfare, but he must have realised the advantages of manoeuvrable ships equipped with light ordnance.

On about 6 September 1589, Phineas' father Peter died. The lease of Hill House was bequeathed to his family. Phineas was left destitute. His brothers, who had remained at the family trade, received him coldly. His widowed mother married the Revd Thomas Nunn, Minister of Weston in Suffolk, taking with her to their new home two daughters, one of whom was Abigail. In 1599 Abigail was murdered by Revd T. Nunn.

In 1590, Phineas was apprenticed to Richard Chapman, the Master Shipwright of Deptford. Phineas was allowed 48s 6d annually for tools and apparel. After serving at Chatham Royal Dockyard, Chapman died in April 1592. Phineas was discharged from the yard. He shipped as a carpenter's mate aboard Edward Graham's privateer the *Edward and Constance*, working the Levant and Barbary coasts. Few prizes were taken, such that when he returned to London in 1594, he was financially no better.

He received from Emmanuel College, Cambridge, the degree of Bachelor of Arts in 1592, and Master of Arts in 1595. In August 1595, he was employed at Woolwich Royal Dockyard by his brother Joseph as an ordinary workman in rebuilding the *Triumph*, a 741/928-ton ship of fifty-eight guns, built in 1561.

The term 'rebuild' was used indiscriminately during the seventeenth century to describe any work from a general overhaul to a complete alteration of structure and design.

Subsequently, he worked under Matthew Baker on the *Repulse*, a ship of 622/777 tons and fifty guns launched at Deptford in 1596. Baker had been Master Shipwright at Woolwich, Deptford and Chatham since 1572. Phineas studied mathematics and draughtsmanship. Over the winter of 1595–6 he received tuition and encouragement from Baker, from whom Phineas gained his greatest enlightenment.

On 15 May 1598 at Stepney church, Phineas married Ann, daughter of Richard Nicholls of Hendon. The marriage was blessed with eight sons and three daughters (Appendix 1).

Phineas did not rely solely on his professional skill to gain advancement. When in employment with his brother Joseph, he spent his earnings on fashionable clothes and preferred the company of men of senior rank to himself. Through Gilbert Wood, Phineas obtained an introduction to Charles Edward Howard, Second Baron Howard of Effingham, First Earl of Nottingham (1536–1624), Lord High Admiral. He was a courtier and a diplomat. Doubtless the ageing Nottingham had known Phineas' father, Peter, and was acquainted with his brothers. It was perhaps due to such heritage that favours were conferred upon Phineas. At Christmas 1598, Nottingham employed him to finish a purveyance of plank and timber in Norfolk and Suffolk for the royal household. This occupied Phineas during the whole of 1599.

The only relaxation with which Phineas indulged himself during his ambitious career was the fashioning of model ships. He made a small model in December 1599, rigged it and presented it to Sir John Trevor. This is probably the earliest instance of an English warship model. No trace has survived.

In June 1600, Nottingham appointed Phineas to succeed John Holding as keeper of the timber yard and other provisions at Chatham Royal Dockyard. This post carried an annual fee of £6 per annum, plus 18d daily, plus an allowance of 16d daily for one servant or apprentice. In October 1600, Phineas obtained a twenty-one-year lease to the Manor House at Chatham. This was vacated by Mr Barker, Lord of the Manor, who had moved to Boley Hill, Rochester. In 1620 the rent for the Manor House and grounds was £2 per annum. By 1653 it had inflated to £20 per annum.

In 1602, at about the time of the birth of his first son, John, Phineas was appointed Assistant Master Shipwright at Chatham Royal Dockyard, succeeding Thomas Bodman. Phineas may have lived at Hill House. Phineas' first undertaking was the repair of a pinnace named the *Moon*. This was achieved on the site of the later gun wharf. In 1603–4, he rebuilt the *Answer* (Appendix 2).

By March 1604 Phineas had built the *Disdain* at Chatham Royal Dockyard for Henry Frederick, Prince of Wales (1596–1612). This pinnace or yacht was a miniature warship fashioned after the *Ark Royal*, built in 1587 by Richard Chapman. The *Disdain* embodied features of a man-of-war, arranged such that the young Prince could practice the art of being a sea captain in the comparative safety of the upper reaches of the Thames. She was handsomely decorated with elaborate gilded carvings by Thomas Rocke, and painted by John de Crete, the King's Sergeant Painter.

Between May and November 1604, Phineas privately built the merchant vessel *Resistance* in David Duck's private yard at Gillingham. In January 1605 Phineas sold one third of her equity to Sir Robert Mansell and another third to Sir John Trevor, retaining the remaining third for himself. The building of this vessel was controversial and created considerable enmity towards Phineas.

The first Charter of the Shipwrights Company granted by King James I in 1605, relating to the art or mystery of Shipwrights of England, named Matthew Baker as the first Master of the Company of Shipwrights.

Phineas' eldest brother Joseph, Master Shipwright at Deptford, died on 15 November 1605. Phineas succeeded him. Phineas was given the annuity which had been with the Petts since 1544. His first major task was the rebuilding at Woolwich Royal Dockyard of the *Victory* and the *Ark Royal* of 1587. Accordingly, in April 1607, he moved his household to Woolwich. When launched on 29 September 1608, the *Ark Royal* was re-named *Ann Royal* (Appendix 2).

On 25 April 1607 he was elected Master of the Company of Shipwrights. He held this office again in 1612 and 1616. Phineas built another ship model. It was garnished with carving and painted, and set under a canopy curtained with crimson taffeta. He presented it to Lord Howard of Nottingham on 10 November 1607. Nottingham arranged for James I to admire it. He was delighted, and commissioned Phineas to build a warship after the fashion of the model. This is the first known instance of a ship model being used to project a new design. This model has long since disappeared.

During the reign of James I, the administration of the navy collapsed into a state of lassitude, corruption and decay. The navy was a melancholic remnant which seldom sailed beyond home waters. Most of its energy was dissipated chasing pirates. The most active were the Barbary pirates from North Africa. They made sorties to the coasts of England and Ireland to carry away the inhabitants into service. During a period of seven years in the middle of James I's reign, no less than 466 English vessels with their crews were known to have defected. Embezzlement within the King's service was common. Men of exalted rank used their position to provide themselves with a private income. Promotion could only be obtained by bribery. Positions of trust were sold and bought lucratively and indiscriminately. Naval supplies were frequently purchased privately and resold to the navy at greatly inflated prices. Large sums of money were allocated to obsolete vessels. The proceeds were divided among officials. Ships' crews were falsely exaggerated in Navy Lists. The money extorted for seamen's pay was divided among the officers. Ships were provisioned by dishonest contractors who charged extortionate prices for poor quality merchandise. Seamen were dressed in rags because their meagre pay could not purchase clothes sold at high profit margins by the ships' pursers. The dockyards were in a piteous condition. Most of the wood held in stock was rotten. The cordage was decayed. Dockyard material was deliberately sold off for private gain.

In order to survive amid the conniving treachery of his contemporaries, Phineas himself was obliged to resort to dubious practices in order to augment his meagre income. In 1608 a Commission of Inquiry, headed by the Earl of Northampton and the Earl of Nottingham, was initiated to investigate abuses in the navy. The tenure of office was two years. Phineas' activities were examined closely. The timber and cordage used in building the *Resistance* of 1604 was alleged to have come from the King's stores. Provisions, ordnance and ammunition used to equip her were allegedly sold to Spain for £300.

The Commissioners of Inquiry themselves came under the cloak of suspicion. They were landsmen who seldom understood the web of intrigue in the navy. There was no evidence submitted to the Inquiry. Nothing was proven. The weight of detailed allegations against Phineas suggested that he was as guilty as anyone else in the King's service. He was not removed from office. This was partly due to his irreplaceable skills as a shipwright and partly due to his being endowed with royal favour. At this period the demand for serviceable King's ships was greater than that for aesthetic morality. The Inquiry resulted in a severe royal reprimand for Phineas.

James I desired a warship after the fashion of Phineas' model. It was to be the greatest challenge of his career so far. The keel of this new ship was laid on blocks in the dry dock at Woolwich on 20 October 1608. By the following summer, the frame was taking shape.

Following the tradition in the *Mary Rose*, the curved frames were made in several pieces. She was double framed, where each piece supported, or gave scarf to, the butts of the adjacent pieces. The original estimate was for 775 loads of timber, whereas 1,627 loads were actually used, with an increase in cost of £5,908. She had two layers of carvel planking. Whether at the rabbet or on the frames, the butt ends of the planks were secured with iron bolts. This was a feature hitherto unknown.

In structure and design, she corresponded closely with the great ships of the later days of Elizabeth I. There was the familiar marked sheer, the same square tuck at the stern, the same broken lower gun deck and the same highly decorated and very impracticable long, low projecting beak, reminiscent of the early galleys. She demonstrated some 200 tons burden increase in size, though differing little in proportion.

Her carving and gilding gave an appearance totally different from that of Elizabethan ships. She was of considerable beauty, being most exquisitely embellished. She was the first ship to have carved work instead of painted panels. This type of decoration remained in vogue for 200 years.

All the carved timber was the work of Sebastian Vicars, at a charge of £441 0s 4d. The painting and gilding was the work of Robert Peake and Paul Isackson, at a charge of £868 6s 8d. Some £164 of this bill was spent on the lodging cabin, and £5 10s spent on the captain's cabin. The total Bill of Costs was nearly £20,000.

The figurehead was mounted on the beakhead and not on the bow. The figurehead took the form of St George slaying the dragon. Above the fore rail was depicted a large knight's helmet surmounted by a crown. The head, its rails, the cat-head and the serpent for the tacks were gilded. She was green above the waist rail with gold relief and white, especially for the impressive Prince of Wales' feathers on the side of the closed quarter gallery. The rails of the waist and half-deck were red.

An entry port was fitted on the port side. A doorway was cut through the thickness of the bulwark. Here was fitted an ornate door. It provided the means for senior naval officers to arrive and depart with dignity. It was applied solely to first rates. This is the earliest recorded example. The entry port is not depicted on G. G. & J. Robinson's etching of the *Prince Royal*. This is not surprising, since with an etching the final print may have been reversed.

She had three galleries at the stern and quarters. The middle gallery was closed all the way around, but the forward end of the lower gallery was left open. Lanterns were placed at the after end of the quarter galleries. She had light spar decks above the forecastle, waist, half-deck and the quarter deck. She carried two complete tiers of guns, with a part tier on her half-deck. The fourteen round ports for the half-deck were carved in the shape of lions' heads.

Her original armament consisted of two cannon petro (twenty-four-pounders), six demi-cannon (thirty-pounders), twelve culverins (seventeen-pounders), eighteen demi-culverins (nine-pounders), thirteen sakers (five-pounders) and four port pieces. Thus, a total of fifty-five guns weighing 83 ton 8 cwt 21 lb. The weight of her broadside was around 330 lb.

Her rigging followed a similar pattern to that of her contemporaries, with four masts, including a small bonaventure mizen mast, and a spritsail topmast carrying a spritsail and a spritsail topsail. She carried topgallant sails at the foremast and mainmast, with square topsails and a lateen sail on both mizen and bonaventure.

Her long boat was 52 feet 4 inches long. It was too large to be hoisted inboard, and was towed behind, to the detriment of the mother ship's sailing qualities.

1. G. G. & J. Robinson's etching of the *Prince Royal* of 1610 (1800). (*G. G. & J. Robinson, London*)

When the time arrived for launching, twelve Master Carpenters were selected from Chatham Royal Dockyard to hammer in wedges under the blocks supporting the keel. This was done in unison to a chant. Thus the keel was raised slightly, and the effects of inertia were reduced.

By 18 September 1610 she was ready for launching.

On Monday 24 September, assisted by his brother Simonson and many friends, Phineas flooded the dock and opened the dock gates, ready to float her out. Tackles were rove, with their falls bent to small windlasses. Screw jacks were used to push her bows off from the dock wall. A strong south-west wind prevented a full tide, and she moved only slightly.

With his retinue of courtiers, James I returned to Greenwich, disappointed at the failure of the launching. Henry, Prince of Wales, chose to remain awhile to discuss the problem with Phineas before leaving. The Prince returned at midnight. At the next high tide, at 2 a.m., the tackles were tightened, and the vessel slipped away from the dock without straining tackles or windlass. She came afloat into the channel. In the strictest sense of the word, she was floated out rather than launched.

Prince Henry christened the vessel. He drank wine from a gold chalice, called out the name of the vessel and sprinkled wine on the poop deck to the four cardinal points. Traditionally, this chalice would have been cast into the sea to prevent its use for toasting ill intent. On this occasion, however, the Prince presented it to Phineas. No trace of this chalice remains. The vessel was named *Prince Royal*, after Prince Henry who had taken a lively interest in her building. She was the first English vessel so named.

Most of the workmen employed on her works were paid off at Deptford on 20 October 1610. The foremast was raised on 1 November. By 6 December she was rigged and ready to go downriver to Chatham. On 9 December she was brought down to her mooring within the chain at Upnor Castle by the pilot, old John a Vale – he was also called Boatswain Vale. He may have been an Englishman. Captain King was her Master, John Reynolds was the Master Gunner and Lawrence Spencer was her Boatswain. Her crew numbered 500 men.

She was sheltered from prevailing winds and inclement weather by surrounding hills. The slow ebb and flow of the River Medway created no hazard from cables breaking or anchors dragging. The mud bottom, free from rocks, was safe for her hull.

The appearance of the *Prince Royal* has been established from several contemporary representations:

1) The earliest draught in the collections of the National Maritime Museum (No. A193) is a mutilated pencil drawing, from the waist forward, of the sheer of a three-decked warship. The suggested lines of the counter, quarter galleries, and after drifts are reminiscent of

the *Prince Royal*. W. Salisbury suggested that this may have been an early shipwright's draught of the *Prince Royal*.
2) John de Critz's (1552–1642) portrait of Phineas Pett (1613) in the National Portrait Gallery (Plate 5) has an inset in the upper right corner. Here is depicted the stern of the vessel as she appeared in the dock during building.
3) An etching of the *Prince Royal*, published by G. G. & J. Robinson, Paternoster Row, London on 22 October 1800, appears in J. Charnock, *An History of Marine Architecture*, Vol. 2, 1801, between pages 198–9 (Illustration 1) This etching probably represents her after a rebuilding, after her beakhead was altered.
4) An oil on panel painting by Adam Willaerts (1577–1664), dated 1622, *The Embarkation of Prince Frederick V, the Elector Palatine and his new bride, the Princess Elizabeth, daughter of James I, on board the* Prince Royal *at Margate on 25 April 1613 for Flushing*. This painting (30.5 inches x 54 inches) passed from Windsor Castle to the National Maritime Museum. The *Prince Royal* fires a salute on the point of departure. The miniature vessel *Disdain*, the *Red Lion* and the *Repulse* accompanies them (Plate 8).
5) An oil painting by Hendrick Cornelius Vroom (1566–1640), *The Arrival of the Elector Palatine and his bride at Flushing in May 1613 aboard the* Prince Royal. This painting is in the Franz Hals Museum at Haarlem, Netherlands (Plate 9). The *Prince Royal* displays the flag of the Lord High-Admiral, the Earl of Nottingham. In the left foreground is the *Red Lion*. On the right is the *Repulse*.
6) An oil painting of the same scene by C. V. Wieringen (1580–1633), also at Haarlem.
7) An oil painting by H. C. Vroom, *The Return of the Prince of Wales and the Duke of Buckingham from Spain, 5 October 1623*. This painting was in the possession of the Earl of Sandwich at Hinchingbrooke, until it passed into the collections at the National Maritime Museum. The flagship *Prince Royal* leads the *St Andrew*, *Defiance* and *Swiftsure* (Plate 11). The vessels are in their winter rig, where the topgallant masts, yards and sails have been removed.
8) An oil painting of the same subject by H. C. Vroom at Hampton Court.

Phineas' unorthodox techniques initiated allegations regarding his incompetency from jealous members of his profession. Objections to experimental features of his design were unfounded. He was indicted with employing poor materials. The evidence against him was irrefutable. Some of the timber was green and unseasoned, and some was too old and in a state of decay. Allegations as to her excessive cost were not substantiated. Phineas was acquitted by James I.

Phineas brought his family back to Chatham. He fitted out an early Arctic expedition, consisting of the *Resolution* and the *Discovery*. They sailed in April 1612 and returned after November.

On 30 June 1612, the keel of a pinnace for the *Prince Royal* was laid in the old dock at Chatham Royal Dockyard. This was probably the dry dock below St Mary's church, which had been used to build a pinnace, the *Sun* of 1586. The new pinnace was fitted with a roomy cabin, and named the *Phoenix*. She was launched on 27 February 1613 (Appendix 2).

On 25 September 1612, a new royal charter for incorporating the shipwrights of England ordained Phineas as the first Master.

Phineas moved his family back to Woolwich. He rebuilt the *Defiance* in 1613–4. This was a three-masted galleon of 441 ton, built at Deptford in 1590 by Peter and Joseph Pett. A model to scale of 1:72 is in the collections of the Merseyside Maritime Museum, Albert Dock, Liverpool (Accession No. 44.33).

On the death of Matthew Baker in August 1613, Phineas completed the rebuilding of the *Merhonour*. Both vessels were launched together from the same dry dock on 6 March 1615.

Phineas and his family removed to Chatham in 1616, when he bought land in the Brook, Chatham, from Christopher Collier for £35.

In 1616 Phineas built a pinnace of 40 feet keel length for Lord Zouch, Warden of the Cinque Ports. The same year he built the *Destiny*. She was re-named *Convertine*. In 1620 he built the 300-ton *Mercury* and the 200-ton *Spy* for the Merchant Committee of the Algiers Expedition (Appendices 2 & 3).

A second Commission of Inquiry in 1618 had a pronounced effect upon Phineas. He was delegated to improving and enlarging Chatham Royal Dockyard between 1618 and 1620 under the supervision of Captain Norreys, an Assistant Commissioner acting as Surveyor, residing at Chatham. There is a memorial to him in the chancel wall of St Margaret's church at Rainham. All new ship construction was done under contract by William Burrell at Deptford. He was a newly appointed Commissioner, and chief shipbuilder of the East India Company until 1626.

The extra income from contract work was consequently lost to Phineas. James I was sympathetic towards him and his outstanding debts. James I gave him a blank patent for a knight baronet, which he managed to sell for £700. He sold another later for £200.

Phineas was joint Master Shipwright at Chatham Royal Dockyard with Edward Stevens in 1621. Phineas repaired the *Prince Royal* in fourteen days at Chatham in 1623. She was strengthened in suspect places. The galley was removed from the hold to the forecastle. Her masts were repaired. The lateen sails on mizen and bonaventure were replaced by square sails. The charge for these repairs was under £1,000.

In 1625, Phineas brought the fifteen-year-old Henrietta Maria from Boulogne to Dover in the *Prince Royal* to marry Charles I. He gave Phineas a valuable gold chain.

Two carvel-built vessels, the *Henrietta* and the *Maria*, were built by Phineas at Chatham Royal Dockyard in 1626–27 (Appendices 2 & 3).

In 1627 he went to Portsmouth Royal Dockyard to equip the fleet for the unfortunate expedition to La Rochelle. Following the custom of Peter, his father, Phineas sought another wife after the death of Anne in 1627. He married Susan Yardley of Eaglesfield (Appendix 1).

The Commissioners, who had been appointed in 1618, were removed from office in 1628. The administration of the Navy reverted to the Principal Officers of the Navy. In 1629, the government of the Navy was strengthened by the appointment of two experienced technical assistants to the Principal Officers, viz. William Burrell and Phineas. Phineas was nominated by Charles I.

In March 1629 the Brethren of Trinity House recommended Peter Pett for appointment as Master Shipwright at Chatham Royal Dockyard. Peter was Phineas' son, born at Deptford on 6 August 1610. He followed closely in his father's footsteps, assisting him in the royal dockyards at Deptford and Woolwich. Peter married Katharine, daughter of Thomas Cole of Woodbridge. The marriage was blessed with four sons and three daughters (Appendix 1).

Phineas built the *Henrietta Maria* at Deptford in 1632. With the assistance of his son, he built the *Charles* at Woolwich in 1632. She was launched on 30 January 1633 (Appendices 2 & 3).

William Burrell died in 1630. In December 1630, Phineas became resident Commissioner of the Navy at Chatham Royal Dockyard. His salary was £200 per annum, with 8*d* daily for his clerk, Charles Bowles, and £6 for petty cash. Additionally, he received his £40 per annum by writ of privy seal granted in 1614. In 1631 he moved his family into his new lodging at New Dock, formerly occupied by Capt. Downing, acting Surveyor of the Navy until 1628 and resident at Chatham Royal Dockyard. Phineas sold the lease of the Manor House to Richard Isackson, the ship painter.

In 1633, Phineas was involved in the 'Brown Paper' scandal with Palmer, the Comptroller; Fleming, the Clerk of the Acts; Terne, Clerk of the Survey at Chatham; and Lawrence, the Storekeeper at Chatham. All were involved in the sale of old cordage, used in the manufacture of brown paper. Allegedly, they had sold cordage without the consent of the other Principal Officers. They were removed from their posts in February 1634. Phineas repaid around £86, his share of the alleged proceeds. On 1 March Charles I granted him a full pardon. The others were similarly restored to their posts.

A contemporary portrait of Phineas is a painting on wood, measuring 39.25 inches by 46.75 inches, attributed to John de Critz (c. 1555–1641/2) (Plate 5). The painting was commenced in the autumn of 1612 when Phineas was working with Thomas Rock at Rochester. This was formerly the property of Earl Hardwicke. It was sold at Christie's on 27 June 1924, Lot 33, and purchased by the National Portrait Gallery (Cat. No. 2035). It went on public exhibition at the National Maritime Museum. For some time it was displayed in the Gallery containing 'Discovery and Sea Power (1450–1700)', until its removal at the inauguration of the new National Maritime Museum in March 1999. In the top left hand corner appear the family arms, granted to Peter in 1583.

From the inscription between these two insets, we realise that Phineas is depicted in his forty-third year. He is immaculately dressed in white doublet with slashed sleeves, and russet coloured breeches accentuated by embroidery. A sword belt edged with gold, and garnished with silver filigree, supports a sword and dagger, both richly wrought. His left hand grasps a rule, while a pen and a partly rolled up document are in his right hand. His bearded face has a fine intellectual quality, with a thin nose, sensitive nostrils, keen, piercing eyes and a high forehead. A white silk cap, garnished with pearls and multifarious motifs, almost conceals his short brown hair. This portrait suggests a self-opinionated, obstinate and conceited individual.

An oil painting, Lot 126, was sold at Sotheby's London Sale No. L11184 on 29 November 2001. This painting was erroneously described as the portrait of Sir William Monson (1569–1643). It measures 33.86 inches by 30.51 inches (Plate 2). A cypher on the front, '67/37', suggests that the sitter was sixty-seven years of age when the painting was made in 1637. Located to the right of the sitter's head is an incomplete cypher, 'Pett. of.' Stencilled on the back are the words, 'The Property of A. R. Harman' and 'PL679'. Formerly in the collections of the National Maritime Museum, it was sold through public auction in November 1995.

Conclusive evidence that the sitter is a member of the Pett family is provided by the discovery of a duplicate seventeenth-century painting held by descendants of the Pett family in Sydney, Australia. This 'Sydney' painting, measuring 31.1 inches by 24.8 inches, (Plate 3) bears the arms of the Pett family. The style of costume worn by the sitter is similar in each painting, and suggests the dating of around 1630.

A later cypher in oil on the front of the 'Sydney' painting claims that the sitter is Peter Pett of Deptford, who died in 1589. The sitter holds a naval commander's baton. Peter Pett of Deptford was not entitled to this as he did not hold a military post. Phineas, however, promoted by Charles I to be a Principal Officer of the Navy in 1631, was entitled to this piece of regalia.

The fact that the *Sovereign of the Seas* was launched on 12 October 1637, with royal patronage, explains why this portrait appeared at this time.

The sixty-seven-year old sitter for the 'London' and 'Sydney' portraits is recognisable as the forty-three-year old sitter in the National Portrait Gallery portrait by John de Critz. Their facial features bear a striking resemblance. We are left with the suggestion that all three paintings may have been the work of the same artist.

Thus, having selected the right man for the task of building this great new ship, Charles I required the means to finance it. This he found through the medium of the Ship Money tax. Doubtless Charles I had good intentions with respect to the Navy. Since he dismissed Parliament in 1629 and began eleven years of personal rule, he was faced with considerable financial deficits. In 1634 he resorted to a traditional fiscal device.

It had become customary in times of war to levy a tax called Ship Money on coastal counties. The ports were required to provide a vessel of determined size, suitably provisioned, equipped and manned, or alternatively to furnish money in lieu. In October 1634, although war had ended some years previously, Charles I levied Ship Money on coastal counties on the plea of the prevalence of piracy. A writ was issued to coastal towns on both banks of the Thames between Westminster and Gravesend, exclusive of the City, to provide a vessel of 500 tons burden with ordnance, stores and tackle and a crew of 250 men for a period of six months. The estimate was for £4,085. The Kentish portion of the assessment was £340 18s 5d.

The Cinque Ports of Kent and Sussex, together with Rochester, Maidstone and the Isles of Thanet and Sheppey, were required to provide a vessel of 800 tons, armed and provisioned with a crew of 260 men for six months service. Though reluctantly, the tax was paid and secured £104,000.

Charles I was emboldened to try the unprecedented measure of extending this tax to inland counties, in addition to that levied for coastal counties. The royal argument was that all should contribute to the safety of all. Charles I ignored the constitutional obligation to secure democratic consent. Writs were issued in August 1635 demanding a payment of exactly twice that raised the previous year.

Kent and the Cinque Ports were required to provide one vessel of 800 ton with a crew of 320 men at a cost of £8,000. By the autumn of 1636, only £20,544 remained outstanding of the £208,000 demanded.

A third writ, dated October 1636, was of similar character to the second writ. It became evident to the nation that Ship Money was to be a permanent and general form of taxation. The tide of bitter resistance by the people started to turn against Charles I. As Sheriff of Kent in 1636–7, Sir George Sandes took no action against those who refused to pay.

In 1638, the Kent assessment was lighter, at £2,750. The writ of 1639 was originally similar to its predecessors. The County of Kent was called upon for £8,000 instead of the expected £6,400. Subsequently, the assessments were greatly reduced, but two-thirds of the tax was never collected. The writs of 1638 and 1639 fell far short of their target. Ship Money was declared illegal by an Act of the Long Parliament in 1641.

Ship Money was the means by which this ambitious venture was financed. The dream of Charles I was manifested by the man selected for the task, viz. Phineas Pett. It was his skill which created the new great ship.

CHAPTER 2

A Great Ship is Born

Charles I called upon Phineas Pett to build this great new ship. She was conceived as an image of power and built as a deterrent against the threat of foreign aggression. This was a political necessity for Charles I's foreign policy.

But it posed a difficult problem for Phineas to solve, in arranging a fixed weight of heavy ordnance along a gun deck less than 170 feet long. This weight was a product of the length of keel, plus the rake of stem, plus the rake of sternpost (Appendix 7). The initial estimate was for ninety guns, but Charles I altered this, not only in the number of guns, but also in their type. By the stroke of his pen, he amended the manuscript list from ninety to 102 guns, without increasing the tonnage proportionately.

This great new ship was the first English vessel to carry a heavy armament of more than 100 pieces. The size of each gunport and the interval between adjacent ports was proportional to the size of the piece upon its carriage. The length of the gun deck was proportional to the size and number of each piece. Therefore, an increase in the armament necessitated an increase in the principal dimensions and tonnage. Therefore, in order to accommodate so many heavy pieces in a vessel of such relatively small dimensions, Phineas resorted to placing them on three full tiers, with a forecastle and a half-deck above. Phineas had devised this arrangement when he built the *Prince Royal* of 1610. In developing this trend, the great new ship became the first warship in the English navy to have three continuous decks without falls.

She was not the first three-decked ship that history records. A Spanish three-decker, the *Philip*, was engaged with the *Revenge*, commanded by Sir Richard Grenville, off the Azores in 1591. The *Philip* carried three tiers of ordnance, with eleven pieces in each tier.

According to the English convention for a three-decker, the main gun deck, being the broadest and strongest both in construction and armament, was termed the lower gun deck. Beneath this deck, below waterline level, was the orlop deck for stores and equipment above the hold. The orlop may not have extended the entire length of the vessel. Above the lower gun deck was the middle gun deck, and above that the upper gun deck. The raised deck above the upper gun deck forward was the forecastle. The fore end of the forecastle terminated with the beakhead bulkhead. Following the trend of the *Prince Royal*, there was a small deck in the prow, forward of the beakhead bulkhead, slightly above the level of the middle gun deck.

The matter became more complex with the raised decks at the stern. She had three such decks. The elevation at the stern was called the half-deck, perhaps because it covered around one half of the length of the upper gun deck. The quarterdeck originally denoted the quarter of the hull between the aftermost end of the main channels and the sides of the stern, terminated by the quarter pieces. The highest and aftermost raised deck at the stern was the poop. It served as a roof to the great cabin. The interval between the forecastle and the forward end of the half-deck was the waist. Like the *Prince Royal* before her, over the forecastle, waist and half-deck was a light spar deck. This was made of long lengths of fir called raft-trees, supported by stanchions and small turned pillars. Across the top was a light grating of deal boards providing a walkway.

Apart from finding accommodation for guns, Phineas sought capacity for powder, shot and provisions. Casks of beer, water, bread or biscuit, salt beef, pork, fish, peas, butter and cheese for a crew of 815 men at sea for six months amounted to 249 tons (Appendix 39).

With these difficulties in mind, Phineas drew up the design on his drawing board. Ships' draughts of this period were conceived with no other tools than a straight edge and a pair of compasses. There was nothing revolutionary concerning Phineas' concept. Some features were considered experimental by his contemporaries. This was a stage in the evolution of warship design from the Elizabethan galleon to the future ship-of-the-line.

Phineas must have had some practical experience of the trades required in the practice of shipwrights, viz. sawyers, carpenters/joiners, caulkers, blacksmiths, plumbers, sculptors/carvers, painters, coopers, hatchellers, spinners and rope-makers, sail-makers and riggers.

He gave her a high forecastle and poop, with a low waist amidships and a pronounced tumblehome. This was the inward curve of her sides above the level of the waterline. The tumblehome provided a reduction in the breadth of the upper gun deck in comparison to that of the lower gun deck. This reduced top weight. This, in turn, lowered the centre of gravity of the vessel and improved stability. It is doubtful if the seventeenth-century shipwrights understood the mathematics of stability. He gave her a projecting beak similar to that of the *Prince Royal* of 1610. From a short fore-foot, the stem rose in a long, graceful curve forwards and upwards, terminating in the stem head forward of the forecastle. Such a stem facilitated the hull turning in response to her steering.

One of those who advised on the design in April 1634 was the Storekeeper at Deptford Royal Dockyard named John Wells, a member of a wealthy established Kentish family which had been involved with shipbuilding on the River Thames for more than 160 years. William Wells was assistant to the Court of the Worshipful Company of Shipwrights on 16 February 1659. Thomas Wells was assistant to the Court from 16 February 1659 and a warden of the Company from 1667 to 1669.

When the designs were completed, Phineas appointed his son Peter to the task of building a model. This was of exquisite and admirable workmanship, curiously painted in azure and gold. The hull was built on the usual single foot-hook system. It was open and unplanked, revealing every main timber. Phineas and his son were both accomplished model builders. Their energies in this field were fully justified. It explained features of the construction not readily realised from the draughts and plans.

On 29 October 1634, this model was conveyed to Hampton Court and there placed in the Privy Gallery. The moment when Charles I first saw this model is immortalised in an allegorical etching by Robert Spence in 1919 (Plate 15). The model was removed to Whitehall; no trace has survived.

In size and dimensions this great new ship was smaller than Henry V's unfinished ship of 1419, but she was larger than anything built for some years. She remained the largest vessel in the English navy until the *Victory*, of 2,162 tons burden, was launched in 1765 at Chatham Royal Dockyard.

Richelieu was inspired to build a large new warship for the French. The intention was to impress Charles I of England. In 1629 this warship was laid down in the shipyard at La Roche-Bernard. She was built by Charles Morieux of Dieppe, aided by Admiral Claude de

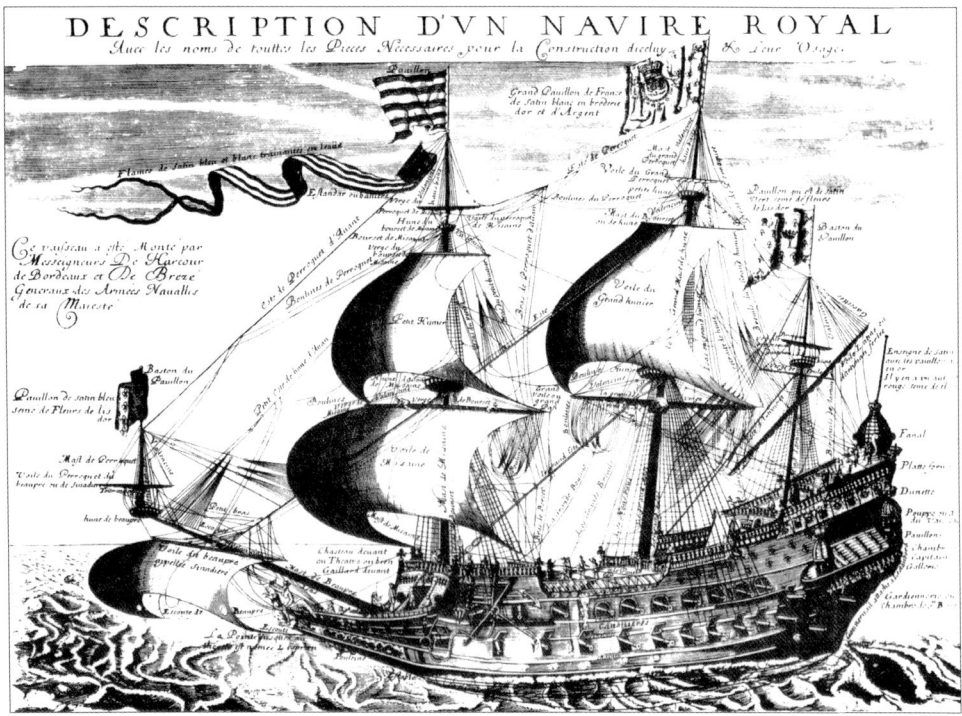

2. Henry Hondius' print of *La Couronne* of 1635 (1626). (*The Mariner's Museum, Newport, Virginia, USA*)

Rasilly. Named *La Couronne,* she was launched on the River Seudre at the beginning of 1635 (Illustrations 2 & 3).

She was double planked, secured with iron at intervals of nine inches. There were six pairs of wales along the length of her hull. She had two flush decks and a half-deck. The cable for the main anchor was 24 inches circumference and weighed 6 ton 7 cwt 3 qr. The main anchor weighed 2 ton 16 cwt 3 qr. There were no catheads. The anchor was released from the forward end of the foremast chain wales.

She was some 957 tons burden and 1,276 gross tonnage (Appendix 6). The hull was a natural wood colour. Above the rail of the waist she was painted blue. The inside of the gun port covers was red. The bulwarks were, like the trimming of the tops, a uniform red. The figurehead was an effigy of Hercules in combat with the mythical Hydra. At the stern was a closed gallery. Two gilded angels supported the royal diadem. Below was the inscription '*Succidit Oceanum*'.

Above the taffrail were three lanterns of gilded copper with square panes of mica. The central lantern was the largest. It was 12 feet high and 24 feet circumference. Each was illuminated by 12 lbs of candles.

Her sides were pierced for sixty-eight pieces of ordnance. Some seventy-two pieces of Spanish bronze ordnance were mounted aboard her. The additional four pieces may have been small swivel pieces mounted on the gunwale.

The chain wales of the foremast were above the gun ports of the lower gun deck. The chain wales of the mainmast were above the lower gun deck, but followed the sheer of the wales. The mizen mast chain wales were at the level of the poop deck. The foremast shrouds were ten aside, totalling 360 fathoms. The mainmast shrouds were twelve aside, totalling 400 fathoms. Under full sail, she carried around 4,820 square yards of canvas.

3. Model of *La Couronne* of 1635. (*Musée Naval, Paris, France*)

Most of her timbers were rotten, because she was not built on a slipway under cover from the elements. After an uneventful life, she was scrapped in 1641.

She was renowned for the model made in 1887 under the direction of Admiral Paris. This model was contained in the Musée Naval, Palais du Louvre, Paris. This model was sent for display at the Watercraft Exposition at Liège in 1940. It was not returned after its repatriation at Boulogne-sur-Mer.

Charles I of England was not merely impressed at the audacity of the French. He was determined to possess a show of superlative strength. It was not mere vanity which prompted him to build such a great ship.

The Masters of Trinity House were appalled by Charles I's intention of building such a great ship. Trinity House was a highly respected body, founded by Henry VIII for the training of pilots and ships' officers. They were hostile to Phineas and protested against such a project. T. Best, Walter Coke and R. Salmon, Masters of Trinity House, submitted in August 1634 a formal petition to Charles I alleging insurmountable difficulties which would ensue with such a large vessel. They protested that there was no English port which could safely harbour the excessive draught of twenty-two feet. Because of the necessity for preposterously heavy anchors and cables, no crew could manage her ground tackle by hand.

The Masters objected to the design for three tiers of ordnance. The lowest tier of ordnance must be so low, they argued, that in strong winds the gunports must be closed to prevent sinking.

The Masters quoted the case of the *Mary Rose*, which capsized and sank in the Solent on 19 July 1545 with the loss of around 640 lives. She was over manned and top heavy. There may have been a language problem. Caught by a sudden gust of wind, she heeled over to starboard. The lower gun deck port covers were open. There was a mere 16 inches freeboard between the lower gunport sills and the water.

Similarly, the Swedish sixty-four gun two-decker great ship *Vasa* of 1627 capsized and sank on her maiden voyage in the Stockholm archipelago on 10 August 1628. Caught by a sudden gust of wind while under full sail with her lower gun deck ports open, she listed alarmingly to leeward and shipped water. Her freeboard of around 42–54 inches was insufficient to stem the rush of flood waters.

Her main dimensions may be listed:

		Feet	Inches
Length of keel		128	0
Length of keel, harping rule	khr	134	3
Beam extreme, excluding wales, dead-flat	bx	38	4
Draught in water		15	5
Displacement tonnage		1,300–1,400 tons	

Her beam of 38 feet 4 inches was too narrow for such a long keel length of 128 feet. This resulted in problems with stability, creating a danger to herself and her crew.

Alternatively, argued the Masters, if there were 5 feet of freeboard, then proportionally, the upper gun deck would be too high and cause unwieldiness. The Masters proposed that two vessels, each of 5–600 tons and forty guns, could be built for the same cost as one

4. Rigged model of the *Vasa*. Port bow view. (*Science Museum*)

great ship. Charles I ignored the Masters. He didn't even write an acknowledgement. He needed a great ship, and such it had to be.

On 14 May 1635 Phineas Pett took leave of His Majesty at Greenwich, and hastened to provide and prepare the frame, timber, plank and treenails. At Chatham Royal Dockyard he instructed his son Peter to prepare the moulds and templates, and to select artisans to sail in a hired Newcastle vessel. Phineas boarded this laden vessel at Queenborough in Sheppey and sailed north. With commissions and instructions he attended upon Bishop Morton of Durham.

By the summer of 1635, a company of shipwrights and sawyers had started work in the woods. Phineas and his son Peter supervised the choice of the most suitable timber. This was selected from His Majesty's parklands at Chapwell Woods on the River Derwent, six miles south-west of Newcastle, and Brancepeth Park on the River Wear, four miles south-west of Durham.

The great new ship was built of timber which had been stripped of bark while growing in the spring and not felled until the second autumn. This technique was known as girdling. It was a means of producing a hard timber before felling, with a shorter period required for seasoning. After forty-seven years, all the old timber in her was so hard as to preclude the driving in of a nail. The girdling of timber before felling was not beneficial. If the tree died, as it could do when divest of bark, then the wood itself would die and result in a poorer grade of building material.

Each timber was worked down to its ultimate size and carefully labelled to enable its correct assembly into the hull.

Futtocks and knees were chosen from compass grained timber. A straight grained timber, when cut into an arc, would split under lateral stresses and strains. Such timbers as futtocks and ribs were not bent by steaming during the early seventeenth century.

The boards for planking the skin and the decks were slash-cut from logs using a large double-handed saw over a saw pit. Examples of the type of saw pit in vogue are displayed at:

1) Weald & Downland Open Air Museum, Singleton, Chichester, Sussex.
2) 'Wooden Walls' Gallery in Chatham Historic Dockyard.

Each board so produced was worked down to the required thickness using a finely honed adze.

That summer, 2,500 great oaks were felled, lopped and hauled by oxen and horses down to the nearest rivers and loaded on squat-shaped coastal vessels to take them south. Timber from Chapwell Woods was shipped at Newcastle. Timber from Brancepeth Park was shipped at Sunderland. The cost of carriage of timber to the water was estimated at £1,190. This charge was borne by the counties of Durham, Northumberland, Cumberland, Westmorland and the North Riding of Yorkshire.

Phineas did not stay long in Durham. By 5 August 1635 he returned home to arrange for the preparation of the keel blocks. Woolwich Royal Dockyard was chosen as more suitable than Deptford Royal Dockyard because of the greater draught of water and span in the Thames. The old dock at Woolwich was made double some time before, in around 1606, lengthened in 1615 to take two of the largest vessels, and rebuilt again in 1626.

Waiting there were shipwrights and carpenters. With authority from Phineas Pett, the work force had been recruited by the Shipwright Robert Newman. He had enrolled suitable men from Captain George Weymouth on 7 December 1635.

On 21 December 1635, the keel was laid on blocks in the dry dock. This was called the old 'Mother dock', which was the largest dock at Woolwich. Most of her frame had by then been safely landed. By Christmas, the last of the laden coasters from Durham had arrived. The keel's length of 127 feet was formed of several lengths of straight elm scarfed together.

Elm was favoured on account of its resistance to rotting in sea water. Lengthening the keel in this manner marked a significant advance in the design of building large vessels. The scarfing involved a tapered joint, of varying complexity, between timbers of similar section at the joint. The keel tapered towards the fore and after ends.

The upper longitudinal edges of the elm keel were worked to form a notch or rebate. This formed the rabbet, which extended along the elevation of the keel from the forefoot to the sternpost.

The stem was worked to the required size and shape while lying flat on the ground. The stem was composed of several lengths of compass-grained timber scarfed together to produce the rounded form of the cutwater. The breadth and depth of the stem increased with respect to height above the keel. This constituted a solid bed for the beak. The stem was raised up and scarfed into the forward end of the keel.

A massive, straight vertical timber was mortised into the after end of the keel to form the sternpost. It was backed by a parallel inner post. Temporary jigs or scaffolding prevented the stem and sternposts from toppling. The overhangs of the stem and sternposts above the keel were termed the 'rakes'. The rake at the stem was greater than the rake of the stern. The sum of both rakes usually equalled the beam extreme of the vessel (Appendix 7).

Between the forward end of the keel and the rise of the stem, and similarly at the after end of the keel and the sternpost, was an interval between the timbers and the planking. This interval, being too limited for framing, was filled with wood. Baulks of oak were laid on top of the keel, one above the other, and secured with long iron nails. This not only consolidated the joint between the horizontal and the vertical members but helped the vessel to grip the water. The rabbet along the keel was continued up either elevation of the stem and sternpost.

Each external contoured frame, as designed in the cross sectional draughts, was set out with dividers and rule full size by the shipwrights, and marked in chalk on the wooden planking of the mould-loft floor. From these chalk lines, joiners cut and trimmed light wooden battens, and nailed them to braces to form templates. The external edge of the template followed the contours of the frame.

The templates were taken from the mould-loft to the timber yard at the dock. There the frames were cut from the logs. Because of the difficulty in obtaining adequate supplies of compass-grained timber, the frames were made in several pieces, viz. floor beams, first, second, third and fourth futtocks, and top timbers. They were not butt jointed, but overlapped each other. Each frame was built up of two contiguous layers of timber, with each joint alternating. This double frame technique produced a strong and rigid hull.

Floor timbers were stepped athwart ships of the keel. They were evenly spaced along its length. The lower end of each frame, known as the futtock heel, slid between two adjacent floor timbers. The floor timbers were spaced according to the timber and room, where the rooms between the floor timbers were filled with the lower ends of the futtock heels. The futtock heels terminated about a foot from the keel. Between each futtock heel was a lateral floor timber. The width of each futtock and floor timber remained a constant 2 feet 6 inches. Thus, a solid band of timbers was created in the lower hull.

There were probably fifty-two frames along her keel. These were evenly spaced with timber and room of an estimated 2 feet 6 inches. This accounted for a length of 130 feet. Between each frame was a filling timber, with a thickness less than that of the frame itself. There were another thirteen frames in the bow and stern. The first five or six frames in the bow were turned 90° to the keel and mounted against massive breast-hooks. This formed a strong but bluff bow.

The frames were assembled while lying on level ground. Each frame was raised up into its proper station straddling the keel. The frames were temporarily trussed up with straps and the whole supported by a jig, into which the frames were fastened by wooden wedges and iron clamps.

Oak beams, constituting the keelson, were laid longitudinally and laterally over the floor timbers. They were similarly scarfed to provide the necessary length for the keelson. Long iron bolts passed through the keel, floor timbers and keelson. The bolts were countersunk into the top and bottom members. The ends of the keel bolts were protected from corrosion by wooden dowel caps.

The step to receive the mainmast straddled the keelson at a point slightly aft of the midships bend.

Joints in timber were secured by the use of treenails. These were tapered wooden pegs from 1 to 3 inches in diameter. There were several types distinguished by their length, viz. 1 foot, 1.5 feet, 2 feet, 2.5 feet and 3 feet. They were produced from the straightest timber from the top of the tree. The rough cut treenails were 'mooted' through a die to the required diameter.

The timbers to be secured were bored using a brace and auger type bit. When bored to a convenient depth, the hole was reamed out to the required diameter using an auger. The head of this tool was shaped like a spear head, with one edge sharpened for cutting. By means of a mallet or maul, each treenail was driven into a hole. The surplus ends of the treenails were trimmed by a chisel or saw.

On 16 January 1636 Charles I, with a retinue of Lords, came to Woolwich to inspect the partly completed frame and floor. He ordered Phineas and his son Peter to build two pinnaces from surplus timber. Pinnace is a generic term describing a small, armed, carvel-built vessel, propelled by oars and sails. A pinnace had two or three masts, and was schooner rigged. Such a vessel was similar to a shallop and smaller than a barge.

On 28 March Charles I returned to Woolwich, accompanied by his brother Charles Lewis, Elector Palatine (1617–80) and Prince Rupert (1618–82), First Duke of Cumberland, Earl of Holderness and Count Palatine of the Rhine, with a retinue of Lords. They stood in the windows of Phineas' lodgings to view the pinnaces launched. They were named *Greyhound* and *Roebuck* (Appendices 2 & 3).

With the ribs and frames of the great ship secured, the deck beams were applied. For the sake of dryness, the decks had a slight camber. The centre line of the deck was higher than at the bulwarks. The joint between the deck beam and the frame was buttressed by oak knees, in compass-grained timber, and some 2 or 3 feet thick. Four such knees secured each deck beam by iron bolts. These knees occurred at intervals around every 20 feet along the length of the bulwarks of each gun deck. Vertical posts between the keelson and the lower deck beams, and also between the decks, imparted further strength.

Men with adzes faired the external surface of each frame. This action pared the timber to provide an even surface ready to receive the planking. Lean frames were chocked, viz. extra timber was applied to bring them into the designed line.

The hull was carvel-planked externally, with planks placed edge to edge. The first strake or plank to be applied was the garboard or keel-strake. It was set into the rabbet, along the length of the keel. The planks below the waterline were of elm, deal or beech, 12–14 inches wide. They tapered in width towards the rabbet at the stem and the stern. To secure the ends of the planks in this rabbet, massive wooden breast-hooks and crutches, made in compass-grained oak, were applied internally.

The planking forming the ceiling was secured above the floor timbers and keelson. The ceiling was strengthened by riders, secured by iron bolts.

Treenails were applied at intervals along the length of each strake to secure it to the frames. To prevent starting, iron bolts were used to secure the ends of the planks, called butts, to the frames. The heads of the bolts were countersunk into the planks to allow for an additional thickness overall. Butts in adjoining strakes were kept as far apart as was conveniently possible.

As planking was applied, the temporary jigs were knocked away. The hull was shored upright by blocks and wedges between the bottom of the hull and the dock floor. She was triple planked, the outer planks breaking joint with those of the inner skin. The planking was not all the same thickness, but varied throughout. By inspection of Appendix 8, it can be realised that the beam moulded was 46 feet 6 inches, and the beam extreme was 48 feet. Thus, the thickness of the planked skin at the point of the midships bend was 9 inches.

One of the hazards of wooden vessels was the destruction of its timbers by the borings of shipworms, of the genus *Teredo*. This occurs in sea water. The creature does not survive where the salt content is low. The damage is not readily appreciated. The outer surface of the wood looks normal, yet the interior may be completely riddled. Between each of the three skins of planking was a generous application of paying stuff. This was composed of a mixture of pitch, tar, tallow, resin, sulphur and horse hair. The procreation of the *Teredo* and other molluscs, similar to barnacles, was inhibited to some limited extent by this treatment.

She was built with a round tuck stern. Below the level of the lower gun deck, the planking was worked continuously to the sternpost. This was achieved by curving the planking gradually around the quarter, and carrying it into the rabbet of the sternpost without breaking the sweep of the planking. This vessel was one of the first to be so designed. The feature of a round tuck prevailed in English first rates after around 1620. It served to distinguish them from their French contemporaries, in which almost the whole of the stern above the waterline was of square transom form. The *Vasa*, similarly, had a square tuck stern.

We have the suggestion, therefore, that the round tuck may have been the result of some new technical innovation in the manner in which timber was artificially heated for bending.

On the level of the waterline and above, the strakes were in oak. As the height of the sides increased, so the width of the strakes decreased.

To produce the delightful sheer so characteristic of seventeenth-century ships, exterior wales were secured to the external skin by the use of treenails and iron bolts. Each wale was around 16 inches by 10 inches in cross section, and therefore too heavy for bending. Each wale was produced in short lengths, butted together and shaped where necessary. To keep her wales clear of the gunports, she developed the practice begun at least twenty years earlier, and carried her wales in pairs. One pair was at the waterline, a second pair was between the lower and middle gun decks, and a single wale was placed between the middle and upper gun decks. There was a sixth and a seventh wale above.

The interval between successive frames decreased proportionately as the beam decreased at the stem and stern. The interval between successive gunports, measured outside the planking of the bulwark, was constant along the length. To avoid concentrating weight in any vertical plane, the gunport above was staggered proportionately. This produced a regular pattern of gunports along the bulwarks. Thus, the weight of ordnance was distributed evenly along the length of the vessel. Unfortunately, it was necessary occasionally to cut away part of a top timber of the frame to provide for a gunport.

The flush-sided construction of the carvel hull facilitated the provision of square gunports piercing the hull. This permitted water tight seals or gunport covers, also with flush exteriors, which could be closed when the vessel was not in action. Each gunport was equivalent in size according to the deck.

The vessel's fittings were applied as she stood on her keel blocks. The hatch coamings, companion ways, bulwarks, rails and bulkheads were assembled before the vessel was launched. Hatch coamings were abaft the foremast. The ornate ship's belfry was abaft the coamings. At the break of the forecastle deck were hand rails and a steep companion ladder at either bulwark. On the upper gun deck in the waist were two hatch coamings. A steep companion ladder rendered access from the waist to the half-deck. In the middle of the half-deck was a small round house. At the break of the half-deck was an ornately carved hand rail. Hatch coamings abaft the mizen mast suggested access below. On three sides of these coamings, except for the starboard, was a hand rail. A companion ladder on the starboard elevation gave access to the quarterdeck and the poop. The flagstaff and great lantern were at the after end of the poop.

The King's cabin and the great cabin were richly painted and gilded. The great cabin had access into the quarter galleries. She had two gunrooms, one under the other. According to a treatise written around 1620, the length of the gunroom was 0.474:1 of the keel length, viz. around 60 feet. The middle deck cabin of the *Prince* of 1610 and the *Sovereign* was merely an unadorned upper gunroom, with neither stern windows nor access to the quarter galleries.

Doorways were fitted in the centre of the bulkheads at the after end of the forecastle deck, the forward end of the quarterdeck and the forward end of the poop. The bulkhead between the waist and the half-deck contained two doorways. Two small doorways were below the beakhead bulkhead.

The main windlass was a heavy member mounted on the lower gun deck, forward of the mainmast. The windlass was turned manually by eight long wooden bars which slotted into each side. Movement against the line of purchase was prevented by iron pawls acting like a ratchet. The windlass was used to provide purchase in weighing the anchors, hoisting the yards and topmasts, and other items of considerable weight. Mounted in the waist was a smaller windlass.

On the forecastle deck were two pairs of bitts, each fore and aft of the foremast. About the mainmast were two sets of main bitts, similar to those on the forecastle deck. The fore set of main bitts was in the waist on the upper gun deck. The after set of main bitts was at the break of the half-deck. There were no bitts on the quarterdeck.

Knights, timber heads, kevels and cleats were made in the workshops and fitted ready to receive running rigging. The head of each knight was carved in the form of a bearded male head wearing a plumed cascade type of helmet. The *Vasa*'s knights were similarly fashioned in human head form.

Scuppers were fitted in the lowest part of the decks. They were probably around 3 inches in diameter, and may have been lead tubes or wooden blocks bored out with a great pump auger and lined with lead or leather. To prevent sea water rushing back when the vessel heeled, the external discharge orifice was covered by a leather flap valve, or had a short length of leather hose attached.

All the tools used in the construction were for use by hand. In the collections of the National Maritime Museum and the Chatham Dockyard Historical Society's Museum are shipwrights' tools of the type commonly used, viz. dogs, bevel, callipers, mallet, brace, draw knife, spar axes, adze with moot and spar plane.

Wood shavings, sawdust and offcuts must have fallen through open hatch coamings and incomplete decking into the bilges. If abandoned there, it would have absorbed water and induced rot in the lower timbers. This debris was removed through the strake adjacent to the garboard strake.

Charles I returned to Woolwich on 3 February 1637, accompanied by Charles Lewis and their retinue of Lords. They made a thorough inspection of the vessel. Being satisfied, they retired into Phineas Pett's lodgings to await the flood tide for their return by barge to Whitehall.

The *Sovereign* has been described as the most highly decorated vessel in the history of shipbuilding. By royal command, the task of devising the decoration fell to Thomas Heywood (1574–1641). He was born in Lincolnshire and educated at the University of Cambridge. According to his own testimony, he wrote more than 220 plays for the English stage. He became a popular actor and playwright at court. His plays exhibited a remarkable talent for dramatic and fanciful situations. He translated the Latin plays of

Lucian and Plautus, from which he borrowed copiously to adorn the vessel. He was a close friend of Inigo Jones (1573–1652), His Majesty's Surveyor General.

Heywood had an instinct for dramatic situations. His prolific creative skill was invaluable for this task. To suit the prevalent fashion, the verses and mottoes were in Latin. They were poetic and freely quoted from classical plays. He was spontaneous and lengthy in his verse. When a single word was needed, however, his artistry was unequal to the demand.

The Clerk of the Cheque was Francis Skelton. The Master Carvers who fashioned the embellishments were John and Matthias Christmas, the sons of Gerard Christmas, who died in 1634. There was a Gerard Christmas working on ships built at Harwich during 1666–68.

Charles I gave Queen's House, Greenwich, and grounds to Henrietta Maria. Inigo Jones was employed to enrich the interior. This was not completed before 1642. The Commissioners of the Navy tried to press Inigo Jones' carvers to work on the great ship. A carver named Thomas James and his apprentice Richard Durkin were pressed for service adorning the great ship. However, by February 1637 they were released from the King's works because they were still employed on the Queen's works at Greenwich.

Although she was most exquisitely carved, no heavy colour scheme was entertained. On 23 March 1636, Charles I personally penned the directions for gilding and painting:

> The head with all the carved work thereof, and the rails to be all gilt, and no other colour used thereupon but black. The stern and galleries to be gilt with gold and black in the same manner, with the rails on them to be all likewise gilt with gold. The sides to be all carved work according to the draught which was presented to his Majesty and that carved work to be all gilt with gold, and all the rails of the sides to be likewise gilt with gold and no other colour to be used on the sides but black. Also the figures in the upper strake to be altered into badges of carved work answerable to the other strake, that runs fair with it, and to be gilt answerable to the rest. [Plate 16]

She was paid, or served, with a homogeneous mixture of linseed oil, turpentine and Stockholm tar. Rosin and brimstone were added to the mixture to prevent fouling.

Stockholm tar, imported mainly from Russia, Eastern Europe and Scandinavia, was favoured for waterproofing wood and cordage. It was prepared by the destructive distillation of pine wood in the absence of air. The distillate was further refined by distillation to remove volatile terpenes, present in the form of turpentine. The black viscous residue, viz. Stockholm tar, was characterised by its pleasant aroma, reminiscent of freshly cut pine logs.

Coal tar was not used on account of the presence of phenols. Similarly, hardwood tars distilled from oak and beech logs contained polyhydric phenols in varying quantities. By their slightly acidic nature, phenols were detrimental to wood, tending to shorten the useful life.

Gilding was achieved by the application of gold leaf. The ornamentations of the *Vasa* were similarly embellished.

Caulking was an essential function in the finishing stages. This required treatment by craftsmen. Skeins of oakum were teased out from old rope and rolled into strands of uniform thickness. The oakum was rolled into the open seams between planks. By means of a caulking iron, a tool similar to a broad, blunt cold chisel, which was hammered with a beetle or a mallet, the oakum was driven into the seam. The oakum was further compressed into the seam by means of a horsing iron. Molten Stockholm pitch was poured from a ladle over the oakum, or brushed into the seam, leaving it proud. When hard and excess pitch was scraped off, it left a water-tight joint. Displays relevant to caulking, including the relevant tools, are displayed in the Chatham Dockyard Historical Society Museum, and the 'Wooden Walls' Gallery in Chatham Historic Dockyard.

The rudder blade was formed of several vertical timbers bolted edgewise to the rudder post. Iron gudgeons mounted around the rudder post and the thickness of the rudder blade pivoted on iron pintles on the sternpost. To improve her steering qualities, the fore end of the rudder was as wide as the sternpost. The after end of the rudder may have been much broader.

There was an embrasure in the counter to accommodate the tiller. The steering room was at the after end of the middle gun deck. There were no guns on either side of the steering room to interfere with the maximum traverse of the tiller. The maximum rudder angle was around 20 degrees each side.

She was steered, not with a whipstaff, as was the *Vasa*, but with relieving tackles. Such tackles rove from either side of the tiller to convenient eye bolts to port and starboard. By hauling away on one fall, and slackening off on another, the rudder could be controlled. The relieving tackles may have been similar to gun tackles. Each relieving tackle was probably a simple two-block three-fold purchase, viz. a luff or a jigger tackle. Mounted on the deck before the tiller was the bittacle, a square frame of deal board in which stood the ship's magnetic compass and night lights.

While his masterpiece was nearing completion, Phineas was experiencing domestic problems. His second wife Susan died in July 1637. The following year he married Mildred Byland of Etherington, but she died the same year.

Almost invariably, the Petts selected their prospective brides from affluent families established in the town or country. When relocated to their new residence near the rivers, these brides died young. Their early demise may have been due to their contraction of the ague, resulting in malaria due to the mosquitoes belonging to the genus *Anopheline*, which bred prolifically in the poorly-drained, low-lying salt marshes along the river banks of Kent and Essex.

Phineas wrote to Charles I, proposing 5 February 1638 as a date suitable for the launch. By then her works would be complete. As she would not require winter moorings, the charge of ship-keepers could be alleviated. Charles I, however, disagreed with this proposal, and wrote in the margin of Phineas' letter, 'And therefore it is fit that the new ship be launched as soon as may be.'

Phineas suggested that the tide on 25 September 1637 would be suitable for the launching.

The impatient monarch replied, 'The sooner the better.'

Thomas Rabinett, the boatswain of the *Greyhound*, was commissioned to prepare the launching site and lay out the moorings. Rabinett was not readily forthcoming for this task, however. The Lords of the Admiralty urged Algernon Percy, Fourth Earl of Northumberland, to send Rabinett to Woolwich Royal Dockyard and appoint another able man as replacement in the *Greyhound*.

Rain dominated the weather on the Thames on Tuesday 29 August. But adverse conditions did not deter the enthusiasm of the carpenters who were employed by Phineas. By 11 a.m., they had hammered in the wedges raising the keel on her blocks. The great ship settled on her launching ways. By 9 September, Peter was at Woolwich with all the men and materials required for the launching.

Charles I and Henrietta Maria, accompanied by their retinue, came to Woolwich on 25 September. The royal barge came alongside the dock steps at noon. The royal ensemble boarded the great new ship immediately. They inspected for an hour, and then retired to rooms at the dockyard previously prepared and furnished for their entertainment. At 2 p.m., the tackles were tightened to haul the vessel off her ways and into the water. Two cables broke under the strain. The tide was slack, and the great new ship moved only slightly. The tackles were abandoned, and the vessel was shored up again. Their Majesties, very disappointed that she could not be launched, returned to Whitehall.

Another launch was attempted some two or three tides later. Similarly, the endeavour met with failure. Phineas was obliged to defer any further attempt until the next spring tide, expected on 12–13 October. The Masters of Trinity House enjoined him to refrain from any further attempts until Sunday 14 October, when their specialists would attend to direct the operation.

At a late hour on Saturday 13 October, by the pathetic light of burning reeds heaped up along the shore, Phineas tightened the tackles and knocked away the shoring props. The weather was fine, with a westerly wind promising a fair tide. It came in so fast that the great new ship was afloat before high water. She was heaved off into the channel and warped safely to her moorings before high water. Neither pomp nor ceremony heralded the occasion. The River Thames was dark, sombre and very quiet.

We can but speculate on the anguish demonstrated by the Masters of Trinity House when they arrived to find that Phineas had frustrated them! A messenger was despatched to Greenwich, to Vice Admiral Sir Robert Mansell, Chairman of the Navy Board. Sir Robert rode to Hampton Court to convey the glad tidings to Charles I. His Majesty was pleased and authorised Sir Robert to christen her. He hastened back to Woolwich Royal Dockyard to perform this task personally. The christening was done by torch light at 2 a.m. It was accomplished with the barest of formalities, according to tradition. After the brief ceremony, the silver christening cup, valued at 40s, was given to Phineas' son Peter. No trace remains of this cup.

In 1633, Sir John Borough, the Keeper of the Records in the Tower of London, published a book, *The Sovereignty of the Seas of England...*, in which he described the sovereignty of the seas as: 'the most precious jewel in his Majesties crown ... and the principal means of our wealth and safety.'

This seems to have impressed Charles I, and may have prompted the inspiration by which the great new ship was named the *Sovereign of the Seas*. During the seventeenth century, proper names were not clearly defined. She was indiscriminately described as *Royal Sovereign, Sovereign Royal* or simply *Sovereign*. A variety of names existed for a number of other Stuart vessels.

She was the second English warship to bear the name *Sovereign*.

The first *Sovereign* was a 500 ton carrack, built in 1487–8 at Portsmouth Royal Dockyard. She was rebuilt at Portsmouth in 1509–10, only a few months before the keel of the *Mary Rose* was laid down in the same dock. This is the earliest dry dock in the world. The *Sovereign*'s prow and stern had a sharp line, suggesting that she was built for rowing. Her frames were made in pieces scarfed into each other. They were secured only by the treenails of the external planking.

Originally, she was clinker built. There were no metal fastenings in the original structure. Guns were mounted on each side of the aft-castle and forecastle. She had three masts, with topmasts and topsails on both fore and main. Her mainmast consisted of a pine stick surrounded by baulks of oak bound together by iron bands. The total diameter of the mast was 4 feet 4 inches.

Her dimensions may be recorded:

Length of keel	around 115–20 feet
Beam (extreme)	around 45 feet
Draught in water	7–9 feet
Burden	385–517 tons
Gross tonnage	514–689 tons

Probably at the time when she was rebuilt, the original planks were stripped off. The notches in the face of the frames were furred, and carvel planking applied. The seams

5. The remains of the first *Sovereign* of 1487–8 as found at Woolwich in 1912. South end. (*Corporation of London*)

between the planking were caulked with oakum and pitch. Across the top of the floor frames were heavy riders secured with iron bolts. In places which needed repair, iron bolts were favoured.

In 1521 she was reported to be lying in a dock at Woolwich. Her timbers were deteriorating. She was laid up pending a survey as to the feasibility of rebuilding her. The keel rested on clean river gravel partly covered with a deposit of silt. Considering her obsolete construction, the decision was delayed until it was not worth the effort of either repairing her or removing her for breaking up. Eventually, she was abandoned.

Part of her remains were realised during excavations on the site of Roff's Wharf, near Woolwich Borough Electricity Works, in November 1912. Her timbers were destroyed before their value could be established. Nothing remains extant other than photographs and drawings made at the time of her discovery.

By 22 October 1637, the *Sovereign of the Seas* was moored off Woolwich, alongside the *Prince Royal* of 1610. Being the largest vessel afloat, her tall masts served to erect the sheer legs to step the *Sovereign*'s masts. During the third week in October, the sheer legs were raised. They were composed of two long masts. The heels rested against the hull of the *Prince Royal*, with the peaks lashed together to form an 'A' frame. This device inclined outward from the perpendicular over the *Sovereign*. Tackles rove from the mast of the *Prince Royal* to the peak of the sheers allowed the sheers to act as the jib of a crane.

Further tackles rove to the peak of the sheer provided purchase in weighing the lower masts into the *Sovereign*'s hull. The falls from both tackles were taken up on the *Prince Royal*'s windlasses. By November, the *Sovereign*'s lower masts were stepped.

In rig, she observed the close of the four-masted era. The bonaventure mizen mast, so usual on the largest warships since the beginning of the seventeenth century, became obsolete. The square mizen topsails, introduced in 1618, had created the possibility of obtaining further sail power aft by increasing the size of the mizen mast rather than by duplicating it. In the fleet which brought Prince Charles and Buckingham back to England in 1623, only two vessels had bonaventure mizen masts. These were the *Prince Royal* of 1610 and the *St Andrew* of 1622. By 1640, no four-masted vessel remained in the English navy.

When the rigging was nearly complete, with some sails bent to the yards, Charles I made a visit of inspection. He commanded that she should be removed farther downriver. For this purpose, 100 men were put aboard to supplement her crew of 200. She was brought to Erith for the winter because of the greater depth of water in which to ride at her moorings. Her Master was William Cooke, who had previously commanded the *Ann Royal*. He was fifty-six years old at that time.

Cooke commanded the pinnace *Henrietta* in 1634 while guarding the Medway against smugglers. As Master of the *Triumph*, the Admiral's flagship, he gave evidence in 1636 concerning the articles presented to Charles I by the Earl of Northumberland, alleging defects and abuses in the Navy. Cooke was one of the governors of the Chatham Chest, and attested at this enquiry that Sir Sackville Crow owed around £3,000 and Sir William Russell around £500 to the Chest.

The winter of 1637–38 brought work to a standstill. Due to the inclement weather conditions which prevailed, and the hazard from ice and wind, her Master obtained an increase in her ordinary ship's company from 60 to 100. By 23 December she had laid out another anchor of 39 cwt. She was then moored by four cables and anchors. Anchor and mooring cables were usually hemp ropes impregnated with Stockholm tar. There was no wind during the frost to enable her to go downriver. In these calm, sheltered waters there was the threat from accretion of ice. To prevent damage to her hull, she was surrounded by a boom of floating spars lashed end to end. Cooke requested victuals to be sent down for her ordinary company.

The type of anchor in fashion is exemplified by models in the Science Museum and the National Maritime Museum (Illustrations 6 & 7). Such an anchor had the flukes, crown, arms, trend, bow and shank fashioned in iron. The arms were made from several wrought-iron bars hot-worked together. Each arm was long, straight and slender, meeting at the crown at a pronounced obtuse angle. The technique of curving the crown and the arms into an arc did not come into general use until 1840, although occasionally the curved form did exist during the sixteenth century. The flukes were broad triangular plates hot-worked on to the tip of each bill. The stock was a long timber drilled in the centre to pass over the top of the shank. The stock was at right angles to the flukes, to enable the means for the flukes to bite into the seabed.

Her original anchors (Appendix 38) cost £2 per cwt. The type of anchor is demonstrated by two specimens in the grounds of the National Maritime Museum, Greenwich (Illustrations 6 & 7).

Together with the *Prince Royal* of 1610, she was provisioned under contract by John Crane (1576–1660) of Loughton, Bucks. In 1635 he became Victualler of the Navy. He held this appointment until 1642. By 5 November 1637, he had supplied provisions to both vessels to the value of £500. By 27 January 1638 this had increased to £730 15s.

Charles I visited her in January 1638. He commanded that when the weather improved, and the danger of the ice receded, the vessel's crew must be reduced from 100 to 60 men.

6. Admiralty pattern anchor, around 1790. (*National Maritime Museum, author's photograph, 9 October 2001*)

Phineas Pett's estimate for building, dated 1634, was £13,860. A paper from the Officers of the Navy to the Lords of the Admiralty, dated 14 July 1636, stated that £8,454 18s 2d had been paid towards building. A warrant was issued on 9 May 1637 to pay to Sir William Russell, Treasurer of the Navy, £10,861 12s over and above the sum of £16,647 4s already issued. A warrant was issued on 19 September 1637 for £2,084 12s, being the estimated cost for launching. On 9 January 1638, the Officers of the Navy issued to the Lords of the Admiralty 'An exact Certificate of the Charge in materials and workmanship expended in the new building and launching of his Majesty's Ship, the *Sovereign of the Seas*.'

The charge was for £41,642 17s 11d. From this may be deducted the sum of £7,796 12s 7d. The actual charge for building and launching was £33,846 5s 4d. From this may be deducted the cost of materials for the launching, viz. £2,600 9s 6d. The charge for building the hull was £31,245 15s 10d (Appendix 9).

An estimate dated 9 January 1637 proposed an additional £12,500 to provision her with a crew of 600 for six months' service at sea. A warrant was issued on 25 July 1637 for the charge of £5,679 2s for cordage and other provisions to rig her for six months' service at sea.

Much work remained uncompleted by 2 March 1638. Peter Pett had undertaken to remedy this as soon as practicable. She berthed in dry dock at Woolwich in 21 March. Her underwater hull was inspected, and cleaned of marine incrustations. Her upper works were also completed.

7. Admiralty pattern anchor, around 1750. (*National Maritime Museum, author's photograph, 9 October 2001*)

Many men were employed on her building. As techniques were primitive, involving manual dexterity, it was to be expected that accidents were common. In 1638, a Chatham surgeon was paid the sum of £43 1s 4d for attending to shipwrights injured in the course of their work upon her. The funds came from the Chatham Chest.

By 14 May 1638, her rigging was complete. She cast off from Erith to anchor at Greenhithe, where she took aboard stores, provisions, ordnance, powder and shot.

Charles I and Henrietta Maria, accompanied by the Duchess of Chevreuse, Marie de Rohan-Montbazon (1600–79), James Stuart, the Duke and Duchess of Lennox, with other lords and ladies dined aboard on 6 June. On their departure, they were honoured by a salute of seventeen pieces.

On 12 July she weighed anchor from Greenhithe and anchored a short distance beyond Gravesend, ready to commence her sea trials. On Saturday 21 July Charles I made another visit. He made a thorough inspection, and was satisfied with what he saw. As he departed, he was saluted with a discharge of seventy-two pieces. Naval gun salutes were invariably odd numbers. This was due to a signal piece fired from the half-deck. The fact that an even number was used could be accounted for by the first warning shot being unnecessary, and that the salute was fired by the prompting of a half-minute hour glass. These were the days before a salute was fired in blanks.

The vessel's size and allure, coupled with keen royal interest, attracted many officers in the service, who vied with each other to secure a position aboard her. Thomas Taylor of the *Ann Royal*, who was recommended by Captain Blythe of the *Prince Royal*, and John Costell were her gunners. Phillip Ward of the *Prince Royal*, together with William Stonehouse, John Yeelding, Gervase Russell and Roger Whotston were her pursers. The purser's duties were clerical, in accounting for the receipt of provisions from the contractor, the daily rations of foodstuffs to the cook and maintaining the roll of all the men aboard.

Her four appointed boatswains were Israel Reynolds of the *Prince Royal*, Thomas Rabinett of the *Ann Royal*, John Garnott of the *Adventure*, and, on the recommendation of Admiral Sir John Pennington, Thomas Broadridge of the *Bonaventure*. The boatswain was the officer in charge of cables, anchors, rigging, sails, flags, colours, pendants, the long boat and its equipment, watches of the vessel and the execution of punishments.

John Ferris was appointed Master Cook on 24 September 1637. He had four mates, namely Stephen Hasnott, John Roberts, Nicky Smithe, who was recommended by the Earl of Dorset, and William Simpson, who was recommended by the Earl of Northumberland and Sir John Pennington.

Robert Hill of the *Ann Royal* and Thomas Williams were her carpenters. Their duties provided for the efficient functioning of every iron and timber.

William Braynt was the swabber. He had two mates, Philip Ward and Thomas Supoe, a violinist of His Majesty's musicians, recommended by Sir Sidney Montagne. All the cabins were maintained in a clean condition by the swabbers.

Together with the *Garland*, the *Sovereign*, with Phineas and his son Peter aboard, cast off from the Goodwin Sands on the morning of 15 August 1638 to the Isle of Wight and back. Her sea trials safely and successfully completed, she put into the Downs around 8 a.m. on Friday 20 August. The Downs is a sheltered stretch of water between the Kentish coast and the shifting Goodwin Sands, in the shadow of Sandown, Deal and Walmer castles. Here sailing vessels waited in safety for a favourable wind before entering either the Thames estuary or the Dover Strait. She anchored as close as possible to Admiral Sir John Pennington in the *St Andrew* of 1622. Pennington replaced the Earl of Northumberland, whose illness prevented his presence. The admiral and all vessels in the roads, which included twenty-four King's ships and seven merchant vessels, saluted with discharges of ordnance. The *Sovereign* replied with a twenty-one-gun salute for the admiral.

By 28 August, she was moored in Sovereign Reach, at the southern part of Gillingham Reach, in the River Medway.

Thus, the great new ship was ready to venture forth upon her career. Her name was included in a list of His Majesty's ships to be at sea in 1638, but she was not ready until late in the year. She lay moored off St Mary's Island, Chatham. An estimate occurred in January 1640 for a sister ship. This proposal never materialised.

The *Sovereign* was at Chatham when, on 9 June 1641, John Evelyn visited her. For the next fifteen years, the *Sovereign* was laid up in the River Medway. As she rode majestically at her moorings in the element for which she was designed, her colossal size and rich adornment must surely have created a focus of attention to all those who could travel to visit her or view her from a distance.

CHAPTER 3

Some Original Drawings, Paintings and Models

Of Phineas Pett's original shipwright's draughts and the builder's model made by Peter Pett, no trace has survived.

Thomas Heywood published a book in 1637. The title page is displayed in Illustration 8. The volume was printed by John Okes in London for John Aston, and was on sale at Aston's shop at the sign of the Bull's Head in Cateaten Street, London, on 7 September 1637. W. Hawkins despatched a copy to Robert Sidney, Second Earl of Leicester (1595–1677) of Penshurst in October 1637.

When the attempted launch failed on 25 September, a slump occurred in the sales. When the vessel took the water on 14 October, a second edition appeared. The title page is displayed in Illustration 9. This was similarly printed by John Okes, 1638. Both editions were dedicated to King Charles I. This second edition quickly sold out in the summer of 1638, and was supplemented by copies of the first edition updated by amendment slips pasted into the pages. The work lapsed into obscurity, and subsequently became a rarity.

There is little difference between the texts of either edition. The second edition contains a register of officers, and an announcement concerning a new engraving by John Payne. This is pasted into the first edition, becoming pages 49 and 50. The title and title page of the second edition varies with that of the first.

Heywood claimed 'A true description ...', though only a meagre description of the vessel herself is contained. Quite casually he mentions three distinct gun decks, the half-deck, quarterdeck and the round house aft. Heywood made many errors and contradictions in his text, which serve only to accentuate his lack of sympathy for the arts of the shipwright. His statement for the number of guns, viz. 126, can not be verified by any other authority.

A frontage in the 1637 edition, probably by William Marshall, is an imaginary portrait of the vessel at sea. This frontage was omitted from the 1638 edition. The authenticity is dubious, because in many important features, it is at complete variance with the text it illustrates.

The ship is depicted in perspective from a position off the port quarter. The prow is the wrong shape. The round house is too far forward, and on the starboard elevation of the vessel. The position of the figurehead is misplaced. The bulwarks from the waterline to the gunwale are encrusted with carvings, which are incompatible with the detail in Chapter 5 of this present work. The quarter galleries have six cupolas aside, instead of three. The panel across the top of the transom and above the upper gun deck, called the frontispiece by Heywood, does not resemble the details of his text. Dominating the stern is the great lantern.

To add further to the confusion, a bonaventure mizen mast is depicted at the break of the poop royal deck, thus constituting a rig of four masts. The steeving of the bowsprit, or angle above the horizontal, is too severe. This defect is more readily appreciated because of the lack of a spritsail and a spritsail topsail.

The crossjack yard is rigged with a square sail, which would, of course, have fouled the projecting forward end of the mizen yard and sail, and so cause its ineffectuality. The mizen yard and sail are excluded by Marshall. Her sails are furled, instead of the more usual practice of farthelling. It is rather odd to have buntlines suspended from the yard-arms. The royal sails are not included. It can be readily appreciated that the artist of this presentation was no maritime specialist.

The most widely reproduced representation of this vessel is an engraving (Plate 17) by John Payne (1607–47). John Payne apparently learnt his engraving skill from Simon and William Pass.

Payne has entitled his work: *The True Portraiture of His Majesty's Royal Ship*, The Sovereign of the Seas, *Built in the Year 1637, Capt Phineas Pett being supervisor, and Peter Pett his son Master Builder.*

Payne further describes it in Latin: 'Praegrandis illius atq celeberr. Navis sub auspicis Caroli. magn; Brit: fra: et hib: Regis ANo. 1637. Exstructae delineatio expressissima.' On translation, this becomes, 'The most accurate portraiture of that mighty and most famous ship which was built under the auspices of Charles, the great King of Britain and Ireland in the year 1637.'

A Latin caption is in the bottom right hand corner: '*Cum privilegio ad imprimendum solum.*'

On translation, this becomes, 'With the right of printing alone.'

Thus, we realise that Payne had exclusive rights to the publication. The engraving, on two plates, shows a broadside view in reverse of the starboard elevation of the vessel. It is printed on one sheet of paper. There is an incongruity in the sweep of the midships wales at the conjunction. This occurs in the centre, running vertically from top to bottom. The colour suggests a reddish brown hue of the hull. The original measures 36.5 inches by 26.5 inches. The identical plates were in existence as late as 1789. They were then in the possession of Mount & Co., Stationers.

The general impression is that the ship is departing harbour, leaving behind a cliff face in the right background. Payne's engraving does not specifically depict a round tuck stern. It suggests a square or transom stern. Trailing in the sea is the port bower anchor. A sailor stands on the stock hooking a single sheave block cat-tackle rove from the single sheave in the cat-head above, to the bow of the anchor.

There are many men, including a dog, on the spar deck amidships. Judging from the disposition of the guns, the spar deck was around 7–8 feet above the upper gun deck. The disposition of the people shown below the spar deck suggests that perhaps a platform, or narrow gangway, projected inboard from the bulwark, above the level of the gun barrels. Another spar deck is above the half-deck, up to the break of the quarter deck. There is a ladder-like companionway leading from the quarter deck to the poop. The stern galleries are level with the decks. The quarter galleries follow the plank sheer.

Payne does not depict an entry port. We are left with the suggestion that, as the engraving is in reverse the entry port may have been on the port elevation only.

An impressive battle array is presented by three and one half tiers of yawning gunports and run-out guns.

Her spritsail topsail, fore and main royals and mizen topgallant are farthelled. Sailors clamber up the main lower shrouds, perhaps with the intention to loose the mainsail. A seaman straddles the main yard. The leads of some of the crane-lines are inaccurate.

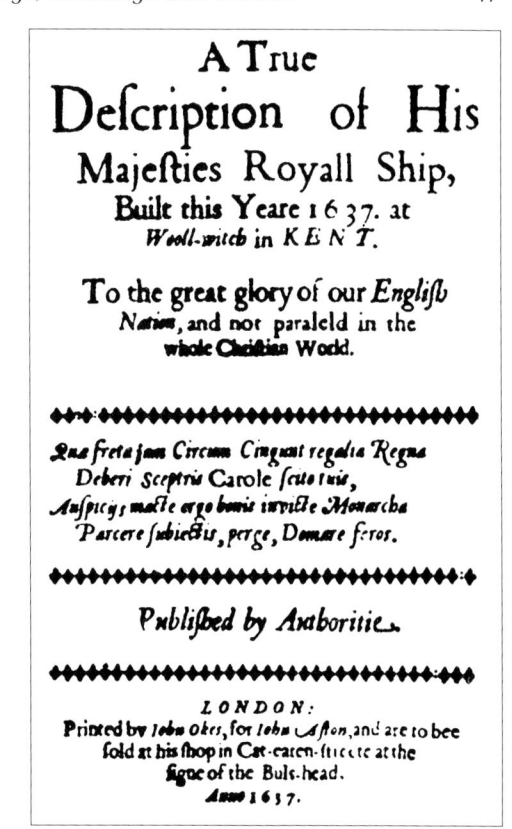

> A True
> Description of His
> Majesties Royall Ship,
> Built this Yeare 1637. at
> *Wooll-witch* in KENT.
>
> To the great glory of our *English*
> Nation, and not paraleld in the
> whole Christian World.
>
> *Quæ freta jam Circum Cingunt regalia Regna*
> *Deberi Sceptris* Carole *scito tuis,*
> *Auspicys mactè ergo bonis invictè Monarcha*
> *Parcere subiectis, perge, Domare feros.*
>
> *Published by Authoritie.*
>
> LONDON:
> Printed by *John Okes*, for *John Aston*, and are to bee
> sold at his shop in Cat-eaten-streete at the
> signe of the Buls-head.
> *Anno* 1637.

8. Title page of 1637 edition of T. Heywood's book, *A True Description of His Majesties Royall Ship ...*, John Okes (1637). (*British Library*)

Crane-lines were backstay pendants which steadied the spritsail topmast to the middle of the forestay by a complicated arrangement of crowsfeet.

Flying from the spritsail topmast is the Union Flag, exclusive to the Navy. The flag at the foremast-head bears a crown and lion encircled by the garter, which is the crest and motto of England. The leopards in the Stuart Royal Standard at the main mast-head romp in the wrong direction. They face towards the mainmast rather than away from it. The flag at the mizen mast-head bears a lion *saillant* within a garter, representing Scotland. At the taffrail is an ensign bearing the Stuart royal arms with lion and unicorn supporters.

A long boat or skiff manned by three is towed aft by a painter.

As the second edition of Heywood's book was on sale during the summer of 1638, Payne's engraving must have been completed and published. Consequently, it was finished before the vessel had her masts stepped, even before she was launched. The engraving was published contemporaneously with the time she was being rigged, before the guns and stores were taken aboard. Therefore, it was impossible that Payne could have patterned his arrangement of rigging from the actual ship herself. It would have taken months to cut his plates. During Stuart times no fixed sail plan was put to the drawing board before the vessel was rigged. The riggers worked to a list of spar lengths and sail areas, rigging the ship according to the prevalent fashion.

Payne acknowledges Peter Pett's initiative for the engraving. In the bottom right hand corner is the Latin inscription: '*Archinaupego Petro Pett juniore: Sculptore I. Payne.*'

This, on translation, becomes, 'Chief shipbuilder Peter Pett the younger: Sculptor J. Payne.'

Payne probably had access to the builders' draughts and plans in the charge of the Master Builder, Peter Pett, for depicting the hull. Payne may have collaborated with Peter Pett to

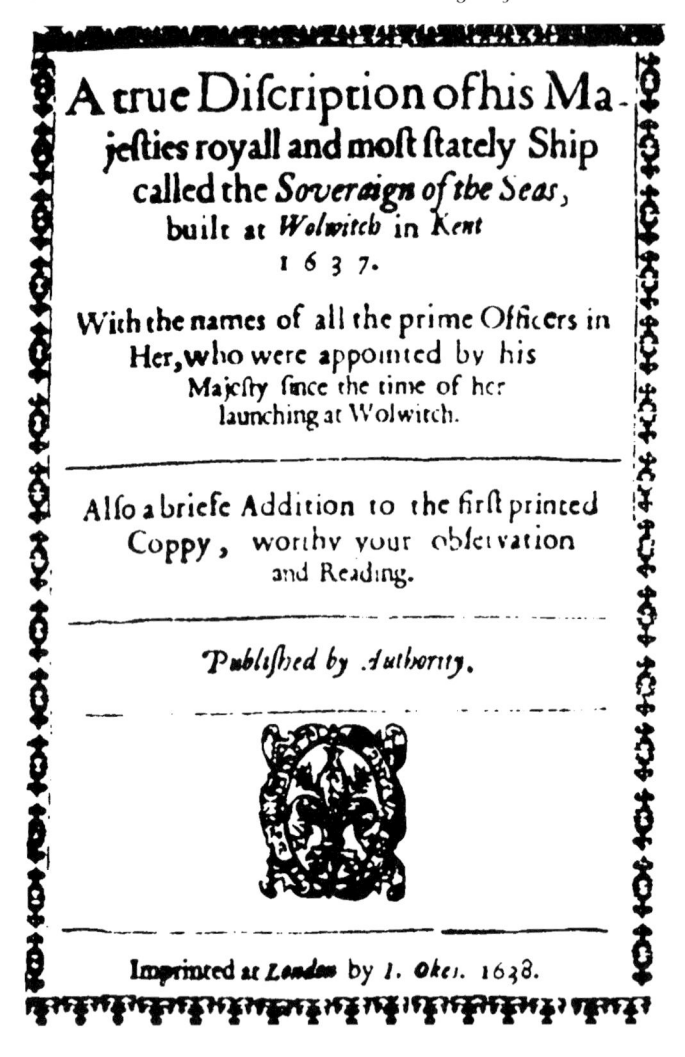

> **A true Discription of his Majesties royall and most stately Ship called the *Soveraign of the Seas*, built at *Wolwitch* in *Kent* 1 6 3 7.**
>
> With the names of all the prime Officers in Her, who were appointed by his Majesty since the time of her launching at Wolwitch.
>
> ———
>
> Also a briefe Addition to the first printed Coppy, worthy your observation and Reading.
>
> ———
>
> *Published by Authority.*
>
> ———
>
> Imprinted at *London* by *I. Okes.* 1638.

9. Title page of 1638 edition of T. Heywood's book, *A true Description of His Majesties royall and ...*, John Okes (1638). (*British Library*)

ensure that the details of the hull were in every conceivable manner as representative of the ship as possible. Peter Pett's model would have proven invaluable in this respect.

Payne's rigging resembles a line engraving by the Dutch artist, Henry Hondius, of one of the largest ships built for the French by the Dutch. This print is called: *Le Navire Royale Faiete en Hollande Anno 1626: A Amsterdam. Chez Henry Hondius.*

This, on translation from the French, becomes, 'The royal ship built in Holland in 1626. At Amsterdam. By Henry Hondius.'

This represented one of five great ships which the Dutch commissioned for Louis XIII of France. It would appear that Payne, Peter Pett and perhaps the Master Rigger at Woolwich Royal Dockyard collaborated in amending the Dutch print to the English mode for the engraving.

This print has been identified to represent *La Couronne* of 1635.

The style and content of Payne's engraving bears a striking resemblance to Hondius' print (Illustration 2). The disposition of the waves, guns, sails, flags and pennants follow a similar pattern. Payne's mizen yard is depicted outside of the shrouds, although behind the crossjack yard, with the mizen course furled. We have the suggestion that perhaps Payne was unfamiliar with the triangular lateen and anticipated a square sail. A similar

10. W. Marshall's drawing of the *Sovereign of the Seas* (1637). Port quarter view. (*British Library*)

condition occurs in Hondius' print of *La Couronne*. Payne's cloths follow the diagonal edge of the port side of the sail instead of the centre line. Hondius' sails are similar. We have the suggestion that perhaps Payne may have known of this print, and may have made use of it as a basis for his engraving of the *Sovereign of the Seas*.

One feature was suspect for some considerable time. Payne includes furled fore and main royals and a furled topgallant sail on the mizen. These sails did not come into general use until nearly 150 years later. As Payne had never seen royals before, we have the suggestion that perhaps he was uncertain how to portray them. The accuracy of Payne's engraving has been substantiated by a manuscript Navy List, dated 1640, from Lord Leconfield's collection at Petworth House. This provided a description of the rigging (Appendix 41). This manuscript was sold in 1928 to the Science Museum. This manuscript was subsequently edited by G. S. Laird Clowes and published ('S.N.R.' 1931 No. 3.) This List includes the 'maintop royall, foretop royall, and mizon topgallant sails of the *Soveraigne*' (*sic*).

There is no reason to question the accuracy of Payne's engraving. But these sails were peculiar to this ship, and were not found in any other contemporary English warship. The engraving was acquired by A. G. H. Macpherson and passed to the Science Museum collections (Inventory No. 1905–163).

Payne's engraving has been the source for many imitations. In 1653, Thomas Jenner published a book, *The Common-Wealths Great Ship Commonly called the* Sovereign of the Seas, *built in the yeare, 1637*. This was printed by Matthew Simmons. It contains extracts from Heywood's book. The most intriguing inclusion is an engraving by Jenner (Plate 18). This is a crude copy, in reverse, of Payne's engraving. Jenner omits the embellishments along the bulwarks, but includes small numbers and a key tabulating some terms of the ship's gear and rigging.

When Samuel Pepys returned home to dinner on 31 January 1663, he found a print of an engraving with an accompanying table, presented by Christopher Pett. Christopher (1620–68) was the eighth son of Phineas by his first wife Ann, née Nicholls. Christopher had four children by his wife, also named Ann (Appendix 1). He was the Master Shipwright at Woolwich and Deptford. On 15 February, Pepys hung this print in his green room. We have the suggestion that this may have been Jenner's engraving.

An oil painting of the *Sovereign of the Seas* was created around 1650–60 by Lorenzo A. Castro (1672–86). He was Master of the Lucas Guild at Antwerp in 1664–65. This painting on canvas measures 96 inches by 54 inches. It is signed L. A. Castro (Plate 19.) This painting bears a close resemblance to Payne's engraving. Castro probably copied Payne's work at first hand. Castro has, however, omitted the comb for the fore tacks. Payne's round tops are small. Castro's round tops are larger and shallower, of the type typical of the period around 1650. Castro's topgallant sails, especially the fore topgallant sail, are loftier than Payne's. Payne's mistake in positioning the mizen yard outside the shrouds does not occur in Castro's painting.

Castro's painting was sold at Christie's in April 1913 for £43 1s. G. E. Manwaring brought it to the attention of the Society for Nautical Research in 1920. It belonged to Lady Henry Grosvenor of Quenby Hall, Leicestershire, who sold it in 1920 for 875 guineas. It is in the collections at Parham Park, Storrington, near Pulborough, West Sussex.

A maritime oil painting on canvas belonging to Sir Richard Worsley, Seventh Baronet of Apuldercombe (d. 1805), passed with his property to his niece, the Countess of Yarborough. It was sold at Christie's (117) by Spink and Son Ltd on 12 July 1929, to Captain Sir Bruce Ingram. He agreed to sell it to Sir James Caird, who was anxious to acquire it for public exhibition. On 14 September 1929, it passed to the National Maritime Museum. It measures 61.75 inches by 56.25 inches (Acquisition No. 1929–1) (Cat. No. BHC 2949.) For many years it was displayed in the King's Ante-room of the Queen's House before transfer to the gallery containing 'Discovery and Sea Power (1450–1700)'. By 1996, it had been transferred back into the Queen's House, where it remained until the inauguration of the new National Maritime Museum in March 1999 (Plate 22).

It is entitled *The Portrait of Peter Pett and the* Sovereign of the Seas.

According to the late Sir G. A. R. Callender's monograph, published in 1930, the stern of the vessel was painted by Willem van de Velde the Elder (1611–93). His son, Willem van de Velde the Younger (1633–1707), painted the portrait of Peter Pett on the same canvas. Later authors have ascribed this painting to Sir Peter Lely (1618–80). P. Kemp has suggested that the painting of the ship was the work of Isaac Sailmaker (1633–1721), while the portrait was by Sir Peter Lely. By no means is the matter conclusive.

It was probably painted when the vessel was laid up at Chatham Royal Dockyard for a rebuilding. This was in the 'Old Single Dock' now called No. 2 Dry Dock. This dock was built in 1623. In more recent times, this dock was commemorated with a stone at the eastern end with a bronze descriptive panel. The original patterns for these cast bronze panels were made around 1946 by three patternmaker apprentices, L. Challis, P. Dawson and H. Reeve.

This was Chatham's only dry dock which could have accommodated her extreme beam of 48 feet. This may have been March 1651, when Peter Pett was forty-one years old. The late Sir G. A. R. Callender dated the work at July/August 1660. This would have been when Peter was forty-nine years old. The uppermost 20 inches of the painting, including the main mast-head banner, is a later addition.

11. Site of the Old Single Dock, constructed in 1623, Chatham Royal Dockyard. Top of stone. (*Chatham Historic Dockyard Trust, author's photograph 27 September 2001*)

12. Site of the Old Single Dock, constructed in 1623, at Chatham Royal Dockyard. Front of stone. (*Chatham Historic Dockyard Trust, author's photograph, 27 September 2001*)

The ship is depicted at sea. The surface of the sea is ruffled by a moderate breeze. This is apparent, not only from the waves, but from the presence of a two-decker in the background to port of the *Sovereign*. The two-decker's courses and topsails billow out as she heels to starboard, tacking under the on shore wind.

The *Sovereign* appears to have a round tuck on the port elevation and a square tuck to starboard (Plate 21). We have the suggestion that the hull below the waterline was painted white. There is the possibility that one side has been touched up. The greater part of the stern was probably concealed by the masonry of the dock side. Even though the artist would have moved in closer to examine details as the need arose, it was probable that some of the hull was concealed by dockyard gear.

Similarly, there is confusion over the depiction of gun muzzles poking out through ports. It was unlikely that the ordnance would have been aboard at the time of refitting. From his relatively elevated position on the dock side, the artist could not have seen the lower tier. Boldly he depicts guns on the half-deck, the upper gun deck and the middle gun deck. The ports here are level with the lower aspect of the quarter galleries. On the lower gun deck he closes, or partly closes the ports, probably because the dock wall left him guessing what to do.

There are four guns visible aside on the upper tier. This is accounted for by the fact that the half-deck has three aside, and the quarterdeck one aside. There are no stern chasers depicted for this tier. There are four stern chasers on the lower gun deck, four on the middle gun deck, and two on the upper gun deck.

On each side is a pair of dead-eyes for lower shrouds. A dead-eye is a flattened block of hard wood, such as *lignum vitae*. The block is drilled to accommodate a laniard, thus securing a pair of dead-eyes in the form of a simple tackle. It is termed 'dead' because the holes, generally three in number, have no sheaves in them, and are therefore lifeless or 'dead'. The fact that these dead-eyes occur between the upper gun deck and the half-deck suggests that they belong to the mizen. The chain-wale for the mainmast is concealed behind open gun port covers of the middle gun deck.

It was hardly likely that the masts and rigging were depicted from reality. If such important features were *in situ*, then the artist would certainly have taken greater care in depicting them. He shows more of the starboard elevation than the port. It is reasonable to expect that the mainmast would appear to the right of the mizen mast. The mainmast, however, is shown to the left. The yards are exactly the same dimensions on either side of the masts, which would not have been expected from the laws of perspective. No doubt the artist consulted Peter Pett's list of dimensions for the masts and spars (Appendix 41). For some reason unknown to us, W. van de Velde the Elder omits the topgallant masts and yards. He also omits the royals. Although she is depicted at sea, her sails are furled and the fore and main yards and the topsail yards sent down.

Peter Pett's countenance is depicted as calm and dignified. The deep forehead and grave eyes are characteristic of the intellectual. The long, supple, well-groomed hands are rather effeminate. Except for the thick wrists and pronounced veins in the back of each hand, they could be mistaken for a woman's. The plain black velvet coat suggests the folly of assuming that Peter Pett may have been a priest or a clerk. The long, natural uncurled hair, and the crushed, semi-stiff collar, suggests that he had just left the dockyard and donned the black velvet to conceal his soiled garments. Perhaps this painting was done at the dock side, when Peter Pett could afford respite from his work.

Both artists have carefully blended their individual techniques to produce an unusual impression. There is no balance about this picture. Indeed, there is a striking contrast. In the bottom left corner is a copious mass of concentrated detail, while the top right corner is a mere background. Both backgrounds are incongruous.

The simplicity of Peter Pett's garments and the vast, unvaried expanse of plain rugged cliffs behind are accentuated by the singular tuft of foliage near the top of the cliff and the pair of dividers loosely held in the right hand. If these two details were omitted, then the effect of the right half of the picture would be significantly altered. The background in the left half is much brighter. There are no two details here which, if removed, would alter the ultimate effect. The whole vessel is a seething mass of intricate detail.

A drawing deposited in the National Maritime Museum (Cat. No. 38) is a pen and ink sketch of the stern of the vessel. This may have been a preliminary sketch for the van de Veldes' *The Portrait of Peter Pett and the* Sovereign of the Seas.

A fine copy of this painting was purchased by the Trustees of the National Portrait Gallery (Cat. No. 1270) from Henry Graves and Co. in 1900. This painting measures 55.5 inches by 61.5 inches. The artist for the portrait may have been Sir Peter Lely (1618–80). The artist for the vessel may have been Isaac Sailmaker (1633–1721) (Plate 25).

The differences between these two paintings serve to identify each of them.

The crown of gold and the chaplet of laurel about the figure of Victory in the frontispiece are missing from the National Portrait Gallery. Similarly, the ribbons for the display of her mottoes are missing. There are no winged heads of cupids signifying the winds. Jason's right hand and arm have discarded the Golden Fleece and dive into a capacious trouser pocket. His steering oar becomes a ragged staff. Hercules acquires a great beard falling heavily on his chest. His club becomes a floriated sceptre. This he grasps with both hands instead of using his left fore finger to point at Aeolus (see the description of the frontispiece in Chapter 5, sections A-G).

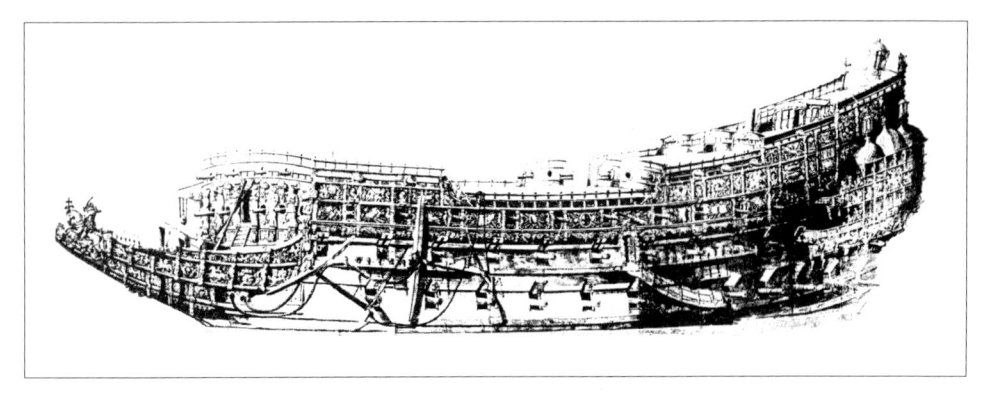

13. W. van de Velde the Elder's broadside drawing of the *Sovereign of the Seas* (1660). Port bow view. (*The late Junius S. Morgan, Junior, New York, USA*)

14. W. van de Velde the Elder's unfinished drawing of the *Sovereign of the Seas* (1661). Starboard quarter view. (*National Maritime Museum*)

Mast-head banners were flown from slender iron staves. They were plugged into a specially shaped mast-head with a fitting similar to an early bayonet. The staff was surmounted by a flattened globe. The banner was attached by ties at the top and bottom and by eight bold loops between. These eight loops are reduced to an inexplicable four in the National Portrait Gallery copy. The National Maritime Museum's banner is a pale yellow cross on a pale blue background. The National Portrait Gallery's banner is a red cross on a dark blue background.

Peter poses against a rocky background. The National Portrait Gallery picture depicts an outcrop with a blurred instead of a sharp outline, and a single tuft of foliage instead of three.

The National Portrait Gallery copy portrays Peter with sleeker hair, more piercing eyes, a more aquiline nose and a thinner moustache, than is apparent in the original National Maritime Museum picture. Peter holds a pair of callipers, dividers or compasses in his right hand. The National Portrait Gallery portrayal of his second finger in the neck of this instrument is an impossible position.

While she was laid up at Chatham Royal Dockyard for her rebuilding in 1659–60, Willem van de Velde the Elder took the opportunity of making a fine broadside drawing in July/August 1660. The original measures 40.5 inches by 14 inches. This was in the private collection of the late Junius S. Morgan, Junior, of New York.

The general impression suggests that van de Velde concentrated on his subject from some distance. He seems to have taken up a position with his drawing board and easel around four points off the port bow and 100 yards distant. Doubtless he moved in closer to examine details of the carvings. He may have withdrawn to a boat or pontoon in the adjacent No. 1 dock. He was to the south, with the sunlight over his left shoulder. The afternoon sunlight highlighted the beakhead bulkhead and the weather decks, leaving the stern in shadow.

The main feature is, of course, the external carvings. To such a skilled and experienced maritime painter as van de Velde, this vessel's embellishments presented a challenge which he could hardly ignore. By 1660, their fame had spread far and wide. The rebuilding of 1659–60 had not altered them.

There is a curious confusion over the outboard fluke of the bower anchor. Aft is another fluke, lightly pencilled in. Although the dock walls concealed most of her form, he includes the entry port and gangway. When in dock, the gangway was slung outboard to render access aboard from the dock side. He depicts a staircase companionway at the starboard break of the poop. Due to the fact that the gun port covers are depicted in the raised position, the port ropes are not apparent. The masts and rigging are excluded, the greater part of which had probably been stripped off by the ship repairers.

Van de Velde the Elder described her in another drawing which he made at Chatham around 1661 (Illustration 14). This torn offset pencil and wash, unsigned drawing measuring 27.75 inches by 14.75 inches was never finished. A jagged seam runs from top to bottom around 3 inches from the right. There is another around 7 inches from the right, and a third seam around 16.75 inches from the right. If it was torn while he was working on it, then one can appreciate why it is unfinished.

The stern, waterline and rail are depicted in perspective from a position aft of the starboard quarter. Though sketchy and incomplete, we are afforded a panorama of the symmetry of the stern. The tuck here is indisputably round. The characteristic tumblehome and the upward tilt of the cat-head are accentuated in the profile of the bow on the extreme right of the drawing. Van de Velde has taken pains to highlight the stern in subtle tones, yet has left the ports and gunwale in the vaguest outline. The location of the middle and upper gun deck ports at the stern is incompatible with the levels depicted along the broadside. The arrangement of the stern decorations and ports suggests the van de Veldes' *The Portrait of Peter Pett and the* Sovereign of the Seas.

On the frontispiece is an effigy of Victory with outstretched arms and wings. Between her and the allegorical adjacent figures of Neptune and Aeolus are oval windows. The original great lantern at the taffrail is replaced by an effigy containing the Royal Arms. This drawing was acquired by the National Maritime Museum in 1935 (Cat. No. VV67).

A Mansion House was built in Blackwall, London, around 1612. The parlour was panelled in oak during 1665. Some part of this panelling was subsequently decorated by a pair of paintings. Here, Isaac Sailmaker (1633–1721) created an oil painting depicting the *Sovereign of the Seas* (Plate 25). The source for his work was Payne's engraving. Sailmaker similarly created a depiction of the *Prince Royal* of 1610 (Plate 24).

The Mansion House was rebuilt in 1678 at Blackwall Yard. A portion of panelling containing these paintings was presented to the Corporation of Trinity House by A. C. H. Wigram in 1889. The painting of the *Sovereign of the Seas* hangs in the passage at the top of the grand staircase near the door leading into the reception room of Trinity House. This large picture measures 66.5 inches by 44 inches. The composition is very poor and the quality of the work inferior to that of Payne. The yard-arm pennants, so conspicuous in Payne's engraving, are omitted.

Sailmaker's painting of the *Prince Royal* of 1610 is displayed opposite to that of the *Sovereign of the Seas* in Trinity House. The painting of the *Prince Royal,* measures 66 inches by 44 inches. It is in poor condition.

Castro's painting formed the source for a sepia drawing in line and wash depicting her port side, entitled, *The* Sovereign of the Seas *built 1637: from an Original Picture by Vandevelde. London. Published as the Act directs. April 21st. 1802 by Cadell and Davis, Strand.* Artist; T. Cadell & W. Davies (Publishers) after J. Payne (Illustration 15). This is published in black & white in J. Charnock's *An History of Marine Architecture* Vol. 2, 1801 p. 286. He states in his text that it was painted immediately after the Restoration of Charles II. The yard-arm pennants, so conspicuous in Payne's engraving, are omitted. The sea and the background vary, as do the position of the anchors and the fore tack and many other details.

An oil painting of the *Sovereign of the Seas* was acquired by William Harvey Hooper, and presented by him in 1831 to the Royal Naval Hospital, of which he was then secretary. It hangs in the panelled room in the President's House. Unfortunately, it is not available for public exhibition. It is of poor quality, and probably based on Payne's engraving.

A painting on vellum depicting the starboard side of the *Sovereign of the Seas* is in the collections of The Museum of Fine Arts, Boston, USA (Cat. No. 32.192). It is attributed to Peter Pett, after Payne. This painting is the gift of J. Templeman Coolidge. The angles and the lines of perspective are reminiscent of Payne's engraving. The embellishments are prolific around partly open gun port covers are decorated with a lion's face. The masts and rigging are not included.

We have a clue that the Boston painting was after Payne from a study of the hancing pieces on the waist. They subdue the severity of change in level between the bulwarks of the forecastle and the waist, and the waist to the half-deck. The starboard hancing

15. T. Cadell & W. Davies' etching of the *Sovereign of the Seas* (1802). After J. Payne. (*T. Cadell & W. Davies, London*)

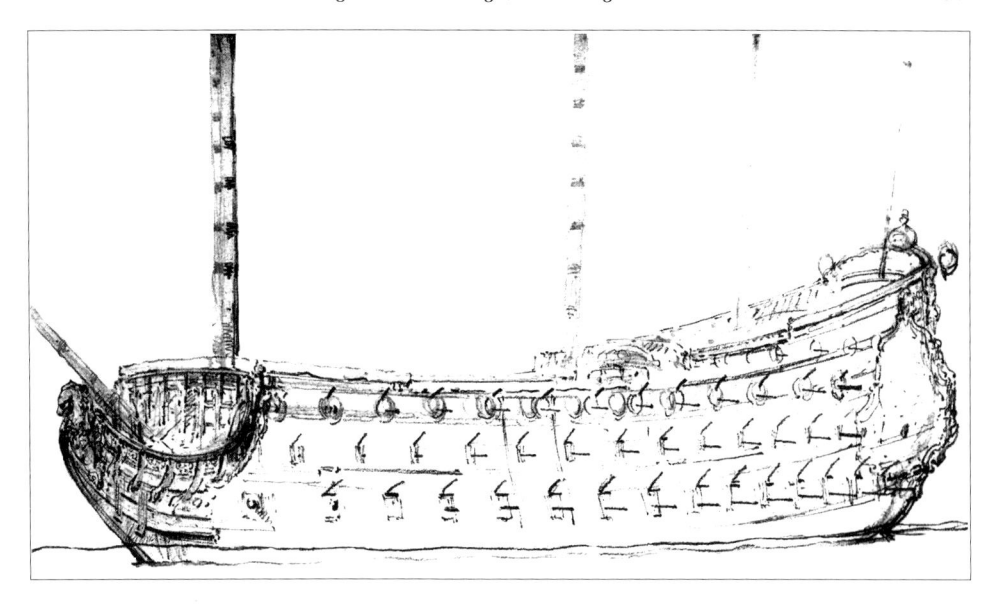

16. W. van de Velde the Elder's drawing of a Man-of-War (*Royal Sovereign*) (around 1685). Port bow view. (*National Maritime Museum*)

pieces are different to those on the port side. These hancing pieces are carved into full-sized figures.

Aft on the port side is Mars, brandishing a sword and shield with a fox to describe his cunning. This is the figure aft on the starboard side of the Boston painting.

Aft on the starboard side is Neptune wearing a spiked crown and carrying his trident, and seated on a sea horse attended by dolphins. This is the figure aft on the port side of the Boston painting.

Forward on the port side is Aeolus attended by the four winds of heaven. This is the figure forward on the starboard side of the Boston painting.

The forward port side hancing piece is not displayed on the Boston painting. We have the suggestion that this painting is after Payne, but is in reverse in depicting the starboard side.

About 1675, van de Velde the Elder made another drawing of the *Sovereign's* port elevation and quarter. The lower right of the drawing is inscribed '*roijal soeverijn*' with the date 1673 or 1675. It has an ink wash, and measures 23.8 inches by 12.6 inches. It is in the collections of The Royal Museum & Art Gallery, Canterbury, Kent (Canterbury City Council) (Reg. No. CANCM 3012.65) (Plate 26).

Only the hull is displayed. The round tuck at the stern is obvious. The profile of the tumble home forward is pronounced. Of the two anchors stowed forward, one is secured alongside the fore chain wale. The stern and quarter galleries are vague in outline. Perhaps van de Velde may have considered his earlier broadside drawing of the *Sovereign* adequate in describing the embellishments. Perhaps we have the suggestion that the stern and quarter galleries may not have incurred any modifications.

On the middle gun deck, slightly forward of the main chain-wale, is the entry port. The steps of the side are omitted. This drawing is unique in depicting skids. These were vertical riders down the side of the hull at the waist. This peculiar English practice was introduced around 1650 to provide a track down which the boats could be hoisted or lowered without fouling on the protruding wales.

There is a multitude of men about her upper decks. Many toil about the long boat, either to launch her or hoist her inboard.

17. W. van de Velde the Elder's graphite drawing of a royal visit to Chatham 1685, for the launch of the *Royal Sovereign* (1684–85). (*National Maritime Museum*)

All ports of the lower, middle and upper gun decks, the quarterdeck, forecastle and poop exhibit protruding ordnance. There is a disguised gun port in the quarter gallery on the level of the middle gun deck. The inside of the gun port covers on the lower gun deck display twin rings. These were used to lash the covers when closed. Each cover on the ports above has only one ring.

The chain wales on the fore and main are between the lower and middle gun decks. The mizen chain wale is omitted. The wooldings on the lower masts are depicted, but no top masts nor rigging are included.

An unfinished drawing of the *Sovereign* was acquired by the National Maritime Museum in 1930 (Cat. No. 488). This pencil and wash work (Plate 27) measures 32.25 inches by 12.5 inches. It is unsigned, but is the work of Willem van de Velde the Younger. From the evidence of the watermark in the paper, it dates from 1675. The starboard broadside is depicted from a point slightly abaft the beam. The drawing was probably based on an offset.

The form of the hull, particularly about the stem and stern, is less accurately expressed than would be expected from van de Velde the Younger at this period. He describes a square tuck stern, which had been altered to a rounded form. The strake curves into the rabbet at too severe an angle to conform to the requirements for a round tuck.

Although the figurehead is equestrian, the beakhead is much shorter than portrayed in any other representation. The quarter galleries and stern works are unfinished. The three cupolas aside and the stern lanterns are vague in form. The omission of detail may have been deliberate, since his father boldly described them in his broadside drawing of 1659–60 (Illustration 13).

The entry port is not depicted. This drawing depicts fenders or skids. The fenders extend from the bulwark rail down to the upper of the lowest pair of wales. Between the fourth and fifth fenders are steps of the side providing the means for sailors to clamber from a boat or jetty alongside to the waist.

Gun muzzles poke through raised ports.

The fore and main channels are depicted, but not that at the mizen. The bowsprit and spritsail topmast are clearly defined, though the foremast is mere outline. Large flags flutter from the spritsail topmast and taffrail. Sailors are in various attitudes over the weather decks.

Some Original Drawings, Paintings and Models 59

An unfinished drawing of an unidentified English three-decker, viewed from the port bow, was acquired by the National Maritime Museum from Colnaghi in 1937 (Cat. No. VV1233). This pencil representation measures 16.125 inches by 10.125 inches (Illustration 16). There is a watermark in the paper. It is unsigned, but may have been the work of W. van de Velde the Elder, around 1685.

The beakhead is boldly depicted. Perhaps van de Velde was trying to record some changes which the rebuild of 1684–85 produced. The figurehead represents a roaring rampant lion. The stem has been rebuilt. The quarter galleries have become a single turret. No entry port is depicted on the port elevation. Skids are depicted amidships.

There are fifteen gunports on the lower gun deck and thirteen on the middle and upper gun decks, with six on the half-deck. Gun muzzles poke through raised ports. The upper gun deck gunports are wreathed. There are several pencil corrections about the midships upper gun deck ports. This unusual disposition of gunports suggests that perhaps she may be the *Charles* after a rebuilding. It is more likely to be the *Royal Sovereign* after a rebuilding.

There seems to be some confusion over the foremast. Two such masts are drawn superimposing upon each other. The wooldings are different on each such mast. The wooldings on the bowsprit and mainmast are obvious. The mizen is very lightly pencilled in.

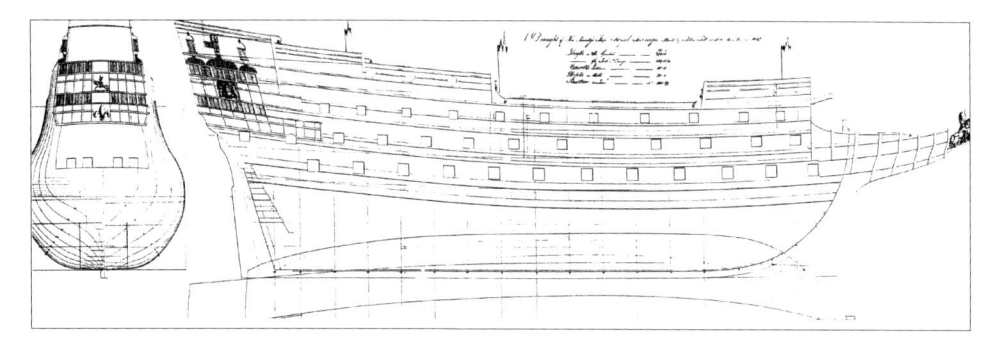

18. Reconstruction draught of the *Sovereign of the Seas* (around 1800). Starboard sheer plan, half breadth plan, body plan and stern elevation. (*National Maritime Museum*)

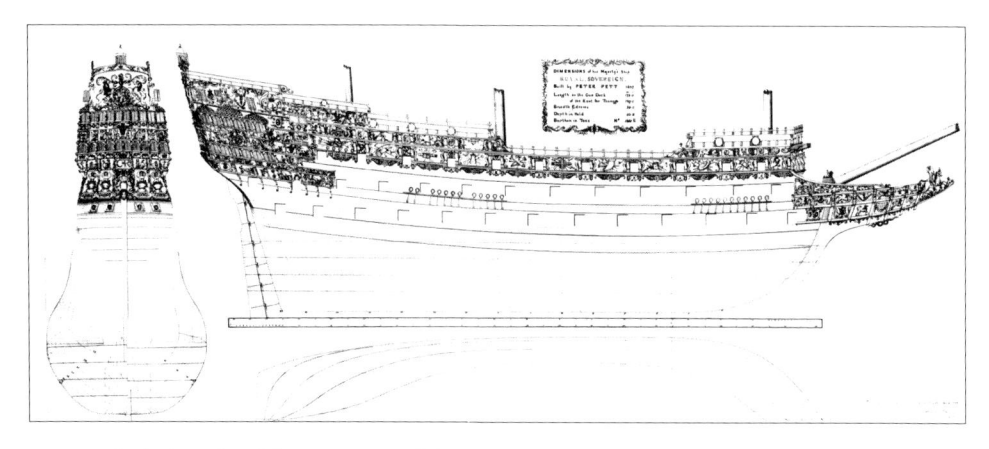

19. W. Edye's draught of the *Sovereign of the Seas* (1817). Starboard sheer plan, half breadth plan, body plan and stern elevation. (*Science Museum*)

20. Contemporary Navy Board rigged model of the *St Michael* of 1669. Starboard bow view. (*National Maritime Museum*)

The Ingram Collection in the National Maritime Museum contains a graphite drawing (Cat. No. VV1224) of a royal visit to Chatham for the launch of the *Royal Sovereign*. This drawing, measuring 24.9 inches by 18.9 inches, is the work of Van de Velde the Elder around 1684. His drawing is very sketchy, and may have been an outlay for a larger work which was never completed.

A pencil drawing acquired by the National Maritime Museum in 1932, shows the *Sovereign* at anchor with the Royal Standard at the main (Cat. No. 660). This crudely made drawing, measuring 21 inches by 14 inches, is inferior to van de Velde the Elder's later work, and may have been the work of his son Adriaen van de Velde the Younger (1636–72). This drawing has been cut at the top left. The vessel is depicted from a position off the port beam. Streamers are suspended from the yard-arms. The upright anchor in the Admiralty flag at the foremast suggests a dating of around 1686.

In the National Maritime Museum is a reconstruction draught (Cat. No. 9521) of the *Sovereign of the Seas* dating from around 1800. This formerly belonged to Lieutenant Gartside Tipping. It measures 70 inches x 21.5 inches, and may have been drawn on three separate sheets of paper and subsequently joined. There are two incongruous seams running down the draught vertically from top to bottom. They are at distances of 13.88 inches and 41.38 inches, respectively, from the left edge. The draught displays the starboard external profile with half-beam plan and stern elevation with body plan. The scale is 1:48. The height between each respective deck is exaggerated (Appendix 20). Over the waist of the ship is a table displaying the main dimensions (Appendix 21). Decoration is minimal. The equestrian King Edgar as the figurehead is displayed. There is no entry port.

In the Science Museum is another draught (Cat. No. 751). In the bottom right hand corner is the caption, 'This drawing was made by the late William Edye, Esquire (*circa*) 1817. Wolphus G. Edye Captain A.2-J.P'. This draught displays the starboard external profile with half-beam plan and stern elevation with body plan. Over the waist of the ship is a table displaying the main dimensions (Appendix 21). Edye's draught is an imperfect copy of some earlier draught. He could not have been acquainted with Heywood's book, nor even the subsequent reproduction of part of the text, viz.,

1) J. Charnock *History of Marine Architecture* Vol. 2, 1801 pp. 281–7.
2) J. S. Clark, S. Jones & J. Jones 'The *Sovereign of the Seas*', Naval Chronicle for 1807 Vol. 17, 1807 pp. 308–9.

Heywood's book describes Aeolus and Mars on the port hancing pieces of the waist, with Jupiter and Neptune in the corresponding positions on the starboard. Edye copied from an original port elevation, but reversed his draught to depict the starboard elevation. He erroneously presents Aeolus instead of Jupiter. He would never have entertained the Royal Arms in the frontispiece if he had been familiar with the van de Veldes' *The Portrait of Peter Pett and the* Sovereign of the Seas.

The frontispiece of the *Vasa* of 1627 contains a magnificently carved and gilded form of the Swedish national Royal Arms. The frontispiece on the contemporary Navy Board model of the ninety gun *St Michael* of 1669 in the National Maritime Museum portrays the Royal Arms of Charles II, finely carved and detailed. Similarly, the Royal Arms are depicted on the frontispiece of a contemporary Navy Board model of the first rate *Royal Prince* of 1670 in the Science Museum.

In the National Maritime Museum is a draught (Cat. No. 9520) of the *Sovereign of the Seas* by Sir Robert Seppings, dating from 1827. Seppings (1767–1840) was Surveyor of the Navy from 26 May 1813 to 9 June 1832. His draught measures 36.75 inches by 13.5 inches. It is printed on two sheets of paper, measuring 14.25 inches by 13.5 inches and 22.5 inches by 13.5 inches respectively. The seam occurs around two thirds of the length from the left. Holes, creases, tears and seams are prolific around the left and right hand edges are soiled and damaged, suggesting that the draught was frequently rolled up carelessly. Like many of the images in this volume, the draught as reproduced has been computer enhanced. The intention is not to deceive, but to facilitate comparison with other draughts.

The draught displays the starboard external profile with half beam plan and stern elevation with body plan. The scale is 1:96. The height between each respective deck is exaggerated (Appendix 20). Over the waist of the ship is a table displaying the main dimensions (Appendix 21).

There is a close similarity between Seppings' draught and Edye's draught. Each has one common feature. They both lack the same authoritative sources. Even van de Velde the Elder's unfinished drawing (1661) had eluded their individual researches. As they appeared within ten years of each other, it is not unreasonable to presume that Edye's draught may have provided the basis for Seppings' draught. There is a close resemblance between both in respect to the embellishments. Both portray the elaborate carvings along the bow, sides and quarters. Both possess the same error in representing the Royal Arms in the frontispiece. Payne's engraving was probably accessible, and was doubtless consulted by Seppings. There is a resemblance between Payne and Seppings with regard to the bow and broadside carvings. The minor irregularities between them may be explained by the difficulty in interpreting Payne's engraving.

Using his own draught, Sir Robert Seppings made, in 1827, a block type of model of the *Sovereign of the Seas* on the orders of the Lords of the Admiralty. Seppings was a pioneer in the field of naval architecture. He delighted in building models to arouse the interest of the Lords of the Admiralty in his novel ideas.

Seppings' model is to the scale of 1:48 (Cat. No. 1637–1, SLRO356) (Plate 28, Illustrations 22 & 23). At the stern is a round tuck. The seams of the deck planks and the strakes at the side are worked in pencil or ink. The hull and fittings are stained and varnished. The deck arrangement is out of character with the known disposition of the *Sovereign*. The embellishments are carved in boxwood. The frontispiece contains the Hanoverian armorial device. The fonds for the panels are painted green. The prolific gilding about the embellishments has the patina of age.

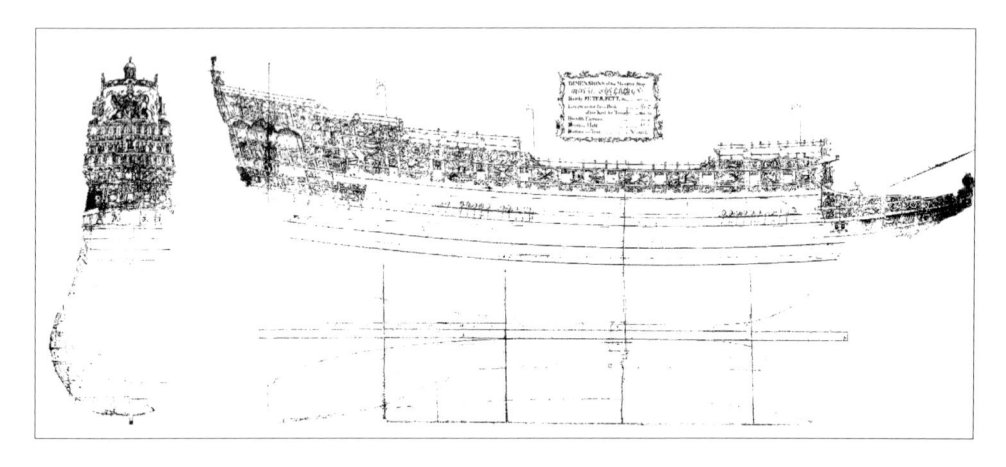

21. Sir R. Seppings' draught of the *Sovereign of the Seas* (1827). Starboard sheer plan, half breadth plan, body plan and stern elevation. (*National Maritime Museum*)

22. Sir R. Seppings' model of the *Sovereign of the Seas* (1827). Starboard elevation. (*National Maritime Museum*)

Due to the perspective in Payne's engraving, only two gun muzzles are visible on the port elevation of his beakhead bulkhead. The third is masked by the cat-head and ship's gear. Seppings misinterpreted Payne and erroneously mounts two guns only on each side of the beakhead bulkhead.

After collecting all contemporary models, and those from previous eras which were available to him, Seppings established the Model Room at Somerset House. This was a commodious and imposing gallery on the second floor in the centre of the south or main building, facing the River Thames. Probably, he modelled her to complete a collection of the most significant vessels then known.

The collection was expanded due to the energies of Seppings' successor Sir William Symonds. In 1864 the collection was transferred to the newly created Royal School of Naval Architecture at South Kensington, where it became accessible to the public. In 1873 a significant proportion, containing Seppings' model of the *Sovereign*, was moved to the Royal Naval College at Greenwich and displayed in the gallery of marine art, which became the painted hall. Together with the Greenwich Hospital collection, which contained important examples presented by King William IV in 1830, this collection was transferred to the National Maritime Museum at Greenwich in 1934. At the opening of this Museum in April 1937, King George VI and Queen Elizabeth, with Queen Mary and the future Queen Elizabeth II, posed for a photograph behind Seppings' model of the *Sovereign of the Seas*.

This model was displayed in the former Neptune Hall. Hence it was moved to the Queen's House. For many years now, it has been consigned to storage at Kidbrooke awaiting restoration.

In 1851 John Fincham published a draught of the *Sovereign of the Seas*. The starboard sheer plan is reproduced in Illustration 24. The body plan, half beam plans and stern elevation are in Illustration 25. The dotted lines surrounding the plans represent the contours of a typical mid-nineteenth-century vessel. In the text before the draught is a table listing the main dimensions (Appendix 21).

The curvature of the beakhead bulkhead is obvious.

Other than the figurehead, hawse-holes, hancing pieces of the waist, and part of the quarter galleries, the embellishments are sparse. Fincham's figurehead is that of St George and the Dragon. The frontispiece in the stern elevation contains a grand representation of the Royal Arms.

The four gunports of the stern chase on the lower gun deck are included, but not those of the middle nor upper gun decks. The aftermost gunport on the broadside of the upper gun deck is missing. The outline may have been lost among the lines of the quarter gallery. Instead of the usual four gunports on each side of the forecastle, Fincham depicts only two.

The chain-wales are depicted.

Fincham's draught and stern elevation bear no resemblance to the text of Heywood, nor indeed to the van de Veldes' *The Portrait of Peter Pett and the* Sovereign of the Seas.

Neither does Fincham suggest recourse to the reconstruction draught, nor those of Edye and Seppings. Perhaps he based his lines on those prevalent draughts during the mid-nineteenth century. His sources have not been identified. Fincham's draught, however, serves to compare her overall size with a vessel typical of the mid-nineteenth century.

In February 1918, Mr Howell, a wealthy ship enthusiast, commissioned Henry B. Culver of New York, the Secretary of the American Ship Model Society, to produce a model. It was created at a great distance from the sources of original informative. War conditions caused a severe handicap for research, yet at a cost of $30,000, this model, on a scale of 1:48, was the most ambitious piece of reconstruction attempted in any country.

23. Sir R. Seppings' model of the *Sovereign of the Seas* (1827). Port bow view. (*National Maritime Museum*)

Culver studied various authoritative sources:

1) J. Payne's engraving of the *Sovereign of the Seas* (1636).
2) W. van de Velde the Elder's broadside drawing (1660).
3) The van de Veldes' *The Portrait of Peter Pett and the* Sovereign of the Seas (1660).
4) R. C. Anderson 'The *Royal Sovereign* of 1637' M.M. 3, 1913 No. 2 pp. 109–12; 3, 1913 No. 2 pp. 168–70; 3, 1913 No. 3 pp. 208–11.
5) A draught in oil on four wooden panels, possibly by Sir A. van Dyck, from the collection of Mr Oatway. The starboard side of a ship, purported to be the *Sovereign of the Seas*, is described.
6) Sir R. Seppings' model of the *Sovereign of the Seas* (1827).
7) W. G. Perrin 'The Autobiography of Phineas Pett' N.R.S. 51, 1918.
8) A manuscript from Lord Leconfield's collection at Petworth House was provided by R. C. Anderson, who subsequently published it (S.N.R. 1958 No. 6 pp. 46–64) 9). R. C. Anderson provided Culver with another manuscript, dated 1640, from the same collection. It was subsequently edited by G. S. Laird Clowes and published S.N.R. No. 3. 1931 (Appendix 41).
10) J. Smith *A Sea Grammar*, 1627.

A solid core, slightly smaller than the outside skin, was constructed in several pieces to facilitate subsequent removal. The stem, sternpost, keel and ribs were built up over this core. The outer planking of spruce 0.25 inch wide by 0.125 inch was nailed in place, and the core removed. A round tuck stern is included. The floor beams, lower decks and bulkheads are built. The embellishments are modelled in plasticine. From this, gelatine moulds were made. Plaster casts were taken from these moulds. The wood carvers employed by Culver worked from the retouched sets of plaster casts to carve the boxwood. The frontispiece is fashioned according to Heywood.

When the whole structure of the vessel was completed, skids, corbels and window frames were cut and secured. Lattices were cast in lead, gilded, and applied to the glass itself of the windows in the stern and quarter galleries. Culver modelled a short flight of steps from the doorway in the fore part of the beakhead bulkhead to the deck below. This feature is omitted by Payne.

The three anchors at the port bow follow Payne. The forward anchor is suspended from its cable. A double sheave block is hooked to the bow of the anchor from the three sheaves in the cat-head above.

Culver's light spar deck over the waist follows Payne. Culver includes a small ship's boat on stocks on this spar deck. His spar deck over the half-deck is open in the centre down the medial plane. The forecastle deck, quarterdeck and round house are made separately but were not secured until all the embellishments, guns and other fittings were ready for assembly.

Gun-carriages for the lower gun deck are fitted. Culver copied Seppings' mistake over the number of guns mounted in the beakhead bulkhead. Culver mounts two guns only on each aside.

Culver's rigging follows Payne. The fore and main royal yards, the mizen topgallant yard and the spritsail and spritsail topsail yards are sent down with the sails fartherled. The fair-lead for the fore-tacks is carved in serpentine form after Payne. The ratlines on the shrouds are made with eyes at the ends, the lashings passing through the eyes and around the outside shroud. The blocks are made of highly polished cocos wood, and are stropped with cord instead of metal. The sails are made of the finest and heaviest quality of Japanese silk, which was stretched and pasted upon beaten aluminium frames. Culver's banners and flags imitate Payne's.

In colour, Culver deviated from authenticity. Below the level of the waterline, the hull is in ochre. The wales are black. Pale blue accentuate the fonds of the panels.

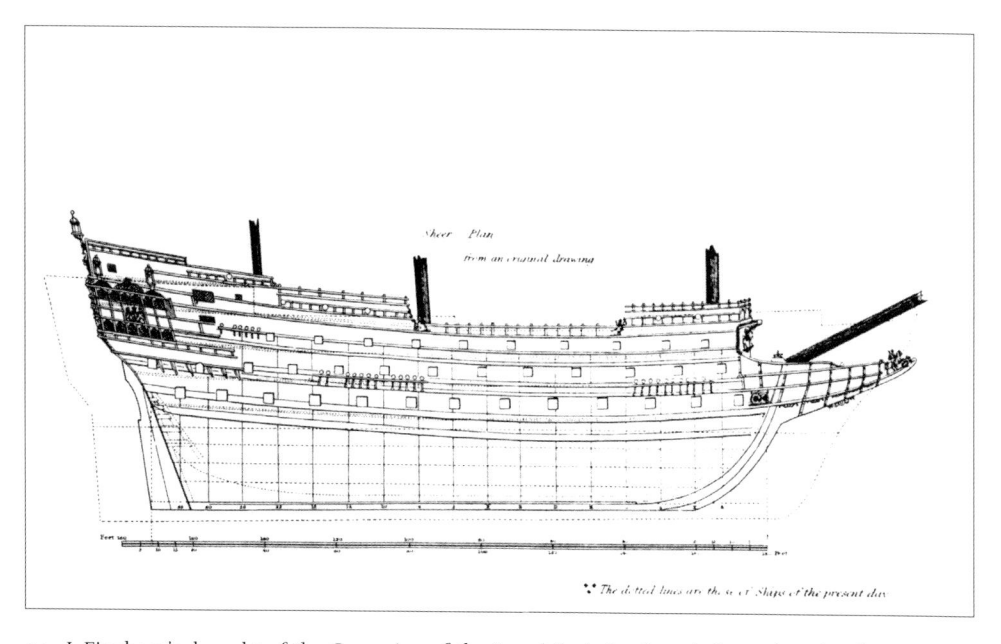

24. J. Fincham's draught of the *Sovereign of the Seas* (1851). Starboard sheer plan. (*Scolar Press, London*)

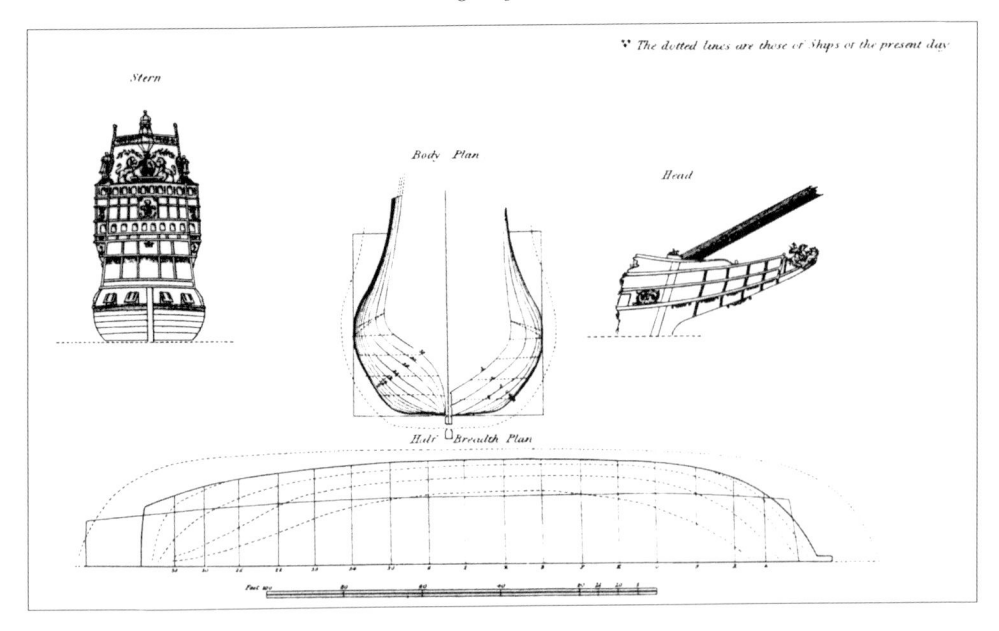

25. J. Fincham's draught of the *Sovereign of the Seas* (1851). Body plan, half breadth plan and stern elevation. (*Scolar Press, London*)

26. H. B. Culver's model of the *Sovereign of the Seas* (1921). Starboard view of waist and main chain-wales. (*Dr A. R. Kriegstein*)

Some Original Drawings, Paintings and Models 67

There is a sparing use of red in the raised decoration, which is prolific in gold. The only use for green is to suggest tarnishing of the guns.

Since completion in 1921, Culver's model remains the most accurate model of this vessel extant. It was purchased from Mr Howell's estate by Richardson Pratt and donated to the Pratt Institute, Brooklyn, New York, where it remained in the library for many years. It has been displayed in the Architectural League of New York and the Museum of Science and Industry. The Kriegstein family acquired it directly from the Pratt Institute around 1980. The Kriegstein family loaned the model to the Naval Academy Museum, Annapolis, Maryland, where it is currently displayed.

Culver's model seems to have been the source for V. H. Green's unfinished model of the *Sovereign*, published by E. Keble Chatterton in 1934.

27. H. B. Culver's model of the *Sovereign of the Seas* (1921). Port quarter view.
(*Halton & Co. Ltd., London*)

Gregory Robinson published a draught of the *Sovereign of the Seas* in 1936. Plate 53 depicts the port sheer plan, body plan and sail plan. The embellishments are included. The close resemblance to Payne's engraving is obvious. The interest in this draught lies in the fact that Robinson suggests the trim about the waterline.

In the Science Museum is a model constructed by A. C. Jackson on a scale of 1:96. It was lent to the Museum in 1943 by his son, R. Jackson (Cat. No. 42/54).

In designing this model, Jackson had recourse to the following sources:

1) J. Payne's engraving of the *Sovereign of the Seas* (1636).
2) The van de Veldes' *The Portrait of Peter Pett and the* Sovereign of the Seas (1660).
3) W. Edye's draught of the *Sovereign of the Seas* (1817).

The hull is shaped from a solid wooden block. He erroneously depicts a square tuck stern. In the centre of the spar deck over the waist are hatch coamings with a capstan forward. This great ship had windlasses, not capstans. Below the level of the waterline, the model is painted white, reminiscent of the van de Veldes' *The Portrait of Peter Pett and the* Sovereign of the Seas.

The bulwarks and prow are black. The embellishments are gilded. The inside of the gun deck ports is red. The inside of the middle and upper gun deck ports is adorned with small gold coloured squares. The lower masts and bowsprit are stepped in place, but carry no rigging.

Subsequently, several excellent models were made in the USA by Clyde Chaffin and John Dupray, both of the Ship Modellers Association of Southern California, and Theodore Pugh of the Ship Modellers Guild of San Diego.

Probably the best modern image of high fidelity and casting richness may be provided in Sergal's model Cat. No. 787, scale 1:78, of the *Sovereign of the Seas*. This kit in 700 pieces may be obtained from Mantua Model, CP 46048, S. Lucia di Roverbella, Mantova, Italy. The model is based on Payne's engraving. But, modellers beware: the representation of the Royal Arms across the frontispiece is after the draughts of W. Edye (1817), and Sir R. Seppings (1827), and not Heywood's original design.

A rigged wood-effect resin model, around 17 inches long, of the *Sovereign of the Seas*, Cat. No. 7635, supplied complete and ready for display, may be obtained from Nauticalia Mail Order Catalogue, The Ferry Point, Ferry Lane, Shepperton-on-Thames, Middlesex TW17 9LQ. A similar model Ref. No. 760014, is available from RNLI (Sales) Ltd., Lifeboat Support Centre, West Quay Road, Poole, BH15 1HZ.

To any enthusiast determined on creating a model of this great ship, as she would have appeared in her original form, the following sources are recommended:

1) J. Payne's engraving of the *Sovereign of the Seas* (1636).
2) The van de Veldes' *The Portrait of Peter Pett and the* Sovereign of the Seas (1660).
3) W. van de Velde the Elder's broadside drawing of the *Sovereign of the Seas* (1660).
4) Reconstruction draught of the *Sovereign of the Seas* (c. 1800).

In all her ornate splendour, she was the epitome of the glory and beauty of the bygone age of sail. This stately ship would be a fitting subject to sail down the tide of skill and patience, to anchor in some hallowed niche around the home.

Reconstruction of Phineas Pett's original masterpiece is difficult. The evidence is flimsy. We are left with the scattered crumbs from a banqueting table of a bygone feast. From such crumbs we struggle to reconstruct the nature of the feast. We can but speculate on the appeal of the vanished delicacies.

A skilled craftsman could successfully demonstrate her exquisite contours and beauty in model form, however great a challenge that may be, but her vast size and increase in tonnage over her contemporaries could only be elucidated by a mathematician.

28. H. B. Culver's model of the *Sovereign of the Seas* (1921). Port bow view.
(*The Studio Ltd., London*)

29. H. B. Culver's model of the *Sovereign of the Seas* (1921). Stern carvings. (*Society for Nautical Research*)

CHAPTER 4

Her Size Calculated in Tonnage

Tonnage is the term describing the magnitude of a vessel. It is a corruption of the term tunnage, derived from tun. This was a large cask for storing and shipping wine. The size of a tun was determined by Act of Parliament in 1423 at not less than 252 wine gallons, which is equal to 40.32 cubic feet. A tun was the largest wine package, and 252 gallons lent itself admirably to subdivision. Consequently, tonnage was originally a statement of the number of wine casks which a vessel could carry. Henry VII's Navigation Act of 1485 inaugurated the measurement of English vessels by the method of tonnage capacity. Standard mathematical systems of determining tonnage began to evolve.

Tonnage capacity was calculated from such measurements as the length of the keel, the beam and the depth in the hold.

A committee, consisting of Admiral Sir John Pennington, Vice Admiral Sir Robert Mansell, Phineas Pett and John Wells, the Storekeeper at Deptford Royal Dockyard, examined Phineas' plans for the *Sovereign* and drew up a schedule of proposed dimensions (Appendix 7). The gross tonnage calculated from the depth in the hold was to be 1,466. When the value for the draught in water was substituted for the depth in hold, the tonnage was to be 1,661, and similarly from the mean beam, 1,836. These proposals were approved by Charles I on 7 April 1635.

Sir John Pennington proposed a slight modification, resulting in the dimensions entered in Appendix 7. By one method of calculation the tonnage was to be 1,522, and by another 1,884. This final modification was endorsed by Charles I on 17 April 1635. We do not know how much of either proposal was used. It is unlikely that the final proposal supplanted the initial proposal. Phineas Pett doubtless used these proposals as a guide rather than as a specification.

On 13 June 1637, a survey was made of her partly completed hull to establish her actual dimensions. His Majesty's Shipwrights, and the chief shipwrights of the Thames, assisted by six experienced seamen from Trinity House, undertook this survey. They realised the dimensions:

1) Length of keel between false posts. This was the 'touch' measure – (kfp) was 127 feet.
2) Beam moulded to inside of planking at the dead-flat position. This was the beam amidships inboard from plank to plank – (bm) was 46 feet 6 inches.
3) Depth in hold from extreme beam to upper edge of keel at dead-flat position – (h4) was 19 feet 4 inches.

30. V. H. Green's unfinished model of the *Sovereign of the Seas* (1934). (*Hurst & Blackett Ltd., London*)

During the early part of the seventeenth century, there were two distinct methods of keel measurement. The 'touch' was the length along the rabbet of the keel, from aft of the sternpost to the point where the rabbet of the stem began to curve upwards. This was compatible to the length between false posts (kfp). These were additional timbers secured to the front of the stem and after end of the stern post to provide strength to the main timbers. Until around 1677, tonnage was calculated using the 'touch' keel measure.

The 'tread' was measured along the bottom of the keel to the angle where the fore edge of the cut-water began to rise. This was as much as she trod on the ground, measured from the heel to the forefoot. The 'tread' measure was always the largest value.

The dead-flat position was the point of midship bend. It was the greatest beam in the transverse section. It was fixed at a point mid-length between perpendiculars. The position was designated on shipwrights' draughts by the use of the Greek letter '*theta*' Θ. This character has been used throughout this chapter and the Appendices. The greatest beam was around 3 feet above the waterline, such that when the vessel heeled under sail the main beam held. This provided stability.

Her Size Calculated in Tonnage

There were two distinct methods of measuring beam. This was done at the point of greatest breadth, '*theta*' Θ. The beam moulded was measured to the inside of the planking (bm). The extreme beam was measured to the outside of the planking (bx), excluding wales at Θ. Later in the seventeenth century, the beam moulded was abandoned in favour of the extreme beam. The extreme beam was always the largest value.

Early shipwrights' designs had an arbitrary keel:beam ratio, viz.,

kfp:bx	2.78:1
Mary Rose	c. 2.82:1
Great Harry	c. 3:1
Prince Royal	2.61:1
Sovereign	2.65:1

Similarly, the depth in hold:beam ratio, viz.,

h4:bm	0.43:1
Mary Rose	c. 0.40:1
Great Harry	c. 0.45:1
Prince Royal	0.42:1
Sovereign	0.42:1

The development of the elongation of the vessel's hull, which improved its ability to sail to windward, was characterised by the ratio, length on deck:length of keel:beam, viz.,

gd:kfp:bx	3:2:1
Mary Rose	c. 3.3:2.8:1
Great Harry	c. 3.5:3:1
Prince Royal	3.5:2.6:1
Sovereign	3.5:2.6:1

The length along the lower gun deck was measured outside of the planking from the rabbet of the sternpost to the rabbet of the stem (gd). The shortest distance between the stem and stern posts was impossible to measure, since along the centre line of the lower gun deck were such obstacles as masts, bitts, windlass and hatch coamings.

The average Elizabethan galleon was characterised by the ratio 2:3:1. Thus, the *Mary Rose* and the *Great Harry* were both designed as carracks rather than galleons. Neither the *Prince Royal* nor the *Sovereign* could be described as a carrack or a galleon, but marked a departure from the early traditions in shipbuilding.

During the early part of the seventeenth century, there were several methods of measuring a vessel for determining tonnage. Elizabethan Navy Lists recorded tons burden. Royal dockyards, even until late in the twentieth century, employed Mathew Baker's method established in 1582. It remained in vogue during the reign of James I. In 1627 John Wells described this technique, which was ratified by an order in Council on 26 May 1628:

(1) Tons burden = (kfp x bm x h4)/100
Where:
kfp = length of keel between false posts, viz. the 'touch'

bm = beam moulded to inside of planking at Θ
h4 = depth in hold from extreme beam to upper edge of keel at Θ

The register ton was defined as 100 cubic feet, hence the divisor of 100.

Customs dues on merchant vessels were charged on tons and tonnage, synonymous with gross tons. This was the gross capacity of cargo in bulk. Barrels of wine were round and curved. Therefore, there was some inevitable interstitial space between each contiguous barrel. In order to obtain the total internal capacity of the hold containing the barrels, the value for the burden required an increase. Elizabethan burden was multiplied by a factor of 5/4 to produce gross tons. Later, this factor was adjusted to 4/3. If we divide the area of a square of side 2 x radius, by the area of a circle of diameter 2 x radius, the product is 4/3.142. When rounded to the nearest whole integer, the product is 4/3.

(2) Gross tons = tons burden x 4/3

A careful survey of the *Prince Royal* taken in 1632 established her dimensions (Appendix 5). When the relevant values are entered into these equations we obtain:

Tons burden = (115 x 43 x 18)/100 = 890.1
Gross tons = 890.1 x 4/3 = 1,186.8

When the relevant dimensions of the *Sovereign* as entered in Appendix 8 are substituted in these equations we obtain:

Tons burden = (127 x 46.5 x 19.33)/100 = 1,141.53
Gross tons = 1,141.53 x 4/3 = 1,522.0

Seventeenth-century shipwrights recorded tons to the nearest whole integer. These values are frequently correctly quoted in the literature. With similar proportions to the *Prince Royal*, the *Sovereign* demonstrated an increase in burden of some 251 tons. Similarly, using the relevant dimensions for *La Couronne* of 1635 (Appendix 6) we obtain 957 tons burden using equation (1), and 1,276 gross tonnage using equation (2).

The second method employed during the early part of the seventeenth century was assumed by the shipwrights of the Thames to be the 'old rule':

(3) Tons burden = (kfp x bx x d3)/94
Where:
bx = Beam extreme excluding wales at Θ
d3 = Draught in water at extreme beam to bottom of keel at Θ

Every 94 cubic feet of the shape represented by kfp x bx x d3 was reckoned as 1 ton.

We may calculate the 'old rule' for the *Sovereign*:

Tons burden = (127 x 48 x 21.083)/94 = 1,367.25
Gross tons = 1367.25 x 4/3 = 1,823

These measurements were determined when the vessel was high and dry, with no tackle nor stores, nor waterline to confuse the measurement. Such relationships were designed primarily for cargo-carrying vessels, but were also applied to evaluating warships.

The third way of determining tonnage was proposed by Edmund Gunter, Phineas Pett, Edward Stevens, Hugh Lydiard and John Wells, who in 1626–7 were required by

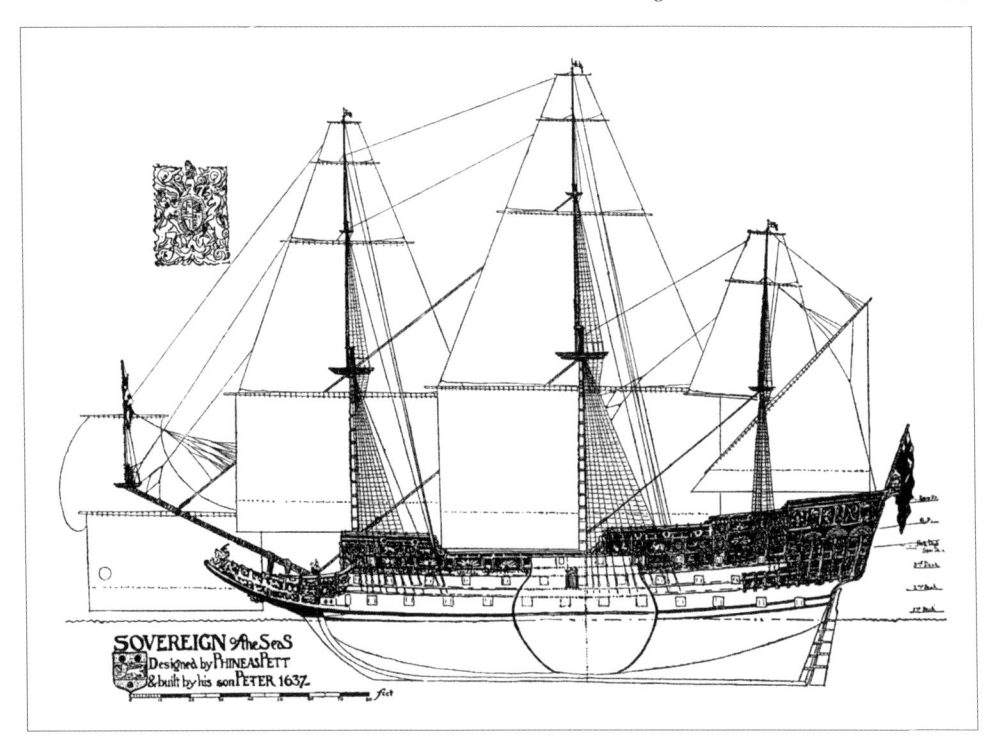

31. G. Robinson's draught of the *Sovereign of the Seas* (1936). Port sheer plan, body plan and sail plan. (*Peter Davies Ltd., & Lovat Dickson Ltd., London*)

32. A. C. Jackson's model of the *Sovereign of the Seas* (1943). Starboard quarter view. (*Science Museum*)

33. J. Dupray's model of the *Sovereign of the Seas* (1982). Ship's bell. (*Ship Modellers' Association of Southern California, USA*)

34. J. Dupray's model of the *Sovereign of the Seas* (1982). Starboard bow. (*Ship Modellers' Association of Southern California, USA*)

George Villiers, First Duke of Buckingham (1592–1628), Lord High Admiral, and the Commissioners of the Navy, to measure the *Adventure* of Ipswich, the greatest bilged vessel in the Thames. From her dimensions, they were required to formulate a rule which might be applicable to other frames.

Their method might be expressed:

(4) Tons burden = (kfp x h3 x bs)/65
Where:
h3 = Depth hold at extreme beam to upper floor of the ceiling at Θ
bs = Mean beam within the ceiling at half of this depth

We may substitute the relevant values for the *Royal Prince* from Appendix 5 into equation (4):

Tons burden = (115 x 16.25 x 36)/65 = 1,035
Gross tons = 1,035 x 4/3 = 1,380

The relevant values for the *Sovereign* produces the relationship:

Tons burden = (127 x 17.167 x 42.127)/65 = 1,413.01
Gross tons = 1,414 x 4/3 = 1,884.01

The value of 1,884 gross tons is compatible with that specified on 17 April 1635. Thus, we have some verification of the use of equation (4).

There was a fourth method of determining tonnage. This was devised by the shipwrights and Masters of Trinity House.

(5) Tons burden = (kfp x bx)/70
The relevant values for the *Sovereign* produces the relationship:
Tons burden = (127 x 48)/70 = 87.085
Gross tons = 87 x 4/3 = 116.114

This method was abandoned early because the values so derived were absurd!

The essentials of formulae (1) and (3) survived to 1694. By which time some of the parameters had become interchangeable.

(6) Tons burden = (kfp x bx x h4)/96
Where:
h4 = Depth in hold from extreme beam to the upper edge of keel at Θ

The internal capacity of the tun is 40.32 cubic feet. By 1687 one ton of shipping was fixed at a capacity of 42 cubic feet. If we divide 40.32 by 42, the product is 0.96. Hence the use of 96 as a divisor.

The relevant values for the *Sovereign* produces the relationship:

Tons burden = (127 x 48 x 19.333)/96 = 1,227.65
Gross tons = 1,227.65 x 4/3 = 1,636.87

The value of 1,637 tons and tonnage occurs frequently in the literature, and may have been based on Heywood. Authors quoting this value have realised the coincidence in numerical identity with the year of her launch.

A skilful and experienced surveyor would have realised no difficulty in measuring the depth in the hold, the extreme beam and moulded beam. But the determination of keel

35. Pugh's model of the *Sovereign of the Seas* (1982). Stern galleries.
(*Ship Modellers' Guild of San Diego, USA*)

36. T. Pugh's model of the *Sovereign of the Seas* (1982). Great lantern. (*Ship Modellers' Guild of San Diego, USA*)

length could only be accomplished adequately when the vessel was high and dry. The rake of both stem and sternposts was not always constant, and fluctuated throughout their length. The determination of keel length afloat always presented a problem. During the 1670s and 1680s the terms 'tread' and 'touch' measures for the length of the keel were applied indiscriminately. Because of this, many anomalies have occurred in Navy Lists.

By order of the Council of State on 2 January 1664–5, another method of defining keel length was established in private and royal yards. This was known as 'Shipwright's Hall Rule'. The keel length was deduced from the harping rule:

(7) khr = pp – 0.6 bx
Where:
khr = Length of keel from the harping rule
pp = Length between perpendiculars. This was measured from the after end of the keel to a perpendicular dropped from the fore side of the stem at the level of the upper edge of the lower main wale or 'harping'
Length of keel from the harping rule = 159.833 – (0.6 x 48) = 131.03

At around 1665 there appeared the relationship known as the 'Builders' Old Measurement Rule':

(8) Tons burden = (khr x bx x 0.5 x bx)/94

From around 1650 onwards, the beam is usually listed as extreme beam. This particular relationship is cited in the Establishment of 1719. It remained in use until 1835. The relevant values for the *Sovereign* produces the relationship:

Tons burden = (131 x 48 x 0.5 x 48)/94 = 1,605.45
Gross tons = 1,605.45 x 4/3 = 2,140.6

The terms tons burden and gross tonnage were employed without distinction, and have created confusion. This dual system of nomenclature ceased shortly after 1660. The use of equation (2) became obsolete.

In Lists for the years 1659, 1686 (Appendix 16), 1688 (Appendix 17) and 1689 (Appendix 18), we find the dimensions:

Keel length (harping rule)	131 feet 0 inch
Beam (extreme)	48 feet 0 inch
Tonnage	1,605 tons

When these values are inserted into equation (8), we have:

Tons = (131 x 48 x 24)/94 = 1605.45 tons

Lists for the years 1660 and 1665 recorded:

Keel length	127 feet 0 inch
Beam	47 feet 10 inches
Tonnage	1,545 tons

80 *Sovereign of the Seas*

37. Sergal's model of the *Sovereign of the Seas*. Various details. (*Mantua Model, Italy*)

When these values are inserted into equation (8), we have:

Tons = (127 x 47.833 x 23.92)/94 = 1,545.84

Lists for 1684 and 1685 record the dimensions:

Keel length	135 feet 6 inches
Length along lower gun deck	167 feet 9 inches
Beam (extreme)	48 feet 4 inches
Depth in hold	19 feet 3 inches
Tonnage	1,683 tons

When these values are inserted into equation (8), we have:

Tons = (135.5 x 48.333 x 0.5 x 48.333)/94 = 1,683.72

As realised from an examination of Appendix 22, there is a remarkable resemblance between the dimensions scaled up from Edye's draught and those similarly produced from Seppings' draught. There is the suggestion that one was copied from the other. When we scale up the measurements from the reconstruction draught, we produce dimensions which are incompatible with Edye and Seppings.

The main dimensions scaled up from Edye's draught and Seppings' draught suggest a similarity with Fisher Harding's *Royal Sovereign*. The third vessel by this name, she was a first rate of 112 guns, built at Woolwich Royal Dockyard and launched on 25 July 1701:

Length of keel, 'tread' (kt)	158 feet 0 inch
Length of keel, harping rule (khr)	141 feet 7 inches
Length along lower gun deck (gd)	174 feet 6 inches
Beam moulded (bm)	48 feet 5 inches
Beam extreme (bx)	50 feet 3.5 inches
Depth in hold (h1)	20 feet 1 inch
Depth in hold (h2)	19 feet 10 inches
Tons burden	1,883

When these values are inserted into equation (8), we have:

Tons = (141.58 x 50 x 0.5 x 50)/94 = 1,882.7

In the National Maritime Museum is a painting of her by Willem van de Velde the Younger (Plate 39). She is flying William III's Royal Standard. A contemporary British Navy Board model of her hull, to a scale of 1:48, was presented as a gift from Queen Anne of England to Peter the Great of Russia in the period 1707–1714. This model has survived and is in the Central Naval Museum, Saint Petersburg, Russia (Illustrations 38–41). The model bears the cypher 'W.R.' On the stern and the figurehead are the armorial bearings of William and Mary.

There was some difficulty measuring the depth in the hold when full of cargo. Therefore, another method of evaluating tonnage developed. By 1720, half the beam was substituted for the measured depth in hold. It seems to have been correct only in instances where the value of the depth in the hold continued to be exactly half of the extreme beam.

It will be observed from Appendix 8 that there were four dimensions for the depth in the hold, viz. h1, h2, h3 and h4. The ratio of the depth in the hold:extreme beam was found to be 0.420, 0.399, 0.358 and 0.403 respectively.

Although equation (1) was eminently satisfactory for shipbuilders, it was difficult to apply it to a vessel with cargo aboard. The custom developed of measuring extreme beam to the outside of the plank, neglecting wales and doubling strakes. The keel length was a function of the length on the deck minus three-fifths of the beam as the overhang forward. The depth in the hold was assumed to be equal to half the beam.

The equation used for warships around 1677 might be expressed:

(9) Tons burden = [(gd – 0.6 bx) x bx x 0.5 x bx]/94
Where:
gd = length along the lower gun deck

The relevant values for the *Sovereign* produces the relationship:

Tons = [(167.75 – 28.8) x 48 x 0.5 x 48]/94 = 1,702.88

The English Tonnage law, enacted in 1773 as the Builders' Old Measurement, made use of equation (9), with the exception that the length along the lower gun deck was substituted by the 'touch' measure of keel length. The Builders' Old Measurement remained in use as the official mode of measurement for ships of the Royal Navy until 1872, when it was replaced by a method to determine tonnage by displacement.

Equation (9) assumes that sixty per cent of the total displacement of merchant vessels was cargo. The remaining forty per cent constituted the weight of the vessel herself complete with stores and equipment. The mean coefficient of fineness, otherwise known as the block coefficient, of seventeenth-century hulls is approximately 0.62. This was the ratio of the volume of the hull immersed compared with the volume of a rectangular box of identical length, breadth and depth. If we assume that the draught in the water was approximately equal to half the beam, and if the length along the lower gun deck was approximately equal to the length between perpendiculars, then by analogy with the length of the keel from the harping rule, the length of the keel could be expressed satisfactorily by the relationship gd – 0.6 bx.

We may, consequently, derive the relationship:

(10) Dead weight tonnage = [0.6(gd – 0.6 bx) x bx x 0.5 x bx x 0.62]/K
Where:
K = volume of 2,240 lb sea water at 62 degrees Fahrenheit, viz. 34.97 cubic feet

The relevant values for the *Sovereign* produces the relationship:

Dead weight tonnage = [0.6(167.75 – 28.8) x 48 x 0.5 x 48 x 0.62]/34.97 = 1,702.78

By simplifying equation (10), we obtain the relationship:

(11) Dead weight tonnage = [(gd – 0.6 bx) x bx x 0.5 x bx]/94

Consequently, we have:

Dead weight tonnage = [(167.75 – 28.8) x 48 x 0.5 x 48]/94 = 1,702.88

As expected, the value of dead weight tonnage from equation (11) is identical to that calculated from equations (9) and (10). During the seventeenth century, however, the concept of tonnage was pertinent to a volume measurement. It is doubtful if the principle of displacement was as advanced at that time as this analysis implies. It is unfortunate that this argument involves several drastic assumptions.

Archimedes' Principle states that the apparent loss in weight experienced by a body when immersed in liquid is equal to the weight of liquid displaced. Hence, the weight of liquid displaced is equal to the weight of the immersed body. This principle of physics has found application in the calculation of displacement tonnage. The mean area of cross section of the water-immersed hull may be deduced for a given draught in water. Hence, the volume of the water-immersed hull may be calculated. This volume, when divided by a function of the density of sea water, produces a value for the weight of water displaced. This, in turn, is equal to the weight of the vessel.

Hence, we may express the relationship:

(12) Displacement tonnage = (cf x wl x d2 x bx)/K
Where:
cf = Coefficient of fineness, otherwise known as the block coefficient (Appendix 22)
wl = Length of hull along waterline from rabbet to rabbet
d2 = Draught in water from waterline to rabbet

The relevant values for the *Sovereign* produces the relationship:

Displacement tonnage = (0.609 x 166.917 x 20.667 x 48)/34.97 = 2,883.64

Alternatively, the expression may be simplified to:

(13) Displacement tonnage = (wl x A)/K
Where:
A = mean area (square feet) of cross section of water-immersed hull, at a draught in water of 20 feet 8 inches (Appendix 19)

The relevant values for the *Sovereign* produces the relationship:

Displacement tonnage = (166.917 x 604)/34.97 = 2,882.98

Hence, the displacement tonnage of the *Sovereign* at a draught in water of 20 feet 8 inches was calculated at 2,883 tons. The displacement tonnage, un-laden, calculated on a draught in water of 19 feet 6 inches, was 2,721 tons. The displacement tonnage, laden, on a draught in water of 23 feet 6 inches, was 3,279 tons (Appendix 39).

A modern approach to tonnage determination is exemplified by the Thames yacht measurement. It was adopted by the Royal Thames Yacht Club in 1854, and the Yacht Racing Association in 1878. This is used in assessing modern yachts and similar light craft. Although irrelevant in establishing the tonnage of a seventeenth-century warship, it is intriguing to make this comparison with modern vessels. The interest lies in its similarity to equations (8), (9) and (11):

(14) Thames tonnage = [(ld – bx) x bx x 0.5 x bx]/94
Where:
ld = length along deck from fore side of stem to after side of sternpost. This is similar to the length between perpendiculars.

The relevant values for the *Sovereign* produces the relationship:

$$\text{Thames tonnage} = [(159.833 - 48) \times 48 \times 0.5 \times 48]/94 = 1{,}370.55$$

This value is similar to the 1,367 tons burden calculated from equation (3). The resemblance between these values is coincidental.

Thus, the keel length, beam and depth in hold, or the draught in the water, were the only functions necessary in evaluating tonnage by the seventeenth-century methods of calculation. The discrepancies in tonnage values as recorded by later historians were due entirely to the differing methods by which these functions were measured. The values for tons burden and gross tonnage remained constant during the lifetime of the vessel. The displacement tonnage may have varied, due to fluctuations in the weight of material parts, stores and provisions.

The weight of timber used for her exquisite carvings was itself a considerable entity.

CHAPTER 5

A Description of her Decorative Carving

Her elaborate ornamentation followed the fashion established by the magnificence of the sixty-four gun *Vasa* of 1627. No other English warship before or since has been bestowed with so much lavish ornamentation as was the *Sovereign of the Seas*. At a period when warships were so urgently needed, it was incredible that so much money was squandered in decoration that stood the hazard of being shot away in action. The cost of embellishment at £6,691 was some 20 per cent of the total cost of building and launching. This extravagance might have been curtailed to pay £5,500-£6,500 for a single forty gun ship, fully equipped with rigging, sails, stores, ammunition and provisions for six months' sea service.

The grandiose appearance of this vessel was intended to reflect and portray the power and prestige of Charles I. Such a creation was intended to initiate dismay and intimidation among foreign powers. However, her building seems to have taken the pride of the English people, and helped to soften the sore blow dealt out by the tax of Ship Money. The ship was an attempt to regain international sea power. It could also have been an attempt to improve Charles I's popularity in the eyes of the English people.

Thus, starting at the forward aspect of the great ship, and referring to the indexed drawing in Illustration 42, we have:

1) The figurehead represents Edgar the Peaceable (944–75). The younger son of King Edmund (r. 939–46), he succeeded in consequence of an uprising against his brother, Eadwig, who died in Wessex 1 October 959. Edgar, nearly sixteen years of age, was accepted as King by the West Saxons. But he was not crowned until 11 May 973 at Bath. Thirteen years of his reign elapsed before his coronation because of the reproval by St Dunstan and seven years penance for his indiscretion upon a lady of noble birth who had assumed the veil as a nun. He sailed to Chester, and in 973 was ceremoniously rowed in his barge along the River Dee from his palace to the church of St John by eight voluntary vassal Saxon Kings, namely Scotland, Cumberland, Westmorland, Anglesey with the Isle of Man and the Hebrides, Galloway, North, South and Middle Wales. Allegedly, he was the founder of the English navy. His reign was remembered as a golden age of peace, security and prosperity. Edgar died 8 July 975 and was interred at Glastonbury.

The portrayal of this warrior king as the figurehead was intended to suggest King Charles I. Van de Velde depicts him mounted on a galloping horse, with plume and crest on its head, and trampling under feet the prostrate crowned kings. The long-haired and bearded Edgar wears a plumed crown. He is in full armour, with a loose skirt billowing from beneath his cuirass. His left arm is flexed across his chest, grasping the reigns. His gauntleted right hand holds aloft a naked sabre. The empty sheath is suspended from his sinister side.

This effigy is reminiscent of the figurehead of the *Prince Royal* of 1610, where St George was depicted slaying the dragon.

According to Heywood, the prostrate Kings of the *Sovereign of the Seas* were: Kynadus King of the Scots {King Kenneth II (971–95)}, Malcolm King of Cumberland and Dufnall, Griffith, Huval, Jacob and Judithil as the Welsh Kings. Though the submission of the Kings seems to have some credibility, the story of Edgar being rowed on the River Dee is probably myth.

Peter Mundy's diary records his visit on 26 September 1639 when her beakhead projected over the bows by 28 feet. Another diarist, John Evelyn (1620–1706), visited her on 9 May 1654. Some years later, when in action with the Dutch, a cannon shot knocked Edgar off his horse.

The contemporary Navy Board model of the *Royal Sovereign* of 1701 in the Central Naval Museum, Saint Petersburg, Russia, depicts the armorial device of William III of Orange (1688–1702) in the figurehead. An effigy of the mounted William III is depicted on the taffrail. Below, on the balustrade of the stern balcony of the quarterdeck, is the figure of Queen Anne Stewart with her armorial bearings. These reflect the union of England with Scotland, and are characteristic of the period 1707 to 1714. Thus, we have in allegorical form, the transfer of power by William III to Queen Anne. These armorial devices are indicative of the period when this model was made (Illustrations 38–41).

The mounted figure of William III depicted on the taffrail (Illustration 41) is similar to that in the painting of the *Royal Sovereign* of 1701 by W. van de Velde the Younger in the National Maritime Museum (Plate 39). We have the suggestion that perhaps W. van de Velde the Younger used this model when composing his painting.

Payne and van de Velde depict the mariner's port side of the *Sovereign of the Seas*, while Edye and Seppings show the starboard side. The carvings on one side are a mirror image to those on the opposite side.

Head-rails curve between the stern of the figurehead and the forward ends of the beakhead bulkhead.

The panels are:

2) A collared dog representing the greyhounds of Henry VII. Edye's animal has developed a mane.
3) The French *fleur-de-lis*, the traditional emblem of the kings of France. This was used in heraldry by the Anglo-Saxon kings. Edward III of England, in making a claim to the throne of France, changed the state seal to include a quarter of the French arms. The seal existed in this form from 1340 to 1801 when George III finally surrendered his title of 'King of France'.
4) The mythical Dragon of Cadwalader, viz. a winged horse. Cadwalader (around 659–89), also spelt Caedwalla, was King of Wessex between 685–9.
5) The crowned Thistle of Scotland is flanked by two indigenous leaves. This plant would be the *Onopordum acanthium*. The panel above contains the initials 'I.D.' crowned by the royal diadem, which was omitted by Edye. The initials are the motto of the Prince of Wales, which is the insignia of the heir apparent, '*Ich Dien*' ('I Serve').
6) A prancing unicorn. The *unicornus* was a mythological animal resembling a horse or a kid with a single spiked horn projecting from the centre of its forehead. This enigmatic fabulous animal was mentioned in the authorised version of the Old Testament as a horned (Ref., Deuteronomy 33:17), very strong (Ref., Numbers 23:22, 24:8) wild animal, difficult to catch and to domesticate (Ref., Job 39:9 fol.) (Ref., Psalms 29:6, 92:10). The unicorn has been identified as the wild ox *aurochs* which roamed Mediterranean lands in Assyrian times, but later became extinct. Van de Velde depicts a spiked collar around

the neck. Attached to this collar is a lead of chain passing between the forelegs, under the chest and over the animal's back. Edye and Seppings omit the collar and lead.

Like the *Vasa*, the exterior carvings were made fast to the hull mainly by the use of iron nails. In the panel above are the crowned initials 'C.R.' This probably signifies the Latin motto, *'Caroli Regis'* (Charles Rex).

7) The crowned Tudor Rose. Above is a panel with the cypher 'H.M.' This probably signifies Henrietta Maria. Both characters are inter-woven, and capped by the royal diadem.

8) Here is a crowned lion *rampant guardant*, as featured in the arms of Scotland. Edye and Seppings portray the opposite side, with the lion's head turned to the right. The portrayal of rampant lions was common with the *Vasa*. The panel above contains the crowned initials 'C.R.' Edye and Seppings interpret these initials as 'E.R.'

The four animals of this frieze stride towards the figurehead. With the exception of the lion, they face forward. The lower frieze contains five panels. Each has a complex floriated background in Payne and van de Velde. This has caused difficulty in interpretation, and was no doubt the reason for minute errors in copying. Below each panel are flourishes and scrolls. There are no brackets under the lower frieze.

The panels are:

9) Two crowned crossed plumes. This is the Prince of Wales' feathers. Edye and Seppings depict a pair of crossed stockinged legs.

10) Both are similar panels containing a prancing horse. This becomes a maned lion in Edye's draught. Van de Velde depicts a horse in the forward panel, with a lion in the after panel.

11) Edye depicts a tapestry or an arras for the Tudor portcullis.

12) The Harp of Ireland is interpreted by Edye as a crowned winged cupid.

13) On either side of the stem are two hawse holes in the strake timbers. An oak timber, called a bolster, faired to the curvature of the strakes, was secured over either pair of hawse holes. The bolster was drilled to accommodate the anchor cable. The bolster prevented the cable chafing. Sheet lead was moulded and nailed in and around the hawse holes and bolsters. This prevented the ingress of sea water in to the open grain of the wood, and prevented chafing of the cable. Each bolster is ornately carved. Van de Velde depicts a nude angel riding on clouds. Her outstretched wings protect either hawse hole. Edye and Seppings neglect the wings. Seppings suggests a mermaid. The portrayal of crowns, mermaids and nude caryatids about the hull was common with the *Vasa*.

14) Here is the comb for the fore-tacks. Payne, Edye and Seppings depict a snake coiled thrice about itself, thus providing three loops in its coils for the tacks. Van de Velde depicts a carved block drilled twice, with no attempt at being serpentine.

15) On top of the stem head is a *couchant* lion, tamed and ridden by a cupid. Under each fore paw, and on either side of the bowsprit is Heywood's motto, 'that Sufferance may curb Insolence, and Innocence restrain Violence'. This was intended to suggest Charles I's mercy.

16) The high beakhead bulkhead follows the pattern of the *Prince Royal*. The *Sovereign*'s beakhead bulkhead is two decks high without a step. It is slightly convex throughout its height. The beakhead is embrasured for six ornately carved ports. The rim of each is a grand floriated design. On top is a crowned *fleur-de-lis*, while underneath is a gargoyle lion head. Each of the eight perpendicular head-timbers crossing between the head-rails has special attention. A magnificently carved wooden caryatid, twice life-size, stands upon a pedestal of acanthus leaves between each port. This is a stylised ornamental motif based on the Mediterranean plant with jagged leaves, *Acanthus spinosus*. Introduced by the Romans in architecture and the decorative arts, it had been popular in furniture decoration since the Renaissance. Edye and Seppings depict nude figures standing on a ledge rather than pedestals. Only figures 20 and 21 are illustrated by Payne, because the remainder are screened by various parts of

the vessel's workings. The pedestals of these two figures are masked by three sailors standing on the beakhead deck.

Van de Velde the Elder presents a more complete picture. All six caryatids are draped in long skirts and stand on pedestals of acanthus leaves. The seven panels with floriated fonds so enclosed, form a top frieze along the side of the beakhead. Below the bulkhead door is a short ladder which leads to the beakhead deck beneath. This is not apparent from Payne, Edye or Seppings.

Enumerating from the starboard side of the beakhead bulkhead, these caryatids are:

17) *'Consilium'* (Counsel) with a folded scroll.
18) *'Cura'* (Carefulness) with a compass.
19) *'Conamen'* (Industry) with a linstock ready to fire. Her right elbow is bent, with the bare forearm flexed before her waist. Van de Velde's collar of the main-stay partly conceals her.
20) *'Vis'* (Strength) with a sword. Her left hand clutches at her skirts which are gathered in front.
21) *'Virtus'* (Virtue or Valour) with a spherical globe, suggesting perfection. Payne depicts her nude. Van de Velde inclines her head to the left. He also splits her skirt from the left knee down.
22) *'Victoria'* (Victory) with a wreath of laurels. Payne and van de Velde depict her in a short knee length skirt. Van de Velde also provides her with a full length skirt beneath, in similar fashion to her five companions. Her right elbow is flexed, with her forearm flexed before her waist. *'Vis'* and *'Virtus'* have short sleeves, while the others have long sleeves. Although all have bodices to their dresses, van de Velde depicts bare bosoms. Heywood saw a moral in these six figures. In all high enterprises there should be 'Council' to undertake, 'Care' to manage, and 'Industry' to perform, and while there was ability and 'Strength' to oppose, and 'Virtue' to direct, then 'Victory' was always at hand to crown the undertaking.

These caryatids were typical of the effigies which Heywood, John and Matthias Christmas, created for the series of Lord Mayor's pageants between 1631 and 1639.

This display of six grandiose caryatids on pedestals before the beakhead bulkhead occurred again on the *Prince*, launched by Phineas Pett (1635–94) at Chatham Royal Dockyard in 1670, and the *Britannia*, launched by Sir Phineas Pett (1635–94) at Chatham Royal Dockyard in 1682. A similar design is apparent in the contemporary Navy Board

38. Contemporary Navy Board model of the *Royal Sovereign* of 1701. Starboard elevation. (*Central Naval Museum, Saint Petersburg, Russia*)

39. Contemporary Navy Board model of the *Royal Sovereign* of 1701. Detail of stern. (*Central Naval Museum, Saint Petersburg, Russia*)

hull of the *Royal Sovereign* of 1701, which is contained in the Central Naval Museum, Saint Petersburg, Russia.

23) At each foremost corner of the forecastle is a cat-head. This is a strong timber mounted under the forecastle deck. The cat-head is canted upwards and forwards, projecting outboard. The outboard end has two mortised sheaves for the cat-tackle. This was used to hoist the anchor clear of the ship's side. A carved snake wriggles along the after side of the cat-head. This is supported by a bracket or knee carved into the shape of a goat legged satyr groaning beneath the burden. A similar effigy supported the cat-heads of the *Prince Royal* of 1610.

Van de Velde's broadside drawing depicts two anchors at the fore chain-wales (Illustration 13). Puddening is served on the ring of the after most anchor. The cable is bent to the ring by an inside clinch knot.

Along the bulwarks are two series of panels forming an upper and a lower frieze. The upper frieze is discontinued by the waist. This is reminiscent of the *Prince Royal* of 1610. This frieze is composed of signs of the Zodiac, alternating with portraits of Roman emperors. Roman warriors and emperors were similarly portrayed on the *Vasa*. Van de Velde's fond for each panel in the upper frieze is carved in a heavy floriated design. On

40. Contemporary Navy Board model of the *Royal Sovereign* of 1701. Detail of bow. (*Central Naval Museum, Saint Petersburg, Russia*)

41. Contemporary Navy Board model of the *Royal Sovereign* of 1701. Detail of taffrail. (*Central Naval Museum, Saint Petersburg, Russia*)

either side of panels 24, 26, 27, 30, 31, 32 and 33 is a fish standing on its chin with the tail uppermost, and its body in an ogee curve.

Starting forward, we have:

24) A globe flanked by mermaids represented Virgo, the virgin. A mermaid was frequently the symbol of a whore. This panel probably represented the differences between sacred and profane love. Edye and Seppings depict a ball flanked by scrolls.
25) The seven circular panels contain busts of Roman emperors surrounded by garlands of flowers.
26) Gemini, the twins, is represented by two seated caressing cherubs.
27) Here is Leo, the lion. Van de Velde depicts him couchant, facing the prow, with gaping mouth.
28) The hancing pieces of the waist subdued the severity of change in level between the bulwarks of the forecastle and the waist, and the waist to the half-deck. These hancing pieces are carved into full sized figures. Aeolus is accompanied by a chameleon, 'which liveth on air', attended by the four winds of heaven.
29) Brandishing a sword and shield is Mars with a fox to describe his cunning. Figures 28 and 29 are bare-headed in Payne and van de Velde.

According to Heywood, the starboard hancing pieces were different. Forward was Jupiter with his thunderbolt, riding on an eagle. Edye's and Seppings' forward figure is a partially-draped Aeolus, wearing a spiked crown and attended by the winds of heaven. Aftermost is Neptune wearing a spiked crown and carrying his trident, and seated on a sea horse (family *Syngnathidae*, order *Gaster-os tei formes*) attended by dolphins. Carvings of Jupiter sitting upon an eagle in the clouds, and Neptune surrounded by nymphs, were included in the sixty gun *White Bear* of 1564 when she was rebuilt in 1598–9.

30) This panel contains Libra, the balance.

The period 23 September to 20 March is sequential, with the exception of *Scorpius* and *Capricornus*, which are omitted. There is no suggestion that the signs of the Zodiac as presented in her embellishments were other than ornamentation.

31) This is Sagittarius, the archer. Here is the figure of a centaur, having the body of a horse and the torso of a man. He holds a drawn long bow, which is not obvious in van de Velde's broadside drawing, even though his left arm is extended.
32) This is Aquarius, the water bearer. He kneels on his left knee holding a vase, from which he decants liquid.
33) Two fish, head to tail, represent Pisces, the fishes.
34) This is Cancer, the crab. Payne and van de Velde portray a crab, whose shell is decorated with a solar face, and surrounded by a regular corona. Edye and Seppings depict the solar face, but omit the crab. Directly above is a small window. Van de Velde and Seppings depict four panes. Only two panes are shown by Edye.

Above this upper frieze, and right aft, above the quarter galleries, is a smaller frieze, containing seven panels. Van de Velde is obscure. He does, however, depict an ornate floriated background to each panel.

35) This panel contains the crowned initials 'C.R.'
36) Here is an eagle with outstretched wings.
37) The initials 'H.M.' are inter-woven with each other and surmounted by the royal diadem. As with the cypher above panel 7, this represents Henrietta Maria.
38) Edye portrays an urn instead of the Harp of Ireland.
39) The crowned *fleur-de-lis*, surmounted by the initials 'C.R.'
40) This panel contains the crowned Thistle of Scotland flanked by two indigenous leaves. Above is a panel with the initials 'H.M.' Both characters are interwoven, and capped by the royal diadem.

41) The crowned Tudor rose. Above is a panel with the initials 'C.R.', which is omitted by Edye. Instead, he depicts a small window with two panes.

The first four vertical posts between these panels are in the form of a male bust. The stern edge of panel 41 is similarly carved. Edye suggests femininity. Van de Velde suggests that the last two posts in this series are carved nude caryatids.

The lower frieze along the bulwark is interrupted by the ports of the upper gun deck. Thirteen decorated panels, containing trophies of war, alternate with the ports. Flanking each panel is an erect sea horse facing inwards towards the panel. The fond of each is composed of an assortment of swords, spears, battle-axes, worms, sponges, rammers, guns, shields, suits of armour, trumpets, drums, muskets, musket crutches, flags and banners. An artillery motif was similarly used in the *White Bear* when she was rebuilt in 1598–9.

42) Here is a close helmet with closed visor.
43) This cuirass suggests a type of Italian brigandine.
44) This is a heavy war shield with a large spike protruding from the central boss.
45) A military side drum overshadows a furled banner.
46) Here is a small shield.
47) This is an escutcheon with a central cross, *argent a cross gules*.
48) This panel contains two crossed pieces of ordnance.
49) Here is the breast plate and paunch of a cuirass. Edye portrays a loose-fitting, sleeveless riding coat. Van de Velde includes tassets below the paunch.
50) Here are two military side drums.
51) This is a complete cuirass with paunch and tassets.
52) This is a plumed helmet surmounting a furled banner and a musket. This panel is particularly long in Payne, Edye and Seppings. It extends over the top of the after port on the upper gun deck. The lower dead-eyes in Payne's mizen chain-wale obscures panel 52.
53) Van de Velde suggests a separate floriated panel abaft 52, and above the after port on the upper gun deck.
54) Here is a small field piece pointing towards the prow. A small panel aft has a shield similar to panel 47.

Van de Velde's last few panels are indistinct.

55) Under the sixth wale, and below the lower frieze, are a series of flourishes, escutcheons and scrolls arranged in short festoons in ogee curves from the luff to the forward end of the quarter galleries. The detail of the festoons vary between all representations, though the essentials were similar. Edye and Seppings depict identical festoons.

The sheer of the wales was greater than that of the decks, and consequently that of the ports also. Therefore, above the four after ports on the upper gun deck is a space provided by the seventh wale as it curves upwards towards the stern. This space is adorned with additional panels. Raised port covers conceal Payne's and van de Velde's panels.

Continuing from the foremost panel between 49 and 50, these panels are, according to Edye and Seppings:

56) A cuirass with tassets similar to an Italian brigandine. A floral design is depicted by Seppings.
57) Here is a close type of helmet with closed visor.
58) This panel contains an eagle with outstretched wings.
59) Van de Velde's broadside drawing (Illustrations 13 & 42) depicts the entry port. Such an elaborate device was fitted exclusively to first and second rates to facilitate their selection as flagships. The earliest entry port recorded was on the port elevation of the *Prince Royal* of 1610.

Payne does not depict this on the *Sovereign*. We have the suggestion that as the engraving is in reverse, the entry port is on the port elevation only.

A Description of her Decorative Carving

The *Sovereign*'s entry port is on the port elevation of the middle gun deck, at the fore end of the main chain-wale between two gunports. The tops of the door posts are carved in the form of nude caryatids. On top of the architrave are two reclining *amoretti* holding a crown over the bust of Charles I.

Neither Payne nor Van de Velde depict the steps of the side. These are pieces of quartering secured to the sides, from the wale upwards, for personnel ascending to or descending from, the entry port. Van de Velde's gangway may conceal these steps. The gangway interferes with the functioning of some of the lower gun deck guns. This suggests that it was not rigged when the vessel was at sea.

When we consider the representations discussed in Chapter 3 of this present work, we find that the *Sovereign*'s entry port is depicted only twice. Both are drawings by W. van de Velde the Elder:

i) Broadside drawing of the *Sovereign of the Seas* (1660) (Illustration 13).
ii) Port elevation and quarter of the *Sovereign of the Seas* (1673 or 1675) (Plate 26).

The contemporary Navy Board rigged model of the first rate ninety to ninety-eight gun *St Michael* of 1669 (Plate 69) in the National Maritime Museum, displays an entry port fitted on the middle gun deck of the port elevation. No steps of the side are displayed.

The contemporary Navy Board rigged model of the *Royal Prince* of 1670 (Plate 71) in the Science Museum, demonstrates an entry port with steps of the side on the port elevation of the middle gun deck.

In the Merseyside Maritime Museum, Albert Dock, Liverpool, is a contemporary Navy Board hull of the ninety gun second rate *Neptune* of 1683 [Accession No. 55.174]. At the forward end of the main chain-wale on the middle gun deck, is a plain arched entry port, without steps on the side, amidships on her port elevation.

The quarter galleries are the epitome of monumental decoration. It became the custom in the *Prince Royal* of 1610, to fit a permanent porch over the doors, providing access to the galleries. There was one such door to port and another to starboard. Most of the *Sovereign*'s quarter galleries are protected by lean-to roofs. This feature lapsed from fashion after around 1640. Three highly ornate half domes are placed over the whole gallery. Payne, Edye and Seppings depict the quarter galleries. This feature is obscure in van de Velde's drawing.

60) The forward end of the lower quarter gallery is open to the elements, while the after end is closed. There were two friezes. The lowest is adorned with the *fleur-de-lis*, the Tudor Rose, the Harp of Ireland and three chariots drawn by pairs of birds and Cadwalader's dragons. The upper frieze contains fourteen similar winged horses.
61) The forward end of the upper quarter gallery is open. The eight panels demonstrate cupids, angels, the Prince of Wales' feathers, two chariots drawn by Cadwalader's dragons, and St George and the Dragon.

There is an upper frieze, similar to that on the lower quarter gallery. According to Payne it contains, continuing from forward:

i) A crowned lion *rampant guardant*, similar to panel 8.
ii) A prancing unicorn, similar to panel 6.
iii) The Dragon of Cadwalader as in panel 4.
iv) A collared dog representing the greyhounds of Henry VII, as in panel 2.

Except for the Dragon of Cadwalader, Edye's figures resemble lions. Seppings depicts the Dragon of Cadwalader and three horses.

62) On the casement of the upper quarter gallery are the Royal Arms. As to be expected from the dating, the reconstruction draught illustrates the type in vogue around 1714–1801.
63) Surmounting the quarter galleries are three turrets to port and another three to starboard. The middle turret is the largest and supports two cupids caressing each other. Edye's figures do not resemble cupids. They are partly attired and carry

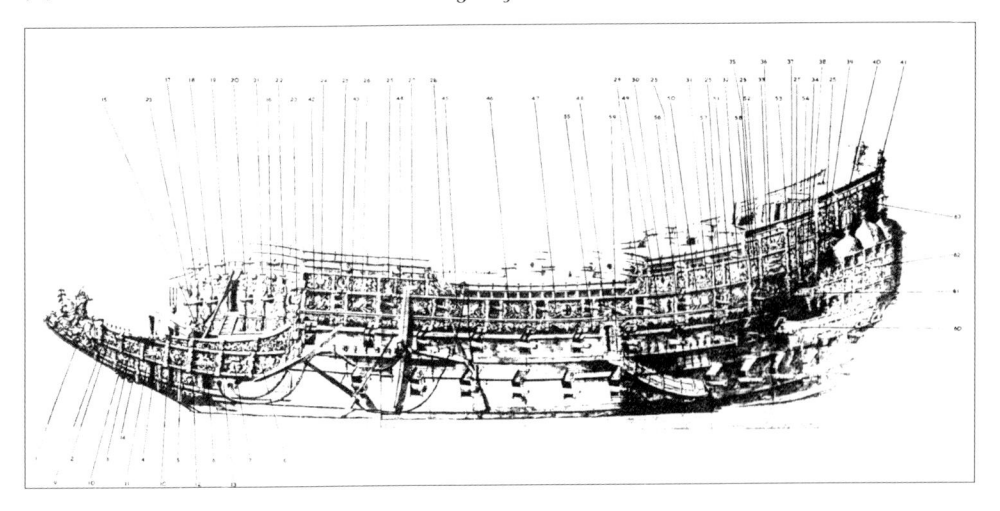

42. W. van de Velde the Elder's broadside drawing of the *Sovereign of the Seas* (1660). Port bow view. (*The late Junius S. Morgan, Junior, New York, USA, indexed by the author*)

nothing. Payne's and Seppings' figures are nude and carry a long bow. On top of each of the fore and after turrets is a lantern.

At the casements of the upper and lower quarter galleries are six windows. The entire after end is delicately carved and overlaid with gilding.

On the upright of the upper-counter, across the top of the transom and above the upper gun deck, is the frontispiece. The *Vasa*'s frontispiece was decorated with the armorial device of the Swedish royal family. That of the *Sovereign* followed a different pattern. In pedantic prosaic vein, Heywood presents a pageant of classical and allegorical figures in carved relief. Our description continues on Illustration 43 with:

A) An effigy of Victory, with outstretched wings and arms, dominates the centre. She stands on a pedestal, is bare-headed and arrayed in a long dress. Encircling her right fore-arm is a crown of gold, and encircling the left is a chaplet of laurels. These imply riches and honour respectively. A sash is suspended over her right shoulder. Here is the motto, '*Validis incumbite remis*' ('Rely upon the strength of your oars'). This was probably an exhortation to Jason, who stands on her dexter side.

B) Jason's fully draped figure carries an oar in his left hand, as befitting the Prime Argonaut. He wears a spiky crown and the mantle of royalty. Over his right arm is the Golden Fleece from the grove of Ares in Colchis. Victory's right hand points to Jason, with the motto, '*Nava*', or more properly; '*Operam nava*' ('Do the work diligently').

C) Here is Neptune, the God of the Seas, astride a sea horse on the crest of a wave and grasping a trident in his left hand. His left shoulder is draped but the right leg and arm are bare. He is bearded and bare-headed. Jason points to Neptune below, with the motto '*Faveto*' ('Do you want help?'). Neptune answers with '*No*' (I swim) ... as if he wanted to respond, 'Many thanks, Jason, but no. I am in my natural element. Look, I can swim.'

D) On Victory's sinister side is a partly draped figure of Hercules, grasping a club in his left hand. He is unkempt. Victory points to Hercules, with the motto '*Clava*' ('club'), ... as if she would say, 'O Hercules, be thou as valiant with thy club upon the land as Jason is industrious with his oar upon the water!'

An effigy of Hercules in combat with the mythical Hydra formed the figurehead of the Swedish sixty-four gun great ship *Vasa*.

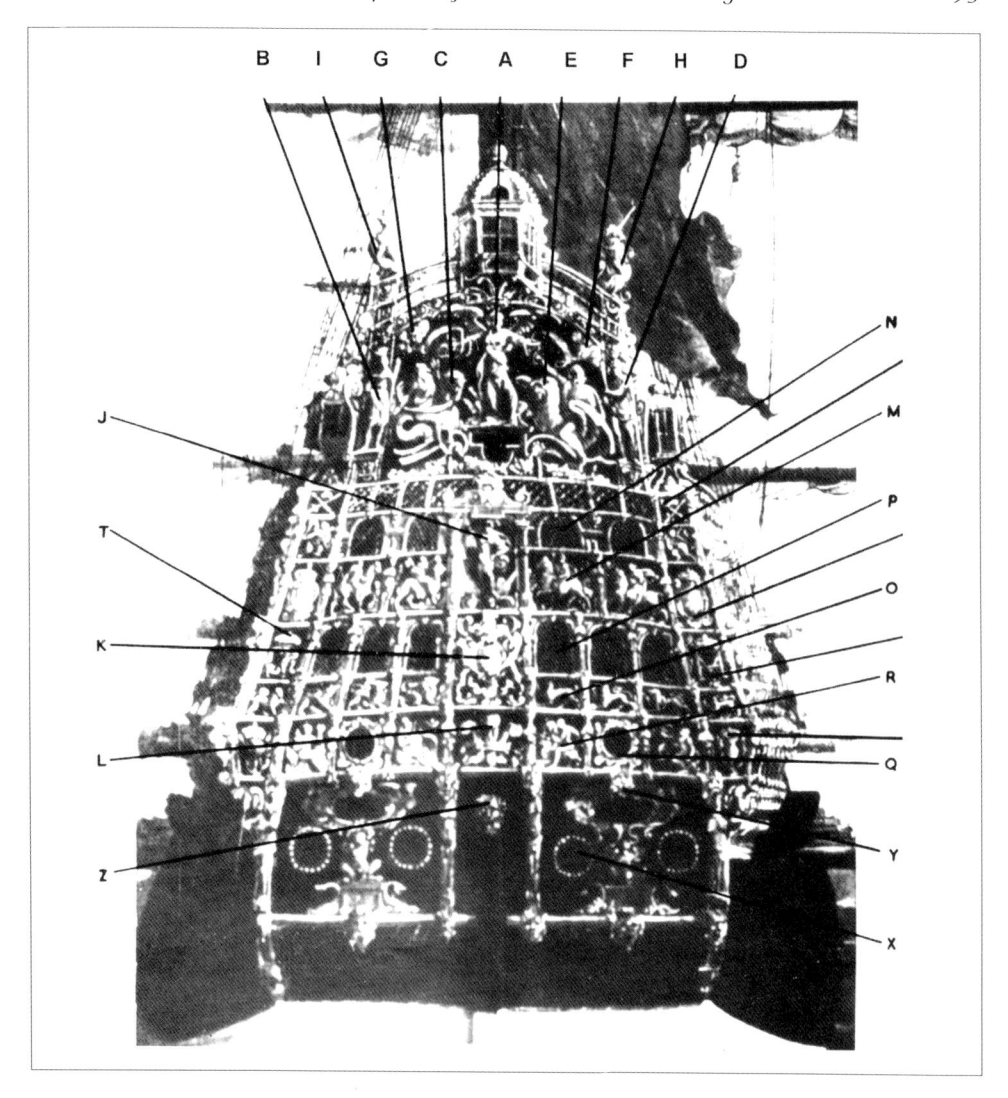

43. The van de Veldes' painting *The Portrait of Peter Pett and the* Sovereign of the Seas (1660). The stern carvings. (*National Maritime Museum, indexed by the author*) (See pages 94–6).

E) Aeolus, God of Winds, rides an eagle above a cloud. He is bearded and bare-headed. His right shoulder is draped leaving the left leg and arm bare. The eagle's wings partly conceal him. Hercules points to Aeolus below with the motto '*Flato*' ('Who blows?'), ... as if he would enquire, 'Are you, Aeolus, in a position by which your Winds could render support?'

Aeolus answers '*Flo*' ('I blow') ... as if he would respond with, 'Look, Hercules, I am here and ready. I blow and my Winds are directed upon your sails!'

F) The head of an admiring small cherub faces Victory.

G) A similar cherub turns its face away from Victory to contemplate Jason's royalty.

We have the suggestion that in all high enterprises when all fulfil their part, Victory was always at hand to crown the undertaking. It is doubtful if the crew, or later historians, ever understood the allegorical creations of Heywood.

Neither Payne nor van de Velde depict the stern carvings. Edye and Seppings depict the Royal Arms in the frontispiece.

On the upper after edge of the taffrail is the motto '*Soli Deo Gloriam*' ('Glory to God alone').

The fifth and largest lantern projects above the after end of the poop above the taffrail. The plan shape is regular hexagonal with a hemispherical domed roof. A spherical finial dominates the whole. Edye suggests the height is 6 feet, with a width of 4 feet, 6 inches. Seppings' height is 7 feet, with a width of 4 feet. Van de Velde suggests a greater width. A door provides access. At least ten people together could stand upright inside.

Illumination was achieved either by lighting a number of tallow candles, or by burning a naturally occurring oil. To prevent loss of flame by the inconstant wind, the panes of each lantern were, like the windows of the quarter galleries and stern, fitted with green, flexible mica. The lattice was small, such that there was no large area which might shatter at the discharge of the guns.

These lanterns facilitated navigation at night. Thus, if two horizontal lights were visible, then swift action was necessary to prevent a collision. If three lights in the form of an inverted 'V' were visible, then the stern view was presented. The broadside was indicated by three lights arranged some distance apart in the form of an 'L' or its mirror image.

Rising above the taffrail, and flanking the great lantern, are two gaunt, solitary allegorical figures, forming the quarter pieces;

H) The right profile of a unicorn *sejant*, characteristic of the Scottish royal arms. About the neck is a garland shaped like a bow tie. The fore paws clutch a sceptre.

I) In similar manner is the sinister profile of a crowned lion *sejant*. The lion represented the arms of England. Similarly, the fore paws clutch a sceptre.

Below the frontispiece is a central panel:

J) A helmeted man faces the port side. He grasps a staff in his right hand. His left hand poises on his hip. He wears a cloak which billows out behind. Considering that the two panels below are regal armorial bearings, this effigy undoubtedly represents Charles I. The Lion of England and the Unicorn of Scotland were considered to be supportive roles to the English monarchy.

The reconstruction draught depicts the sinister profile of an equestrian figure reminiscent of King Edgar.

The sinister profile of the mounted figure of William III of Orange, flanked by cherubs, was depicted on the taffrail of the contemporary Navy Board hull of the *Royal Sovereign* of 1701 in the Central Naval Museum, Saint Petersburg (Illustration 41).

K) The Royal Arms with the heraldic lion and unicorn.

L) These ostrich feathers form the Prince of Wales' crest. In the reconstruction draught (Illustration 18) this panel contains a large *fleur-de-lis*.

M) Here are horsemen in each panel. The sinister profile is shown in the starboard pair. The right profile is shown in the port pair. Two of these riders carry staffs, while another has a battle-axe. The *passant* horses are prancing. The motif of armed knights flanking the Royal coat of Arms is similarly depicted in the *Vasa*.

N) The upper balcony is closed by paned windows.

O) The sinister profile of four lions *passant guardant*, with the dexter fore paw raised and head turned to face the spectator. Their tails curl over their backs. They face towards the port side where there are four similar unicorns *passant guardant* in dexter.

P) The lower balcony with paned windows.

Q) The decorated port for the starboard chaser on the upper gun deck.

The after edge of the quarter galleries contains panels similar on either side, but with the exception of panels S and T:

R) A man riding on a sea horse. A similar panel is on the other side of the port. Each figure faces the port side. Two similar figures on the opposite side face the opposite way.

S) The panel on the starboard side of the lower balcony contains the cypher 'H.M.', superimposed and surmounted by the royal diadem.
T) Here is the crowned cypher 'C.R.' on the port side of the same balcony. This is analogous to panel 8.
U) The sword, sceptre and orb of royal office are represented. The sword and the sceptre cross over each other.
V) The centre of this crowned heraldic device is an escutcheon surrounded by superfluous scrolls.
W) The crowned Thistle of Scotland is flanked by two indigenous leaves. Panel 5 on the top frieze at the flank of the beakhead, and panel 40 above the quarter galleries, are identical.
X) The counter is embrasured for four stern chasers on the middle gun deck. Around each port is floral decoration.
Y) On an elaborate pedestal is a small man sitting on his haunches. On his shoulders rests a large orb. This is Atlas supporting a globe. On either side of this orb are the head and shoulders and wings of angels. Flanking the pedestal is a fish, lying on its chin with its tail curling forward over its head. Over the top of the orb, and at the base of the pedestal, are grotesque gargoyles. This effigy is duplicated on the port side of the ship.
Z) The head of the rudder post is in the form of a carved gargoyle. The head of the tiller of the *Vasa* was carved in the form of a lion's head.

Towards the bottom of the counter, and flanking the rudder post, is Heywood's Latin motto, '*Qui mare, qui fluctus, ventos, navesque gubernat, Sospitet hanc arcem, Carole Magne, tuam*'. On translation, this becomes, 'May He who governs the tides and the winds and the ships keep safe this great ship of yours, Oh Great Charles.'

There is no decoration below the counter. Four big guns, comprising the stern chasers on the lower gun deck, poke their muzzles through very ordinary square embrasures.

It is conjectural whether any of this magnificent decoration was altered during the course of the great ship's career. Her prime design function was to carry an optimum weight of ordnance into conflict against an enemy. When in battle, some material parts must have been shot away. When repaired or replaced, it is difficult to believe that the reparation was affected in the same manner as the original.

CHAPTER 6

The Nature and Disposition of her Armament

At the commencement of Henry VIII's reign, large numbers of guns were imported. Most of the copper required for the home production of ordnance was, similarly, imported. This dependence on foreign supplies caused some uneasiness in England, and prompted Henry VIII to encourage the mining of copper and calamine. This was a general term given to zinc ores. Men skilled in the arts of mining and smelting such ores came to England from Germany. In 1561 a vigorous search for copper and calamine commenced. In 1565 a rich copper deposit was discovered at Newlands, near Keswick, Cumberland. Ore mined here was smelted in works at Brigham. In June 1566 deposits of calamine were discovered on Worle Hill on the Mendips in Somerset. This land belonged to Sir Henry Wallop.

Copper alloys were common until Henry VIII established the production of cast iron at Buxted in Sussex, around 1543. Even though copper alloys were more expensive than cast iron, and were more readily worn by firing iron shot, they were favoured because of their resistance to the effects of corrosion relative to cast iron. Cast iron was liable to dangerous fractures during casting. Copper alloys had a lower melting point. For this reason they could be re-smelted and recast. The nature of the alloy varied according to the gunfounder. The art of producing a sound piece was a matter of experience. The Dutch and Belgians had a very high reputation in this respect.

Any copper alloy used for making ordnance was indiscriminately described as brass. This was an alloy of around 60–90 per cent copper, the remainder being mainly zinc. The term bronze is properly used describing alloys of copper with tin, the tin being around 5–10 per cent. Sometimes, bell metal was added to produce an alloy of around 96.8 per cent copper, 1.6 per cent tin and 1.6 per cent lead. Hard bronzes were made with 18–20 per cent tin. The specific gravity of brass is 8.4–8.7, and bronze 8.7–8.9.

Fragments of metal sampled from several seventeenth-century English bronze pieces in the Royal Armouries in Leeds were analysed by the laboratories of the Government Chemist. The four most predominating constituents were copper, tin, zinc and lead.

A saker (Museum No. XIX.23 Cat. No. 36) of 1601 made by Richard Phillips, gunfounder of Houndsditch, weighs 19 cwt 3 qt 10 lb, measures 9 feet 8 inches, with a bore of 3.75 inches. The gunmetal contains 85.3 per cent copper, 6.25 per cent tin, 0.25 per cent zinc and 3.30 per cent lead.

In 1638 John Browne made five model pieces for Prince Charles, later Charles II (Museum No. XIX.24–28 Cat. No. 40). They are 2 feet 5.5 inches long, with a bore of 1.3 inches (Illustrations 44–46). The metal contains 83.3 per cent copper, 1.0 per cent tin, 1.60

per cent zinc and 12.2 per cent lead. They are inscribed, 'JOHN BROWNE MADE THIS PEECE 1638' In relief is the cypher and motto of the Prince of Wales, *'Ich Dien'* ('I Serve'). There is also the cypher 'C.P.', which signifies *'Caroli Princeps'* (Prince Charles). The muzzle of one of these five pieces (Illustration 44) displays damage by a fire in the Grand Store House in 1841.

A nine-pounder made in 1672 for Charles II weighs 19 cwt 2 qt 21 lb, and is 5 feet 1 inch long with a bore of 4.2 inches (Museum No. XIX.34 Cat. No. 42). This metal contains 86.0 per cent copper, 5.4 per cent tin, 1.0 per cent zinc and 2.3 per cent lead.

Thomas Western, Ordnance Brass Founder, made a mortar in 1687, 3 feet 4 inches long, weighing 47 qt 14 lb, with a bore of 7.2 inches (Museum No. 131 Cat. No. 96). This metal contains 85.3 per cent copper, 0.5 per cent tin, 0.85 per cent zinc and 3.00 per cent lead.

A three-pounder made in 1694 by Philip Wightman, Brass Founder of the Ordnance, weighs 8 cwt 2 qt 27 lb, is 7 feet 1 inch long, and has a 3.25 inches bore (Museum No. XIX.173 Cat. No. 44). This metal contains 89.7 per cent copper, 5.4 per cent tin, 0.45 per cent zinc and 1.05 per cent lead.

In 1568 the first great copper mining company, which had been in operation since 1564, was incorporated, and became known as the Mines Royal. The firm of Sir William Humfrey and Christopher Shutz was granted a patent by Elizabeth I on 17 September 1565 to manufacture brass. This evolved in 1568 by charter of incorporation into the company, 'The Governors, Assistants and Society of the Mineral and Battery Works'.

This company was granted wide powers, with exclusive rights to mine calamine, make brass and engage in the process of sheet and wire drawing. The smelting of brass began at Bristol Castle. It was later removed to Tintern Abbey in the Wye Valley. Here, calamine from Somerset was made into brass. Initially, the process was experimental. Brass was not produced successfully until 1568. This was by the calamine process, which remained the sole method of production until 1850.

Fragments of copper were heated with a mixture of charcoal and calamine in a closed crucible to a temperature of around 2,370 degrees Fahrenheit. The calamine was reduced to a zinc vapour, which diffused into the copper melt. English gunfounding progressed. By the close of the seventeenth century, ordnance was exported to the Continent.

In 1619 a decree was issued confining gunfounding to Kent and Sussex. Ordnance could only be landed at, and shipped from, the wharf of the Tower of London. East Smithfield was the sole market place for sale or purchase. Before each piece went into service, it was tested or proved. The place of proving was Ratcliff Fields in Stepney. All pieces were required to bear at least two letters of the founder's name, with the year of making and the weight of the piece. Moorfields and an old artillery ground near Spitalfields later became the sites for proving. Somewhere between 1667 and 1680 the proof of ordnance was transferred from Moorfields to Woolwich Royal Arsenal.

During the seventeenth century, the casting and production of ordnance was an art rather than an exact science. There was no attempt at standardisation, such that variations occurred between gunfounders and each successive piece. Each was made individually.

Although the *Sovereign* was built in Woolwich Royal Dockyard, it was the practice of the Board of Ordnance to obtain supplies from private contractors, at least until 1716. Her original armament was made by John Browne, son of Thomas Browne.

The Browne family were famous gunfounders. Thomas became the official Crown iron gunfounder in 1596. In 1609 he was casting guns at Ashurst. In 1612 he was granted a pension of 18*d* daily for life. In 1615 his son John succeeded as holder of the patent (Appendix 27).

By 1613 John Browne employed 200 men at his foundry at Horsmonden (TQ 695412) and Brenchley in Kent. His trade was mainly with the Dutch. In 1614 he was granted the monopoly of providing iron and brass guns for the Navy. In 1615 he was granted the office of Gunstone Maker for life, a post previously held by Ralph Hogge. In 1618 John

Browne was appointed one of the King's Founders of Iron Ordnance afloat and ashore at 18d per day.

In 1626 he gained a reward of £200 for casting lighter and more robust guns. A patent was granted in October 1635 conferring upon him the right to make, sell and transport ordnance and shot, in consideration of his payment of £12,000 to Charles I.

His grant of arms consisted of *'Gules a Griffin passant and a Chief Or.'* The crest was: *'Upon a Helm with a Wreath Or and Gules A Falcon wings inverted and addorsed proper armed legged and belled Or preying upon a Mallard's Wing Proper, Mantled Gules doubled Argent'.*

At an estimated cost of some £1,000, he modified his foundry in 1637 for the purpose of casting ordnance for this great ship. It was in the parish of Horsmonden and Brenchley, some half a mile north-east of Horsmonden Heath, Kent. The pond survives as Furnace Pond.

The importance of this furnace relied on the availability of timber for fuel and its comparative proximity to the River Medway which facilitated transportation to the Tower of London.

The foundry had a depot on the south bank of the Medway at Millhall Wharf, Aylesford. During the seventeenth century, this was the highest reach upstream which could accommodate navigable craft. The use of this wharf continued into the Millennium.

In 1637 the inhabitants of Cranbrook petitioned a complaint that John Browne had seized a greater part of the woods, to the detriment of the weaving industry. John Browne was appointed the King's Gunfounder on 16 May 1640.

Each piece was cast by the *cire perdue* ('lost wax') method. A full-size wooden model of the piece to be cast was prepared. Relief decorations, cyphers and trunnions were modelled. The trunnions were lugs at either side and below the medial axis to support the piece on the gun-carriage near the fulcrum of the axis of centre of gravity. The weight of the piece behind the trunnions was slightly greater than the weight before the trunnion. Thus, the piece tilted down at the cascable. The trunnions were sited according to the equation:

(15) $d = l \times 0.472$
Where:
d = distance of trunnions from end of cascable
l = total length of piece

A wax replica was modelled from the wooden pattern. Palm oil, lard or hogs grease was smeared over the wax replica. Sifted red clay was moistened with water and beaten with an iron bar to form a paste. Horse dung and flax or hair were added to consolidate the paste. This was compacted over the model in successive stages to form the mould for casting.

The mould rested horizontally on trestles at either end, and was rotated by cranking manually over a smouldering charcoal fire to dry the clay. Molten wax from the model was allowed to drain away. The mould was strengthened by the addition of iron plates or bars placed along its length. Further layers of clay were applied, followed by drying.

A suitable iron spindle of square or octagonal cross-section was bound around with rope. Beaten clay containing horse dung and hair was smeared overall. The outer surface was smoothed and polished. The correct diameter of this core was judged by the use of a template. This core was dried over a charcoal fire, and then placed in the centre of the mould to produce the concave cylinder or bore in casting. The mould, with the core inside, was placed in a vertical position in a pit, with the muzzle pointing upwards to facilitate pouring the molten metal. The lower end of the core was provided with a crown iron to prevent movement of the core within the mould. After cooling the mould was broken away, and the surplus metal at the muzzle was reamed. The vent was drilled. The outside of the barrel was smoothed with a steel chisel mounted on a lathe, and the inside was reamed out.

A large armament was not uncommon before this great new ship. She was not, as so many authors have stated, the first 100 gun ship in the English navy. The *Regent*, a four-masted carrack of around 1,000 tons, built at Smallhythe in 1489, carried more guns than any other ship in history – 225 of them, all mounted either side of the upper deck and the after-castle and forecastle. They were mainly serpentines, with a bore of a mere 1.5 inches, firing a half-pound shot.

The *Henri Grace a Dieu* (*Great Harry,*) a four-masted carrack of 919 tons burden and 1,225 gross tons built at Erith between 1512–4, carried twenty-one heavy bronze muzzle loading pieces and 130 assorted iron breech loading pieces mounted on wooden beds. Each breech was provided with one or two movable chambers, into which the powder was loaded. Her sides were pierced with gunports. Below the waist she carried two tiers, one of six and the other seven ports per side. When rebuilt in 1540, her armament was reduced to nineteen bronze and 103 iron pieces.

When rebuilt at Portsmouth Royal Dockyard in 1536, the *Mary Rose* had ninety-six muzzle loading and breech loading pieces. These numbered ninety-one when she sank in July 1545.

The designed complement of guns for the great ship was increased from ninety to 100 by Charles I, merely by a stroke of the pen. Phineas Pett resorted to using drakes and cutts, which were lighter and shorter versions of the standard pieces typical of the period.

The term 'drake' described a piece which was a Dutch invention of the 1620s. A drake was taper-bored, viz. the bore in the rear of the chamber was less than that at the muzzle. A drake was lighter in weight and shorter in length than a conventional bore. Because of this, the drake was easier to handle in repeated action. A drake used only sixty-seven per cent of the charge of powder. The lesser charge decreased muzzle and terminal velocity. Unfortunately, the range of the shot was reduced. The discharge at close range, however, was more devastating than that produced by a conventional bore. The whelps of 1628 were the first vessels to carry drakes.

The term 'cutts' described a piece which was shorter than a standard piece.

The original armament of the *Sovereign of the Seas* consisted of 102 pieces distributed among 118 gunport positions. Several ports were left empty. On either side of the lower gun deck were twelve ports, each 32 inches square. The spacing between these ports was around 8 feet.

There was some irregularity in the spacing between ports on each tier in the reconstruction draught. The lower gun deck ports were 37–38 inches square. The spacing varied between 9 feet and 10 feet 10 inches. One port was missing from the quarter. Seppings depicted lower gun deck ports 38 inches square, spaced between 9 feet 7 inches-11 feet.

The gunport covers on the lower gun deck were made of six planks secured with iron bolts. The covers on the upper decks were made similarly from four planks. The inner vertical planks were cut slightly shorter than the outer horizontal planks. This provided a rebate which matched a corresponding rebate in the bulwark. This provided a water-tight fit for the covers when closed.

The square port covers on the lower, middle and upper gun decks were hinged from the upper edge of the cover. The type of iron hinge was exemplified at the fore chase on the lower gun deck of van de Velde the Elder's broadside drawing. An iron ring bolt in the centre of the internal lower edge was used to lash the cover on the inside when closed.

The inside of the gunport covers of the sixty-four gun *Vasa* of 1627 were each decorated with an effigy of a snarling lion's head. The inside of these covers was painted red, suggesting that the bulwarks of the gun decks were also red.

Payne depicts nothing more than a ring bolt. He could not have seen the inside of the gunport covers. Van de Velde the Elder's broadside drawing depicts a cross, similar to the cross of St Andrew, on the inside of the middle and upper gun deck port covers. He did not realise those on the lower gun deck. The van de Veldes' *The Portrait of Peter Pett and the* Sovereign of the Seas does not depict the inside of the gunport covers. At the time van de Velde the Elder made this drawing, the ordnance was not aboard. Probably, the covers were closed and concealed by dock yard gear. Seppings' covers are in the closed position. The inside of Jackson's covers is red. Small gold-coloured squares adorn the inside of the covers of the middle and upper gun deck port covers. We are left with Jackson's suggestion that prevalent fashion may have been observed, and the inside of the gunport covers may have been painted red at some stage in her later life.

The port sills were around 2 feet above deck. When un-laden, the lower gun deck ports were around 5 feet above the waterline. This was reduced to 1 foot by the additional displacement when six months stores were aboard (Appendix 39).

Some twenty ports along the sides and quarters of the lower gun deck were provided with twenty cannon of VII drakes, each 9 feet long, and totalling 45.7 tons (Appendix 29).

In contemporary Lists (Appendices 23 & 24) cannon of VII weighed some 6–8,000 lb with a length of 8.5–10 feet and bore of 8 inches. It fired a shot of 58–60 lb. In a List dated 1639, the service charge weight for the cannon of VII was half the shot weight. The charge weight for a drake was 75 per cent of the service charge.

Payne is presumptuous in depicting a piece protruding from the foremost gunport on the lower gun deck, adjacent to the hawse-holes (Plate 17). Similarly, many artists have followed Payne's error:

1) T. Jenner's engraving (1653) (Plate 18).
2) L. A. Castro's painting (1650–60) (Plate 19).
3) I. Sailmaker's painting (1665) (Plate 25).
4) W. van de Velde the Younger's unfinished drawing (1675) (Plate 27).
5) W. van de Velde the Elder's drawing (around 1685) (Illustration 16).
6) H. B. Culver's model (1921) (Plate 30 & Illustration 28).
7) A. C. Jackson's model (1943) (Illustration 32).
8) Sergal's model (Plates 35–37).

Van de Velde the Elder displays an array of run-out guns poking through open gunports in his broadside drawing (Illustration 13). He depicts a closed gunport adjacent to the hawse-holes. We have the suggestion, therefore, that no piece was installed here.

Because of the inward curve of the bow strakes, the foremost gunport on the lower gun deck was hindered by the anchor cables passing through the adjacent hawse-holes and along the lower gun deck. Therefore, the fore chase, consisting of two demi-cannon drakes of 11.5 feet length totalling 5 tons, was mounted in the second port from the stem, one to port and one to starboard.

In contemporary Lists (Appendices 23 & 24), the demi-cannon's weight varied between 4–6,000 lb with a length of 10–12 feet and a bore of 6.4–6.75 inches. It fired a 32–36 lb shot. The charge weight for a brass demi-cannon in excess of 4,000 lb was calculated on the basis of 5.5 oz charge per 100 lb weight of piece, viz. 13.75 lb. In service, gunners reduced this charge to 3.75 oz per 100 lb weight of piece, viz. 9.375 lb.

No piece was mounted in the port immediately adjacent to the hawse-holes of the National Maritime Museum models (SLRO222, SLRO408 & SLRO409) of the first rate *Royal William* of 100 guns, launched in 1719. The collection of contemporary ship models in the National Maritime Museum demonstrates that by the end of the seventeenth century, no gunport was provided immediately adjacent to the hawse-holes.

The bows abaft the chase was the third port from the stem. Here were two demi-cannon drakes of 11 feet totalling 4.3 tons.

The remaining four ports were in the stern chase. The spacing between ports here was less than 8 feet. Here were four demi-cannon drakes of 10.5 feet totalling 11.4 tons. The stern chase of the *Royal Charles* and the *Prince Royal* consisted of four demi-cannon.

The lower gun deck carried twenty-eight pieces, weighing a total of 66.4 tons (Appendix 29).

There were twenty-six ports along the luffs, broadsides and quarters of the middle gun deck. The foremost eleven ports aside were 30 inches square. The reconstruction draught incorrectly suggests these ports were 34–6 inches square with a spacing varying between 9 feet 3 inches and 11 feet 2 inches. Seppings' middle gun deck ports are 36 inches square. The spacing varies between 9 feet 5 inches and 11 feet 4 inches. The aftermost two ports aside, immediately beneath the quarter galleries, are circular with circular port covers hinged from the upper edge.

The position of the entry port did not effect the symmetrical arrangement of ports. Van de Velde's broadside drawing depicts one port closed to permit the gangway to be lowered from the entry port to the dock side. This gangway was not aboard when the vessel was at sea.

Along the luffs, broadsides and quarters of the middle gun deck were twenty-two culverin drakes, each of 9.5 feet in length and weighing a total of 30.4 tons Appendix (29.) The culverin was a long, slim piece. The name originated from the Latin for snake, *colobrina*.

The twenty-four-pounders of the *Vasa* weighed 2,500 lb each and totalled forty-eight. They were cast from a bronze containing 92 per cent copper.

The foremost two ports on the middle gun deck near the cat-heads constituted the fore chase. Once again, van de Velde provides a clue. His piece mounted here inclines forward. Here were two fortified culverins. These were the standard home-bored full weight pieces. Being full weight guns, these lasted longer than the drakes. We can suggest two pieces each of 11.0 feet length totalling around 4.8 tons.

In contemporary Lists a fortified culverin weighed 4–4,840 lb, with a length of 11–13 feet and bore of 5.2–5.5 inches. It fired a shot between 15–24 lb (Appendices 23, 24 & 25). For the proving of brass culverins in excess of 4,000 lb, the charge weight was 75–80 per cent of the shot weight, plus 3.5 oz. In service, the charge weight was 0.44 times the shot weight, plus 3.5 oz

The bows abaft the chase was the second port from the stem. Here were two demi-culverin drakes 8–9 feet in length, and weighing a total of 1.9 tons.

According to contemporary Lists (Appendices 23 & 24), the weight of an average demi-culverin varied between 3–3,400 lb with a length of 9–12 feet and bore of 4.0–4.75 inches. It fired a shot of 8–13 lb. For proving and for service, the charge weight was calculated as 67 per cent of the shot weight, viz. 6–8.5 lb. In a List dated 1626, the charge weight was equal to the shot weight in demi-culverins and lesser pieces. Demi-culverin drakes of 2,900 lb were allowed in service 2.75 oz charge weight for every 100 lb of piece.

There were another four circular ports in the stern chase, which may have been closed by an internal double door hinged on the vertical. Here were mounted four fortified culverins. It is uncertain which of the *Sovereign*'s six fortified culverins listed in Appendix 29 were mounted here. We can, however, suggest four pieces of length 11.5 feet totalling around 10.2 tons.

Thus, all the ports on the middle gun deck were occupied by thirty pieces with a total weight of 47.3 tons (Appendix 29).

The upper gun deck had twenty-two ports, each 28 inches square, along the broadsides and quarters. The reconstruction draught incorrectly suggests the upper gun deck ports are 29–30 inches square, with a spacing varying between 10 feet 4 inches-11 feet 8 inches. Seppings depicts 31 inches square ports, each 10 feet 5 inches-12 feet apart.

The five upper gun deck ports between the hancing pieces of the waist did not display a gun port cover. This is exemplified in Payne's engraving, van de Velde's broadside drawing, and Sir Robert Seppings' model. Perhaps these covers may have been in two halves and side hung on the vertical, opening internally like a pair of doors.

On the upper gun deck were mounted twenty-two demi-culverin drakes of 8–9 feet in length, weighing a total of 21.1 tons.

The fore chase on the upper gun deck was mounted in the beakhead bulkhead. Neither Payne nor van de Velde depict covers for the six circular ports here. They were probably closed by an internal double door, hinged on the vertical. Because of the hazard of fouling by the rigging on the bowsprit, four of these ports were left unoccupied.

Only two guns formed the fore chase, and they were raked at an angle. Here were two demi-culverins fortified of 10 feet length with a total weight of 2.8 tons.

In the Merseyside Maritime Museum, Albert Dock, Liverpool are Navy Board models of the ninety gun *Neptune* of 1683 [Accession Number 55.174] and the ninety-six gun *St George* of 1708–14 [Accession Number L29.11 (LL 671)]. On either model, only two upper gun deck ports were provided in the beakhead bulkhead.

These pieces were intended for emergencies only. The blast from their muzzles was likely to damage the head rails and the rigging about her bowsprit.

The reconstruction draught omits the middle and upper gun deck stern chasers. Seppings omits the stern chase on the upper gun deck.

The two ports in the stern chase of the upper gun deck were circular. To avoid damaging the decorations, these ports may have been closed by an internal double door hinged on the vertical. The stern chase contained two demi-culverins fortified, of 10 feet in length and totalling 2.8 tons.

The four demi-culverins fortified of the fore and stern chases do not appear in Browne's record of proving the guns, as they were cast separately by Thomas Pitt, acting as subcontractor to Browne. They were probably the first pieces cast for the *Sovereign*. The cancelled debenture itemising them is dated 12 September 1638.

The upper gun deck carried twenty-six pieces of total weight of 26.7 tons (Appendix 29).

The tier above the upper gun deck had 8 circular ports in the sides and head of the forecastle. The two ports aside were circular. The four ports in the head were square with semi-circular upper edges.

The forecastle had eight demi-culverin drakes of 9 feet in length and a total of 7.7 tons.

There were six circular ports on the half-deck. The ports on the forecastle and half-deck had no covers. These decks were light spar decks with no bulwarks, therefore a port cover was unnecessary.

The half-deck contained six pieces similar to those on the forecastle, totalling 5.7 tons.

The two circular ports on the quarterdeck had no covers. The reconstruction draught (Illustration 18) omits a port at this position. Here were mounted two demi-culverin drake cutts of length 6 feet and a total weight of 0.8 tons.

The major bulkheads were built in a series of bays or sponsons. This was designed to give a wider arc of fire to the small guns mounted behind these bulkheads. This facilitated a cross-fire over the open decks when boarded. The forecastle bulkhead aft was embrasured for four circular ports. The half-deck bulkhead forward had six circular ports. Two circular ports were in the quarterdeck bulkhead forward. These twelve ports were within board.

Within board pieces were not practicable, except for repelling enemy boarding parties. There was a hazard of tackle and deck gear being shot away if such pieces could not be trained to fire outboard. There were many loopholes in the cabin and bulkheads within board for small arms fire. The only within board position to mount pieces was the bulkhead abaft the forecastle. Here were two culverin cutts of 6.0 feet in length, totalling 1.3 tons.

The Nature and Disposition of her Armament 105

The forecastle, half-deck, quarterdeck and bulkhead abaft the forecastle carried eighteen pieces weighing a total of 15.5 tons.

When originally armed, she had 102 muzzle loaders with a total weight of 155 tons 19 cwt 2 qt 15 lb (Appendices 28 & 29).

The Officers of the Ordnance, on 27 July 1637, provided an estimate of £20,592 13s 6d for ninety pieces of brass ordnance. There was an expectation of an additional provision for another ten pieces. On 9 August 1637 £1,000 was paid to this account. A revised estimate appeared on 18 December 1637 for 102 pieces at £24,447 8s 8d. Another estimate was issued on 16 April 1638 to provide an additional £3 per piece for adorning 102 brass pieces with a cypher and motto appointed by Charles I.

Thus, each piece was provided with a cypher in relief consisting of an anchor with cable, crossed sceptre and trident, with a Tudor Rose and crown. The rose and crown cypher was used on ordnance to signify their English manufacture for the Board of Ordnance from the mid-1500s to the mid-1700s.

Beneath was the Latin motto '*Carolvs Edgari sceptrvm stabilivit aqvarvm*'.

This, on translation, became 'Charles has established Edgar's sceptre of the waters.' This was an allusion to the Saxon King Edgar.

John Browne petitioned, on 17 June 1638, for an increase over the previous estimate to provide the outstanding four demi-cannon drakes for the stern chase on the lower gun deck. This accounted for 11.4 tons at a cost of £1,700. The final account for these four pieces, dated 20 June 1638, was £1,688 4s 6d. A minute passed at Greenwich on 27 June accepted this increase. We realise that the total cost of casting and cyphering 102 pieces was £26,441 13s 2d. The total weight was around 155.9 tons. The price per ton was around £169 12s 2d. John Browne's account for the *Sovereign*'s guns was paid by February 1641.

The *Sovereign*'s guns were proved in May, June and July 1638.

There are scattered references to various pieces from the *Sovereign* in later years. Two of her cannon of VII were in Ireland in 1685; Castle Ney, Cork (No. 16, Appendix 28) and Athlone Castle (No. 8, Appendix 28). Both are recorded as 9 feet in length. One of her demi-cannon drakes was in the storehouse in Dublin in 1685 (No. 6, Appendix 28). Another similar demi-cannon drake was in the storehouse at Athlone Castle (No. 8, Appendix 28). Three fortified culverins were still in service in 1696. Two were emplaced as garrison ordnance at Portsmouth and one was in store at the Tower of London. A culverin

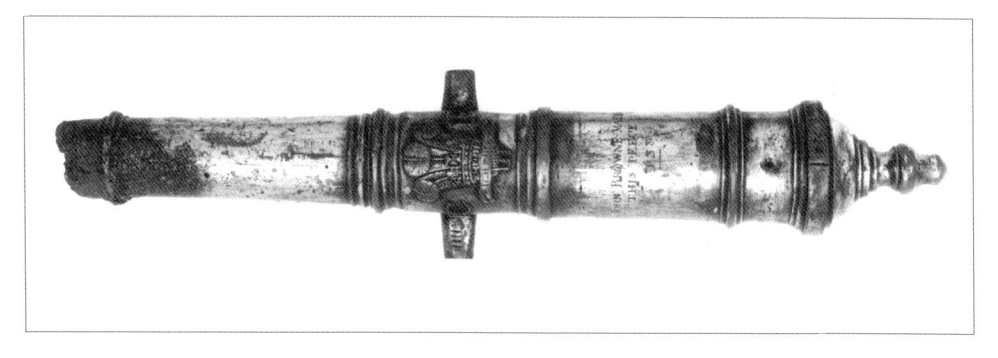

44. Small bronze gun, inscribed 'JOHN BROWNE MADE THIS PEECE 1638'.
(*Royal Armouries Museum, Leeds*)

45. Small bronze gun and carriage, inscribed 'JOHN BROWNE MADE THIS PEECE 1638'. (*Royal Armouries Museum, Leeds*)

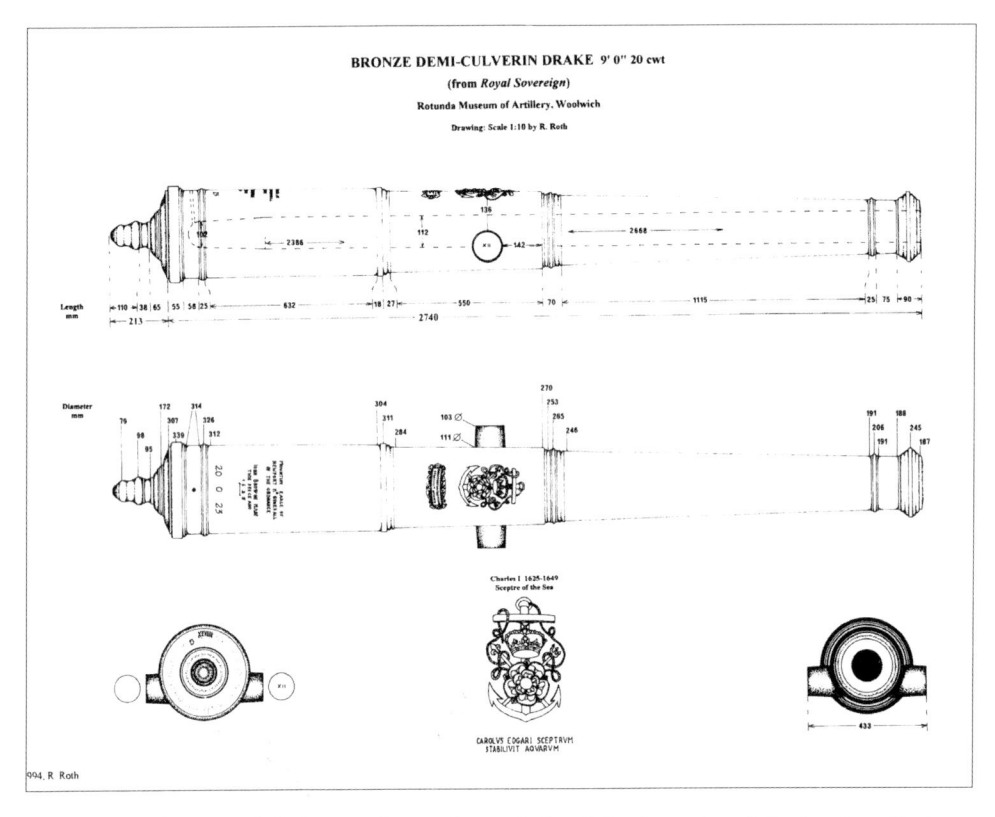

46. R. Roth's drawing of the bronze demi-culverin drake of the *Sovereign of the Seas* inscribed 'JOHN BROWNE MADE THIS PEECE ANO 1638' (1638). (*Jean Boudriot Publications*)

drake (No. 17, Appendix 28) was in Carrickfergus Castle in 1685. Only one fortified demi-culverin survived to 1696. It was held in the Tower of London. A demi-culverin drake (No. 11, Appendix 28) was recast in the Royal Brass Foundry in 1718.

A similar demi-culverin drake (No. 31 Appendix 28) passed into the collections of the Rotunda Museum of Artillery (Cat. No. 2/17). This brass demi-culverin drake formerly lay at the north west corner of the Horse Guards Parade, near the Master Gunner's House in St James's Park. It was removed in 1803. By 1917 it was in store at the Rotunda, Woolwich. For many years it lay in Chatham Historic Dockyard. It was returned in June 2000 to the Royal Artillery Museum at Woolwich (Cat. 2/17) for public display.

On the first reinforce is the incised motto (Illustration 50, Plates 43, 44, & 45), 'MOVNTIOY EARLE OF NEWPORT, Mr. GENERALL, OF THE ORDNANCE. JOHN BROWNE MADE, THIS PEECE ANO, 1638, 20–0–23.'

Mountjoy Blount, Baron Mountjoy and First Earl of Newport (1597–1666) replaced Sir Thomas Stafford as Master-General of the Ordnance in 1634, and was in turn succeeded in that office by John, First Earl of Peterborough in 1642.

On the second reinforce is a cypher in relief consisting of an anchor with cable, crossed sceptre and trident, with a Tudor Rose and crown. Beneath is the Latin motto in relief (Plate 46): '*Carolvs Edgari sceptrvm stabilivit aqvarvm*'.

Just below the base ring are the letters 'D XXVIIIII' (Illustrations 51 & 57). This suggests an absurdity, until we realise that probably the original number 'XVII' was subsequently altered. Stamped into the face of the muzzle is '71'.

The length is 9 feet, bore 4.4 inches and weight 20 cwt 23 lb. Over the surface is the patina of green malachite corrosion. This piece could have formed part of her original armament in the forecastle or half-deck. It is number 31 in Appendix 28. This piece is a surviving relic of the *Sovereign* (Plates 43, 44 & 45).

In the Royal Armouries at Leeds is a four-pounder bronze gun (Museum No. XIX.182 Cat. No. 38), inscribed 'CAST IN PRESENCE OF HIS MAJ OCTO THE FIFTH 1638. MOVNTIOY EARLE OF NEWPORT M GENERALL OF THE ORDNANCE. JOHN BROWNE MADE THIS PEECE.'

In relief is a Tudor Rose cypher between the initials 'C.R.', signifying Charles I. The length is 4 feet 2 inches, bore 3.2 inches and weight 2 cwt 3 qt 5 lb. The surface has been worn smooth by polishing. Below the cypher is a serial number 14522, which was recorded in the Ordnance Survey of 1696.

By tradition, this piece formed part of the vessel's original armament. At a later date it was mounted on the bastion of what was then known as the Royal Victoria Yard Deptford, together with guns of a similar weight, as a defence against the threatened Dutch attack of 1667.

In the same collections is a pair to this piece, but in better condition. In relief is a crowned Tudor Rose cypher between the initials 'C.R.' This piece (Museum No. XIX.170 Cat. No. 39) is inscribed. 'MOVNTIOY EARLE OF NEWPORT Mr. GENERALL OF THE ORDNANCE. JOHN BROWNE MADE THIS PEECE 1638.'

The length is 4 feet 2 inches, bore 3.25 inches and weight 2 cwt 2 qt 25 lb. This was exhibited at the Royal Naval Exhibition at Chelsea in 1891. It belonged to the Rotunda Museum Woolwich until 1930 when it was transferred to the Royal Armouries in the Tower of London. Neither of these later two extant specimens could have formed part of her main armament. Probably, they may have been minute or signal guns used to fire a warning shot before a gun salute (Illustrations 52 & 53).

Each piece was supported by its trunnions on a purpose built carriage. Lengths of elm, square in cross section, were fastened edgeways with long iron bolts to form two similar flanks, called cheeks. Elm was favoured on account of its resistance to splintering if struck by flying debris. To match the narrowing diameter of the piece, the cheeks sloped towards each other at the fore end. The cheeks were held by oak transforms, fore carriage and cross beams. At each forward lower outside corner of the gun-carriage was a small truck

47. Millhall Wharf, Aylesford. (*Author's photograph 28 April 2002*)

48. Millhall Wharf, Aylesford. Detail of early masonry. (*Author's photograph 28 April 2002*)

or wheel of elm mounted on an iron axle-tree. Each truck was reinforced by a pair of iron straps secured across the face at right angles to the grain of the wood. As can be seen in Illustrations 45 & 54, there were no such trucks at the rear. Here was a half rounded lateral timber forming a skid. Such a carriage provided for maximum elevation of the piece. It also dampened down the effect of the recoil after firing. The upper edge of each cheek was grooved to accept the trunnion. A curved iron strap called the cap-square, secured by a forelock, prevented the trunnion disengaging from the carriage. A piece around 12 feet long and weighing nearly 3 tons was mounted on a carriage 5.5 feet long. A demi-cannon's carriage was 5 feet long.

An account, dated 1 May 1639, was drawn in favour of Matthew Banks, Master Carpenter for the Office of the Ordnance, for the sum of £558 11s 8d. This included the cost of gun-carriages for the *Sovereign*. This document describes all her gun-carriages as having whole trucks and half trucks. There is also a record of eleven pairs of rear trucks to carry the half trucks of the carriage clear of the deck. By this means, the rear end of the carriage could be jacked up, and a pair of conventional trucks slid on the axles to facilitate movement across the deck. This design was unique to the *Sovereign*; it had the advantage of providing an increase in the elevation of the shot.

Cast iron was common for making shot. This had a specific gravity of 7.1–7.7. A cast iron ball weighing a trifle over 48 lb had a diameter of exactly 7 in. From this fact, we can calculate the specific gravity of cast iron shot as 7.40. Hence, we can calculate the weight of the ball knowing its diameter, or the diameter knowing its weight:

(16) $w = 0.140 \times d^3$
(17) $d = w^{1/3} \times 1.926$
Where:
w = weight of shot in pounds
d = diameter of shot in inches

Some shot was made from lead and stone. Molten lead was cast about a stone core in the proportion of around five parts of lead to one part stone. This produced a weight comparable to that of a cast iron shot of similar diameter.

The propellant, used to discharge the shot from the piece, was gunpowder. It was also known as blackpowder. This is a homogeneous mixture of saltpetre (potassium nitrate), sulphur and charcoal. This was manufactured privately under licence at Ospringe, near Faversham. This was a most suitable location, being situated on a natural tidal creek near to the River Thames, with ease of transportation by boat between the London and Medway arsenals and the Channel ports. Faversham had an abundant supply of running water, providing the motive power for the grinding mills.

The sea port here facilitated the import of saltpetre from Italy and India. Sulphur was imported from Italy and Sicily. Faversham had an abundant supply of timber for the manufacture of charcoal.

Blackpowder was produced at the Home Works (TR 0161) Faversham between around 1560 and around 1925. Under the private ownership of Daniel Judd, these mills produced two tons of powder weekly in 1653. Blackpowder was also produced at Chilworth, Surrey (TQ 0348) between around 1635 and 1920.

Francis Vincent of Canterbury was appointed, in 1634, official 'saltpetre man' for Kent, Surrey and Sussex. He was required to supply 6 cwt each week. His raw materials included the product of Kentish dovecotes. Thomas May, of Norton near Faversham, entered into an agreement in December 1635 to cover the floor of his dovecote with earth a foot deep, to provide a source for saltpetre. Naturally occurring saltpetre was purified at Northfleet and Maidstone during the reign of Charles I. The raw material was dissolved in water, filtered through clean sand and purified by recrystallisation.

49. H. B. Culver's model of the *Sovereign of the Seas* (1921). Detail of port bow view. (*Halton, Truscott Smith Ltd., London*)

Imported native sulphur was purified by slowly melting in an iron or copper vessel, skimming off the surface and straining the melt through dry, linen cloth.

Hazel, willow or ash trees, cut in May or June, were debarked, and burnt slowly in the absence of air. Before the charcoal could oxidise completely to ash, it was quenched with moistened earth.

During the early seventeenth century powder formulation varied considerably (these values are percentages):

Saltpetre	66.6	69.4	75.0	75	71.4
Sulphur	16.7	13.9	12.5	15	14.3
Charcoal	16.7	16.7	12.5	10	14.3

The manufacturing process was an art in itself. The three ingredients were mixed together in the required proportion and ground to a fine powder in a mortar with pestle. Typical examples of seventeenth-century bell metal and bronze mortars and pestles are displayed in Maidstone Museum and Art gallery, St Faith's Street, Maidstone, Kent (Maidstone Borough Council).

The powder was dampened slightly with fresh water, vinegar or brandy to reduce the hazard of spontaneous combustion during subsequent working. The selection of vinegar or brandy depended largely on the manufacturer. It was added to prevent deterioration if sea water was inadvertently absorbed into the powder keg.

In Upnor Castle, Kent, are a quantity of replica powder kegs, made in 1986 to hold 100 lb black powder (Illustration 55). These conventional wooden kegs are bound in copper. Iron, which would have induced the risk of sparks, is omitted from their construction.

Corning was a simple process to improve the efficiency for heavy ordnance. Corned powder had greater power, provided greater ranges, and higher muzzle velocity to the shot. Powder moistened with water was pressed through thick parchment punctured with small holes. The powder formed small uniform grains. Unlike a finely ground powder, a granular material could not compact in the chamber and hence exclude air. Oxygen, contained up to 20 per cent in the atmosphere, was vital to the chemistry of combustion. Later in the seventeenth century, corned powder was sealed in a cartridge made of paper royal or canvas, glued or stitched into a cylindrical form. The diameter of the cartridge was similar to that of the shot.

Powder which had not been corned was called serpentine. This finer grade was used to prime the vent, and for hand guns.

During repeated loading and firing, the concave cylinder of the piece became fouled due to deposits from the incomplete combustion of the charge. Not all this deposit was removed by the worm and sponge. The heat generated by the exothermic chemical reaction of the exploding charge was absorbed by both the piece and the shot. Consequently, the shot expanded and the bore decreased. Therefore, the diameter of the shot was always less than the bore of the piece. The difference between the bore of the piece and the diameter of the shot was called the windage. In sixteenth-century artillery this had a constant value of 0.25 inch. During the seventeenth century, the bore divided by the diameter of the shot was a constant value. For English pieces, the ratio was 21/20 or 1.05. The French ratio was 27/26 or 1.04 (Appendix 26).

In April 1652, a report to Parliament appeared on the cost to the Navy with an estimate for purchasing 335 pieces which the *Sovereign* and other vessels required. If the pieces were to be brass, then the estimate was £67,200. If the pieces were to be of iron, then the estimate was for £13,520. Apparently, the estimate was too high to be met, because a warrant on 10 May 1652 from the Council of State ordered a re-arrangement of vessels' armament. The brass guns aboard the *Swiftsure, Foresight* and *Laurel* were ordered to be transferred to the *Sovereign* and the *Resolution*. The deficiency was to be made up with iron ordnance. The *Sovereign* was rated as a 100 gun ship for war at home, and a ninety gun ship for war abroad, or peace at home and abroad.

A List of 1654–55 suggested a total of ninety-five guns for the *Sovereign* (Appendix 30), made up of nineteen cannon drakes, nine demi-cannon, twenty-eight culverins, thirty demi-culverins, five sakers and four twelve-pounders.

She was to be provided with 2,850 round shot, 720 double-headed shot, 330 kegs of powder, 300 muskets, twenty blunderbusses, 200 pikes and 100 hatchets. This arrangement seems to have been a project, rather than an actual state of affairs. The *Resolution* and *Naseby* were comparable with similar armament, yet they were only eighty gun ships.

50. Bronze demi-culverin drake of the *Sovereign of the Seas*, inscribed 'JOHN BROWNE MADE THIS PEECE ANO 1638'.
(*Royal Artillery Historical Trust, Woolwich, author's photograph 7 August 2001*)

51. Bronze demi-culverin drake of the *Sovereign of the Seas* (1638). Detail of inscription on base ring.
(*Chatham Historic Dockyard Trust*)

A List dated 18 May 1664 suggested that the *Sovereign*'s armament of ninety guns be made up of twenty cannon of VII, eight demi-cannon, twenty-eight culverins, twenty-six demi-culverins and eight demi-culverin cutts.

This List was based on the availability of ordnance in store for use in the event of war. This List seems to have been a proposal rather than an actual state of affairs.

A List of 1666 recorded between ninety-two and ninety-four guns, made up of twenty-two cannon of VII, either six or eight demi-cannon, twenty-eight culverins and thirty-six demi-culverins. Probably, some of the ports of the upper gun deck were left empty.

According to Sir Anthony Deane's List of 1670, her 100 brass guns weighed 176 tons, and cost £26,400. Her 54 tons of shot cost £728. Her 400 kegs of powder cost £1,200. The cost of the gunner's stores as new was £1,678 (Appendix 13).

According to a List of 1677 (Appendix 35), she had 100 guns for war at home, with a total weight of around 177 tons, and ninety guns for peace or war abroad with a total weight of 162 tons. Her lower gun deck had twenty-six cannon of VII of 54–65 cwt, bore of 7 inches which fired a 42 lb shot. This was a total weight of 78 tons. Two of these pieces were removed for peace or war abroad. Her middle gun deck had twenty-eight cannon petro of 34–36.43 cwt, bore of 5.875 inches which fired a 24 lb shot. The total weight was between 47.6 and 51 tons. Two of these pieces were removed for peace or war abroad. Her upper gun deck had twenty-eight demi-culverins of 27.14–30 cwt and 4.25 inches bore which fired a 9 lb shot. The total weight on this deck varied between 38–42 tons. Two of these pieces were removed for peace or war abroad (Appendix 35). The quarterdeck carried ten light sakers of 11–13.43 cwt with a length of 6 feet, bore of 3.6 inches which fired a 6 lb shot. The forecastle carried four similar pieces. The total weight of these fourteen pieces was between 7 tons 14 cwt and 9 tons 8 cwt. Four of these pieces were removed for peace or war abroad. The poop carried four falcons for war at home and also peace or war abroad. They weighed 4–7 cwt, had a 2.9 inch bore, and fired a 3 lb shot. The total weight of these pieces was between 0.8 and 1.4 tons. Four extra ports would have been required on the quarterdeck and another two on the poop.

The Ordnance Office, dated 1 January 1684–5, proposed 100 guns for the *Sovereign*, made up of twenty-six cannon of VII, twenty-six twenty-four-pounders, twenty-eight twelve-pounders and twenty sakers. There is no evidence to indicate that this proposal was either approved by the Navy Board nor sanctioned by the King. It did, however, suggest some trend towards standardisation of a vessel's armament where there was a benefit to be gained in reducing the variation between pieces.

By 1687–88 her armament had been reduced to a mere eighty-two brass pieces, consisting of twenty-six cannon of VII, seventeen twenty-four-pounders, nineteen twelve-pounders and twenty fortified sakers (Appendix 36). It seems likely that these pieces were subsequently consigned to the *Britannia*.

By the time of the 1696 survey, the *Sovereign*'s armament had been reduced to ninety iron pieces consisting of twenty-two cannon of VII, twenty-six culverins and forty-two demi-culverins. They were numbered 6864 to 6953 sequentially (Appendix 37). The total weight was 170 tons 3 cwt 0 qt 19 lb. None of these pieces were drakes. Some were old and some were new. There was no sign of uniformity. Two demi-culverins, which formed part of the armament of the *Sovereign of the Seas* have survived.

Number 6923 weighs 31 cwt 0 qt 13 lb, and is 10 feet long. It was supplied on 14 February 1691, and is now in Barbados.

The other, bearing the number 6953 incised on the second reinforce, was probably cast by John Banning and supplied to the Navy Board on 4 April 1691. The total length is 7 feet 7.5 inches, bore 4.25 inches and weighs 16 cwt 2 qt 2 lb. There is a heavily corroded cypher in relief depicting a crowned Tudor rose at the second reinforce. The right or starboard trunnion has broken off. This piece was in storage at No. 3 slip, Chatham Historic Dockyard (Illustrations 56 & 57) until February 2008, when it was painted and transferred into the Chatham Dockyard Historical Society's Museum for public display.

The sequence of operations necessary to load and fire the piece was no art. Here was a disciplined military exercise carried out with precision. This drill was practised many times before the gun crews saw action.

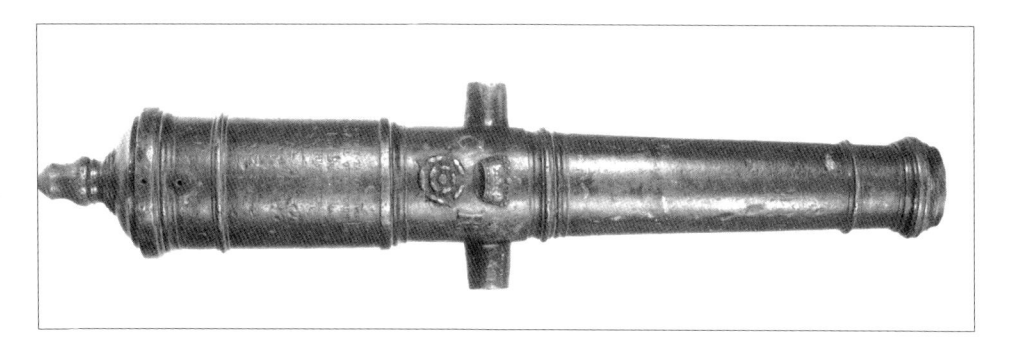

52. Bronze four-pounder gun, inscribed 'JOHN BROWNE MADE THIS PEECE 1638'. (*Royal Armouries Museum, Leeds*)

53. Bronze four-pounder gun, inscribed 'JOHN BROWNE MADE THIS PEECE 1638'. Detail of cypher. (*Royal Armouries Museum, Leeds*)

1) "Put back your piece."
The muzzle lashings were released. The centre of the recoil rope was looped and seized about itself around the cascable. Each end of the recoil rope was hooked to an iron ring bolt in the bulwark on either side of the port. The ring bolt was "barbed". When hammered into the internal timbers of the bulwark, it remained incredibly secure. The recoil rope was loosed.

The breeching tackles were slackened off. These hemp ropes were hawser laid. The breeching tackle was probably a luff or a jigger on the smaller pieces, and a six-fold purchase tackle on the heavier pieces. One end of the breeching tackle hooked to an iron ring bolt on the outside of each carriage cheek. The other end hooked to an iron ring bolt in the bulwark on either side of the port. The train tackle, rove between the drag hook in the centre of the carriage's rear transom and the deck, was hauled in. The piece was drawn inboard to the fullest extent of the slack breeching tackles and slack recoil rope.

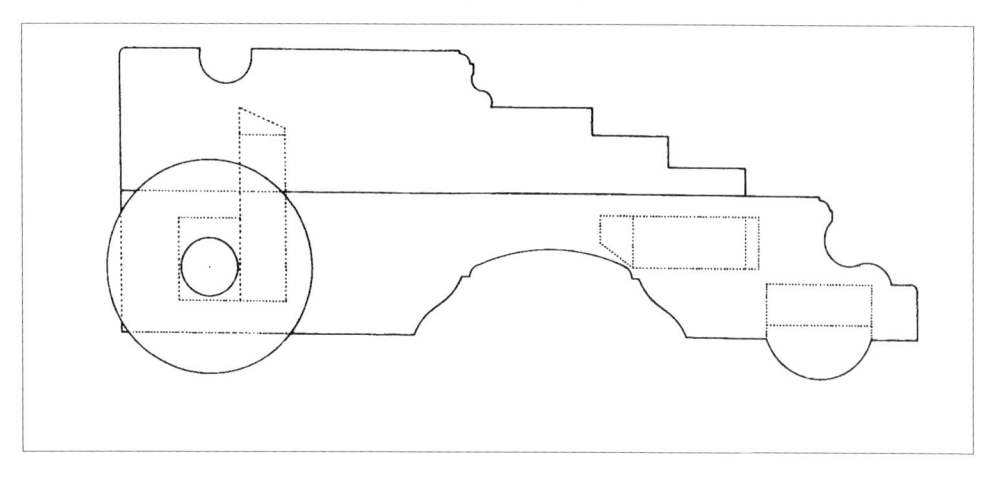

54. T. James' profile of a carriage for a gun for the *Sovereign of the Seas* (1638). (*Jean Boudriot Publications*)

55. Replica powder kegs at Upnor Castle. (*English Heritage, author's photograph 4 April 2002*)

2) "Order your piece to load."
When not in service, the internal cylinder was protected by a wooden or cork plug called a tampion, rammed into the muzzle and covered with tallow. This tampion was removed on the order.

3) "Search your piece."
An iron worm like a corkscrew on the end of a wooden staff was thrust down the muzzle, twisted, and pulled out. Any debris was withdrawn. In the upper part of the rear of the chamber was a hole drilled through the metal. This vent was cleared with an iron spike or wire called a priming iron, pricker or vent auger.

4) "Sponge your piece."
A sponge was a fragment of lambskin secured to the end of a wooden staff. This sponge was dipped into a wooden bucket of sea water and thrust down the muzzle to extinguish any lingering sparks and to cool the piece.

5) "Fill your ladle."
The ladle was copper, in the form of a half cylinder rounded at the open end. The opposite end was attached to a wooden staff. The ladle was filled by dipping into the powder keg.

6) "Put in your powder."
The filled ladle was thrust into the muzzle. For safety, the loader stood to one side.

7) "Empty your ladle."
The ladle was twisted sideways to empty the powder into the chamber.

8) "Put up your powder."
A wooden cover was placed over the powder keg. As a precautionary measure, it was also moved aside.

9) "Thrust home your wad."
Wads were usually made up on board ship. The gunner's stores contained pieces of old rope and cable, known as junk. In 1655, the *Sovereign* had 50 cwt of junk for this purpose. The wad was placed down the muzzle. The wad and charge were thrust down the cylinder by a rammer. This consisted of a wooden staff. At one end was a cylindrical block of wood which neatly fitted inside the cylinder.

56. Iron demi-culverin of the *Sovereign of the Seas* (1691). Muzzle end (No. 6953).
(*Chatham Historic Dockyard Trust*, author's photograph May 2002)

57. Iron demi-culverin of the *Sovereign of the Seas* (1691). Cascable end (No. 6953). (*Chatham Historic Dockyard Trust, author's photograph May 2002*)

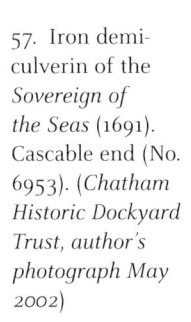

10) "Regard your shot."
A shot, of diameter suitable for the piece, was selected from the rack which extended down the length of the gun deck and placed into the muzzle.
11) "Put home your shot gently."
The rammer was used to thrust the shot on to the wad.
12) "Thrust home your last wad with three strokes."
A second wad was pushed down the cylinder by the rammer. The rammer was used to compact the shot on to the first wad. Gauging the exact degree of ramming was part of the gunner's art.
13) "Prime your piece."
The vent was cleared using a vent auger. Approximately a pound of serpentine powder was poured from a powder horn into the vent and covered with an apron of lead or dried sheepskin to keep the powder dry, and also to prevent premature firing. This operation was done by the gunner himself.
14) "Run out your piece."
The lashing securing the port cover was slackened off. The cover hoist was hauled in and secured to a fair-lead on the bulwark at the side of the port. By hauling on the falls of the breeching tackle, the carriage rumbled across the deck to thrust the muzzle outboard through the open port.
15) "Gage your piece."
The piece was trained on to its target by the breeching tackles. The carriage was manoeuvred into position using handspikes. These were straight or curved wooden levers 5–6 feet long. One end was flattened and the other was tapered. The elevation, and hence the range, was controlled by adjusting a wooden wedge called a quion between the rear transom of the carriage and the rear of the piece.
16) "Fire."
The apron was removed from the vent. The powder in the vent was touched by a lighted linstock. This was a wooden staff around 2–3 feet long. At one end was a cock or screw to hold the slow match. At the other end was a sharp spike. This was thrust into the deck to hold the linstock upright and therefore safe. The ball was discharged and the piece recoiled violently, being restrained by the recoil rope.

The firepower of this great ship at close range was devastating. At longer range her ability was limited. Repeated broadsides must have had an exhilarating, yet terrifying psychological effect on her crew. The discharge must have been deafening. The gunners could not possibly have heard audio commands. The shock waves created by the recoil must have caused strain on tackle and rigging.

CHAPTER 7

Her Masting and Rigging

The *Sovereign of the Seas* relied upon the vagaries of weather and wind to provide the means of motive propulsion. The laws of classical physics were applied to a unique design. Tall wooden masts carried hemp cordage which supported long wooden spars spreading stitched canvas sails.

English soils could not support the growth of the huge conifers necessary for the spars of the expanding deep-water fleet. The demand developed for long-grained softwoods. Such timbers minimised weight aloft, and assured the suppleness which indigenous hardwoods could not provide.

The Baltic fir, Riga fir (*Pinus sylvestris*) was the Navy's prime choice of mast timber. The criteria required was strength and supple resilience. These depended on the presence of gummy resins characteristic of conifers. The mast's resilience and durability were due to the retention of resins long after felling. Because of the proximity of rival naval forces, the traditional supply of mast timber, hemp, canvas and wood oils from the Baltic ports was rather precarious.

The navy's second choice of mast timber was the New England white pine (*Pinus strobus*). A ship-load of pine masts was imported from Penobscot Bay, Maine, in 1634. To forestall the crisis in replacing masts damaged in action, and to build up a reserve for warships still on the stocks, mast transports were despatched by the Navy to New England in 1652. Their return during the following season marked the beginning of an annual trade in mast timber which continued until 1775. Thus, mainmasts, foremasts and bowsprits came from New England, where the virgin forests furnished 40-inch-diameter spars which, through over harvesting, were scarcely obtainable in the Baltic.

The lighter masts and spars came from Norway, where the spruce has an excellent toughness when young.

Soon after felling, a mast or spar was stripped of its bark. In the forest clearing it was worked with an adze, to produce a partly dressed timber of sixteen sides in cross section. In this form it was shipped across the seas.

To prevent drying out and splitting, mast and spar timber were normally stored under fresh water in ponds in the dockyards. It lay here for some years until needed. To retain the essential springiness, a mast was usually replaced every ten years. This process seasoned the timber, allowing the sap to die back without drying out the resins. A mast, selected for length and thickness, was hauled into the mast-house and placed horizontally across several wooden trestles. It was allowed to dry out gradually in air.

Her Masting and Rigging

The mast-houses were connected to the mast pond by a short slipway. Because of the simple equipment needed for mast making, there was little difference between a working mast-house and a mast-house for storing mast timber. The masts for the *Sovereign* were brought from the mast pond at Deptford.

The original lower masts were pole-masts, viz. they were in one piece. The mast was cut to the required length. Damaged ends were removed. Specialist shipwrights with adze and plane worked to produce a full rounded mast of the required size.

During the early part of the seventeenth century, the length of the mainmast was dependent on the vessel's beam. The length of the *Sovereign's* mainmast in 1640 was calculated from the relationship:

(18) MM = K x bx
Where:
MM = Length of the mainmast, in feet, above the step
K = Constant of 2.354
bx = Beam extreme, excluding wales, at Θ

The constant was arbitrary, but the value of 2.354 was specific to the *Sovereign*. Other contemporary vessels exhibited a similar ratio, viz.:

Bear of 1618	2.43
Sir Henry Mainwaring dated 1623	2.4
La Couronne of 1638	2.15

Substituting the relevant values from Appendix 8, we have:

Length of mainmast = 2.354 x 48 = 112.99

The length and maximum diameter of the *Sovereign's* masts from a List of 1640 are displayed in Appendix 41.

Sir William Monson suggested a different empirical relationship by which the length of the mainmast was calculated:

(19) MM = 2(d1 + bx) – (bx – 20)
Where:
d1 = Actual draught, waterline to bottom of keel. We assume that the draught was 22 feet 6 inches

Substituting the relevant values from Appendix 8, we have:

Length of mainmast = 2(22.5 + 48) – (48 – 20) = 113

At around 1660, we find another relationship to determine the length of the mainmast:

(20) MM = (0.5 x khr) + bx
Where:
khr = Length of keel in feet, from the harping rule

Substituting the relevant values from Appendix 8, we have;

Length of mainmast = (0.5 x 131) + 48 = 113.5

During this period, the fraction was ignored and the product taken to the whole integer. This simplification accounted for anomalies in Lists. The resemblance between the products from equations (19) and (20) and those obtained from equation (18) may not necessarily be coincidental.

The maximum diameter of the mainmast was 2.8 per cent of its length. The point of maximum diameter of a lower mast occurred at the partners. These were timbers bolted to the deck beams to secure the lower mast and reinforce the breached deck at the point where the lower mast passed through the thickness of the upper gun deck.

The foremast's maximum diameter was 84 per cent of that of the mainmast. The maximum diameter of the mizen mast was 76 per cent of that of the mainmast. With respect to length and diameter, the bowsprit was similar to the foremast. The maximum diameter of the bowsprit was 2.8 per cent of its length.

The diameter tapered towards either end at 1 inch/3 feet of length. Expressing the diameter of the mainmast at the partners as 100 per cent, the diameter at the heel was 67 per cent and at the hounds 75 per cent. The hounds were shaped timbers fore and aft of the fore and main lower mast-head. The forward end of the bowsprit tapered to 50 per cent of its maximum diameter.

The ends of the lower masts, comprising the heels and mast-heads, were square in cross section. The removal of the rounding at the mast-head facilitated the addition of the hounds. The length of the lower mast-head was around 10.4 per cent of the length of the mast, viz. 1.25 inches/feet of length.

Large-diameter masts had a tendency to split when drying out. To prevent this tendency, wooldings were applied. While supported horizontally across several trestles, several riggers worked simultaneously on one mast. Wooldings, consisting of thirteen consecutive turns of rope, were spaced regularly along the length of the mast. A wooden band, around 1.5 inches wide, was nailed to the mast above and below each woolding. This served to make it fast. There were twenty-two turns of wooldings on the bowsprit, nineteen on the mainmast and fifteen on the foremast. No wooldings were applied to the mizen mast.

The heel of the mainmast was sited slightly abaft the middle point between the stem and sternpost. This was the plane of maximum beam. The heel fitted into a step straddling the keel.

The foremast was stepped on a deck beam because the heel was forward of the forefoot. The foremast's step was consequently higher above the keel than the mainmast's step. Because of this, the foremast's length was not a ready measure of its height above the upper gun deck. Thus, the effective height of the foremast above the level of the upper gun deck was increased, such that the foremast-head was almost level with the mainmast head.

The heel of her mizen mast was placed midway between the mainmast and the taffrail. The step was on the keel.

Each mast inclined from the vertical. Her spritsail topmast and foremast both raked forward by 2 degrees. This had the effect of pressing her head into the sea. The mainmast raked aft by 3 degrees. The mizen mast raked aft by 4 degrees. The effect was to give the vessel more way. Thus, the foremost lower dead-eye was further aft. When the vessel was correctly trimmed in the water, the fore topmast was vertical.

The stem head of the *Prince Royal* of 1610 rose above the level of the middle gun deck. To provide a firm seat for the heel, the bowsprit was stepped beside the stem head. This was due to insufficient space forward of the foremast to allow the heel of the bowsprit to be stepped on the keel. Alternatively, the heel of the bowsprit was secured by a pair of bitts on the orlop deck.

The *Sovereign* followed this same trend. Payne and van de Velde the Elder's broadside drawing depict the stem head on the left of the bowsprit. Thus, it passes on the starboard side of the stem head and foremast. Edye and Seppings, in depicting the starboard side

Her Masting and Rigging

elevation, portray the stem head to the right of the bowsprit. Seppings' model, however, depicts the bowsprit centrally above the stem head. The *Sovereign*'s bowsprit entered the hull below the beakhead bulkhead where it met the prow deck. This was located around 1–2 feet above the level of the middle gun deck. This provided clearance for the two guns forming the fore chase of the upper gun deck mounted in the beakhead bulkhead. Similarly, the bowsprit of the *Royal Prince* of 1670 was stepped beside the stem head.

The steeving of the bowsprit, viz. the angle from the horizontal, prevented it from dipping beneath the waves on a turbulent sea. This would entail disastrous consequences. The angle of steeving varied with each authority:

W. Marshall's frontispiece	28 degrees
J. Payne's engraving	24 degrees
W. van de Velde the Elder's broadside drawing	28 degrees
Sir A. Deane's List of 1670	30 degrees
W. van de Velde the Younger's unfinished drawing	44 degrees
W. Edye's draught	24 degrees
Sir R. Seppings' draught	24 degrees
Sir R. Seppings' model	24 degrees
A. C. Jackson's model	35 degrees

The masts were steadied and the stress was distributed throughout the hull by means of standing rigging (Appendix 42). This was a permanent installation of rope tackles, shrouds and back stays aside the vessel, with stays in a fore and aft direction, forming a pyramidal support for the masts.

Hemp was the traditional fibre used in manufacturing ropes for rigging. Hemp was produced by the plant *Cannabis sativa* of the family *Cannabaceae,* grown naturally in temperate climatic zones on the steppes of southern Russia. This plant was harvested and exported through the Baltic ports, which gave rise to the name Baltic or Riga hemp. Fibres were extracted from the stalks of the plant by a series of operations. These long, straight fibres were excellent when applied to the manufacture of strong cordage.

When wet hemp retains water, it shrinks, and is prone to rot. On drying out, the fibres expand again. Frequent adjustments were necessary to control the tension in the standing rigging. To effect stabilisation and prevent rotting, the yarn was treated with hot Stockholm tar. Using the motive power provided by a manual windlass or capstan, the yarn was drawn through a vat of hot tar. The tarred yarn was laid up in storage to dry until it was ready to be formed into strands.

Rope has been made at Chatham Royal Dockyard since 1618. Here is contained the sole surviving commercial rope-making company, viz. Master Ropemakers Ltd., using traditional methods of manufacture.

The first standing rigging fitted on the vessel started with the bowsprit. The heel was lashed to a deck beam close to the foremast. Where it emerged from the hull, the bowsprit was lashed to the stem head.

Forward of the stem head were a pair of gammonings. These multiple lashings alternated over the bowsprit and under the knee of the head without a slot in the timber of the *Prince Royal*. The *Sovereign* followed the same trend, but her gammonings rove through slots in the knee of the head. The circumference of her gammonings was around 34–40 per cent of the mainmast's diameter. They were laid right handed. There were around ten turns of rope. Each turn was seized to the previous turn, and the end was eventually seized to one of the earlier turns. The gammonings were prevented from slipping down the bowsprit by thumb cleats, one above the bowsprit, and one on either side. Payne omits the lower part of the gammonings. Van de Velde the Elder depicts squares of canvas draped over them where they passed over the bowsprit. We have the suggestion, therefore, that the bowsprit was in place when van de Velde made his drawing.

At the upper parts of the hounds were the cheeks. Below were a pair of trestle-trees in oak, each bolted fore and aft on either side. The length of her trestle-trees was 27 per cent of her extreme beam. Quarter round timbers called bolsters were fitted to the upper edge of each trestle-tree to ease the angle of the standing rigging and prevent chafing. Slots around 1 inch deep across the upper surface of the trestle-trees supported a pair of cross-trees, which were similar oak timbers placed athwart ships. The iron work about the mast-heads was forged by hand by the dockyard blacksmiths.

Over the trestle-trees and cross-trees was a wooden platform, called the top, projecting like a circular scaffold around the mast-head. A deck was formed of timber around 2–3 inches thick and around 6 inches wide. Knees radiating out around the perimeter, supported the planking around the sides which produced a saucer shape. The diameter of her mainmast top measured around 13 feet at the base, and 18 feet at the rim. A similar structure was provided at each lower mast-head and the forward end of the bowsprit. Payne depicts extraordinarily small tops. Obviously, he was working from documents and not from the vessel herself.

Van de Veldes' *The Portrait of Peter Pett and the* Sovereign of the Seas offers the best portrayal of her tops.

Doubtless, Phineas Pett specified the mast and spar lengths and diameters and designed the sail area. The manner in which the vessel was rigged was performed essentially by the Master Rigger according to prevalent fashion.

58. J. Dupray's model of the *Sovereign of the Seas* (1982). Gammonings. (*Ship Modellers' Association of Southern California, USA*)

Her Masting and Rigging

The first standing rigging fitted over the mast-head were the pendants for the burton tackles. Each was formed of one single block, one single hook-block, one double block (or a fiddle block), a pendant, a runner and a fall. This was the means to steady the masts and to set up or tighten the shrouds. The tension in the standing rigging varied according to changes in atmospheric humidity. Burton tackles were also used to hoist gear about the vessel. The fore and main masts had a pair aside. Each was made by doubling the pendant and seizing it to form a bight in the centre which passed over the mast-head. The starboard pair went on first. Only one tackle per side was provided on the mizen mast, with the pendants cut spliced over the mast-head.

The entire length of each pendant was served to prevent chafing. A single block was spliced in each end of the pendant. The runner rove through this block. One end of the runner was secured to the chain-wale. The other end was spliced to a double block. Through this double block rove the fall. One end of the fall was spliced to a single hook-block secured to a iron ring bolt in the chain-wale. The other end of the fall rove through the single hook-block, back through the double block and was belayed to a timber head inboard of the bulwark.

Chain-wales provided the means to spread the standing rigging to support the mast, and to prevent chafing against the bulwark and gunwale. The chain-wale was a timber bolted to one of the external wales and following its sheer. The forward end of the chain-wale was abreast of the middle line of the parent mast. A chain-wale's width, half that of the parent wale, was sufficient to maintain the standing rigging clear of the bulwark.

When originally built, the chain-wales of the *Prince Royal* were slightly below the upper gun deck. They were moved lower when she was rebuilt in 1623. The fore and main chain-wales of the *Sovereign* were on the fourth wale, between the lower and middle gun decks. Her mizen chain-wale was nothing more than a thickening of the sixth wale, between the middle and upper gun decks. Underneath each chain-wale were curved iron brackets securing it to the hull.

Over the tackles went the shrouds. They were fitted in pairs, each pair made by doubling the shroud and seizing it to form a bight in the centre which passed over the mast-head and descended between the cross-trees. The bight was served to prevent chafing. The foremost starboard pair went on first, then alternated with the foremost port pair, etc. There were an odd number of shrouds on the fore and mizen masts. The last shroud on each side was cut spliced over the mast-head.

Shrouds were secured with a pair of dead-eyes and a laniard. The lower end of each shroud was doubled about itself and seized to form a bight around the upper dead-eye.

The width of a dead-eye approximated the radius of the parent mast. At the beginning of the seventeenth century, a dead-eye was pear-shaped. The pointed end was uppermost on the shroud, but was set downwards on the lower dead-eye. The score around the outer edge prevented it from slipping from the bight. Grooves in the inboard face allowed the laniard to follow a gentle curve, thus avoiding harsh corners which could cause chafing.

The end of cable laid or left handed rope rove under the dead-eye from right to left, passed the standing part of the shroud and emerged on the right hand side. The end of right handed rope rove from left to right finishing on the left side of the shroud. A throat seizing secured the end with the standing part. The end was secured by two round seizings, then whipped and cut to length.

One end of the laniard was stopped with a Matthew Walker knot. The laniard rove outwards through the hole in the upper dead-eye furthest from the end of the shroud. It rove through the corresponding hole in the lower dead-eye, outwards through the middle and uppermost hole in the upper dead-eye and successively through the three remaining holes. It was drawn taut, passed up behind the upper dead-eye, over the standing part of the shroud, between the throat seizing and the dead-eye and passed under itself to make a half hitch.

59. J. Dupray's model of the *Sovereign of the Seas* (1982). Main top.
(*Ship Modellers' Association of Southern California, USA*)

Around the score of the lower dead-eye was an iron strap which passed through a notch in the outboard edge of the chain-wale. The lower end of the strap was secured to the hull below the chain-wale by an iron bolt called the chain-plate. Her mizen chain-plates were shaped to fit around the wale and were made fast to the hull immediately beneath. The centre line of the foremost dead-eye was level with the after side of the parent mast. The chain-plates radiated in a straight line from the mast-head. The foremost chain-plate was vertical. Each successive chain-plate was raked gradually.

The lower dead-eyes were arranged along the length of the chain-wales to provide clearance for the opening of the gunports of the upper and middle gun decks. Payne depicts these lower dead-eyes evenly distributed along the length of the chain-wales. His engraving was completed before he had the opportunity to appreciate the open gunports for himself. Edye and Seppings depict a spacing between the fifth and sixth lower dead-eyes at the foremast. Similarly, they had a spacing between the tenth and eleventh lower dead-eyes on the mainmast. There was a spacing between the fifth and sixth lower dead-eyes on the mizen mast. These spacings prevented the shrouds from fouling the opening of the gunports.

Abaft the figurehead, Payne depicts five shrouds aside the bowsprit. They were prevented from slipping down the bowsprit by cleats. The perspective of Payne's shrouds is reversed. Van de Velde the Elder depicts six lower dead-eyes for shrouds aside the bowsprit.

She had eleven shrouds at the foremast. Van de Velde the Elder's broadside drawing depicts nine lower dead-eyes, with a tenth and eleventh lightly pencilled in forward. His confusion over the number of lower dead-eyes suggests that perhaps the shrouds were not rigged when he made his drawing in 1660. The *Prince Royal* had eleven shrouds on the mainmast. The *Sovereign*'s mainmast had twelve shrouds. Van de Velde the Elder's broadside drawing depicts fourteen lower dead-eyes. The aftermost two were partly concealed by a run out gun. In his unfinished drawing he depicts nine at the foremast and ten at the mainmast. The mizen mast had seven shrouds. Van de Velde the Elder depicts six in his broadside drawing. The reconstruction draught and Edye depict six.

The shrouds were the same size as the tackle pendants. The circumference of main shrouds was around 25 per cent of that of the mainmast's diameter. The fore shrouds' circumference was 85–90 per cent of the main shrouds, and the mizen's 55–67 per cent of the main shrouds.

A laniard called a ratline passed horizontally across each shroud where it was secured by a clove-hitch. The fore and after ends of the ratline were seized to the foremost and aftermost shrouds respectively. Further ratlines were applied above at intervals of around 13–15 inches to form a network for men clambering aloft.

A small eye was spliced in the upper end of the fore-stay. The fore-stay passed through the bight. A mouse or lump was worked in the bight to prevent it closing up. This device was rigged in the *Prince Royal* and the *Sovereign*. The bight was served to prevent chafing. This bight passed over the tackle pendants and shrouds at the foremast-head. The lower end of the fore-stay was seized about an upper dead-eye in similar fashion to the shrouds. The lower dead-eye was secured to the bowsprit by a spliced collar and round seizing. Thumb cleats prevented the collar slipping down the bowsprit. Dead-eyes were common in English ships until around 1690 when they were replaced by hearts.

The main-stay was rigged in similar fashion to the fore-stay. The main-stay was the heaviest rope in the rigging. The circumference was slightly more than the radius of the mainmast.

The rope for the collar had a circumference around 75 per cent of that of the main-stay. The collar rove through a slot in the knee of the head abaft the gammonings. Van de Velde the Elder's broadside drawing depicts the collar served where it passes abaft the stem head on either side of the bowsprit, and where it enters fair-leads below the rail of the beakhead bulkhead. The collar crosses over itself between the bowsprit and the beakhead bulkhead. The loop of the collar finishes abaft the foremast with a seizing about the lower dead-eye. We have the suggestion, therefore, that the lower masts were in place when van de Velde made his drawing.

The lower end of the mizen-stay was secured in like fashion to the mainmast above the partners.

The burton tackle pendants, shrouds and stays were cable laid. Three right-handed hawser laid ropes were laid up together left handed. Cable laid rope was less likely to twist than hawser laid rope.

The height of the lower mast was increased by the erection of the topmast. The heel was stepped forward of the lower mast-head, between the trestle-trees. The topmast passed through the cap on the extreme peak of the lower mast-head. The length of the topmast head was around 10 per cent of the length of the topmast. The taper for the lower part of the topmast head was 70 per cent and that for the upper part of the mast-head was 55 per cent of the diameter of the heel of the topmast.

At the forward end of the bowsprit was stepped the spritsail topmast. It stood in a cap secured to the top of a knee stepped at the forward end of the bowsprit.

Top-ropes were used for hoisting and lowering the topmast. The top-rope was running rigging, applied to the standing rigging. The standing part of the runner was secured to an eye bolt beneath the cap of the lower mast-head by a throat and round seizing.

60. J. Dupray's model of the *Sovereign of the Seas* (1982). Sprit topmast top. (*Ship Modellers' Association of Southern California, USA*)

The runner passed through a sheave athwart ships in the heel of the topmast, and rove through a block hooked or seized beneath the cap opposite to the runner. There was a tackle on the lower end of the runner. The fall rove through the fourth sheave in the knight abaft the mast.

Over each topmast head were fitted topmast shrouds, rigged with a pair of dead-eyes and laniard in similar manner to the lower shrouds. The top extended the spread of the topmast shrouds to render greater support. An iron futtock-plate around the score of the lower dead-eye rove through a hole in the rim of the top. An iron bar called the futtock-staff was seized horizontally outboard the lower shrouds. It was placed as far below the top as the mast-head extended above it. Each topmast shroud had a futtock-shroud below the top. The upper end of the futtock-shroud had an eye-splice securing a hook, which passed through the futtock-plate. The lower end of the futtock-shroud was secured by a half-hitch around the futtock-staff and one of the lower shrouds and was seized to the lower shroud.

The futtock-shrouds were the same circumference as the topmast shrouds and 50–60 per cent of the circumference of the lower shrouds.

Ratlines were secured to the topmast shrouds and futtock-shrouds in similar fashion to those on the lower shrouds.

The lower shrouds were kept taut against the outward pull of the futtock-shrouds, by the addition of catharpins. This system of ropes passed between the futtock-staffs of the port and starboard sides. Two three-holed dead-eyes were each stropped to a single block. The legs of the catharpings rove through the holes in the dead-eyes forming a six-fold purchase to each. Each leg was secured to a lower shroud. The fall started from one block, rove through the two blocks and was made fast between the block and the dead-eye on the opposite side from the standing part.

Topmast stays were rigged over the mast-heads in similar fashion to the lower stays. The fore topmast stay led to a complicated tackle rove between blocks on the spritsail topmast top and the bowsprit. The lead for the main topmast stay rove through a block stropped to the foremast-head slightly above the top then descended abaft the foremast. There was a fiddle-block at the end, and a single block hooked to an eye bolt in the deck with a four-fold tackle. The mizen topmast stay was rigged to the aftermost shroud on the mainmast by a pendant and crowsfeet.

Above the fore and main topmasts was stepped the fore and main topgallant masts respectively. The heels and mast-heads were square in cross section. The fore topgallant trestle-trees were similar in size to the spritsail topmast trestle-trees. With respect to length and diameter, the fore and main topgallant masts were similar to the spritsail topmast.

The royals on the fore and main topgallant and the mizen topgallant masts were simple pole masts rigged in the mast-head with a fitting similar to an early plug bayonet. The length and maximum diameter of these masts may be estimated by assuming that the ratio of royal mast/topgallant mast was the same as that for the parent topgallant mast/topmast, viz. 0.5.

Top-ropes were rigged for hoisting and lowering the topgallant masts in similar manner to the topmasts.

The topmasts and topgallants were steadied by the use of burton tackles. There was one such tackle aside the topmast and topgallant mast. Each tackle had two single blocks and a three-part fall. They were rigged in similar manner as those on the lower masts.

In having tops on all three topmast heads, and also on the topgallant mast-heads on the foremast and mainmast, she was unique. These upper tops were constructed in similar manner to the lower tops, but were only half their width.

The topgallant shrouds and futtock-shrouds were similar to the topmast rigging, but without ratlines. Payne depicts five shrouds aside the spritsail topmast. Payne's shrouds on the topmasts and topgallants are concealed by billowing canvas. Van de Velde the Elder does not portray shrouds at the lower mast-head and above, because she was not rigged at the time of his drawing.

The topgallant stays had a long eye-splice over the mast-head, without the use of the mouse. The fore topgallant stay led to a pendant and elaborate crowsfeet on the spritsail topmast shrouds. The main topgallant stay rove through a block abaft the fore topmast head and descended to the fore top.

Running back stays were fitted over the shrouds on the mast-head in similar fashion to the shrouds. The back stays were simple pendant and whip type. One back stay was rigged abaft each topmast, topgallant and royal mast. The pendants descended on either side of the mast to below the level of the top. A block was spliced into the lower end. The falls started and finished on the bulwark rail, or a timber head inboard of the bulwark, abaft the shrouds. The spritsail topmast back stay had a pendant and complex crowsfeet secured to the fore-stay.

In the first quarter of the seventeenth century, the circumference of the mainmast back stay was slightly greater than the radius of the mainmast. The back stays were the same circumference as the lower shrouds.

Thus, her masts were well supported against the stresses and strains imparted by the vagaries of the wind on the yards and sails.

Her square sails were spread from yards suspended from the centre on the forward aspect of the mast. Timber with a straight even grain, free from knots, was selected for use as yards. They were worked individually in similar fashion to the masts. The yards were at right angles to the mast, athwart ships of the keel. Such sails received the wind on the after side only. Although the angle to the keel line could be altered to receive the wind squarely on the after surface, the centre always remained along the keel line.

The length of the main yard was dependent on the keel length of the vessel. The length of the *Sovereign*'s main yard in 1640 may be calculated from the relationship:

(22) MY = R x kfp
Where:
MY = length of the main yard, in feet.
R = ratio of 0.894.
kfp = length of keel between false posts, viz. the 'touch'.

The ratio was arbitrary, but the value of 0.894 was specific to the *Sovereign*:

1) dated 1600	0.8
2) *Bear* before 1618	0.87
3) after 1618	0.79
4) J. Smith dated 1627	0.83
5) Sir William Monson dated 1623	0.833
6) Sir Henry Mainwaring dated 1623	0.833
7) 1650–1700	0.8–0.95

Substituting the relevant vales for the *Sovereign* from Appendix 8, we have:

Length of main yard = 0.894 x 127 = 113.54

The length and maximum diameter of the *Sovereign*'s yards from a List of 1640 are displayed in Appendix 41.

The point of maximum diameter of each yard occurred at the centre. Yards tapered from the centre out towards the yard-arms, where the spar diameter was around 33 per cent of the maximum diameter. The yards were round for their whole length.

With respect to length and maximum diameter, the crossjack and main topsail yards were similar in a List of 1640. The spritsail topsail, mizen topsail and main topgallant yards were also similar to each other.

The length of the masts and spars as displayed and scaled up from the van de Veldes' *The Portrait of Peter Pett and the* Sovereign of the Seas follow the trend of the values for 1640.

The masts and spars were not painted nor varnished. No treatment was afforded to the bare wood. The gummy resins present in the spars provided for their resilience. This condition was permitted to weather naturally.

1. D. Mytens' portrait of King Charles I. (*National Maritime Museum*)

Left: 2. J. de Critz's portrait of Phineas Pett (1637) (London painting). (*Henri P. Richard, Maroubra, Australia*)

Below left: 3. J. de Critz's portrait of Phineas Pett (1637) (Sydney painting). (*The Boucher/Thevenin family*)

Below right: 4. The arms granted to Peter Pett in 1583, from the portrait of Phineas Pett (Sydney painting) (1637). *(The Boucher/Thevenin family)*

5. J. de Critz's portrait of Phineas Pett (1613). (*National Portrait Gallery*)

6. D. Mytens' portrait of Charles Edward Howard, First Earl of Nottingham.
(*National Maritime Museum*)

7. J. de Critz's portrait of King James I (*circa* 1610). (*National Maritime Museum*)

8. A. Willaerts' painting *The Embarkation of Prince Frederick V, the Elector Palatine and his new bride, the Princess Elizabeth, on board the* Prince Royal *at Margate on 25 April 1613 for Flushing* (1622). Port bow view. (*National Maritime Museum*)

Above: 9. H. C. Vroom's painting *The Arrival of the Elector Palatine and his bride at Flushing in May 1613 aboard the* Prince Royal (1613). Starboard elevation. (*Franz Hals Museum, Haarlem*)

Right: 10. H. C. Vroom's painting *The Arrival of the Elector Palatine and his bride at Flushing in May 1613 aboard the* Prince Royal (1613). Detail of the starboard beak. (*Franz Hals Museum, Haarlem*)

11. H. C. Vroom's painting *The Return of the Prince of Wales from Spain, 1623* (1623?). Starboard elevation. (*National Maritime Museum*)

12. C. de Vries' painting of the *Prince Royal*. Starboard elevation. (*Chancellor Press*)

13. Sir A. van Dyck's portrait of Queen Henrietta Maria. (*National Maritime Museum*)

14. C. de Vries' painting of the *Vasa*. Port bow view. (*Chancellor Press*)

15. R. Spence's etching of Charles I and a model of the *Sovereign of the Seas* (1919). (*National Maritime Museum*)

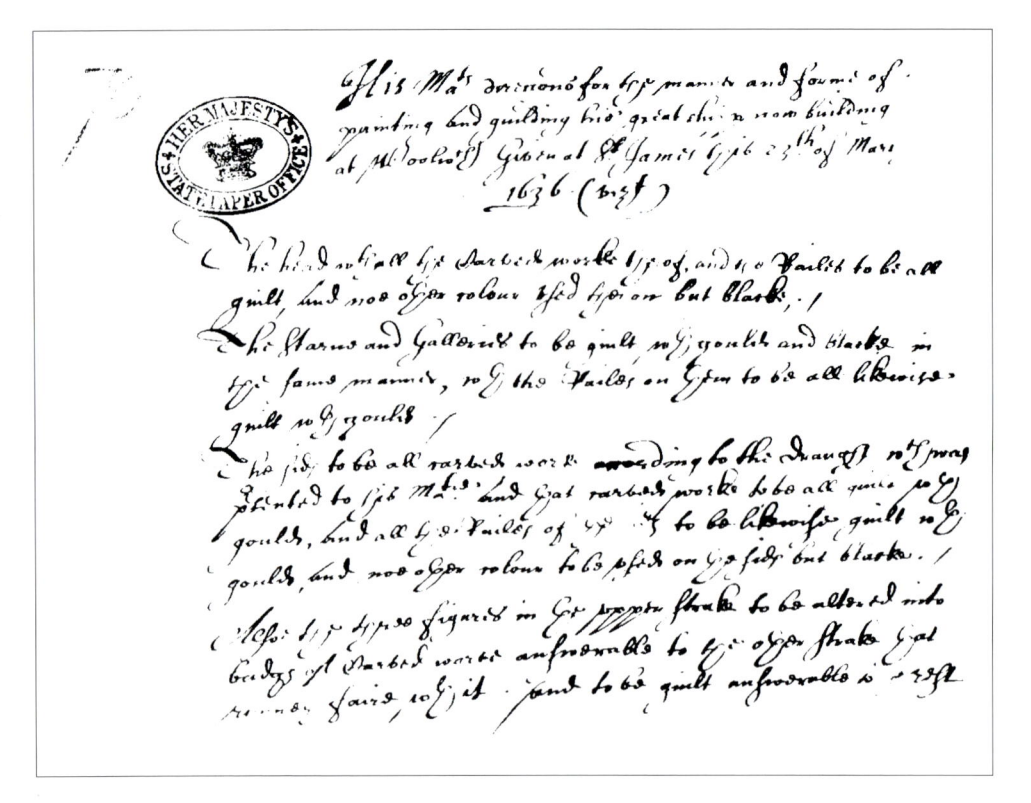

16. Directions given by Charles I for gilding and painting the *Sovereign of the Seas* (23 March 1636). (*Public Record Office*)

17. J. Payne's engraving of the *Sovereign of the Seas* (1637). Port elevation. (*National Maritime Museum*)

18. T. Jenner's engraving of the *Sovereign of the Seas* (1653). Starboard elevation. (*National Maritime Museum*)

19. L. A. Castro's painting of the *Sovereign of the Seas* on canvas (1650-60). (*Michael Hemsley*)

20. C. de Vries' painting of the *Sovereign of the Seas*. Port bow view. (*Chancellor Press*)

21. The van de Veldes' painting *The Portrait of Peter Pett and the* Sovereign of the Seas (1660). The stern carvings. (*National Maritime Museum*)

22. The van de Veldes' painting *The Portrait of Peter Pett and the* Sovereign of the Seas (1660). (*National Maritime Museum*)

23. Unidentified painting, *The Portrait of Peter Pett and the* Sovereign of the Seas. (*National Portrait Gallery*)

24. I. Sailmaker's painting of the *Royal Prince* (1663). (*Antique Collectors' Club*)

25. I. Sailmaker's painting of the *Sovereign of the Seas* (1665). (*Antique Collectors' Club*)

26. W. van de Velde the Elder's drawing of the port elevation and quarter of the Sovereign *of the Seas* (1673 or 1675). (*Royal Museum & Art Gallery, Canterbury*)

27. W. van de Velde the Younger's unfinished drawing of the *Sovereign of the Seas* (1675). Starboard elevation. (*National Maritime Museum*)

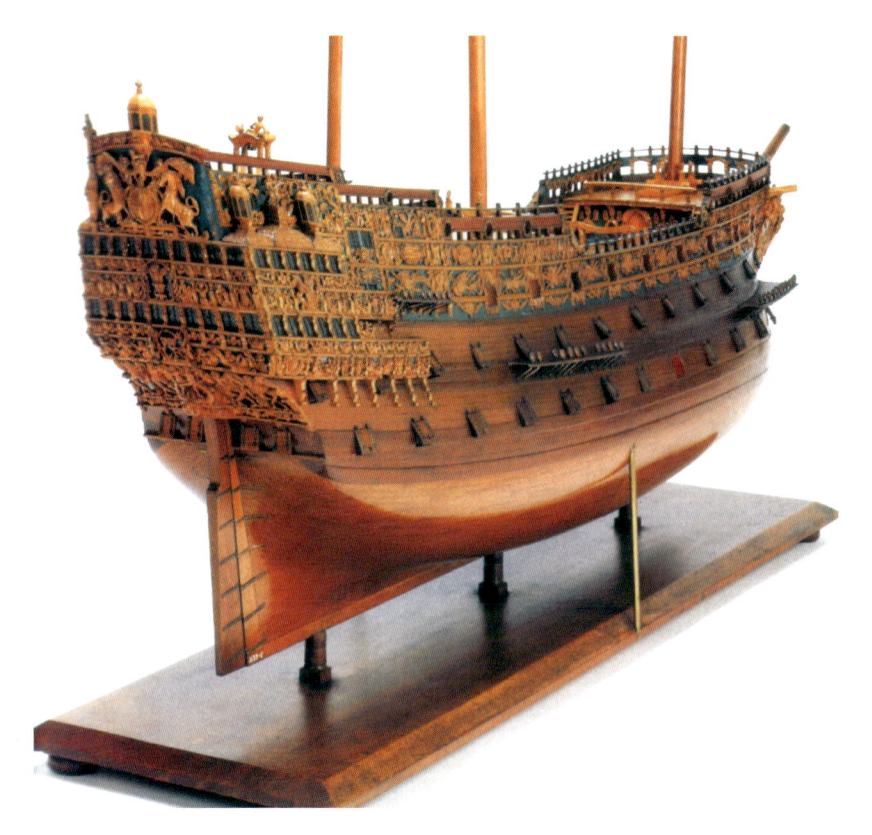

28. Sir R. Seppings' model of the *Sovereign of the Seas* (1827). Starboard quarter. (*National Maritime Museum*)

29. H. B. Culver's model of the *Sovereign of the Seas* (1921). Starboard elevation. (*Dr A. R. Kriegstein*)

30. H. B. Culver's model of the *Sovereign of the Seas* (1921). Starboard view of prow. (*Dr A. R. Kriegstein*)

31. H. B. Culver's model of the *Sovereign of the Seas* (1921). Starboard view of waist and fore chain-wales. (*Dr A. R. Kriegstein*)

32. H. B. Culver's model of the *Sovereign of the Seas* (1921). Starboard quarter. (*Dr A. R. Kriegstein*)

33. H. B. Culver's model of the *Sovereign of the Seas* (1921). Stern carvings.
(*Dr A. R. Kriegstein*)

34. C. Chaffin's model of the *Sovereign of the Seas* (1982). Starboard elevation.
(*Ship Modellers' Association of Southern California, USA*)

35. Sergal's model of the *Sovereign of the Seas*. Aerial view. (*Mantua Model, Italy*)

36. Sergal's model of the *Sovereign of the Seas*. Various details. (*Mantua Model, Italy*)

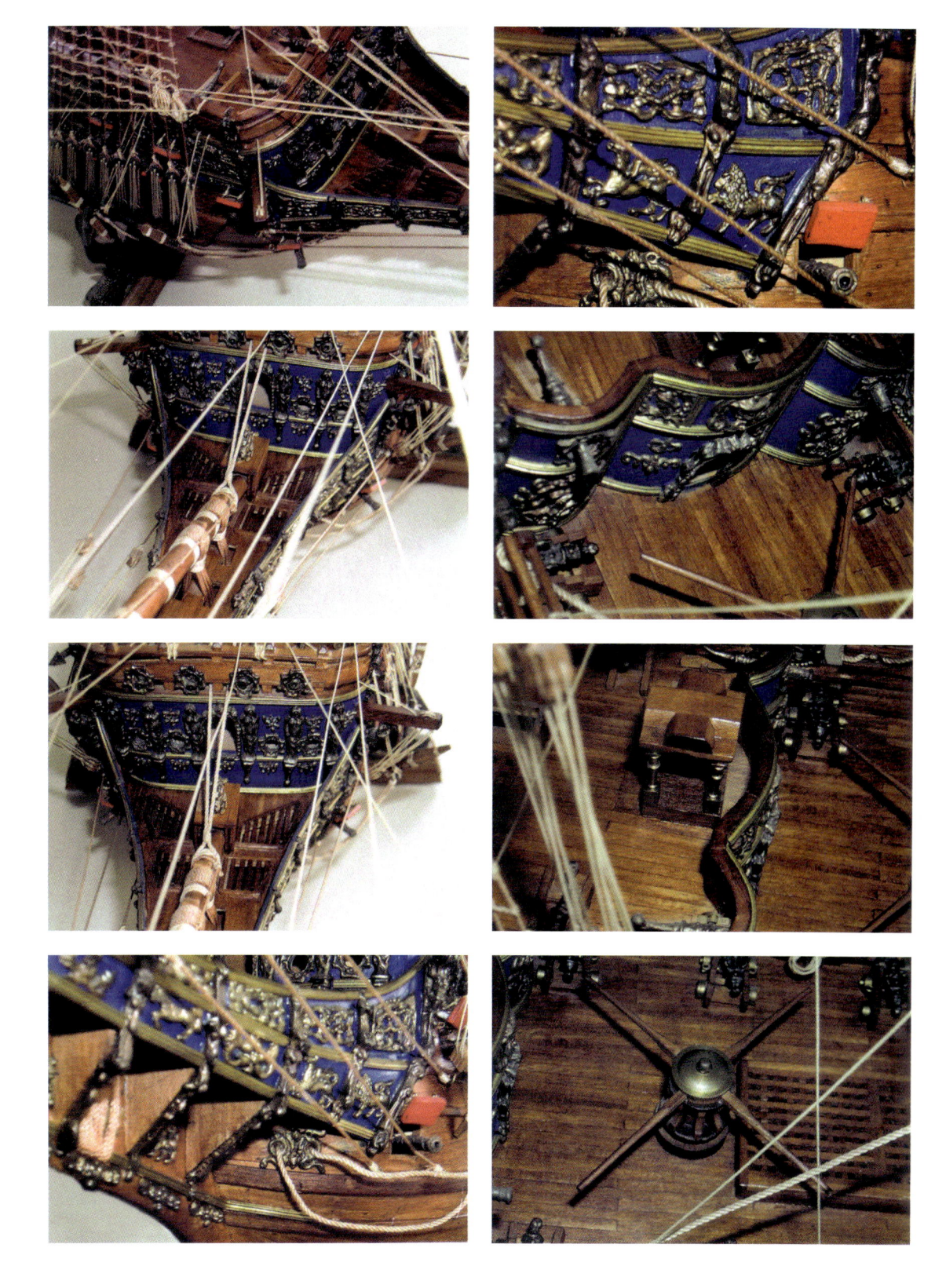

37. Sergal's model of the *Sovereign of the Seas*. Various details. (*Mantua Model, Italy*)

Right hono:ble

Wee have according to yor Lopps Warrant of the 14:th of May last, called sir Ma:ts Ch:fe Shipwrights and divers of the Ch:fe Shipwrights of the Thames w:th halfe a dozen of the auntientest and most experienced Seamen of the Trinitie house to assist us, who have in our presence taken an exact Survey of the Dimensions of his Ma:ts new royall Ship, built at Woolwich, this daie, and thereupon have testified that according to his Ma:ts rule of measuring Ships,

	Feet	inches
Shee is in length by ye keele	127	0
In bredth without side ye plancke	46	6
In depth from the upper edge of ye keele to the extreame bredth	19	4

Which being cast up and divided by 100. the product in bare tunn = 1141. Whereunto adding one third Shee is in tunn and tunnage = 1522.

But measured by the old rule, as they terme it the Ships burthen is in 1367 tunn, to w:ch a third being added makes 1823 in tunn and tunnage. And so presenting our service, Wee humbly rest,

13:o Juny 1637

As your Lopps Comands

W: Russell.   .....   Ken: Salisbury   .....

/33

38. Dimensions of the *Sovereign of the Seas* (13 June 1637). (*Public Record Office*)

39. W. van de Velde the Younger's painting of the *Royal Sovereign* of 1701 (1703). Starboard quarter view. (*National Maritime Museum*)

Above: 40. Jan K. D. van Beecq's painting of the *Royal Prince* of 1670 (1679). Starboard quarter view.
(*National Maritime Museum*)

Left: 41. Contemporary Navy Board rigged model of the *Royal Prince* of 1670. Port bow view.
(*Science Museum*)

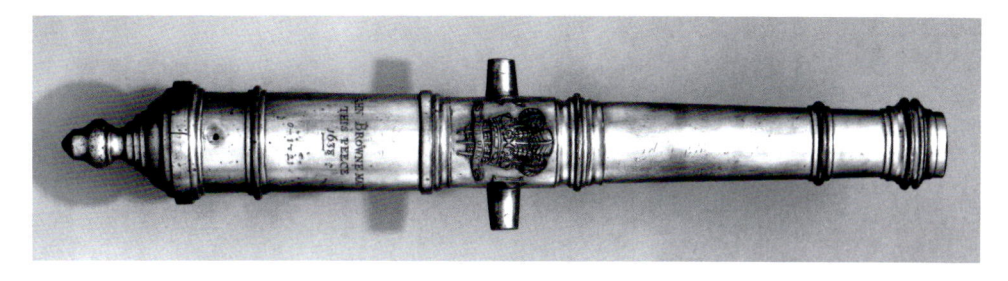

42. Small bronze gun, inscribed 'JOHN BROWNE MADE THIS PEECE 1638' (Weight 0–1–21). (*Royal Armouries Museum, Leeds*)

Above left: 43. Bronze demi-culverin drake of the *Sovereign of the Seas*, inscribed 'JOHN BROWNE MADE THIS PEECE ANO 1638'. Muzzle end. (*Royal Artillery Historical Trust, Woolwich*)

Above right: 44. Bronze demi-culverin drake of the *Sovereign of the Seas*, inscribed 'JOHN BROWNE MADE THIS PEECE ANO 1638'. Cascable end. (*Royal Artillery Historical Trust, Woolwich*)

45. Bronze demi-culverin drake of the *Sovereign of the Seas* (1638). Detail of inscription on first reinforce. (*Chatham Historic Dockyard Trust*)

46. Bronze demi-culverin drake of the *Sovereign of the Seas* (1638). Detail of cypher on second reinforce. (*Chatham Historic Dockyard Trust*)

47. Scratched drawing of a spritsail topmast vessel around 1660 at Upnor Castle. (*English Heritage*) (*Author's photograph 4 May 2002*)

This drawing was found under some layers of whitewash in April 1949 when Upnor Castle was being repaired. Messrs. Charles Mitchell and Michael Robinson were consulted about it and have reported as follows:-

"There is a quite clear Spritsail Topmast which could not appear in big ships after 1720. The curved shape of the head would pass for anything after 1660. There is one obscurity. The figurehead has the appearance of the fiddle head type which means a date about 1800. In the late 17th or early 18th century there would have been a lion figurehead but this is a crude drawing and what looks like a fiddle is very probably shorthand for a lion figurehead. There is one other explanation, namely, that this is a consciously archaic but inaccurate drawing of an older ship drawn by a man who lived in the days of the fiddle head but that is a remote and unlikely possibility. The Spritsail Topmast would have passed from the memory of most seamen by 1800. We incline to date the drawing about 1700."

48. Scratched drawing of a spritsail topmast vessel around 1660 at Upnor Castle. Caption. (*English Heritage*) (*Author's photograph 4 May 2002*)

49. Sir A. van Dyck's portrait of Oliver Cromwell. (*National Maritime Museum*)

50. Sir P. Lely's portrait of George Monck, First Duke of Albemarle. (*National Maritime Museum*)

51. Sir G. Kneller's portrait of Samuel Pepys (1689). (*National Maritime Museum*)

52. W. van de Velde the Younger's painting of the Battle of Solebay 28 May 1672 (1687). (*National Maritime Museum*)

53. W. van de Velde the Younger's painting of *The Burning of the* Royal James *at the Battle of Solebay 28 May 1672* (1680). (*National Maritime Museum*)

54. N. de Largilliere's portrait of King James II. (*National Maritime Museum*)

The yards and sails were controlled by running rigging (Appendix 44). This was a complicated arrangement of cordage rove through blocks. Three stranded hawser laid hemp rope formed the major part of the running rigging. To minimise handling difficulties, this was not impregnated in tar. Most of the falls were belayed to the bulwark rails or to timber heads beneath.

The centre of each yard was made fast to the parent mast by a parrel. This consisted of a lacing through holes drilled in trucks and ribs which passed thrice around the circumference of the mast. The trucks were wooden balls with one hole. The ribs were wooden battens with three holes. There were three trucks between two ribs. A breast rope, or truss, passed over the parrel and around the yard on either side of the mast. This flexible system was designed to permit the raising, lowering, rotation and tilt of the yard.

A parrel was not rigged on the crossjack yard. Instead, it was secured by a truss. The crossjack was hoisted by slings. A block was stropped in the centre of the yard. Through the block rove a rope with an eye in one end. The two ends of the runner passed up outside the trestle-trees on opposite sides. The plain end passed round abaft the mast-head and through the eye where it was hitched.

Payne omits the parrel and slings on the spritsail yard. This yard was suspended below the bowsprit slightly forward of the fore-stay by slings. The rope had an eye-splice in one end. It passed around the yard and was seized to itself near the eye. Hence, it passed over the bowsprit and around the yard again. It was seized to itself close to the yard. The fall was taken over the bowsprit and through the eye, where it was seized.

Two separate tackles used for hoisting, carrying and lowering the yards were ties and halliards, and jeers. The *Prince Royal*, when rebuilt in 1641 and re-named *Resolution*, used both systems. We have the suggestion, therefore, that the *Sovereign* followed the same trend.

The tie was the same size as the shrouds. The end of the tie was doubled about itself, seized, and secured to the centre of the yard by a cow hitch. The runner rove through one of the cheeks at the mast-head, then through a hole in the upper part of a 3-sheave halliard block. It passed by the same route on the other side of the mast to the centre of the yard where it was secured by a cow hitch.

The halliards started from an eye bolt on the side of the knight abaft the mast and rove through a sheave in the halliard block then through a sheave in the knight. The runner rove through the halliard block and knight for several passes. The fall was belayed to the knight itself.

The spritsail yard had no tie. The simple halliard started from the forward end of the bowsprit, rove through a single block at the centre of the yard, through another single block at the forward end of the bowsprit and was belayed near the gammoning cleats.

The jeers tackle was quite separate. It supplemented the function of the ties and hoisted the yard. A single block was secured to the centre of the yard. Two similar single blocks were pendant aside the mast-head. The standing end was lashed to the yard. The runner rove through one of the mast-head blocks, through the block on the yard and through the other mast-head block. The fall descended beside the mast to the gunwale under the shrouds.

The lowest spar on the mizen mast was the mizen yard. It was rigged fore and aft. The peak, or after end, was higher than the nock, or forward end. The mizen yard parrel had two rows of trucks. A dead-eye with two holes was seized in the bight at the end of the parrel rope. The two parts of the rope were seized to the strop of the jeer block. The ends rove through the truck and ribs of the parrel, round the mast then through the holes in the dead-eye. They were spliced together. The effect was to hold, not the yard itself, but the strop of the jeer block close to the mast. The parrel was rigged to allow the mizen yard to pass on either side of the mast with change of wind direction.

The jeers, ties and halliards of the mizen yard were similar to those on the courses.

There were no cleats on the yards to secure the parrel ropes, ties, nor jeer blocks. Such a feature did not came into fashion until around 1654. There were, however, a pair of cleats nailed on the fore and after sides of each yard-arm.

The lifts were tackles to maintain the yard horizontal or for hoisting it by the yard-arms. A single block was stropped at the mast-head and one at each yard-arm. The runner started at a seizing to the two parts of the stay, rove through the mast-head block, then the yard-arm block, then back up to the mast-head block and descended to the gunwale.

The mizen yard had one lift rigged on the peak.

The yards were hauled down by the truss tackle.

Braces were essential in controlling the angle of the sail with respect to the keel line. This process, known as tacking, enabled the sail to catch the wind. A single block was spliced in the end of a pendant from each yard-arm. The runner started at the standing part of the stay, rove through the block at the yard-arm, and back to a block secured to the stay nearer to the mast than the standing parts. The fall was belayed to the vessel's quarters.

The braces on the spritsail yard were assisted by garnets which worked midway out along the yard. Payne's garnets are depicted in three parts. The standing part was secured to the fore-stay below the braces. The runner rove through a block on the yard, back to a block on the fore-stay below its standing part and through a block in the head. The fall was belayed at the beakhead.

Payne's crossjack braces have short pendants. The standing part leads forward and is made fast to the aftermost shrouds on the mainmast. The leading block is lower down on the same shroud. The runner returns to the mainmast rigging above its standing part hence aft to the mizen top and descended below.

The van de Veldes' *The Portrait of Peter Pett and the* Sovereign of the Seas depicts the crossjack braces leading to the aftermost timber on the poop.

There were no braces on the mizen yard. There were a pair of tackles, with the confusing name of bowlines. The runners passed through holes in the nock. They were knotted, then rove through blocks on the aftermost main shrouds. The falls descended to the rail for belaying.

The raw material for sails was canvas. This was a stout fabric probably named after *Cannabis*. Hemp and flax were traditionally used to produce sails. It was also favoured for hammocks, awnings, cabins and hatch covers. The terms sailcloth and canvas were used synonymously.

Canvas was woven on a loom producing fabrics of width around 28 inches. The weight per unit area was arbitrary. The product was made up in rolls called bolts.

The cloths were the widths of canvas sewn together to form the sail. Their direction was arranged to provide optimum strength. They were joined by overlapping seams sewn along each side. On some sails, the width of these seams tapered between around 1.2 inches–3.5 inches at different points along their own length. This taper was not constant throughout the sail, but varied in adjoining seams to mould the sail to specified requirements.

She carried twelve square sails, four bonnets and one lateen sail with a total of 5,513 square yards of canvas. One complete suit of sails cost £404. She was unique in carrying royal sails on the fore and main topgallant masts, and a topgallant on the mizen mast.

Her courses were rectangular in shape. Consequently, the corners were perfect right angles. The topsails, topgallant and royal sails were quadrilateral in shape. The foot of the sail was greater than the head. This resulted in the bunt bulging forwards, enabling the sail to gather more wind.

The rectangular spritsail was small in area and could be handled easily. The quadrilateral spritsail topsail was bent to a yard on the spritsail topmast. This combination exerted

61. J. Dupray's model of the *Sovereign of the Seas* (1982). Sprit topmast top, detail. (*Ship Modellers' Association of Southern California, USA*)

considerable leverage. It was useful in bringing the ship's head about when tacking. This feature was fashionable until the close of the seventeenth century. The spritsail topsail was the precursor of triangular head sails.

Her lateen was a triangular-shaped sail with its longest edge bent along the mizen yard. The opposite corner of the lateen was an obtuse angle. The mizen yard was suspended on the leeward side of the mast. This sail could receive the wind on either side. Thus, it enabled the vessel to sail much closer to the wind than was possible with a square sail.

The edge of the sail was turned over and sewn down, forming a hem called tabling. This varied along its own length for the purpose of shaping the sail. For example, the tabling on the leech of the lateen was wider at the peak than in the centre of the yard. This gave the leech, or trailing edge of the sail, a slight outward curve, which straightened out under load. Various additional cloths were sewn in position to strengthen the sail. Linings took their names from the position they occupied. Mast cloths on the after side prevented chafing against the mast. Buntline cloths on the fore side prevented chafing by the buntlines. The middle band ran horizontally across the sail.

A bolt-rope was sewn around the finished edges of the sail. This provided reinforcement. The upper corners of the bolt-rope were spliced to form an eye. This constituted a head-earing cringle.

A short length of a single strand of rope was rove through the left hole. It was brought against its own part, and laid up following the original lay. The longer of the two ends rove through the right hole, and was laid up against itself. The ends were spliced into the leech-rope.

The bolt-rope was doubled about itself at the clue. The loop so formed was seized at the throat. This formed a clue cringle.

The sails were bent to the yard by robands. This lashing rove through holes immediately below the head rope, and around the diameter of the yard. The roband at the centre became worn by abrasion against the mast.

The setting and control of the sail was achieved by clue-garnets, sheets, tacks and bowlines. The clue-garnets on the after side of the sail hauled the clues down and forward. The sheets on the after side hauled the clues down and aft. The tacks on the fore side hauled the clues down and forward. The bowlines on the fore side hauled taut the leeches.

The clue-garnets, sheets and tacks were connected together and to the clue cringle.

The standing part of the clue-garnet was secured to the yard by a timber-hitch. The runner rove through a block at the clue. The clue block was stropped at the clue with a seizing through two eyes in the ends of its strop. The clue-garnet rove to another block on the yard. The fall descended to the gunwale where it was belayed.

Payne depicts double clue-garnets on the spritsail. The runner passes from the yard, down through a block at the clue, back to a block at the yard just inside the standing part, through blocks in the head and is belayed at the forecastle rail.

The fore-sheet passed from a ring bolt on the wale below the upper gun deck, forward of the main chain-wales. The fore-sheet was secured with a throat and round seizing. It rove through a block with an ordinary strop over the clue, back to a sheave in the bulwarks above its standing part, and was belayed to an inboard cleat or kevel.

The spritsail sheets had long pendants. Payne depicts both ends of the sheets passing over the bulwarks forward in the waist.

The tack was a single rope rove through the strop of the clue-garnet block below the sheet block. The tack rove through a fair-lead forward and was belayed inboard.

The fore-tacks rove through a double ornamented comb under the knee of the head. They passed inwards and upwards through the head, crossing each other on the way, and were belayed at the forward corners on the forecastle.

Like the *Prince Royal* of 1610, the *Sovereign's* main-tacks rove through fair-leads called chess-trees, abaft the fore shrouds on the upper deck. The tack was belayed to an inboard cleat.

The rigging on the spritsail imitated that of the courses, except for the fact that tacks were omitted.

The lateen had a single sheet and a single tack. Sheets and tacks were cable laid to minimise twisting.

There were two parts in the bowline bridles on the fore course, and three on the main. The connections were made by *lignum vitae* bulls-eyes. The legs of the bridles were secured to the leech cringles by a bowline knot.

The fore bowlines rove through two blocks, seized to the bowsprit close to the lower dead-eye of the fore-stay. The two falls passed from these blocks to the forward corners of the forecastle, where they were belayed.

The main bowlines rove through blocks near the gammoning cleats.

She followed the contemporary trend and carried bonnets. These were small rectangular sails laced to the foot of the spritsail, and the fore, main and mizen courses. The bonnet was about one third as deep as the sail to which it was laced. This was a simple and effective way of increasing sail area. Bonnets went out of fashion around 1680.

When she carried a bonnet, the clue-garnet block, sheet and tack block were rigged to facilitate easy removal. The clue-garnet block had an ordinary strop which passed through and over the clue. The tack had a big knot at its end. The tack passed through the clue with the knot aft. The strop of the sheet block had two legs with a knot on each. These two legs passed through the clue above the tack, where they were seized.

The bowline bridles could be varied to suit the course alone, or course with bonnet laced.

The clue-garnets, martnets or leech-lines, and buntlines were devices used to gather the sail up to the yard for furling.

Martnets were common at the beginning of the seventeenth century. They hauled in the leeches up to the yard. After around 1660 they were superseded by the simpler leech-lines, which operated on the fore side of the sail. The buntlines, operating on the fore side of the sail, gathered up the bunt to the yard.

Martnets were complicated. Essentially, they consisted of two dead-eyes connected by a bridle. Each had runners through its three holes. These runners were connected at each end, and to the leech, in a crowsfeet arrangement. The bridle rove through the lower of a pair of sister blocks. The fall from the strop of a single block suspended on a pendant from the topmast head, rove through the upper sister block, up to the pendant block and descended to the deck.

Payne depicts three buntlines on the spritsail. The falls were belayed at the forecastle.

He also depicts six buntlines on the fore sail. They rove between blocks on the yard and corresponding blocks under the tops. The buntlines were secured to cringles at the bunt by bowline knots. The buntlines probably worked in pairs. They were belayed to cleats aside the mast.

The parrels on the upper yards were similar to those on the courses. They were simpler, with only two rows of trucks.

The topsails were hoisted by ties and halliards. The tie was secured to the yard by a cow hitch, then rove through a sheave in the topmast below the cross-trees. The tie had a block at the end. Through this block rove a runner secured to the side of the vessel and well aft. The runner had a block at its free end. The halliard worked through this block and descended to the opposite side of the vessel to the standing part of the runner.

The topsail lifts functioned also as topgallant sheets. They started from the clues of the topgallants, rove through single blocks at the topsail yard-arms, rove through blocks pendant from the mast-head inside the stay and beneath the trestle-trees and descended down the mast to the top.

The fore topsail braces imitated the fore braces, except for the fact that they were based on the main topmast stay instead of the main-stay.

The main topsail braces started from near the mizen top. They rove through pendant blocks and returned to a pair of blocks secured to the mizen shrouds, and hence descended to the deck.

The mizen topsail braces led aft to the peak of the mizen yard.

The clues of the upper sails did not require both sheets and tacks, because the clues were hauled down to the yard-arms beneath. The sail was trimmed by means of the lower braces.

The rigging about the mizen topsail imitated the fore and main topgallants. The main difference was due to the fact that there was no sail beneath the crossjack yard.

The rigging about the mizen topgallant imitated that on the fore and main royals.

Topsail bowlines imitated those on the courses. The bridles ran in three parts on the fore topsail and four on the main topsail. The main topsail bowline rove through a pair of blocks secured to the main topmast stay, and hence through the two sheaves of a double block secured under the fore top.

Martnets on the topsails imitated those on the courses.

The van de Veldes' *The Portrait of Peter Pett and the* Sovereign of the Seas portrays martnets on the fore and main yards.

Payne depicts martnets on the fore sail and main topsail only. He depicts leech-lines on the fore topsail, fore topgallant sail, main topgallant sail and mizen topsail.

The leech-lines passed from the lower of two cringles on either leech, through the inner of two leading blocks on either half of the upper fore side of the yard, through one of a pair of sister blocks, through the outer leading block and to the upper cringle. The fall started from the topmast head above the shrouds and descended abaft the topmast to the upper of the two sister blocks, hence to a block on a short pendant from the topmast head and descended through the topmast rigging and the top to the deck.

Payne depicts buntlines on the fore sail, but omits them from the topsails.

Topgallant lifts started from the caps and rove through single blocks at the yard-arms and beneath the trestle-trees. They were belayed in the tops.

The rigging of the spritsail topsail yard imitated that of the topgallants. The parrels had two rows of trucks. The tie was single, and rove through a sheave cut fore and aft in the spritsail topmast. The halliard was a whip starting from, and returning to, the cross-trees of the spritsail topmast top.

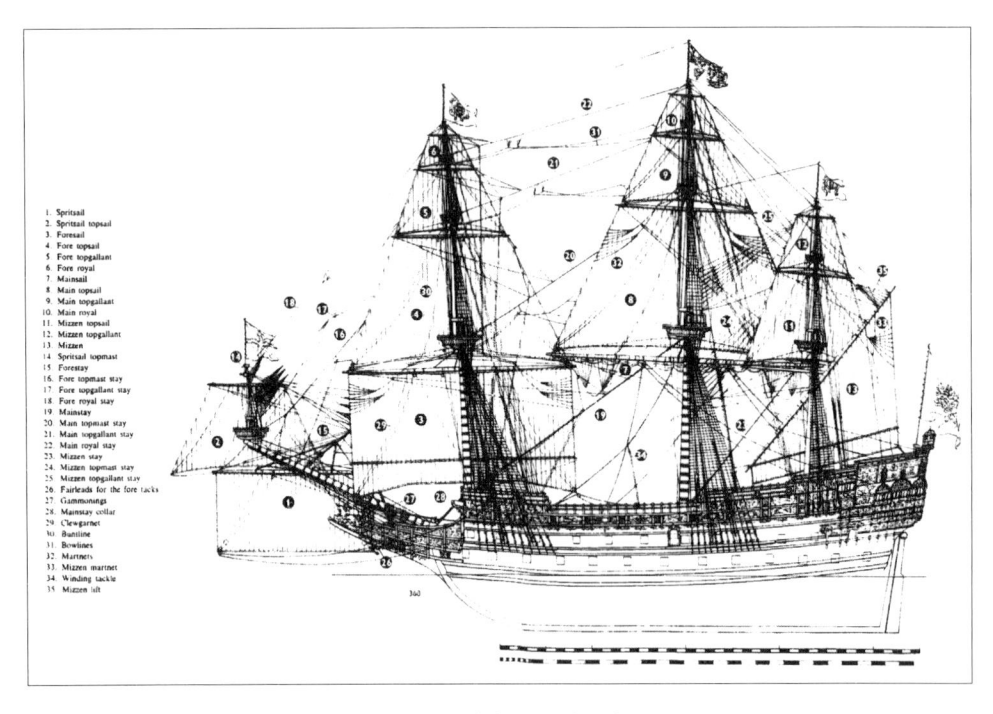

62. B. Landstrom's sail plan of the *Sovereign of the Seas* (1961).
(*Olof Landstrom, Stockholm, Sweden*)

The lifts of the spritsail topsail yard had two parts with blocks at the yard-arms. The standing parts and the upper blocks were secured to the mast-head. The falls were belayed in the top.

The fore topgallant braces were based on the main topgallant stay. The main topgallant braces were based on the head of the mizen topmast in similar manner as the main topsail braces.

The standing part of the braces of the spritsail topsail yard was secured to the fore-stay. The pendants on the yard were short. The falls were belayed at the beakhead.

The spritsail topsail clue-garnets imitated those of the topgallants. The lifts of the spritsail yard also served the function of spritsail topsail sheets.

The topgallant bowlines imitated those on the topsail. The main topgallant bowlines rove through blocks on the main topgallant stay and blocks on the fore topmast shrouds and were belayed in the fore top.

Leech-lines and buntlines were not rigged on the topgallants.

The royal yards and sails were rigged in imitation of the topgallant rigging, but tended to be simpler. The sheave for the royal yard tie was cut into the royal mast below the riggingstop.

Following the normal seventeenth century practice, the royals, mizen topgallant sail and spritsail topsail were furled by farthelling. This is exemplified in two representations:

1) Payne's engraving of the *Sovereign of the Seas* (1636) (Plate 17)
2) The van de Veldes' *The Portrait of Peter Pett and the* Sovereign of the Seas (1660) (Plate 22)

The bunt was farthelled against the mast, the bottom of the bundle was brought down to the top and the clues lifted up horn-wise to the yard.

A purchase secured to the main-stay and used to hoist gear in and out of the hold was called a garnet. It had a pendant from the mainmast head with a single block at the end. This pendant was seized to the main-stay such that the block was suspended above the main hatch. The runner had a hook at one end and a fiddle-block at the other. The fall started from a block with a hook beneath and four-fold purchase. When in use, the runner was hooked to the weight to be lifted and the lower fall block hooked to some convenient eye bolt on the deck. When not in use, the garnet was carried along the main-stay with its two hooks lashed to the collar of the main-stay.

The winding tackle was a purchase with a pendant from the mainmast head. It had a guy to the foremast-head. The upper block was a fiddle-block and the lower block was double. This gave a four-fold purchase tackle. It was useful for hoisting guns or boats inboard and out.

Her sails had no reef points. A single reef in the topsails on the fore and mainmasts of large vessels came into fashion around 1655. Staysails appeared after around 1655. Stun-sails appeared after around 1660. Newly built vessels were rigged with these features. It is doubtful if the *Sovereign*'s rig was ever amended to include them.

From the mast-heads and the yard-arms of Payne's engraving stream pennants. These are slit into two tails at the fly. At the hoist was the cross of St George, which had been the principal emblem of England since the fourteenth century.

The Union Flag flies at the spritsail topmast in Payne's engraving. By order of Charles I in 1634, this device was restricted solely for use in the King's own ships.

Payne's main mast-head banner portrays the Royal Standard of Charles I, laced nine times about a staff.

W. van de Veldes' main mast-head banner in *The Portrait of Peter Pett and the* Sovereign of the Seas has a pale yellow cross on a pale blue background. It is loosely laced to a slender iron staff plugged into the main royal mast-head. The upper end of the staff consists of a flattened globe. It is made from two solid hemispheres in bronze or brass soldered together at each planar surface, resulting in an oblate spheroid shape. The staff passes through a hole drilled in the globe, its upper end being hammered over to form a button similar to a rivet. A small gap remains between the peak of the staff and the banner. The lacings on mast-head banners survived, in the case of admirals' flags and ensigns, to 1783. From 1793 no vestige of lacings survived.

Flying above the taffrail of W. van de Veldes' painting is a bold red ensign. Similarly, the Royal Standard is at the main mast-head in a pencil drawing of the *Sovereign of the Seas* (c. 1686) by Adriaen van de Velde the Younger in the National Maritime Museum (Cat. No. 660).

At around 1660, the weight of rigging for a first rate was around 33 tons. The weight of sea stores in respect to ground tackle and other cordage was 60 tons 8 cwt 2 qt 14 lb.

By 1670, the method of calculating the length of the mainmast had changed. Deane's List of 1670 postulated the relationship:

(23) $M = 0.6(kfp + bx + bs) - (bx - 27)$
Where:
bx = extreme beam (Deane's value is 47 feet)
bs = mean beam within ceiling at half of depth in hold

Substituting the relevant values for the *Sovereign* from Appendix 8, we have:

Length of mainmast = $0.6(127 + 47 + 42.167) - (47 - 27) = 109.70$

63. Sir A. Deane's mast and rigging plans of a First Rate of 1670. Starboard sheer plan and sail plan. (*Pepysian Library, Magdalene College, Cambridge*)

Her Masting and Rigging

The length and maximum diameter of the *Sovereign*'s masts from Deane's List of 1670 are displayed in Appendix 41.

A mast made from a New England spar had a maximum diameter of 1 inch/3 feet of length. The diameter in inches at the partners of a New England mainmast was equal to the length of the mainmast in yards, viz. 36.5. The mainmast and foremast tapered to the hounds where the diameter was 66 per cent of its maximum diameter. The mizen mast and bowsprit tapered to 50 per cent of their respective maximum diameter.

Deane made a positive attempt to standardise the measurement of masts. The diameter of each was a constant 15–16 inches/3 feet of its length. With respect to length and diameter, the fore and main topgallant masts were similar. With the exception of the fore and main topmasts, Deane's masts were slightly shorter and slimmer than those of the 1640 List. His plans showed only slight departures from Payne's rigging.

The planking around the sides of the tops was removed to produce a flat structure, but otherwise there was no significant difference.

Deane's upper yards on the fore, main and mizen masts were similar to those in the 1640 List. With respect to length and maximum diameter, Deane's crossjack and main topsail yards were similar to each other, and those in the 1640 List. Deane's spritsail topsail, mizen topsail and main topgallant yards also possessed similarity.

Ties and halliards and also jeers were rigged on the foremast. Only jeers were on the mainmast.

Foot-ropes, otherwise called horses, were used on the main yard only. There were two foot-ropes, eye-spliced around the yard-arms and rigged on the inside of both the brace pendants and the topsail sheet and lift blocks.

Following a contemporary fashion, Deane's crowsfeet work was diminished in comparison to Payne's engraving.

Appendix 13 provides some of Deane's costs for items of rigging.

By 1685 another system of establishing the length of the mainmast was in vogue. This may be explained by the use of the equation:

(24) MM = K x bx
Where:
K = constant of 2.406

Substituting the values for the Sovereign, we have:

Length of mainmast = 2.406 x 48 = 115.49

The length and maximum diameter of the *Sovereign*'s masts from a List of 1685 are displayed in Appendix 41.

This relationship resembles equation (18). We have the suggestion that this methodology reverted to the earlier system. Perhaps not all dockyards accepted Deane's system.

With respect to length and diameter, the spritsail topmast was similar to the fore topgallant mast.

With the exception of the bowsprit, mizen mast and main topgallant mast, the length of masts in the 1685 List resemble closely those in the 1640 List. We have the suggestion that the 1685 List is a departure from the attempt at standardisation proposed by Deane's List of 1670.

With respect to length and maximum diameter, the fore and main topgallant yards in the 1685 List are similar to each other. With the exception of the fore, main and crossjack yards, the length of yards in the 1685 List resemble closely those in the 1640 List.

Perhaps by 1685 the masts and spars were made by a variety of craftsmen working from incompatible Lists of dubious dating in different dockyards. There is also the probability that adequate standardised raw materials were not always available.

The Lists of 1640, 1670 and 1685 neglect the mizen topgallant yard and the fore and main royal yards. The length and maximum diameter of these missing yards may be estimated by assuming that the ratio of royal yard/topgallant yard was the same as that for the parent topgallant yard/topmast yard, viz. 0.5.

The length and maximum diameter of the *Sovereign*'s yards from the Lists of 1640, 1670 and 1685 are recorded in Appendix 41.

An examination of Appendix 41 demonstrates that she was re-masted and re-sparred at least three times during her lifetime. During her rebuilds of 1644, 1651, 1659–60, 1666, 1673, 1684 and 1686–8 she went into dry dock (Appendix 48). Her rigging may have been removed to storage. The lower masts may have been left stepped in position to assist in raising sheer legs to lift heavy gear. Therefore, there were many opportunities to modify her rigging style. If, after repairs or rebuilding, she was launched late in the year, then it is probable that she may not have been re-rigged until the spring of the following year. In this manner, the riggers had sufficient time to prepare her gear and make any necessary modifications prevalent at the time.

On 9 May 1686, King James II visited Chatham Royal Dockyard with S. Pepys. He examined the famous New England tree of diameter 39 inches which was being made into a mainmast for the *Sovereign*. King James dined in the old Commissioner's House, which was the residence of Sir Phineas Pett (1635–94), the Commissioner of Chatham Royal Dockyard (1686–89). James II met the Dockyard Officers in the adjacent walled gardens. To avoid further expense upon Sir Phineas, King James subsequently enjoyed his meals aboard his yacht.

While at Chatham Royal Dockyard in February 1689, the *Sovereign* was provided with new masts which were made of several pieces. The sophisticated built mast was a necessity forced on ship builders because of the shortage of suitable mast timber. A mainmast was prepared from six Riga trees in a fortnight by forty-five men at a cost of £490. The foremast was similarly prepared from six Riga trees in a fortnight by forty men at a cost of £440. About one ton of iron work was required for each mast. There were two fletchers available which would serve as cheeks for the mainmast, but none for the foremast.

Because of the pronounced curve of her stem, resulting in a short fore-foot set well back along the keel, it was difficult for her to work close to windward. The rudder blade was narrow, and did not allow ease of steering. The long beakhead shipped water in a heavy sea, causing her head to press lower in the water, making her sluggish. Her sail area was below the requirements for a vessel of her incredible size and tonnage. She carried only 45 per cent of the sail area in a ship of comparable dimensions of around 1840. There was little value in having such devastating fire power, if it could not be brought quickly to tactical advantage.

When running before the wind, or with the wind on the quarter, the spritsail had the disturbing effect of pulling the bows lower into the water. When changing to another tack, the mizen yard was swung almost vertical to reset the sail on the lee of the mast. When running before the wind, there was the hazard that in gusting winds the leverage so far out from the vessel's centre of gravity could cause capsizing.

Man's inspiration and purpose has guided his restless ambition in harvesting such prolific naturally occurring resources as wood, tar, hemp and flax. His ingenuity and skill transformed the green virgin forests into the means to master the elements of Nature. Of all Man's inventions and creations, perhaps the finest and most beautiful ever achieved is the creation of the wooden sailing vessel.

In spite of her disadvantages, the *Sovereign of the Seas* must have been a delightful sight. She sailed across many a sea of adversity, a monument to the skills of the men who had created her.

CHAPTER 8

The English Civil War 1642–49

The *Prince Royal* was rebuilt at Woolwich in 1638–41 by Peter Pett. The bonaventure mizen was removed. Her armament was increased to ninety guns. Hence, she became a three-decker. Her main dimensions remained as original.

Of the 280 loads of timber used for this rebuilding, 200 loads came from Sir Perceval Hart's park at Lullingstone and 80 loads from Aylesford. The timber was felled from the extensive woods at Tottington and Cossington, below Blue Bell Hill. The estimated cost for her rebuilding was £16,019. The carving and painting work was estimated at £2,000, plus an addition of £40 for the use of elm. The actual charge for carving was £756 and £2,571 for gilding. The charge for launching and conveyance to Chatham was £2,160.

A Woolwich medical practitioner was paid the sum of £33 11s 4d for the care of shipwrights working upon the *Prince Royal*. The funds came from the Chatham Chest.

The designer of the *Sovereign*'s decorations, Thomas Heywood, died in London on 16 August 1641 aged sixty-seven years.

The Civil War erupted in 1642. Robert Rich, the Second Earl of Warwick, became Lord High Admiral for Parliament. The fleet and the dockyards adopted the Parliamentary cause, in the hope of obtaining better conditions of service. Colonel Sir John Seaton and Colonel Edwin Sandys, with a troop of soldiers, were despatched from London specifically to take Chatham Royal Dockyard for Parliament. Phineas Pett surrendered the dockyard and some 300 pieces of ordnance, about to be conveyed to the King, on Saturday 20 August 1642. Upnor Castle and the warships in the River Medway, including the *Sovereign* and the *Prince Royal*, were similarly surrendered by Phineas on Monday 22 August.

For his loyalty to Parliament, Phineas was confirmed in his post of Commissioner of the Navy at Chatham Royal Dockyard. His salary and allowances remained unchanged. Up to this time, he had not received any salary from Charles I.

Captain Peacocke and 200 armed soldiers were ordered by James Temple, on 4 July 1643, to secure Chatham Royal Dockyard and the *Sovereign*.

Sometime during 1644 she underwent a total rebuild. Most of her underwater frame was renewed. This work may have been done with recourse to Phineas' original drawings. Navigating a tall sailing ship against the tides, through the narrow and shallow waters of the River Thames, upstream to Woolwich Royal Dockyard was hazardous. Therefore, it was decided prudent to take her to the expanding facilities at Chatham Royal Dockyard.

The *Sovereign*'s rebuild was probably done in the 'old single dock' built in 1623. This was the only suitable dock to take her beam. This is No. 2 dry dock, which is the southernmost surviving dock in Chatham Royal Dockyard (Illustrations 11 & 12).

During the seventeenth century, this dry dock was a broad, deep trench excavated into the river bank. Hinged water-tight wooden gates prevented the ingress of river water. Water was drained from the dock at low tide by gravity. Wooden shoring between the timber lining at the sides of the trench and the hull provided stability while mechanical operations were performed on the hull.

The renewal of her underwater frame suggests that she may not have been seasoned in frame. This was a process which involved leaving the frames open to the air for several months before the hull was planked. In this manner, the frames were seasoned naturally by air circulation. The explanation for the omission is obvious when we remember Charles I's impatience to get her launched!

Peter Pett built a privateer, the *Constant Warwick*, at Ratcliffe for the Earl of Warwick in 1645. She was allegedly the first English frigate.

Her dimensions may be recorded

Length of keel	Around 85 feet
Beam (extreme)	25 feet 5 inches
Depth in the hold	14 feet
Burden	315 tons
Gross tonnage	420 tons
Guns	30, then 32

She was sold to the State in 1648, but was re-taken. She was rebuilt at Portsmouth Royal Dockyard in 1666. She was taken by the French on 12 July 1691.

From 1642 onwards, Phineas Pett remained quietly at Chatham Royal Dockyard, perhaps too infirm to take any active part in current affairs. He remained in salary in office until his death in his seventy-seventh year of age. He was interred in August 1647 in St Mary's church, Dock Road, Chatham. Thorpe's *Registrum Roffense...* accounts for all the monuments in this church as they were by 1769. However, he does not list Phineas' memorial plaque of 1647. No will or administrative act of Phineas has been found.

Thomas Smith succeeded Phineas' (1570–1647) post as Commissioner at Chatham on 28 August 1647.

John Payne, famous for his excellent engraving of the *Sovereign of the Seas*, died in indigent circumstances in 1647.

In 1648, at the age of thirty-eight, Peter Pett was appointed Commissioner at Chatham with a salary of £250 per annum, an allowance of £8 for boat hire, £6 petty cash and 8*d* daily for each of his two clerks. He was appointed on the first board of Navy Commissioners in 1651. He was permitted to own a private shipbuilding yard at Woodbridge, and to build royal or merchant ships by contract. Following the custom of his father and grandfather, Peter remarried. He wedded Mary, daughter of William Smith of Greenwich. Peter was Master Shipwright at Chatham 1664–67. He was MP for Rochester in 1659 and 1660, and a Fellow of the Royal Society.

There was a temporary revulsion of feeling when, in 1648, a Royalist rebellion occurred in Kent. Chatham Royal Dockyard, under the control of Peter Pett, remained loyal to Parliament, though rebels occupied Upnor Castle and some warships anchored in the Medway. Peter Pett took the necessary measures to avert local danger. On 24 May 1648, he ordered Captain Jervoise with the twenty-eight gun vessel *Fellowship* of 1643 and 366 tons burden, down-river to Gillingham for safety. Three days later, Royalist insurgents seized

The English Civil War 1642–49

her and brought her to Upnor, where her powder and shot were removed. The Royalists ordered her gunner, Pratt, to collect forty kegs of powder from the *Sovereign* and the *Prince Royal*. Peter Pett refused to permit this to happen.

The following day, Dirkin, assisted by some of the principal gunners of the Navy, led a company of Royalist insurgent musketeers with the intention of taking Chatham Royal Dockyard. Peter Pett closed the gates and stood his men to arms. Realising the futility of their cause, Dirkin seized the *Sovereign* and the *Prince Royal*. From these vessels he confiscated twenty-five kegs of powder, which were sent to the insurgents at Gravesend and Deptford.

Following the defeat of the Royalists at the Battle of Maidstone on 1 June 1648, Royalist remnants tried to make their escape in the *Fellowship*. Peter Pett frustrated their attempts. With a boat of musketeers, he boarded and seized the vessel. The following day he similarly recovered the *Sovereign* and the *Prince Royal*. Pett's courage and resolution saved the situation at Chatham.

Charles I's rule during a period of rising aspirations for greater political and religious liberties provoked civil war. This resulted in his execution in his forty-ninth year. At 2 p.m., on 30 January 1649, he stepped outside from an upstairs window of the Banqueting House of Whitehall, London, on to a specially erected scaffold draped in black to face death on the block by decapitation before a crowd of thousands. He was interred a week later in St George's Chapel at Windsor, in the same vault as occupied by Henry VIII and Jane Seymour.

Upon the death of Charles I, the administration of the Navy was controlled by the Council of State. Thomas Taylor was re-appointed gunner to the *Sovereign* on 24 October 1649. John Blundell was appointed her purser on 16 December 1650.

On 16 December 1650, the Council of State instructed the Admiralty Committee to confer with the Master Builders and carpenters with regard to improving her sailing qualities. Although a fortune had been lavished upon her, she was not successful as a fighting vessel. She was too high, causing her to roll excessively when under shortened canvas in a heavy sea. Thus, the broadside ordnance was hindered from bearing down on to its target. The arrangement by which the decks rose in steps to the prow and the stern, leaving a low waist amidships, weakened the vessel's sides. Her armament was too heavy for her rig. She had a high, square beakhead bulkhead similar to that in the galleys. This presented an ideal target to the enemy, who could rake her fore and aft by firing directly into the bows. A similar disadvantage was provided by the broad, square stern. Such a strategy could sweep the entire length of the gun decks, and so effectively and dramatically reduce a vessel's firepower.

While at Chatham Royal Dockyard, shortly after 1 March 1651, the height of her upper works was reduced by 6 feet. The light spar deck above the forecastle, waist and half-decks was removed. The level of the bulwarks on the forecastle was reduced to the top of the gunports. Similar modifications were made aft. The after round house was removed. The length of the half-deck was reduced by cutting away part of the forward end. The topgallant poop was dismantled. The raised decks at the stern were subsequently termed, enumerating from the waist, the quarter, the poop, and the poop royal decks respectively. Other changes included shortening the long, projecting beak and the removal of the forward open ends of the quarter galleries.

These extensive alterations did not influence the keel length, beam, and depth in hold. She was so reduced in dead weight that her draught in the water was reduced by 1 foot. Her dead weight or displacement tonnage was reduced by around 140 tons correspondingly.

During the period of the Commonwealth, 1649–60, she was styled *Commonwealth*. Because of political reasons, however, this name never became established.

Edward Hawthorne, purser of the *Sovereign*, petitioned the Admiralty Committee on 10 March 1651 for the continuance of the servants which had formerly been allowed to him.

These servants had been taken from him for other duties. Edward Hawthorne was the Mayor of Rochester until his death in 1651.

In contravention of orders, the Master Caulker, William Thompson, had, for two years up to December 1651, neglected to caulk her. Thompson frequently went up to London without leave, and employed dockyard men to cut up and carry out firewood for his personal use at home. He was, however, not unique in this type of misdemeanour.

A deplorable state of affairs prevailed at Chatham Royal Dockyard. The men had not been paid for years. In November 1651, complaints were laid by some subordinate officials at Chatham against Peter Pett. It was alleged that members of the family worked into each other's hands. Stores were wasted or misappropriated. Higher wages were charged than were paid. False musters were kept.

A special inquiry was ordered in January 1652. Peter had little difficulty in proving that the charges were malicious.

John Browne continued to cast ordnance and shot for the Commonwealth. In addition to his own forge at Brenchley, near Horsmonden in Kent, Parliament gave him control of forges at Cowden and Ashurst in Kent, Brede at Powdermill Farm in the parish of Udimore, Sussex, Imbhams at Boremill copse in the parish of Chiddingfold, Surrey, and Connop and Lydbrook in the Forest of Dean. He was buried in St Margaret's church, Horsmonden on 13 June 1651. Originally, there was a large black marble and alabaster tomb monument dedicated to John Browne. This disappeared during the nineteenth century.

The family business continued under the sons George (1649–85) and John (1662–1735) until around 1685 (Appendix 27).

The rivalry for colonial free trade between the established maritime powers of England and Holland developed into a state of enmity. Each vied fiercely with each other in an attempt to assert their own nation's pretentious sovereignty over the seas.

CHAPTER 9

The First Anglo-Dutch War 1652–54

By Parliament's Navigation Act of 1651, only English vessels could be permitted to carry English imports, while exports could only be conducted by English vessels, or ships belonging to the country to which these goods were destined. This Act was clearly intended to damage the successful and established maritime trade of Holland.

The Council of State ordered the completion of preparations for the fleet. Recently rebuilt, the *Sovereign* was prepared for her first sea engagement with an enemy. In January 1652, the Council of State ordered the *Sovereign* to be made ready for summer service. By 8 March, the Admiralty Committee ordered men, guns and ammunition to be placed aboard her.

Thomas Arkinstall petitioned the Admiralty Committee on 6 January 1652, for arrears of pay owing to him by the Treasurer of the Navy. He occupied the post of Assistant Master Attendant at Chatham Royal Dockyard between 1645 and 1660.

On 15 March 1652 the Council of State ordered the Commissioners of the Navy to prepare the *Sovereign* and the *Resolution* for sea service to implement the summer guard. On 16 April a Report to Parliament appeared on the Charge of the Navy, estimating £21,600 for preparing the *Sovereign* and the *James* for six month's sea service with a crew of 900 in each. Some 335 pieces of ordnance were required for the summer fleet. If they were brass, the estimate of cost was £67,200. A mere £13,520 was needed for iron pieces.

In May 1652 a Dutch ship in the Channel refused to recognise English sovereignty by the traditional salute of dipping their flag or topsail when passing English men-of-war. The inevitable confrontation erupted into the beginning of the First Anglo-Dutch War. The first encounter took place on 19 May 1652 off Dover, between Robert Blake (1599–1657), General-at-Sea, and Maarten Harpertszoon Tromp (1598–1653), Lieutenant Admiral of the United Provinces.

The Council of State, on 22 June 1652, intended to strengthen the fleet. Together with the *Resolution, Vanguard* and *James,* the *Sovereign* was part of the contingent of ten warships reinforcing the thirty merchant ships which formed the main body of the fleet.

On 30 June 1652 the Council of State instructed the Officers of the Ordnance to supply such brass pieces as the Tower of London could provide for the *Sovereign.* The Council of State, on 11 and 12 July, ordered Peter Pett to carry the *Sovereign* down to Bishop's Ness, and there to stay aboard until a master or captain came to take command. On 12 July 1652 the Council of State required the Masters of Trinity House to propose three able persons, from which would be selected the master of the *Sovereign*. A similar order was given to the Commissioners of the Navy on 17 July.

On 19 July, the Council of State received the names of three persons proposed for master of the *Sovereign*. Thomas Rabinett, who had been the Boatswain of the *Sovereign*, was the favourite choice. In 1643, Thomas Rabinett was appointed one of four Masters Attendant of the Navy. He replaced the deceased Captain Thomas Austin at Chatham Royal Dockyard. In 1645, Rabinett was in the pinnace *Henrietta* guarding the Medway. Rabinett died in 1658 through age and infirmity. His post was not filled. Boatswains acted as deputies in the absence of the Master Attendant.

The Officers of the Ordnance were instructed to hasten the supply of guns from London to the *Sovereign*. The victuallers were instructed to hasten supplies to the *Sovereign* lying at the Nore. She remained in the Hope on 19 July awaiting a master, crew, provisions, guns, ball and powder.

On 20 July the orders of the Council of State provided for twenty of the able seamen who had volunteered for service to be selected for reward. Ten were granted Master's pay, and ten granted mate's pay. At this time an able seaman's pay was around £1 4s per twenty-eight day month, while a Master's pay was £7, and a mate's pay £3 6s (Appendix 49).

By 21 July, the Officers of the Ordnance were instructed by the Council of State to prepare gun carriages for the *Sovereign* and the *Antelope* with all possible speed.

Available brass ordnance was despatched from the Tower of London. She took aboard shot and powder, which required great care in handling.

On 26 July the Council of State ordered the Lord General to provide 200 men for the *Sovereign* and the *Antelope*. Hewett's commission to be master of the *Sovereign* was rescinded. Thomas Scott was his replacement. The command of the *Sovereign* finally fell upon the forty-seven year old Captain Nicholas Reed. This was his first and only naval appointment. On 29 July 1652 he was ordered to select some honest and able minister to go to sea with him in the *Sovereign*. The Admiralty Committee were required to consider a suitable allowance for the minister.

Because of a misdemeanour, Thomas Stevens was relieved of his position as her Lieutenant on 2 August.

On 16 August the Council of State ordered Col. Ingoldsby to provide 100 of his men to supplement her crew. On 22 August the *Sovereign* in the Downs received these soldiers. Richard Mayo was selected on 17 August as her minister. The Navy Commissioners were required to provide oatmeal, sugar and other spices aboard her for the relief and comfort of such men who might fall sick.

Such a vessel during warfare required a larger crew than was warranted during peacetime. Her effectiveness as a fighting vessel depended on the skill and size of her crew. This was dictated by the type and number of guns which consequently controlled her tonnage.

According to the Establishments of 1672 and 1677, a crew of fifteen men were required for each cannon of VII drake and its opposite number on the far side of the lower gun deck. Her twenty-four-pounders required fourteen crews each of ten men. Her twenty-eight demi-culverins required 112 men. Her fourteen sakers needed forty-two men, and eight men were required for her four three-pounders. To fill and handle black powder, some sixteen men were required and some thirty-eight boys carried powder from the magazine to the guns. The Master Gunner had two mates, four quarter gunners, an armourer and a gunsmith. Thus, some 560 men were necessary to handle her guns.

The surgeon and his crew were eight men, with another twelve to carry the wounded down into the cockpit. The carpenter and his crew were at least six men. The purser and his crew accounted for six. Crewing the three ship's boats, including the boatswain and two mates, required thirty. The tops needed ten, and more if she was a flagship. There were two helmsmen and another two to con the ship. Some eighty men manned the sails and rigging. The yeomen, trumpeter, sentries, marksmen or soldiers numbered eighty. She needed a cook, a steward and mate, eight midshipmen, six Master's Mates or pilots, a Lieutenant and a Master. Consequently, 815 men were required to handle such a vessel in battle.

Navy Lists invariably recorded a complement of 600–15 for peacetime service at home and abroad, 710 for war at home and 815 for war abroad. Thus, any significant decrease in the established complement would not only have impaired her fighting capabilities, but could have created a potential unmanageable hazard to vessels in her vicinity.

On 20 August 1652 the *Sovereign,* together with other ships, was required to come out of the Thames to augment the fleet. On 21 August, the Council of State ordered Robert Coytmor to go downriver to hasten the *Sovereign, Antelope, Lion, London, Little President* and the *Renown* into the Downs. The Council of State ordered various vessels to guard the *Sovereign.*

Captain Nicholas Reed was instructed by the Council of State on 21 August 1652:

1) To take the *Sovereign,* together with other vessels, into the Downs.
2) To take and seize all Dutch or French vessels and secure them in some convenient Commonwealth port.
3) To burn, sink or destroy any resisting enemy vessels.
4) To take command of the other captains and officers in company with the *Sovereign.*
5) To observe orders from the Parliament, Council of State, General Robert Blake or Sir George Ayscue.

After his engagement with Sir George Ayscue (1615–72) off Plymouth on 16 August 1652, the Dutch Lieut. Admiral Michiel Adriaenszoon de Ruyter (1607–76) continued cruising in the Channel, searching for home-bound Dutch merchantmen.

On 27 August 1652, the Council ordered General-at-Sea Robert Blake to intercept a French squadron from Le Havre. Blake took to sea in the *Sovereign* in the lead, followed by his flagship, the *Resolution* of eighty-eight guns, and several other warships. The French, under Commodore de Menillet, found themselves overwhelmed. He ordered supply vessels to retreat northwards. The English took several prizes and returned triumphantly to Dover. Captain N. Reed ordered a victory salute of all the Sovereign's guns. The deafening thunderclap was disconcerting to the local population.

By mid-September de Ruyter's squadron was running low on provisions. The merchantmen, already under escort, were anxious to reach the safety of port. Because of his failure to protect the Dutch herring fishing trade from the ravages of Blake, Tromp was dismissed. His commission was occupied by Admiral Cornelis de Witt (1623–72). De Ruyter returned home and joined up with the Dutch. The Dutch under de Witt with around forty-four vessels, intent on attack, suddenly appeared off the Goodwin Sands on 25 September.

The English were anchored in the Downs under the command of Blake in the *Resolution,* with Vice Admiral William Penn in the *James* and Rear-Admiral John Bourne. The main fleet was hastily reinforced to number sixty-eight sail.

Early on Tuesday 28 September the English weighed from the Downs under a westerly wind, searching for the enemy. They rounded the North Foreland and at noon sighted the Dutch with sixty-two sail, hove-to close under the lee of the Kentish Knock. This is a sand bank in the Thames estuary, fifteen miles north-east of the North Foreland.

The Dutch were organised in four squadrons; de Ruyter had the van, de Witt the centre and G. de Wildt the rear. J. Evertsen with the fourth formed a reserve.

The wind shifted to the south-west and moderated. The main action began around 5 p.m., and lasted for three hours. The encounter became known as the Battle of the

Kentish Knock. Trouble and discontent beset the Dutch. The crew of Tromp's former flagship, the *Brederode*, refused to allow de Witt to board her.

The English kept the wind and closed upon the Dutch. By means of skilful manoeuvring during the initial stages, Blake's *Resolution* gained the weather-gage of de Ruyter, but as a consequence, ran aground in less than three fathoms on the Kentish Knock, together with the *Sovereign, Andrew* of 1622 and the *James*.

The grounded ships regained their draught by tacking to the south-east. The *Resolution* was first off the sandbank. She was south-south-west of the Dutch, who now tacked to meet him. Blake's mishap became a tactical advantage. As the four English warships cleared the sand bank, they fell upon the Dutch. The main fleets charged each other, sailing through the opposing formations. The fighting was particularly fierce in the van. The Dutch, having tacked, were standing towards the south, with the English to the north and west.

The vessels were drab in appearance in their black paint. But the *Sovereign* retained her gilded appearance. This provided the enemy with a ready means of recognition. Though the four English warships which had cleared the sand bank were outnumbered 20 to 4, the superior gunnery of the English wrought havoc among the Dutch. The *Sovereign* tacked through their line of battle, creating havoc on either side. At one time there were twenty Dutch vessels about her, but they could not match her firepower. She sank one ship with a single broadside. One of her broadsides brought down a Dutch ship's masts. The *Sovereign* sustained some damage to her rigging, and lost twenty men dead. She had some 300 shot in her bulwarks. Most of the shot stuck in her; only a few had enough momentum to pass through her timbers.

It was this type of action which epitomised the *Sovereign* throughout her active life. The Dutch christened her the *Golden Devil*.

As de Witt's squadron withdrew from Blake's isolated but furious bombardment, it was met by Bourne's rearguard squadron coming fresh into action from the south. Two Dutch warships were dismasted. Captain John Mildmay in the frigate *Nonsuch* boarded and took a Dutch frigate of thirty guns, and a larger vessel. Captain Badiley's ship was severely damaged, but managed to regain port. The main action moved off southwards, developing into a series of irregular combats between individual ships and groups of ships. The larger English ships finally won the day due to Blake's sudden attack and the reluctance of the Dutch crews to engage. The battle continued furiously until nightfall.

The Dutch lost two ships taken and two sunk. Many more were severely damaged.

The following day, Wednesday, the English chased after the Dutch. About 4 p.m., some English closed with the enemy. The *Sovereign* came within shot, and fought fiercely until darkness prevented further action. She sustained damage with some of her rigging carried away. She put into Portsmouth Royal Dockyard to winter. In the eight general actions of the First Dutch War, this was the *Sovereign*'s sole encounter.

Cromwell believed that the Dutch intent was destroyed, and sent part of the fleet into the North Sea and Western Approaches on convoy escort duty. Blake was left with forty-five ships in the Downs.

Thomas Taylor, Gunner of the *Sovereign* petitioned the Admiralty Committee:

1) There was a shortage of powder during part of her last engagement. This was due to the delay in sealing the powder into cartridges.
2) The range of the *Sovereign*'s ordnance was less than that of the Dutch.

The first of Taylor's concerns was due to insufficient men to fill the cartridges with powder. There were insufficient boys to carry the powder to the guns.

Taylor's second concern was due to the fact that the *Sovereign*, like many vessels in the fleet, was equipped with drakes. This, with a reduced powder charge, produced devastating damage at short range. This weapon was useless at long range. The Dutch used long straight-bore guns which discharged shot with square grooved indentations. With an increase in powder charge, the weapon had a long range. This was a feature of ordnance design rather than a fault in operation.

In November 1652 General George Monck was appointed one of three generals-at-sea.

By 7 December 1652, the *Sovereign* was at Portsmouth Royal Dockyard. She was listed among vessels required to be ready for sea service by 14 February 1653.

Peter Pett wrote to the Admiralty Committee on 22 January 1653, informing them of the shortage of masts supplied from London for the ships at Portsmouth. Only a main yard was available for the *Sovereign*. If there were no masts at Deptford mast pond, then recourse would have to be effected to secure masts from the New England ships at London.

On 6 January 1653, Mr Pointer, Cheque of the *Swiftsure*, was appointed Cheque of the *Sovereign*. Mr Hedges, Master of the *Marston Moor*, was appointed Gunner of the *Sovereign*.

On 4 February she was careened on one side. The planking on the exposed side was cleaned by breaming. Here, the fouling was burnt off. The bottom was then paid with sulphur, tallow, pitch etc. to inhibit the growth of worms in the planking. The other side was cleared the following day.

Marine incrustations such as barnacles and sea grass fouled her water-immersed hull and inhibited her sailing qualities. One of the effects of the rebuild of 1644 in dry dock was to remove such deposits. Sometimes a dry dock was not always available. In such circumstances, careening was necessary. In this process, the guns, shot, powder, stores and boats were discharged from her. Her rigging above the level of the lower tops was removed. She was towed close inshore at high tide and beached on some suitable sandy shore as the tide receded. The warship was heeled over by shifting ballast. Multiple tackles rove between the lower mast heads and bitts on the deck of an attendant hulk. The hulk's windlass weighed on the falls until her lower futtocks broke the surface of the water. Considerable strain was imparted on the wales and side timbers where the vessel came into contact with the beach.

On Monday or Tuesday next it was intended to have her ready for provisioning. But there was a shortage of crew.

The *Sovereign*, *Prince* and *James* were refitted at Portsmouth, and therefore were not present at the Battle of Portland on 18–20 February 1653. In the opinion of her purser, Edward Hawthorne, the *Sovereign* needed another four months to complete preparations for sea. On 17 February, Mr Newberry, Officer for the Ordnance at Portsmouth Royal Dockyard, was required to provide from London enough ordnance for the *Sovereign*'s lower gun deck. Thomas Arkinstall was due to take charge of her on 3 March to expedite preparations. She was still short of her lower tier of ordnance and full complement on 7 March.

On 13 March she put into Stokes Bay, off the south-west coast of the Gosport, for provisions. By 18 March men from the *Martin*, *Merlin*, *Drake* and *Nonsuch* (ketch) were taken for manning the *Sovereign*. The Admiralty Committee ordered that the *Sovereign* should be ready for sea service by 1 May 1653.

Blake, although ill due to wounds sustained in the Battle off Portland, visited her on 1–2 June 1653 at Portsmouth to personally inspect the refitting. By 6 July she was ready to take aboard provisions. Due to insufficient crew, she could not be brought out of harbour. Being too late in the year for useful service, the Council of State ordered that she should be kept rigged and fitted out ready for any unforeseen contingency.

On 20 July, General George Monck wrote to the Admiralty Committee requesting a supply of drinking water, and suggesting the appointment of John Hancroft, the Boatswain of the *Sovereign*, to Master Attendant at Chatham Royal Dockyard in place of Thomas Rabinett. Seaverne, Boatswain of the *Andrew*, succeeded as Boatswain of the *Sovereign*.

A List of Ships dated 3 September 1653 included the *Sovereign*, with no named commander.

The Council of State required her readiness for sea by 14 February 1654.

The Treaty of Westminster brought the First Anglo-Dutch War to a close on 15 April 1654 on terms favourable to England. The Dutch made large concessions, and agreed to the striking of the flag to English ships in the narrow seas. In a List of Blake's fleet for 1654 and in another for 1656, the *Sovereign* was not mentioned. Her Master during 1654 was L. Lane.

Matthias Christmas, Master Carver at Chatham Royal Dockyard, who had worked on the *Sovereign*'s embellishments, died in August 1654 aged forty-nine years. His post seems to have been occupied by his son-in-law, Thomas Fletcher, until his death on 10 June 1685 aged sixty-four years. Elizabeth, daughter of Matthias Christmas, and wife of Thomas Fletcher, died on 29 July 1710 aged seventy-five years. All three were similarly interred in St Mary's church, Chatham. There was a Gerard Christmas working on ships built at Harwich during 1666–8.

Her first Master, William Cooke, was one of the four Masters of Trinity House in 1642. He is recorded as going to sea as Master of the *James* in 1645. He was still in office in 1650. He died in retirement on 21 December 1654 aged seventy-two years, and was interred in the church yard of St Mary Magdalene at Gillingham.

She was rebuilt at Chatham Royal Dockyard in 1659–60 by the resident Master Shipwright, Captain John Taylor. This was in the 'old single dock', now called No. 2 dry dock. She was warped into the dock stern first. She was structurally recreated in her body and underwater form, though her embellishments remained unaltered. The only outward change was her new head and the quarter galleries. The long, low projecting beak was shortened. The unbroken line of the head-rail swept down from the figurehead and up again before the cat-heads, terminating in a large gargoyle. The ornate friezes on either side of her prow were re-fitted between the head-rails. Her figurehead changed. Thomas Fletcher, Master Carver of Chatham, received £109 for his work on her. The quarter galleries lost the old fashioned open portion which projected aft. They had always presented a hazard in action on account of the temptation it provided to the enemy intent on tossing a lighted torch in to the open gallery to set fire to the vessel.

On 2 March 1660, Sir Edward Montagu (1625–72), First Earl of Sandwich, and General George Monck (1608–70), were jointly appointed 'Generals of the Fleet' for the next summer expedition. They immediately put to sea with the fleet. They lay in the Channel off Dover for some time before proceeding to Breda to bring back the King. Samuel Pepys (1633–1703) sailed with Sir Edward Montagu as his secretary. They embarked aboard the *Swiftsure*. On 2 April they transferred to the *Naseby*. She was re-named *Royal Charles*.

On 25 May 1660, His Majesty Charles II landed at Dover from the *Royal Charles*. He was met there by General George Monck. His Majesty raised Monck to the peerage as First Duke of Albemarle, in recognition of his contribution towards a peaceful restoration of Stuart rule. Charles II processed triumphantly through Canterbury and arrived with an escort of cavalry at the city of Rochester between 4 and 5 p.m., on Monday 28 May, to a fanfare of trumpets. Suspended across the crowded streets were exquisite garlands curiously made of expensive scarves and ribbons.

Amid cheering, His Majesty, with the Dukes of York and Gloucester, alighted from his coach to refresh himself at the home in Crow Lane of Master Francis Clarke, an ardent Royalist who had been instrumental in securing the monarch's return from exile. The home was then occupied by Colonel Richard Gibbons, who together with Master Francis Clarke, received His Majesty.

Col. Gibbons, whose regiment was quartered in Rochester, had been honoured and rewarded by Oliver Cromwell for his services to Parliament. Gibbons must have been

64. Rigged model of the *Naseby* of 1655. Port elevation. Reconstruction model by Robert Spence around 1943. (*National Maritime Museum*)

somewhat apprehensive on this occasion, anticipating dispossession on the Restoration of the Monarchy. His Majesty wisely confirmed Gibbons' lands.

This red brick property was favoured by the Dukes of York and Gloucester as their lodgings. The ground plan of the house is a letter 'E', in honour of Elizabeth I. The two outer projections form wings, with the porch in the centre. The oak roof is covered with red tiles. Most of the window frames, mullions, etc., are of oak, but some are moulded brick.

His Majesty was conducted over Chatham Royal Dockyard by Peter Pett. They saw the *Sovereign* and other vessels. He dined with Peter, probably at Hill House. His Majesty returned to the Crow Lane mansion around 8 p.m. In the Panelled Hall, together with his brothers and hosts, he entertained Kentish noblemen at supper.

The following morning, between 4 and 5 a.m., the City prepared for the royal departure. The Mayor, Aldermen and Councillors, after solemn procession to the Crow Lane mansion, presented His Majesty with a basin and ewer of silver gilt, valued at £100, to commemorate his stay at Rochester. He knighted Master Francis Clarke, William Swan of Denton in Kent, Baynham Throckmorton of Gloucestershire, and George Rese of Twayte, Suffolk. His Majesty formally ordered Sir Francis Clarke to rename his house 'The Restoration House'. It survives in private possession.

As His Majesty departed in his coach for London, the Kent Militia lined the streets. Groups of maidens scattered herbs and flowers across the road. The bells of the cathedral and St Margaret's church pealed out merrily. Cheering and a fanfare of trumpets joined in the joyful expression of feeling. The guns of the warships in the Medway, with those in the Block Houses and Upnor Castle, joined in the royal salute to celebrate the Restoration of the Monarchy.

From 1660 until its abolition in 1832, the Navy Board was responsible for the management of the Royal Dockyards. The Navy Board was responsible to the Lord High Admiral, James the Duke of York (afterwards King James II), a post for which he was destined almost from the cradle. The Navy Board consisted of four Principal Officers; Sir George Carteret as Treasurer, Sir John Mennes as Comptroller, and Sir William Batten as Surveyor. Samuel Pepys was appointed Clerk of the Acts by Sir Edward Montagu. There were also two full Commissioners; Sir William Penn, Lord Berkeley, and Peter Pett as local Commissioner and Supervisor of Chatham Royal Dockyard with a salary of £350 per annum.

With the Restoration, officers were required to confirm their loyalty. Thomas Taylor had been a gunner in His Majesty's ships since around 1620, many of them having been in the *Sovereign*. She was renamed *Royal Sovereign*. In June 1660 Taylor was considered suitable for the post of Master Gunner of England, in lieu of John Wemis who had been deposed because he had borne arms for Parliament. In August 1660 her Carpenter, Robert Moorecock, petitioned for confirmation of his post. He had served the crown for thirty-four years, twenty of which had been in the *Sovereign*.

Willem van de Velde the Elder's broadside drawing of the *Sovereign of the Seas* (Illustration 13) depicts two anchors as they were in 1660. In the grounds of the National Maritime Museum is an Admiralty pattern anchor, of similar type, which formerly belonged to a ship-of-the-line around 1750. This specimen was recovered off Sheerness, Kent (Illustration 7).

Originally she was equipped with three small boats; a long boat, a pinnace and a skiff. Hayward's Navy List, dated 1660, suggests that there had been no change in the sizes of these boats (Appendix 40).

After her rebuilding, she was launched on 26 August 1660. This process probably imitated her original launching. The dock was flooded, and the dock gates removed. She awaited for the next favourable high tide. She floated off majestically, and was warped into the channel.

In company with other warships, she spent the next few years laid up in the River Medway. Sixty men on full pay were kept aboard to keep her clean and to wait on visitors. Her moorings were upstream, off Upnor Castle, in Chatham Reach, below what was later to become New Dock Yard. The draught of water here at low tide is around 22 feet. In line with other King's ships, this was her normal allocated berth when not at sea nor in dock.

Samuel Pepys' first sight of the *Sovereign* occurred on 17 January 1661. Pepys and his wife were escorted by Captain Roger Cuttance (Mayor of Weymouth) and Captain Blake by barge along Ham Creek, through the Faversham marshes and into the East Swale, south of the bank which later became Harty Ferry, to the vessels anchored in the Medway. Lady Sandwich with her daughter Jemimah, Mrs Browne (probably Elizabeth, who remarried George Browne in 1653), Mrs Grace, Mary (probably wife of the John Browne who was christened in 1645), and the page, Mrs Pepys' servants and Samuel Pepys, all in frivolous mood, went into the *Sovereign*'s great lantern together.

Pepys enjoyed a late supper at Hill House, Chatham on 8 April 1661. He slept overnight in the Treasurer's Chamber. This was his first sight of Hill House. He was pleasantly impressed.

The *Sovereign* lay in Chatham Reach when Pepys visited her on 9 April 1661. He went down by barge with a group of ladies, singing all the way. Pepys and his party was escorted by William Castle (a shipbuilder of Deptford) and Captain Phineas Pett (this Phineas {1619–66}, Clerk of the Cheque, was the seventh son of Phineas by his first wife Ann {née} Nicholls). In frivolous mood, Pepys took Lady Batten, Mrs Turner, Mrs Hempson, and the two Mrs Allens into the great lantern and there kissed them, demanding such as a fee due to a Principal Officer.

Pepys and Peter Pett (1610–74) visited the *Sovereign* at her moorings on 4 August 1662. They were satisfied that she was well maintained, but there were only a few officers aboard.

John Hancroft was her Boatswain in October 1662, when Captain John Cox recommended him to the Navy Commanders for service with Captain Brook.

At around 11 p.m., on the evening of 12 July 1663, Pepys, together with Mr Whitfield (clerk), walked down to Chatham Royal Dockyard and there took a boat with crew. On this pleasant moonlight night they rowed down to the guard ships moored in Chatham Reach. They found no officers aboard the *Sovereign*. There were no arms fixed, and no powder nor shot for her few guns. He found none awake aboard the *London*. Pepys spent all that night in a state of despair visiting the neglected ships at their moorings, and was distraught to find no officers aboard, and all the crews asleep.

Pepys was anxious concerning the irresponsible manner in which Peter Pett had been managing Chatham Royal Dockyard. Peter had neither the financial resources, the necessary materials, nor the manpower to implement his orders. Pepys visited the *Resolution* (formerly the *Prince Royal* of 1610) when she was laid up in dock at Chatham on 10 April 1661. She had been there since 1660, being rebuilt by Phineas Pett. The seventh son of Phineas (1570–1647), he was knighted in 1663.

Pepys visited Hill House, Chatham, on 11 July 1663. After dinner he travelled by coach through pouring rain to the dockyard to board the *Sovereign* to witness the launch of the *Resolution*.

Hill House was abandoned during the early eighteenth century and lay derelict. It was demolished around 1804 to accommodate the new Royal Marine Barracks then being built.

The *Royal Sovereign*, the expensive product of many labours and endeavours, survived to serve in the role for which she was designed. In company with other vessels, she remained laid up in ordinary in the River Medway awaiting the opportunity for action again.

CHAPTER 10

The Second Anglo-Dutch War 1665–67

England declared war on the Dutch 4 March 1665, and thus began the Second Dutch War. The Captain of the Fleet was Sir William Penn. The *Sovereign* was laid up in ordinary at Chatham Royal Dockyard in April, where she had been since August 1660. The first action was the Battle of Lowestoft, between 3 and 4 June 1665. The *Sovereign*, being short of some 200 men, was not in action that day. The *Prince Royal* of eighty-six guns and 700 men, the flagship of Edward Spragge, with Sir Roger Cuttance as Flag Captain, was in the Blue Squadron. She suffered some slight damage. The Dutch were heavily defeated in this action.

Richard Sellar, a young long-shore fisherman from Kilnsea near Scarborough, was seized by the press gang on Scarborough pier in 1665. He was taken aboard the *Prince Royal*, the flagship of Edward Spragge. Sellar was a conscientious objector, namely a Quaker. His faith prevented him taking up arms. In consequence, Sellar suffered punishment and humiliation aboard the flagship. During action against the Dutch, Sellar was employed looking out for fire ships and carrying down the wounded to the cockpit. In this, he distinguished himself. Spragge, impressed with his courage, devotion and faith, discharged him from the King's service with a personally signed certificate confirming his freedom.

Edward Spragge was knighted by Albemarle. Sir William Penn retired from sea service. His sphere of activity lay at the Admiralty, where he did excellent work. Sir William died in 1670, aged fifty years. He was interred at St Mary Redcliffe, Bristol. His son, the famous Quaker and founder of Pennsylvania, USA, kept his name green for years to come.

Peter Pett (1610–74) was on his way to inspect her at Chatham on the morning of 7 July 1665. He witnessed the effects of the parting of the strap on a block, which killed one man and injured several others. Peter ordered a new strap to be fitted, praying that further mishap might be avoided. There was a mere thirty tons of hemp in store. He ordered more from Samuel Pepys. On 8 July Peter requested Pepys to supply 100 seamen and 200 soldiers to man her. Every effort was urged to complete her preparations to get her down to Sheerness. This dockyard was well sited for the servicing of ships stationed at the important naval anchorage at the Nore. This was a sandbank in the Thames estuary extending from Shoeburyness in the north to Sheerness in the south.

By 11 July, she was being rigged and taking aboard beer and provisions. Repairs were completed the following day, with some provisions stowed below deck. John Evelyn visited her on 1 August at the Buoy of the Nore. She still awaited her full provisions, ammunition and complement. Thirty-nine select men were transferred to her from the *Bendish*. These were replaced by thirty-two soldiers. Trinity House recommended to the Navy Commanders on 3 August the suitability of Captain Brooks as her Master. Samuel Pepys visited her at the Nore on 18 August to enquire about her readiness for sea. The following day General George Monck, the First Duke of Albemarle, ordered her and some other vessels out to sea to strengthen the fleet. Albemarle commanded the fleet during the Second Anglo-Dutch War.

On Monday 28 August 1665, the *Sovereign* came in from the Gunfleet and joined the main fleet. She was in the Red Squadron, under the command of Sir Jeremy Smith. William Coleman was her Second Lieutenant and George Perkins her Third Lieutenant. Sir Jeremy Smith returned from Harwich to his command. But he was ill. The following day, he was put ashore at Lowestoft to recover. The fleet sailed from Harwich on 31 August. Pepys reported that the fleet consisted of 100 ships, both great and small.

Pepys visited his benefactor, Sir Edward Montagu, First Earl of Sandwich, aboard the *Sovereign* at Gravesend on 18 September. She was at sea during a storm on the night of 31 September, some forty-five miles from the Texel. She sprang a leak which wetted forty kegs of powder in her hold. The *Diamond* lost her bowsprit, foremast and main top mast. She was sent into Harwich for repair. Some forty men were taken out of her to augment other vessels' crews.

Pepys wrote on 25 November concerning the difficulty of finding a master for the *Sovereign*, because Sir Jeremy Smith was ill.

On Saturday 9 December 1665, Sir Thomas Allin, commanding in the *Royal James*, went aboard the *Sovereign* to examine her condition for himself. The following day, Allin sent a boat with seventy men, his boatswain, two mates, two hawsers and a small anchor to bring her to her moorings. She gained her moorings above Upnor Castle on Monday 11 December. On Wednesday 13, Mr Sneddell was sent up to fetch one warp and one anchor for the *Royal Katherine*, which the *Sovereign* had allowed to slip. On Saturday 16 December, Allin received an order regarding the disposition of the mooring of the ships in the Medway. The *Prince* was at the *Sovereign*'s moorings, and the *Old James* ahead of her. Here, in the shelter provided by the River Medway, the fleet was laid up in ordinary for the winter.

Her name was omitted from a List of the Fleet dated 16 March 1666. Her Master on 14 May was Captain John Cox. Her Lieutenants were L. Bellamont, Christopher Mason and Robert Parkes. On 21 May she was short of provisions. She was short of her full crew. She needed another 300 soldiers. Due to unfavourable winds, she waited seven or eight days before being able to leave Sheerness.

There were four vessels left behind when the main fleet sailed from the buoy of the Nore, around 23 May 1666. The *Sovereign* remained at Sheerness. The Generals-at-Sea had already sacrificed the fourth rates *Charles V* and *Westfriesland* to allow their crews to supplement the *Sovereign*'s complement. But, she was still short of around 300 men when the fleet sailed. In some exasperation, the Lord High Admiral, James the Duke of York, consented to despatch the *Sovereign* with five other short handed vessels down to the fleet by 31 May 1666. She was provided with 100 additions to her crew. Her commander was Captain John Cox, of the Red Squadron. The *Colchester*, a fifth rate of twenty-eight guns and 110 men, commanded by Arthur Laughorne, was assigned to the *Sovereign* to protect her from fire-ships.

The Dutch anchored off Dunkirk on 1 June 1666. The fleet strengths were:

	Dutch	English
Warships	85	80
Guns	4,615	4,460
Crew	21,909	21,085

Each fleet was divided into three squadrons:

Dutch

Van	Centre	Rear
C. Evertsen	De Ruyter	C. Tromp

English (Albemarle)

White	Red	Blue
G. Ayscue	Prince Rupert	T. Allin

De Ruyter was in the eighty-gun *Zeven Provincien*. To the south was Cornelis Tromp (1629–91). The van was in the north.

The English were under the joint command of Prince Rupert in the *Royal James* and Albemarle in the *Royal Charles*. Admiral Sir George Ayscue commanded the *Royal Prince* with ninety-two guns and 620 men. For some days previously, Prince Rupert with his twenty-four ships had been detached from the main fleet to intercept a French force of around thirty-six ships allegedly coming to the aid of the Dutch.

The action which followed, the Four Days' Fight in the Channel, 1–4 June 1666, was one of the most prolonged and hard-fought sea actions of all time.

Albemarle sighted the enemy in thick weather off the North Foreland early on 1 June. With the wind in his favour, he ordered an attack, despite his numerical inferiority. By midday, in a very close line ahead formation, Albemarle attacked Tromp's squadron. The Dutch scarcely had time to cut their anchor cables and take to the fight, moving south. The English gave Tromp a hard time for some hours.

By 4 p.m., Albemarle was forced to change to a westerly course, because of the proximity of the Flanders coast. De Ruyter and Evertsen engaged the English. The superior Dutch numbers started to take effect. The vice admiral of the White Squadron commanding the *Swiftsure*, Sir William Berkeley, was killed. His ship was taken. The *Essex* was similarly captured by the Dutch. Sir John Harman aboard the *Henry* fought a heroic battle, repelling several Dutch ships and three fire-ships. He managed to quench the fires in his rigging, killed Evertsen with the last salvo of his decimated ordnance, and brought his battered ship to safety at Harwich.

By evening both sides had lost several ships. During the night some damage was repaired. Ships no longer capable of fighting were sent to the rear. Vice Admiral De Vries took command of the Dutch van.

Before dawn on 2 June the Dutch received reinforcements of sixteen ships. Albemarle retained the weather-gage, and attacked the Dutch. The opposing fleets were sailing parallel to each other again. The odds were forty-four English ships to eighty Dutch. Ayscue in the *Prince Royal*, the only remaining flagship in the White Squadron, took his station at the head of the line to provide leadership in that crucial position. Tromp tried to take his fleet to the rear of the windward side of the English, but found himself in a very critical situation. De Ruyter was obliged to bring ships to his aid. The Dutch lost all semblance of order. Albemarle was unable to take advantage of the enemy's misfortune, due to his numerical inferiority. After both sides had lost several ships, Albemarle broke off the attack and reluctantly stood towards his own coast. He hoped that Prince Rupert would soon return.

The end of the day found that each side had lost three ships, sunk, burnt or blown up. Both fleets spent the night repairing their rigging.

By 3 June, Albemarle had only thirty ships fit for action. He withdrew westwards. De Ruyter, with his damaged ships, could not reach Albemarle. Only a few shots were exchanged. At around three p.m., Prince Rupert with his twenty ships returned to reinforce Albemarle.

At 5 p.m. on 3 June, Ayscue's flagship, the *Prince Royal*, drawing around 22 feet, grounded on the Galloper Sands, twenty miles off the coast of East Anglia. The Galloper is a linear shallow orientated N.N.E. – S.S.W. The most dangerous section is a stretch some three miles long and 300 yards wide. The *Royal Charles* and the *Royal Katherine* similarly grounded twice on the Galloper, but managed to regain their draught. De Ruyter sent two ships to take the *Prince Royal*. The *Royal James* bore away just in time. No English vessel was able to approach to render support because the tide was adverse. There was a prevalent fear aboard the *Prince Royal* of the imminent approach of two Dutch fire-ships. Ayscue was forced by his terrified crew to surrender because they were surrounded.

Of the initial complement of 620, only Ayscue and some 500 remained. They were taken off into captivity. The rising tide raised the *Prince Royal* from the sand. But her rudder was damaged and her head would not swing around. With English fire-ships approaching fast, the Dutch set her on fire and abandoned her to sink. Her drifting pyre lit up the night sky. Shortly before midnight a powder explosion sent her to the bottom. The *Prince Royal* sank at position 51°48′ N and 01°58.30′ E.

Next morning, 4 June, both exhausted fleets sought a final decision.

The Dutch had nearly seventy ships. The English had fifty-six, half of which were damaged. They both sailed westwards, with the Dutch to windward. The English van sailed faster than the main body. A gap developed in the English line. The Dutch Rear-Admiral van Nes entered this gap with fourteen ships of his van squadron. Simultaneously, Tromp with his rear squadron, came about on the lee of the English rear. The centre and rear of the English came under fire from both sides. De Ruyter broke through the centre of the English line. Both fleets suffered heavy losses in the ensuing struggle.

The *Royal James* lost her main topmast. The *Royal Charles* was severely mauled by the *Zeven Provincien*.

Immediately after the *Zeven Provincien* had driven off the *Royal Charles*, she came alongside the *Sovereign* and received a hot reception. With her main topmast shot away, and her side timbers badly broken, the *Zeven Provincien* reeled away from the *Sovereign*. Cox had been left to engage Col. Willem Joseph van Ghent's sixty-four gun ship *Gelderland*. She carried a crew of around 335–50 men. Van Ghent was saved by the wits of his crew. As the *Sovereign*, *Fairfax*, *Lion* and *Triumph* closed in to demand his surrender, the Colonel of Marines dropped an anchor. The powerful ebb tide rushing from the Thames swept the astonished English past him to leeward.

Cox also engaged van Gelder's *Klein Hollandia* and Maximiliaan's *Wassenaar*. These three Dutchmen suffered a severe mauling from the *Sovereign*. Shortly before 3 p.m., she was attacked by a Dutch fire-ship which she sank with gun fire.

By 4 p.m., the Dutch centre streamed south in full retreat.

Having almost exhausted their stock of powder and shot, the Dutch turned for home. The English finally broke off the engagement. By evening the action was over.

The English lost ten ships of the line and six fire-ships, with 5,000 men killed and 3,000 men taken. The Dutch lost four ships of the line and five fire-ships, with 2,000 men killed. This was de Ruyter's greatest victory. His successes in battle have been attributed to his development of an effective combat order, stressing fleet discipline.

De Ruyter blockaded the River Thames for some time. The English were by no means destroyed.

On 13 June, Captain Howard of the *Garland* was ordered to deliver thirty men from his crew of 110. They were selected by Captain Cox for service, other than as officers, aboard the *Sovereign*. On 14 June a fire-ship was allocated to serve with her. Her complement had been augmented by men from the *Fairfax*. Captain Cox was ordered on 18 June to deliver these men to the *Coronation*.

On 1 July the *Sovereign*'s Boatswain, John Hancross, was detained at Chatham Royal Dockyard on business. Thomas Swan, gunner of the *Royal Charles*, brought 120 brass pieces from the Tower. Fifteen were consigned to the *Sovereign*.

De Ruyter, commanding the eighty-gun *Zeven Provincien*, left port with fifty-nine ships on 25 June 1666, followed shortly after by other Dutch ships, with van Nes, Cornelius Tromp, Meppel, and De Vries. Admiral John Evertsen commanded the *Walcheren*. The Dutch numbered eighty-eight warships, including eight new ships of war, and twenty fire ships. They arrived off the English coast on 3 July, blockading the mouth of the Thames.

Under the command of Captain John Cox, the *Sovereign* was in the fleet which put out from the Nore on 19 July. The English sailed on 22 July and anchored off Orfordness, with the Dutch to the south-east.

Each fleet was divided into three squadrons:

Dutch

Van	Centre	Rear
J. Evertsen	de Ruyter	C. Tromp (junior)

English (Albemarle)

White	Red	Blue
T. Allin	Prince Rupert	J. Smyth

Prince Rupert and Albemarle, in the *Royal Charles*, were in joint command of the English. Sir Thomas Allin commanded the *Royal James*. Admiral Jeremy Smyth commanded the *Loyal London*. John Kempthorne in the *Defiance* was the rear-admiral of the blue. The English had eighty-one ships of the line and frigates, twenty-three of which were new. There were also around eighteen fire ships. The Dutch had a total of around eighty-eight ships.

Both fleets came in sight of each other at 4 p.m. on 24 July. The Dutch held the weather-gage. On 25 July 1666 (St James' Day), both fleets were thirty-six miles off Orfordness, with the wind at N.N.E. Then followed the action of the St James' Day Fight. This is also known as the Battle of the Gunfleet, North Foreland and also Orfordness. Thus, we have some indication that the action was fought off the Thames estuary. This was a justifiable threat to London.

At around 9.30 a.m., the Dutch fired at the leading English ships. Sir Thomas Teddiman, the Vice Admiral of the White Squadron in the *Royal Catherine*, was the first to receive Dutch fire. Together with the *St George*, she had to haul out of action. The two van squadrons engaged each other closely. The *Resolution* was set afire and blew up. Vice-Admiral Sir Joseph Jordan in the *Royal Oak* joined in the fray.

By 1 p.m., the English had disabled two Dutch ships. Evertsen died at about the same time, causing his ship to run into five others. A running fight developed in an easterly direction, with the English to windward. In a short time, all the admirals in the Dutch van were killed.

The *Royal Charles*' rigging was so disabled that she was forced to withdraw. Her place in the line was taken by the *Sovereign*. The *Royal Charles* completed her repairs and bore down on de Ruyter. She struck a sandbank near the Gabbard, but backed her sails and fell away. The *Sovereign* also brushed the sandbank, but did not strike.

At around 3 p.m., the Dutch ships withdrew, followed by Allin's squadron. Tromp's rear squadron pursued some English ships, leaving de Ruyter's centre squadron to face a superior number of English ships.

Together with the *Fairfax*, *Lion* and *Triumph*, the *Sovereign* engaged the *Zeven Provincien* and so disabled her that de Ruyter was obliged to anchor. His main topmast was shot away and his rigging severely lacerated. The *Sovereign* sank a fire-ship which de Ruyter sent out towed by a long boat. De Ruyter cut his cable and stood in again, to cover the withdrawal of Colonel Willem van Ghent in the *Gelderland*. The *Royal Oak* exchanged many broadsides with de Ruyter.

At 4 p.m., the Dutch gave way and both divisions drifted apart, severely damaged. In a masterful manner, de Ruyter, with twenty ships, covered the withdrawal of the Dutch.

Banckert quitted his ship the *Tholen*, of sixty-six guns. She and her crew were captured and the vessel set on fire.

Throughout the night and the following morning the English continued their chase. Tromp, with only eight ships, was out of sight. De Ruyter, behind the shallows off Flushing, covered the arrival of stragglers. Tromp was in danger of being cut off, but arrived safely home the following day. De Ruyter's masterful conduct saved the Dutch from destruction.

The Dutch lost twenty ships and 4,000 men and 3,000 men wounded. They lost five flag officers and several captains. The English lost only the *Resolution* and two or three fire ships, 300 men and one captain.

The English maintained control of the sea.

De Ruyter blamed Tromp for the Dutch defeat. In August 1666, this resulted in the withdrawal of Tromp's commission and his resignation from the navy until 1673, when de Ruyter and Tromp were reconciled.

At a Council on 28 July, it was decided to send the damaged *Royal Charles* home. Her masts and rigging were shattered. The fleet were ordered up the Dutch coast as far as the Texel. The wounded men from the fleet were set ashore on Saturday 28 July. On 29 July, Allin sought to transfer the *Sovereign*'s wounded to the *Mary*. The bell of the *Royal Charles* was given to the *Sovereign*'s gunner.

On 29 July 1666 a small English squadron, under the command of Sir Robert Holmes, destroyed 160 Dutch merchantmen in the Texel. This action became known as 'Holmes' bonfire.'

Prince Rupert, with Albemarle, had to find another flagship. At 3 p.m. on 30 July they took the *Royal James*, with Albemarle as Flag Captain.

Consequently, Sir Thomas Teddiman instructed Allin, the commander of the *Royal Charles*, to remove himself and his goods to the *Sovereign*. Allin was ill with his wounds at the time, and Mr Chorley, surgeon of the *Prince Royal*, warned him of the dangers of making such a journey. Allin, however, was obliged to comply with orders, and moved to the *Sovereign*. In spite of her size, she had not previously been favoured as a flagship. The reason is uncertain. It may have been due to the lack of cabin space aft. This would have been somewhat cramped for senior naval officers.

On Monday 30 July, Allin was appointed Admiral of the White Squadron in the *Sovereign*. Captain Cox, her commander, was transferred to the *Royal James*. Although he was still Captain of the *Sovereign*, he was acting Flag Captain in the *Royal James*.

On Friday 1 August 1666, the fleet weighed anchor and stood to the south. About noon, they discovered the Dutch. Similarly, they stood to the south. In striving for the weather-gage, the pilots mistook their soundings. At 3 p.m., the *Royal Charles*, the *Sovereign*, and Captain J. Roch's ship, the *Antelope*, brushed south east of the Gabbard Bank, but did not go aground. The *Royal Charles* drew less than four fathoms of water. As the tide was running, they backed their sails and cleared with no damage. His Highness ordered a gun to be fired to warn the rest of the fleet of the danger of the shallows. After lying at anchor for four days, the fleet worked its way northwards.

The English anchored off the Texel on 7 August.

On 18 August 1666, Prince Rupert and Albemarle removed to the *Charles*. Allin returned to the *Royal James* on Tuesday 21 August. On 22 August John Langley arrived with fresh water.

He delivered it and went for more on the same tide. The water was distributed to the *Sovereign* and the *Montagu*. On 29 August the victualler's agent was ordered to replace 1,300 lb of defective bread in the *Sovereign*.

Although badly in need of repair, the *Sovereign* remained at sea with the fleet. She lay at anchor on 18 September, while the main fleet saw action. She leaked so much that by 20 September Captain Cox was anxious to go about in her.

The fleet left St Helens road and sailed for home. The *Sovereign* and the *Slothany*, a Dutch prize of sixty guns, were in danger if they met another storm at sea. Most of the *Sovereign*'s crew was distributed among those ships in need. The *Royal James* took 325 of her men. With only 120 men aboard, the *Sovereign* put into Portsmouth Royal Dockyard on 21 September 1666 for repair.

The economic situation of England had been devastated by the epidemic of the Great Plague, which swept London and Kent between the spring of 1665 and the autumn of 1666. The Fire of London in September 1666 added to the dilemma. The resultant high taxation and unemployment led to social unrest. To aggravate the seriousness of the situation, the English and Dutch were at war on the high seas.

After the last victory against the Dutch, the English decided to save money by laying up the majority of the fleet in the River Medway. Most of the crews were paid off. Mutiny was prevalent since the sailors had not been paid for several months.

With complete surprise, the Dutch fleet of eighty ships under the command of Admiral de Ruyter mounted an offensive. On 7 June 1667 they appeared in the Thames estuary. The Dutch Vice Admiral van Ghent, with seventeen sail, bombarded Sheerness Fort on 11 June. They landed a force of around 800 men on Sheppey and hoisted the Dutch flag. Hastily mounted guns at Sheerness Fort collapsed under the first discharge. Within an hour the Dutch seized the fort and secured all useful stores.

The Dutch, assisted by a strong easterly wind and unusually high tide, advanced up the Medway. The half-rigged *Royal Charles*, mounting thirty-two guns, lay aground and abandoned. A Dutch boarding party of nine men re-floated her and sailed her back to Holland. The Dutch sailed on and burnt the *Royal James*, *Loyal London* and *Royal Oak* moored below Upnor Castle. The *Royal Oak*'s commander, Captain Douglas, refused to leave his post and perished in her (Illustration 65).

Further Dutch successes were prevented by the turn of the tide. The *Sovereign* remained at Portsmouth Royal Dockyard, where she had been repaired and wintered, and therefore escaped the devastation wrought upon the English.

The Dutch retired for the night and harassed Gillingham village. On 13 June they resumed their attack with a bombardment of Upnor Castle. With the turn of the tide, the Dutch withdrew downriver to Queenborough. On 21 June they abandoned Sheerness Fort and withdrew. Van Ghent blew it up. The magazine full of stores was deliberately burnt.

As a scapegoat, Peter Pett was arrested at Chatham Royal Dockyard under a warrant issued by the House of Commons. He was committed to the Tower of London on 17 June 1667. Under charges of sedition and misdemeanour on eight counts, preferred by Albemarle, Peter was brought to trial on 19 June with all documentation relevant to the Medway. He confessed to saving the model collection rather than the King's ships, and consequently the *Royal Charles* was captured by the victorious Dutch. Peter was accused of bestowing greater care upon his collection of ship models than the warships themselves. He was dismissed and threatened with impeachment.

On 8 July 1667, a warrant from Lord Arlington to the Lieutenant of the Tower allowed Anne, Peter's sister, to visit him in his prison.

The Second Dutch War ended with the Treaty of Breda on 31 July 1667, giving advantageous terms to Holland. It achieved some relaxation of the Navigation Act. Dutch ships were permitted to carry goods from the River Rhine to England. The Dutch gave up the New Netherlands in North America. The English renamed it New York and New Jersey.

65. Pieter van den [sic] Velde's painting *The Burning of the English Fleet off Chatham 20 June 1667*. (*Rijksmuseum, Amsterdam*)

Peter was released from imprisonment on 20 December 1667, on surety of £5,000 bail provided by Rowland Crispe of Chatham, his son in law, and Samuel Hall of London. The articles of impeachment were conveyed to the House of Lords, but no further prosecution resulted. Peter was appointed Commissioner at Deptford on 17 December 1668. He was permitted to retire quietly. He died in obscurity around 1674.

The only English first rate to survive by the end of the war was the *Sovereign*. She remained laid up in the River Medway, with a very small crew to keep her clean. Her Lieutenants during 1668 were Richard White and Lawrence Wright.

The office of Commissioner of Chatham Royal Dockyard remained vacant for two years. The Master Attendant at Deptford Royal Dockyard, Captain John Cox, was appointed resident Commissioner of Chatham Royal Dockyard in March 1669.

During repair work on the gatehouse of Upnor Castle in April 1949, a crude drawing was found beneath layers of whitewash on a plastered internal wall. The port bow of a spritsail topmast vessel, of the type common before around 1720, is depicted. The fore course, fore topsail and fore topgallant sails are billowing. Gunport covers are open. The shape of the head is typical of the period after around 1660. The figurehead may be a lion, but the drawing is crude and inaccurate. This may be a first hand contemporary impression of a warship laid up in the Medway (Plates 47 & 48).

To prevent the repetition of such an ignominious defeat as had been inflicted by the Dutch raid, additional defences were provided. By February 1669, Sir Bernard de Gomme, the King's Chief Engineer, had surveyed the Medway between Rochester bridge and the Mussell Bank. He designed a system of artillery defences to protect the river approaches to Chatham Royal Dockyard and the anchorage for warships which occupied the 3.75 miles of reaches below Rochester bridge.

A bastioned fort was erected at Sheerness to protect the battery at Garrison Point. Both land and sea fronts here mounted 150 guns. At the entrance to the Medway were three earth fortifications at Grain, called Buda, Middle and Quaker Batteries. By April 1669 construction began on the forts at Cockham Wood and Gillingham. Two batteries between Cockham Wood and Upnor Castle were called Middleton's and James', or Bird's Nest.

The function of Upnor Castle changed. It became a store for gunpowder to supply the warships in the Medway. In 1691 it stored more gunpowder than any other depot in England, but still retained a defensive armament on its river facade as a second line of defence.

Cockham Wood Fort is on the north bank of the river, 1.25 miles downstream of Upnor Castle. Almost due south, on a wide bend called Short Reach, on an island near salt marshes at the mouth to St Mary's Creek, was a similar defence known as Gillingham Fort.

These two forts formed the most powerful defences of their time on the Medway. They were surrounded by a rampart and ditch on the landward side, and were entered over a drawbridge. They consisted of a redoubt and flat gun platforms behind low revetments. Cockham Wood adapted to the slope of the contour of the hillside. There was a line of gun embrasures along the edge of the river, and a second tier at a higher level behind. Gillingham Fort was diamond-shaped in plan, with the guns along two facets facing the river. Cockham Wood's redoubt was bastion-shaped in plan, while Gillingham's was square. These redoubts were in brick with stone cladding and dressings. These three-storied towers served as storehouses and a retreat for the gunners in case of need.

The first definitive list of guns actually mounted in place dates from 1698, following the allocation of August 1669. Cockham Wood Fort mounted sixteen demi-cannon, nineteen culverins, three demi-culverins, two six-pounders and four sakers.

Gillingham Fort mounted forty culverins, ten demi-culverins, three six-pounders and one three-pounder. This was an increase over Gillingham's allocation of August 1669, which recorded eight demi-cannon and nineteen culverins. An abstract of 1680 recorded that ship's gun-carriages were provided for the guns at Gillingham and the lighter nine guns at Cockham Wood. Most of the demi-cannon and all the culverins at Cockham Wood were on standing carriages. The six-pounders, sakers and three-pounders were mounted on top of the redoubts.

Upstream of the boom was the sheltered anchorage of Sovereign Reach. In the shadow of the protection afforded by Gillingham Fort is water with a draught of around twenty-two feet at low tide. This haven was a mooring site for the *Sovereign* and other warships. She was visited here on 6 June 1669 by Cosimo III, Hereditary Prince, afterwards Grand Duke of Tuscany.

In 1637 the charge for building the hull was listed at £31,245 15s 10d. In Navy Lists of 1670 and 1685, the value of the hull complete from the builder was £29,840, at a cost per ton of burden of £20. Deane's Navy List of 1670 recorded the *Sovereign*'s value and the cost for provisioning for six months (Appendix 13).

By the early 1700s Hill House was no longer in naval use. The building was completely restored in 1703. Its use for naval purposes ceased around 1720. Until around 1750 it was used as a Pay House. It became known by that name. In 1749 the Admiralty decided to let Hill House and use another building as a Pay Office. Hill House lay abandoned for some years until around 1758, when it opened as an inn. The Admiralty were planning to create extensions to Chatham Royal Dockyard. The Admiralty purchased Hill House in 1777 from James Gordon for the sum of £420. Hill House was demolished in 1805 to accommodate the new Royal Marines Barracks which was built on the same site. There is no plaque nor stone to commemorate the site of the former Hill House.

Cockham Wood Fort elapsed into desuetude heralding a period of decay. It passed into private ownership during the nineteenth century. A remnant of the red brick revetment to the

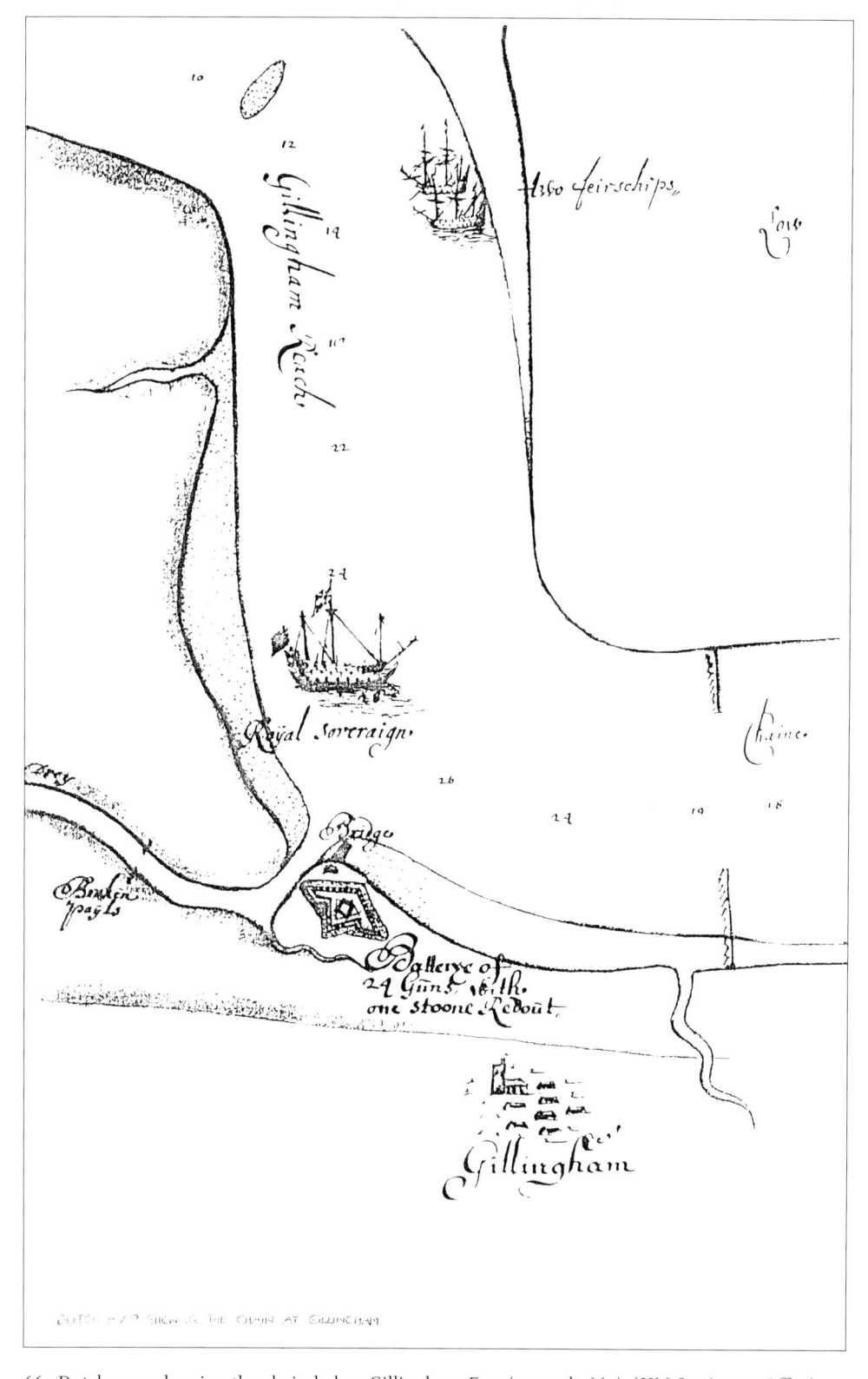

66. Dutch map showing the chain below Gillingham Fort (around 1669). (*HM Stationery Office*)

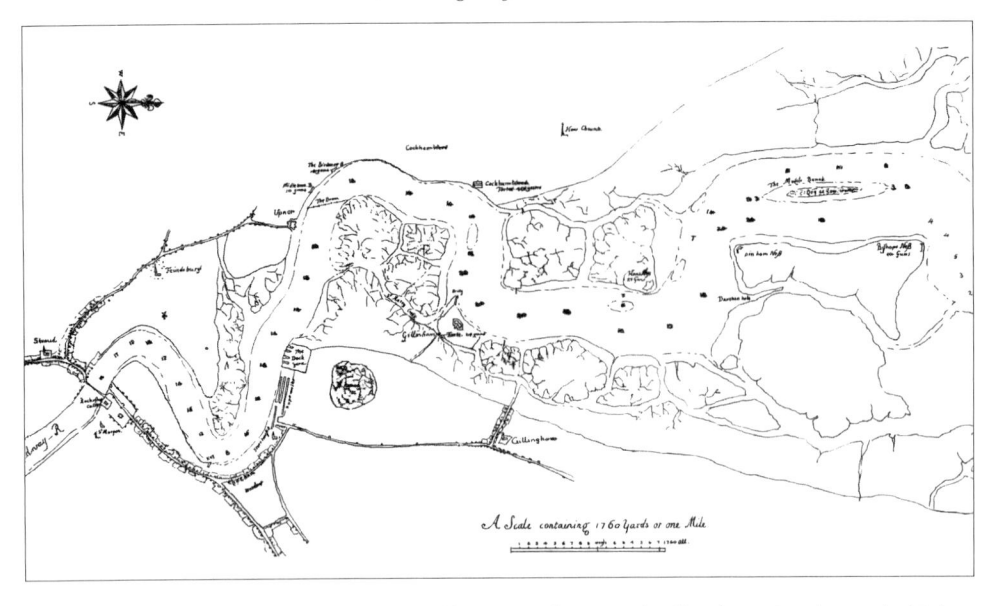

162   Sovereign of the Seas

67. Map of the River Medway showing Cockham Wood Fort and Gillingham Fort (around 1685). (*HM Stationery Office*)

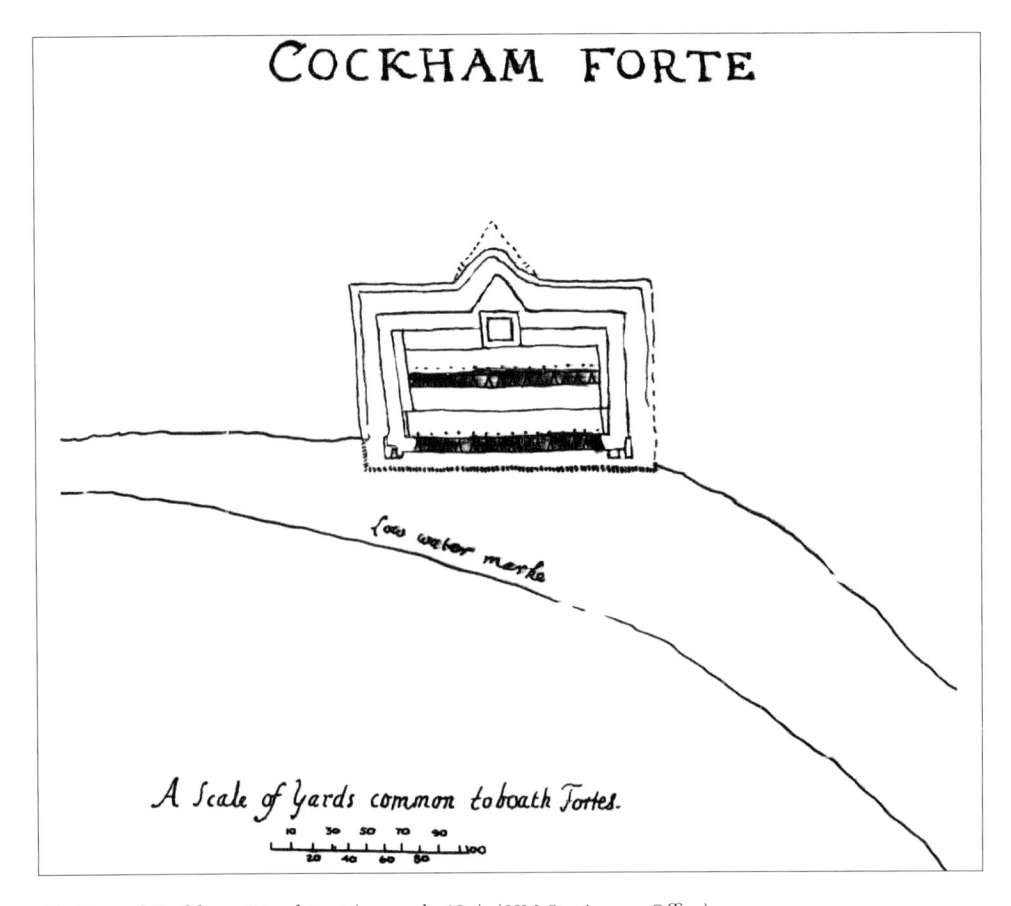

68. Plan of Cockham Wood Fort (around 1685). (*HM Stationery Office*)

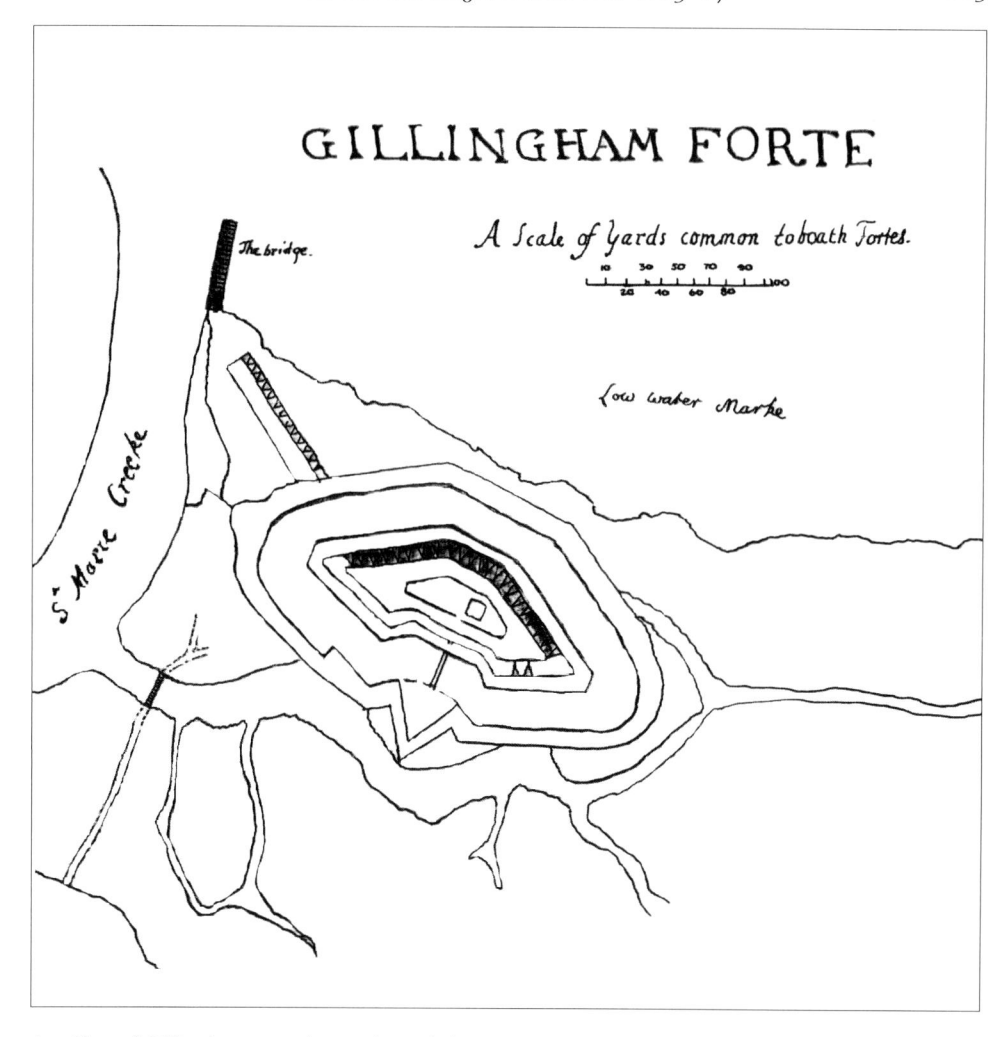

69. Plan of Gillingham Fort (around 1685). (*HM Stationery Office*)

lower gun battery, which was part of the west bastion, survives. The ruins extant comprise the lower part of the redoubt and a flat area of earth, overgrown with vegetation, which formed the rear or upper battery. The eastern end of the fort has been severely eroded due to tidal action.

During the 1860s the Royal Navy was converting from sail to steam, and from wood to iron. Extensions to Chatham Royal Dockyard became inevitable. The purchase of some 185 acres comprising St Mary's Island was completed in 1854. Gillingham Fort was demolished in 1865 to provide for extensions. Interconnecting dock basins and graving docks on the site of St Mary's Creek, together with a river wall and embankment, were completed by 1883. This extension to the north of the original yard provided 380 acres to the existing 97 acres. Consequently, the older part of the yard remains largely unaltered and survives substantially as it had been in the days of sail.

The site of the former Gillingham Fort lies beneath the site of Collier Dock, between Bull's Nose Locks and Gillingham Pier. The site of the fort remains a matter of speculation for the local historian. There are no visible remains.

CHAPTER 11

The Third Anglo-Dutch War 1672–74

The year 1672 commenced with preparations for conflict with Holland. James, the Duke of York, Lord High Admiral of England (later King James II), raised his flag in the *Royal Prince* of 1670, the flagship of the Red Squadron. Captain John Narbrough joined her on 5 January 1672 as First Lieutenant. Without vacating his post as Resident Commissioner at Chatham Royal Dockyard, Captain John Cox was appointed her Flag Captain on 15 January. Her Master was Captain Christopher Gunman. Cloudesley Shovel entered as Midshipman on 22 January.

While patrolling the Channel, an English squadron commanded by Sir Robert Holmes made an unprovoked attack on 12 March 1672 on a wealthy Dutch convoy, homeward bound from the Mediterranean. Sir Robert was acting under orders from Parliament.

Charles II convinced a hostile Parliament to vote funds for fitting out the fleet by reminding the Members of the humiliation suffered from the Dutch at the Medway raid of 10–14 June 1667. On 19 March 1672, Charles II declared war on Holland. He entered into an agreement with Louis XIV of France to assist the French in their endeavour to destroy the Dutch by conflict both on land and sea. On 27 March, Louis XIV declared war on Holland.

The initial intention was to wage war upon the sea. For the Anglo-French plans to succeed, it was necessary for the coalition to have mastery of the North Sea. It was imperative to destroy de Ruyter in a decisive naval battle.

So began the Third Dutch War.

Together with the *Royal James* and the *George*, the *Sovereign* joined the fleet on Saturday 23 March. During part of 1672 at least, the *Sovereign*'s Captain was Stephen Pyend. Philip Lately was First Lieutenant, James Watts Second Lieutenant, Nordash Rand Third Lieutenant, with Maximillian Keech as another lieutenant. Over sixty per cent of the *Sovereign*'s crew, and that of the fourth rate *Leopard,* were pressed into service. These were the days when a commander resorted to using soldiers or volunteer seamen organised into press gangs to apprehend likely recruits to make up deficiencies in a vessel's crew. Press gangs never chose landsmen. Instead, seamen or fishermen were chosen, because such men knew seamanship.

On the evening of Wednesday 3 April Sir Joseph Jordan, the commander of the *Sovereign,* hoisted the red flag at the mizen mast-head as Rear-Admiral. He boarded her on 18 April. The following day the blue flag was hoisted to her foremast-head. Sir Edward Montagu, Earl of Sandwich, in the *Royal James* of 1671, commanded the Blue Squadron.

Sir John Harman bore the red flag at the mizen mast-head of the *Charles.* They were allied with the French under Vice- Admiral Comte Jean d'Estrées of the White Squadron.

As First Captain of the Fleet, Cox was knighted on 27 April by Charles II on board the *Prince Royal* at the Nore.

The Dutch, withdrawing from Orfordness, were sighted on 11 May.

The Duke of York joined the French under Admiral Comte d'Estrées at Brest on 21 May. D' Estrées, who had been an army general before 1668, commanded the *St Philippe* of seventy-four guns. The French were divided into three squadrons under d'Estrées, Vice Admiral Duquesne and Rear-Admiral De Rabesnière. On 31 May the combined fleet arrived at Southwold Bay to revictual. During the seventeenth century this bay was a considerable indentation on the Suffolk coast.

The fleet strengths were:

	Dutch	Allies
Ships of the Line	75	65 (+ 33 French)
Total Ships	around 130	150
Guns	4,484	6,018
Crew	20,738	34,496

Each fleet was divided into three squadrons:

Dutch

Van	Centre	Rear
Banckert	De Ruyter	Van Ghent

Allies

White	Red	Blue
d'Estrées	Duke of York	Earl of Sandwich

The Dutch were commanded by Admiral de Ruyter in the *Zeven Provincien* of eighty-two guns.

The Duke of York commanded the *Royal Prince* of 102 guns as Admiral of the red. Sir John Cox served as his First Captain. Sir John Narbrough was his Second Captain. Her master was Captain Christopher Gunman. Vice Admiral Spragge commanded the main. The Earl of Sandwich in the *Royal James* of 104 guns, commanded the centre of the Blue Squadron. Richard Haddock served as his Captain. Vice Admiral Sir John Kempthorne held the rear guard.

This was the only action of the two Dutch Wars of Charles II's reign from which Prince Rupert was absent. On 2 May the Duke of York, Lord High Admiral, was required by Charles II to attend the fleet bound to sea. The Duke may have been a little anxious regarding his personal future. He required some authorised person to take care of affairs at the Admiralty. He desired Prince Rupert to accept this responsibility in the Duke's absence. Prince Rupert was commissioned Vice Admiral on 16 July 1672. This appointment was confirmed by patent in the following October.

The first fleet action of the Third Dutch War was the Battle of Solebay (otherwise known as the Battle of Southwold Bay) on 28 May 1672. The action was fought around four leagues from the shore. The sea was calm, and the weather was hot with good sunlight.

De Ruyter sailed from the Maas on 28 May, with the wind in his favour. In a wide formation, he attacked the Allies anchored in Southwold Bay. The Allies cut their anchor cables in their frantic haste to get under way. The close proximity of the coast forced both fleets to turn south-east. With difficulty, the Allies manoeuvred away from the coast in the prevailing easterly wind. The English kept together as they stood to the north.

The inexperienced French failed to follow. The French had learnt their tactics from the Dutch. D'Estrées took his squadron south, leading off on the wrong tack. He was intercepted by Banckert with part of the Dutch van. The French attempted a long-range artillery duel against these ships, but did not commit themselves to action.

On the starboard tack, standing towards Lowestoft, the *Sovereign* led the van with most of her division in a line behind her. De Ruyter's Dutch lay to windward. The main body of the Dutch fell upon the English. A fierce action ensued at close quarters.

Van Ghent was killed around 10 a.m.

Between 7 and 8 a.m., the *Sovereign* engaged in a hotly contested action with de Ruyter, a vice-admiral and a rear-admiral with five or six great ships, and four or five fire-ships. They strove to regain the weather-gage, but the *Sovereign*, having no fire-ships, was loath to surrender it. They fought together for about an hour, the *Sovereign* endeavouring to hold the wind. Quite unnecessarily, Sandwich sent a boat with instructions to this effect. The fact that she kept close to the wind caused her adversaries to tack. In this manner, the Dutch lost the wind to her. In the smoke and confusion, Jordan, commanding the *Sovereign*, could hardly discern one fleet from the other. He did however, discern the Duke of York to leeward of the enemy's van, and endeavoured to close to support him. The fact that the enemy bore away to leeward gave the *Sovereign* some advantage in this manoeuvre.

De Ruyter, with seven Dutch ships, hotly engaged the *Royal Prince*. Between 9 and 10 a.m., Captain Sir John Cox was standing near the Duke of York on the poop. In his forty-ninth year of age, Cox was killed by a great shot. His memorial is in St Mary's church, Chatham.

At about 11 a.m., the enemy tacked. The *Sovereign* chased after them, keeping the wind and maintaining her fire power.

Between 11 a.m. and 12 noon, the *Royal Prince*'s main topmast was shot away. She was towed northwards. Her fore topsail was similarly shot away. Two fire ships approached the unsupported vessel. Narbrough ordered two boats to tow her out of reach of the enemy. In recognition of his gallant behaviour during this action, John Narbrough was subsequently promoted to Flag Captain. The Duke of York was obliged to transfer his flag to the first rate *St Michael*, commanded by Sir Robert Holmes. The *St Michael* sprang a leak. The Duke transferred to the *London*, commanded by Sir Edward Spragge, Vice Admiral of the Red Squadron.

At the height of the struggle, the Earl of Sandwich in the *Royal James* was attacked by two fire ships, quickly followed by Jan Danielsz van Rijn's fire-ship the *Vrede*, which grappled the *Royal James*. She was destroyed by fire (Plate 106). Sandwich had to retire in a boat. This became so overcrowded that she sank. All aboard were drowned. The Earl's body was found some days later on a sandbank, dressed in his uniform with the insignia of the Garter. He was interred in Henry VII's chapel in Westminster Abbey.

At around 2 p.m. the *Sovereign*, with six or seven vessels, gained the wind of the Dutch, and kept along with them, firing until 6 p.m. The bitter fighting continued until dark. At 8 p.m., Kempthorne in the *St Andrew* and Sir John Harman in the *Charles* assembled together with another thirty English ships. They tacked northwards. After some fourteen hours' hard fighting, the Dutch, of around seventy sail, retired southwards.

Between 8 and 9 p.m., the *Sovereign* joined up with the Duke of York. The battle continued between the two centres. Both fleets drifted with the feeble wind past Lowestoft towards the south, until they came near Aldeburgh.

The Third Anglo-Dutch War 1672–74

In the evening, Banckert rejoined de Ruyter. The French squadron joined the Duke on the following day. A strong feeling prevailed among the English that the French had failed to provide adequate support for them.

The English lost the *Royal James* and three fire ships, all burnt and sunk. Some 2,500 men were lost. The Dutch lost the *Jozua* of sixty guns, the *Stavoren* of forty-eight guns, and another warship which blew up during the night. The Dutch lost 2,000 men.

With this attack, de Ruyter had frustrated a planned invasion of Holland. This action was, once again, a strategic success for de Ruyter, who again retired into the coastal shallows with his fleet, awaiting the moment for his next engagement.

At 6 a.m. on 29 May, the Duke of York with some of his squadron and the *Sovereign* with hers, tacked and stood westwards. By 9 a.m., they joined the remainder of the fleet. The English sailed homeward. By 1 June they returned to Southwold Bay.

By Sunday 28 July some 100 of the *Sovereign*'s crew lay sick. There was a shortage of water and beer. By 3 August the sick numbered over 140. The main fleet weighed anchor on 21 August. She borrowed men to weigh anchor.

Because of the large diameter of the anchor cable, it was impossible to bend it around the spindle of the windlass. Therefore, as the cable lay along the lower gun deck between the hawse-holes and the anchor locker access forward of the mainmast, a lighter endless cable called a messenger was laid alongside. The cable was nipped every 2–3 feet of its length by a clove hitch on a laniard. The messenger was turned several times around the windlass. Wooden windlass-bars, 12 feet long, were slotted into the windlass head. Teams of two to three men per bar heaved the windlass round, and so drew in the nipped cable. Agile boys called 'nippers' loosed the clove hitch close to the windlass, and ran forwards with the laniard to secure another lashing. As the slack cable passed aft, it passed the riding bitts, and into the anchor locker. It took several hours working in relays, with twelve to eighteen men in each crew, to haul in the anchor.

On the morning of 16 September 1672, the *Sovereign* arrived in the River Medway off Chatham.

By 24 March 1673 she was in the 'old single dock', now called No. 2 dry dock at Chatham Royal Dockyard, for repairs to her under water frame. The work was supervised by the Commissioner, Rear-Admiral Sir Richard Beach. She was launched again on 8 April. The *Charles* took away her long boat on 15 April, together with similar craft from adjacent vessels.

An unfavourable wind on the 19 April prevented her departure from Chatham. By 22 April the wind was westerly, and she was brought to Sheerness Royal Dockyard.

From the ninety to ninety-eight gun first rate *St Michael* of 1672, Prince Rupert sent an instruction on 29 April 1673 to Sir Richard Beach to send all the riggers from Chatham Royal Dockyard, and all the available seamen, on board the *Sovereign*. The riggers became aware of this instruction even before it was issued. Wary of being pressed into service as seamen, many made their escape from the dockyard. Some went to the fishing trade. By 3 May most of the remaining riggers had volunteered for service aboard the *Victory* and the *Sovereign*, thus hoping to outwit the press gangs. The moorings about these two vessels were, in consequence, abandoned.

Sir Richard Beach complained to the Navy Commanders on 5 May that all the riggers aboard the *Victory* and the *Sovereign* had absconded for fear of being pressed into service as seamen. So acute was the shortage of manpower that work came to a standstill.

Sir Richard was endeavouring to bring these warships out into the river. Because of a northerly wind, the *Sovereign* could not get out. By 8 May the wind had veered southerly, and by 3 a.m. preparations were in hand to bring both vessels out. Sir Richard Beach despatched one of the Masters Attendant to convey Augustine Purnett to pilot the *Sovereign*. Sir Richard went down to Sheerness himself to instruct her Master, Captain John Hayward, to prepare her skeleton crew of 150 men to raise her anchor. The wind was fair, and everything was made ready to receive the pilot aboard in time to reach the Nore on the tide. When Purnett came aboard he refused to raise the anchor and get her under way because the weather had deteriorated.

By 9 May, the *Victory* and the *Sovereign* still lay at Sheerness under an adverse north-easterly wind. The *Sovereign* and some other vessels were still short of crew on 10 May.

By 12 May some twenty to thirty of the riggers who had deserted had reappeared to work on the fitting of the moorings. The *Sovereign's* moorings were rotten. Two cables had lain under water for two years, and another two cables were immersed for three years. Prince Rupert instructed Sir Richard Beach, on 15 May, to replace the *Sovereign's* rotten moorings with those from the *Golden Hind*.

It was not until 24 May that the moorings for the *Sovereign* and the *Royal Prince* were replaced, due to the anxieties among the riggers caused by the soldiers from Rochester impressing men into service as seamen.

The English, allied with the French, planned an invasion of Holland. Their strategy at sea was aimed at blockading the coast, defeating the smaller Dutch and then landing an expeditionary force. On 20 May the English weighed from the Gunfleet, and arrived off the Dutch coast. The French squadron joined in the Channel.

The strengths of the fleets were:

	Dutch	Allies
Warships	52	49 (+ 27 French)
Fire-Ships	25	35
Guns	3,171	4,812

Each fleet was divided into three squadrons:

Van	Centre	Rear
C. Tromp	De Ruyter	Banckert

Allies

Red	White	Blue
Prince Rupert	d'Estrées	Spragge

Prince Rupert in the *Royal Charles* commanded the Allies. This vessel was launched at Portsmouth in 1673 as a 100 gun first rate. Sir Edward Spragge in the *Royal Prince*, as Vice Admiral of the Blue Squadron, was Rupert's second-in-command. George Rook served as First Lieutenant. The *Victory*, *Diamond* and the *Sovereign* joined the main fleet on Saturday 24 May within the Ooster Banks.

On 25 May the Allies sighted the Dutch lying at its anchorage in the Schooneveldt, a long narrow basin guarding the entrance to the Scheldt estuary. De Ruyter positioned himself ideally amid a maze of shoals and sandbanks. This forced the Allies to hesitate for three days.

On 28 May 1673, the Allies approached on a westerly wind in a broad line-abreast formation. The Dutch emerged with the west-north-west wind in their favour. At noon, a running battle ensued. This was the First Battle of Schooneveldt. De Ruyter broke the French centre, but then had to withdraw to aid the hard-pressed Banckert. Tromp was cut off by the superior English van and was in difficulties. He had to change his flagship three times.

De Ruyter abandoned his action with the English rear and moved with Banckert to aid Tromp.

The fleets disengaged in the evening. De Ruyter anchored off the coast. Prince Rupert anchored off the Oster Bank to his west.

The French lost two ships. The Dutch *Deventer* of seventy guns foundered during the night.

For the next five days the opposing fleets repaired their damage in full view of each other.

On 2 June, Prince Rupert decided to shift his flag from the cranky *Royal Charles* to the *Sovereign*. Prince Rupert had his baggage transferred to the *London* ready to transfer to her. The following evening, Prince Rupert boarded the *Sovereign*, the flagship of the Blue Squadron. On taking Rupert's flag, she became flagship of the Red Squadron. The Union Flag was broken at the main mast-head. Sir Richard Haddock and Anthony Young followed as flag captains. Rupert's secretary was a Mr Hartgil Baron. The *Royal Charles* went into the vacated position.

On Wednesday 4 June, Prince Rupert returned to the *Royal Charles* to select some 250 men to transfer to his new flagship. At around 10 a.m., Spragge of the *Royal Prince*, with the Earl of Ossory, rowed some six miles across to the anchored *Sovereign* for a discussion with Prince Rupert. When Spragge drew level at about noon, the *Sovereign* signalled the approach of the enemy fleet by loosing her fore topsail. Rupert had little to say to him, but urged his return to the *Royal Prince*, where his squadron lay waiting for orders. The fleet weighed anchor. As there was insufficient crew aboard the *Sovereign* to effect this properly, Prince Rupert ordered the cable cut.

During the afternoon, at the Second Battle of Schooneveldt on 4 June 1673, the *Sovereign* was only two or three places ahead of the French Vice Admiral d'Estrées in the *Reine*. The *Sovereign* inflicted severe damage on the *Waesdorp*, commanded by Ruyter's son, while sustaining only slight damage herself.

The wind suddenly turned to the east, placing the Dutch in the windward position. De Ruyter attacked immediately. The Allies were unready. They sought to escape. There was no manoeuvring on either side. The opposing fleets sailed side by side on the starboard tack with the Dutch to windward. The action ran on to the English coast. Only Tromp and Spragge entered into serious fighting.

After some six hours, de Ruyter broke off the action. This was as fierce as before, but inconclusive. With only slight losses, he again frustrated an attempted invasion. Holland could once again bring in precious convoys.

The Allies were compelled to leave the Dutch coast to repair and refit.

By 9 a.m. the following day, the *Sovereign* was around twenty-one miles off Lowestoft, and under sail in a east north-east wind. At about 5 p.m. the Dutch engaged the English. On approach the Dutch bore away. On Friday 6 June, the *Sovereign* anchored around two miles below the Middle Ground Buoy in eight fathoms of water. By Sunday she had anchored one mile below the Nore. The remainder of the fleet was in attendance. Many vessels were in need of repair. Sir John Narbrough visited Prince Rupert aboard her on 8 June. The following day there was a strong easterly and east by south-east wind. She was forced to strike her topmasts.

On Tuesday 11 June, Charles II and James, Duke of York, dined aboard her. Charles II came out from Sheerness to dine aboard her again on Wednesday. His Majesty and James took their leave and departed in yachts for London. On 15 June 1673, James resigned from the office of Lord High Admiral.

On Monday 16 June Sir Richard Haddock sent the *Barbabella* to London to fill the *Sovereign*'s water cask. She took aboard a ship of beer of some sixty tons. By 20 June, the frigate had returned with sixteen tons of water for the *Sovereign*.

At 2 p.m. on Thursday 26 June, a Council of flag officers was held aboard the *Sovereign*. On 1 July Sir Richard Haddock was appointed Commissioner of the Navy. Sir William Reeves and Sir John Wetwang were appointed flag captains under Prince Rupert in her. The Second Captain, Anthony Young, was transferred to the *Edgar*. On Monday 7 July Narbrough sent Second Lieutenant Henry Carverth aboard the *Sovereign*. He was instructed to command a fishing vessel which went into Sheerness Royal Dockyard on 8 July to be fitted as a fire-ship.

The selection of the *Sovereign* as flagship, and the demands of war, created an opportunity among the fleet for promotion. Thus, there were many changes in her officers during 1673. Ralph Saunderson was Second Captain during part of the year. Joseph Perry and Charles Thorowgood were each First Lieutenant, Adrian Scroope was Second Lieutenant. The position of Third Lieutenant was occupied by Thomas Allen, Thomas Trapps and John Wood. Theophilus Downing was Fourth Lieutenant. Peter Whitley was another recorded Lieutenant.

Charles II, in his yacht *Cleveland*, visited the fleet at Sheerness on 16–17 July. W. van de Velde the Elder followed him in the yacht *Kitchen*. His Majesty visited the French Rear-Admiral. Charles II attended a Council of flag officers on 18 July in the *Sovereign*'s great cabin. In his own handwriting, Samuel Pepys recorded the Council's resolutions which were to form Prince Rupert's Battle Instructions. Together with the fleet, she cast off from Sheerness on 19 July for the Dutch coast.

Prince Rupert commanded the allied English and French when they engaged the Dutch off their own coast. A military force was mobilised at Yarmouth, ready to land on the shores of Zeeland if the naval operations proved successful. Bad weather kept both fleets at anchor for several days. On 11 August the Dutch came out in strength to defend their coast.

The fleet strengths were:

	Dutch	Allies
Warships	75	62 (+ 30 French)
Fire-Ships	22	28

Each fleet was divided into three squadrons:

Dutch

Van	Centre	Rear
Banckert	De Ruyter	C. Tromp

Allies

White	Red	Blue
d'Estrées	Prince Rupert	Spragge

Prince Rupert commanded the *Royal Charles*. Sir Edward Spragge commanded the *Royal Prince* of 100 guns. Kempthorne acted as his Vice Admiral, with the Earl of Ossory as Rear-Admiral.

During the night, with an easterly wind, de Ruyter succeeded in putting himself between the Dutch coast and the English. Enjoying the weather-gage, de Ruyter attacked at dawn on 11 August 1673. The resultant action is known as the Battle of the Texel (otherwise known as Camperdown).

Sailing on a southerly course, the parallel fleets were matched; Banckert engaged d'Estrées, de Ruyter fought against Prince Rupert, with C. Tromp (1629–91) in the *Gouden Leeuw* of eighty-two guns versus Spragge. D'Estrées tried to surround the Dutch van, but Banckert broke the French line and threw it into complete confusion. Delegating a few ships to watch the French, Banckert returned with the rest of his squadron to aid the centre. D'Estrées avoided further conflict. In consequence, the brunt of the action fell upon the English centre and rear squadrons.

Prince Rupert's ships in the centre suffered heavy casualties before eventually breaking free. The new vessel *Royal Charles* gave an unsatisfactory performance for Rupert. He therefore transferred his flag to the *Sovereign*. De Ruyter in the *Zeven Provincien* engaged Rupert, who had van Nes in the *Naagd van Dordrecht* on his weather bow. The *Sovereign*'s Flag Captain, Sir William Reeves, was killed at Rupert's side on the quarter deck. Some sixty men were killed or dangerously wounded aboard her. Gradually, Rupert moved his centre westwards, to keep de Ruyter at a distance.

In deliberate defiance of Prince Rupert's orders, Spragge waited for Tromp, leaving the Red Squadron unsupported. The rearward squadrons clashed immediately, and remained locked in combat. The *Royal Prince* was disabled; her main and mizen masts were shot away. She survived after a magnificent defence. Spragge was obliged to shift his flag to the *St George*. Similarly, his adversary Cornelis Tromp had to change to the *Comeetstar*. The *St George* became so damaged that Spragge had to shift his flag to the *Royal Charles*. A shot struck the barge in which he was transferring. He was drowned alongside.

Rupert was hard pressed by de Ruyter, who was reinforced by Banckert. Both main bodies eventually turned to join the battle astern of them. The conflict continued fiercely until nightfall, when d'Estrées eventually returned, and De Ruyter withdrew towards his home coast.

The English sailed home, abandoning the attempted landing. Rupert had fought his last battle. Other than fire ships, no ships were sunk, except for the English yacht *Henrietta*, but a great number on both sides were severely mauled. The Allies loss in men amounted to around 2,000. The Dutch lost half this number.

The English alleged that their French allies had deliberately avoided taking any risks in the serious part of the action. Disgusted with them, the English made peace with Holland at the Second Treaty of Westminster on 9 February 1674. The Battle of the Texel was the last great naval engagement fought between the English and Dutch. Holland was free of the threat from the sea. A large East India convoy could be brought home to Holland in safety. De Ruyter was promoted to Vice Admiral, in recognition of his victory.

So ended the Third Anglo-Dutch War.

The effect of the indecisive actions towards the close had incurred severe damage to the English vessels. The *Sovereign* was among those vessels needing repair. During the fifteen years of peace which followed the Third Dutch War, great progress was made in the organisation of the Navy.

Abandoned by naval commanders on account of her instability, the *Royal Prince* was laid up for the next nineteen years. The high cost of repair was deemed wasteful. There were other vessels which took priority in the demands of war.

Prince Rupert boarded the *Sovereign* at the Nore on the morning of 4 September 1673. He called a Council of War with the Red and Blue Squadrons, ordering all officers to prepare their vessels for sea. Prince Rupert was instructed to lay her up at Sheerness, and the remaining first and second rates at Chatham Royal Dockyard. The crews were paid off, and the vessels brought to their moorings for repair ready for sea service the following year. She went into Sheerness on 14 September. On the morning of 16 September the *Sovereign* retired to winter at her moorings in Chatham Reach in the River Medway.

Sir John Wetwang was in command of her when, on 7 October, Pepys instructed him to obtain leave of the Treasurer and Controller, Sir Jeremy Smith, at Chatham. Wetwang went up to London to assist in the prosecution of Lieutenant Edwards. One of the Masters Attendant resided aboard during his absence. By 29 October she had gained her moorings. Wetwang was transferred to the *Newcastle* on 11 November.

In February 1676 Pepys conferred with the Navy Board concerning the suspension of Mr Minors, the *Sovereign*'s purser. He had caused some misconduct during his absence from duty. On 19 October Charles II promoted the purser of the *London* of 1670, John Stevenson, to that office aboard the *Sovereign.* The vacancy aboard the *London* was occupied by Mr Pugh.

Due to his service aboard the *Sovereign,* Captain Richard Vittles was the First Boatswain of England. According to his traditional right of succession, he petitioned on 6 January 1678 to be advanced to the vacancy of Master Attendant at Chatham Royal Dockyard. He occupied this post, together with Simon Dunning, between 1679–89.

Phineas Pett (1635–94), the second son of Peter of Deptford (1592–1652), was knighted and appointed to the Navy Board in 1680. He was succeeded as Master Shipwright at Chatham by Robert Lee. He had been Master Caulker, and became Assistant Master Shipwright in 1677, succeeding John Lawrence who was promoted to Master Shipwright at Sheerness. Robert Lee married Elizabeth Pett (*née* Houghton), the widow of William Pett.

The surveys made on the *Sovereign* after the Third Dutch War suggested that she was in a poor state. The officers at Chatham Royal Dockyard were dissatisfied with her form. When due for a large repair, they wished to modernise her. The report, dated 21 August 1675, proposed that she be stripped from the top of her side to the foot of the upper pair of futtocks. The whole of the stern down to the keel was to be taken out. Her stern was to be 6 feet wider at the transom to give her a better seat in the water. Her length aft would be increased by 6 feet. The greater part of her rake was to be removed. All her decks were to be raised to eliminate the hog which she had developed. Her quarters aft were to be lowered. The estimate for this work was £16,000.

On 12 July 1676 it was reported that she was so decayed that she could not be made seaworthy without a full repair. Nothing was done. Indeed, in those years half the Navy was lying in wait for repair.

The survey dated 21 August 1675 was repeated in the periodical reports of 16 August 1678, 27 March & 26 June 1679.

On 16 January 1680 the surveying officers presented another report. In her hold her riders, foot-waling, beams, knees, standards and cross-pillars were sound. Her deck planks, beams, knees from the lower gun deck upwards were similarly sound. Her outboard works were also sound. The main defect was in the camber of her decks, her stem and the timbers abaft in the bread room. The officers were unable to present an estimate of cost until she was in dry dock. This report was signed by Phineas Pett, John and Thomas Shish, Robert Lee and others.

On 27 May 1680, Phineas Pett and Robert Lee reported that after the launching of the *London,* the *Sovereign* could be docked. This was done in the 'old single dock' which is now No. 2 dry dock. It was essential to grave and caulk her, to eliminate the many leaks which she had acquired. She had not been graved or caulked since about 1673.

The funds for the Navy were scanty and much in demand. The Admiralty sought the means to reduce the estimate of £16,000. When docked the Admiralty called upon the Shipwrights' Company for another survey. This proposed that she be stripped down to the channel wales. The riders would need to be lifted and re-faired. Some needed replacement. The stem, sternpost and keel were not mentioned. They proposed to rebuild the stern and galleries. The estimate was £4,255. This did not include masts. She needed new main and fore lower masts, and a fore topmast. The Admiralty welcomed this lower estimate.

The *Sovereign* was rebuilt at Chatham Royal Dockyard in 1684–5 under the supervision of Robert Lee. Because she was the largest and best vessel in the Navy, the shipwrights were anxious to bring her up to date. More and more of the fabric needed attention as the work progressed. The ship was almost rebuilt. They probably exceeded the proposed estimate of £4,255. The report on the *Sovereign*'s rebuilding was among papers which Pepys took away with him.

To provide better steering qualities, the stern transom was widened by 6 feet.

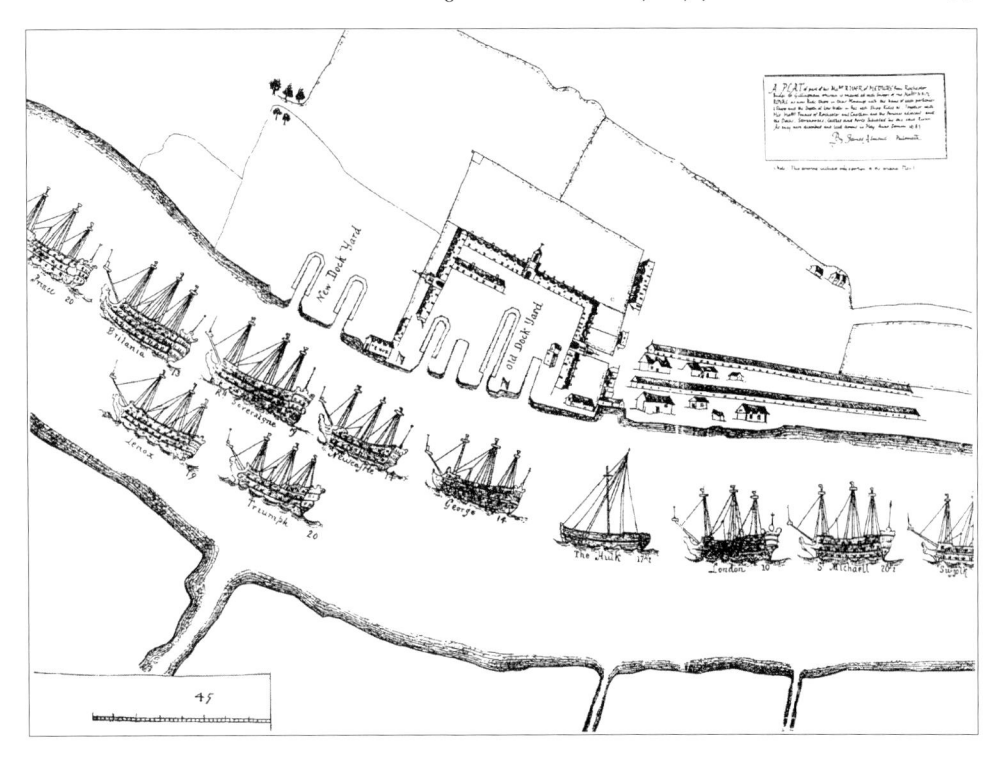

70. J. Almond's map of Chatham Dockyard (1685). Detail of mooring sites. (*HM Stationery Office*)

The distinctive three turrets in the quarter galleries were changed to a single turreted quarter gallery.

The upright fashionable stem as proposed was not applied. This would have increased her keel length forward by 4 feet. Up to 1660 she had kept her original figurehead. This was replaced by the fashionable roaring, crowned, rampant lion of the period. Cheeks were fitted below the bolsters of the hawse holes. An entry port was fitted to the starboard elevation in like manner to that to port.

The first occurrence of an entry port on both the port and starboard elevations is found on a Navy Board hull of a first rate of the *Royal James* of 1671. This is in the National Maritime Museum (SLRO372). Her entry ports are decorated simply, unlike the elaborate ports on similar models of this period. Steps of the side are also included.

A model of Sir Phineas Pett's (1635–94) *Britannia*, launched at Chatham in 1682, was formerly in the collections of Charles Sergison at Cuckfield Park, Surrey. Hence it passed into the collection of Col. Henry Huddleston Rogers, New York City. It was bequeathed by him to the United States Naval Academy Museum, Annapolis, Maryland, as part of his collection of British Admiralty seventeenth- and eighteenth-century Navy Board models. This model illustrates an entry port with steps on the side on both the port and starboard elevations.

In the same collection is the contemporary Navy Board rigged model of the second rate ninety-six gun *St George* of 1701. Similarly, it has an entry port complete with steps of the side, amidships on both the port and starboard elevations.

The contemporary Navy Board hull of the *Royal Sovereign* of 1701, in the Central Naval Museum, Saint Petersburg, Russia shows an arched entry port, complete with steps on the side, amidships on the middle gun deck on both the port and starboard elevations. The tops of the door posts are carved in human form. Above is the cypher 'A.R.', signifying Queen Anne Stuart.

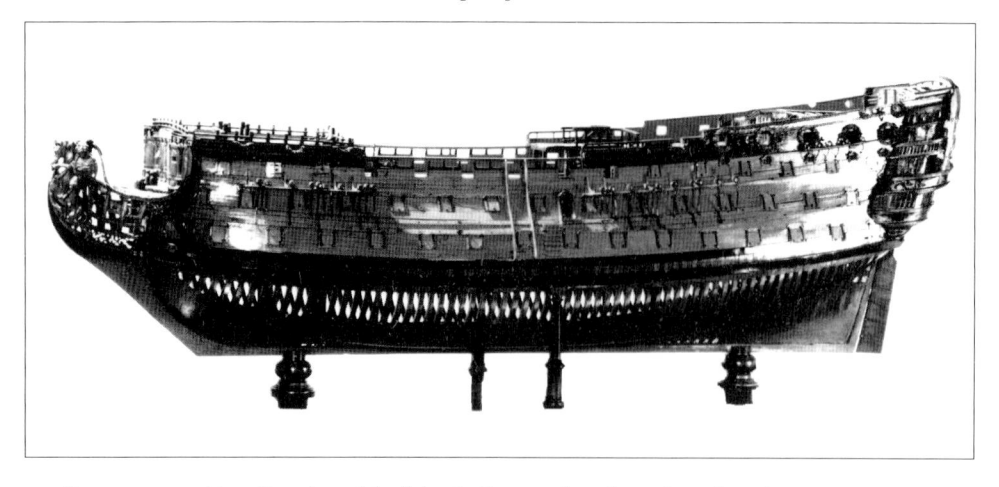

71. Contemporary Navy Board model of the *St George* of 1708–14. Port elevation.
(*Merseyside Maritime Museum, Ron Davies Photography*)

Similarly, the contemporary Navy Board hull of the ninety-six gun first rate *St George* of 1708–14 in the Merseyside Maritime Museum has an entry port complete with steps of the side, amidships on both the port and starboard elevations.

Van de Velde the Elder made two drawings of the *Sovereign* on the occasion of this rebuild. Neither drawing depicts an entry port. Illustration 16, depicting the port elevation, describes the skids only.

She was launched on 30 September 1684.

At the completion of the work, Robert Lee applied to the King for a piece of plate for rebuilding the *Sovereign*. Due to the fact that Pepys removed the records, the decision on Lee's application cannot be found. Pepys had little faith in Lee's ability. This may have created a clash of personalities between Lee and Pepys.

Robert Lee wrote in 1687 that the *Sovereign* was not altered in her principal dimensions since her first building. An examination of the Navy Lists in Appendices 16, 17 & 18 suggests that the length of the keel remained unaltered.

In 1685 King James II came to the throne. The severely neglected fleet required attention. A Special Commission was initiated on 17 April 1686 to supersede the Navy Board and undertake the work of repair. It consisted entirely of experts including Sir John Narbrough, Sir Anthony Deane and Sir Phineas Pett (1635–94). Sir John Narbrough died in May 1688. Deane was called out from retirement to undertake the task and was offered £500 per annum, with permission to continue his many lucrative private enterprises. He was an honest man who knew his worth. He requested, and was granted, double this salary, such that he could devote himself to the King's service. Phineas Pett was christened on 29 April 1635 at Deptford, the second son of Peter of Deptford, and grand nephew of Phineas of Chatham.

The budget was £400,000 annually for three years. This Commission was an experiment in organisation for which Pepys was largely responsible. During its tenure of office, the Commission repaired and rebuilt a total of thirteen vessels, viz. *St Michael*, *Royal Katherine*, and *Britannia* at Chatham Royal Dockyard, the *St George* and *Monck* at Portsmouth Royal Dockyard, the *Happy Return* and *Oxford* at Woolwich Royal Dockyard, and the *Portland* and *Phoenix* at Deptford Royal Dockyard. The *Royal Prince*, *Victory*, *Royal Oak*, and *Kingfisher* were also included.

The *Sovereign* was not included in the work of this Commission, because she had already benefited by a major rebuild at Chatham Royal Dockyard in 1684–85.

The work of this Commission was successfully completed after only two and a half years tenure of office, and was dissolved on 12 October 1688. The system of government by principal officers was restored.

William Bagwell, carpenter of the *Royal Prince,* was appointed First Master Shipwright at Chatham Royal Dockyard in 1689.

Thomas Fletcher, Master Carver at Chatham Royal Dockyard, had worked on the S*overeign*. He died on 10 June 1685 aged sixty-four years. Elizabeth, daughter of Matthias Christmas and wife of Thomas Fletcher, died on 29 July 1710 aged seventy-five years. Both were interred at St Mary's church, Chatham.

The *Sovereign* was in harbour awaiting repairs on 25 March 1686. She received a visit from James II on 9 May 1688. Her repairs were completed by 18 December 1688, though she was not at sea that year. The estimate of her defects was £2,134. The final charge was a mere £1,349. The value of rigging and sea stores was £5,181.

CHAPTER 12

The War of the English Succession 1689–97

Charles II died due to natural causes on 6 February 1685. His younger brother James, Duke of York and Lord High Admiral, succeeded to the throne. This precipitated changes in political and religious constitution. James II was a staunch Catholic in an Anglican-dominated society. James II crushed a revolt led by his nephew, James Scott, Duke of Monmouth. During the rebellion, James II had dispensed with the Test Acts (passed in 1673, this measure disqualified Catholics from holding office) and appointed Catholics to military command. This led to a confrontation with Parliament. James II attempted to win support by ending religious restrictions.

The birth of his son, James Francis Edward Stuart on 10 June 1688, suggested a Catholic succession. The opposition leaders invited William of Orange, to take the English throne. He was the son of William II of Orange and Mary, daughter of King Charles I of England. William landed in England in November 1688 and marched on London. He was hailed as a deliverer. James II, deserted by his troops, fled to France, where he was supported by King Louis XIV. In 1690, with a small body of French troops, James II landed in Ireland in an attempt to regain the English throne. He was defeated in battle and returned to France.

William of Orange had married the fifteen-year-old Mary. She was the daughter of James, Duke of York, by his first wife Anne Hyde, daughter of Edward Hyde, Earl of Clarendon. Mary had been brought up as a Protestant.

William III with his wife Mary II were crowned as joint rulers in April 1689. This accession brought about further hostilities. Louis XIV endeavoured to invade England to return James II to the throne. William III and Mary II's policy was simply to destroy Louis XIV's power. The Dutch and the English were allied against the French in the War of the English Succession. This campaign was otherwise known as the War of the League of Augsburg, The War of the Grand Alliance, King William's War and The Nine Years War.

After fifteen years of peace, the Navy had been re-organised and placed in a state of readiness. On 5 January 1690 a list included the *Sovereign* as the flagship of Sir Ralph Delaval, Vice Admiral of the Blue Squadron, with Humphrey Sanders and Joseph Hartnell as Flag Captains, with Fleetwood Emms and George Simonds as her Lieutenants. This list was intended to come into operation in the early part of 1690.

But events changed, and Admiral Arthur Herbert, the Earl of Torrington, took her as his flagship. In February 1690, he witnessed the field trial at Woolwich of a new type of gun carriage. He was so impressed that he secured an order from William III to provide the new gun carriages for his flagship.

In February 1690, Torrington informed Edward Gregory, the Navy Board Commissioner at Chatham Royal Dockyard, that he required the lanterns of his flagship, the *Sovereign*, to be made from the new stone-ground glass, to replace the green flexible mica which was traditionally fitted to lanterns. In this manner the navigation lights would be visible from a greater distance.

Both Gregory and Robert Lee, Chatham's Master Shipwright, were reluctant to make the change. They considered that Torrington should be content with the lanterns already fitted. Robert Lee had confused notions towards the project. Samuel Pepys wrote a report to the King in 1686, observing that Lee had never built a ship, that he was full of gout, and not as capable as former master shipwrights at Chatham. The Admiralty ordered the modified lanterns to be made. Torrington approved the sketch of the proposed lanterns. They were made and fitted to the *Sovereign*.

Edward Gregory was born in 1639, the second son of Edward Gregory (died November 1682). He served as purser in the *Sovereign* during the early 1660s. He purchased this post from his predecessor. He was associated with the Chatham Chest Charity. He served as Clerk of the Cheque 1661–72. He succeeded his father in this capacity on 1 April 1665. He suffered ill health. William Brown was appointed his deputy. Edward Gregory was appointed Resident Commissioner at Chatham from 1689 until 1703. Edward was knighted in 1691.

Robert Lee served for eighteen years as Master Shipwright at Chatham Royal Dockyard. He died on 1 April 1698 in the sixty-sixth year of his age. He was interred at St Mary's church,Chatham under a monument with his arms, *'Gules, a cross gold between four unicorns heads razed gold for Lee, impaled with sable, three bars silver for Houghton.'*

Lee's wife, Elizabeth, died in 1711 aged seventy-five years.

Lee was succeeded by Daniel Furzer, who had been the first Assistant Master Shipwright at Chatham from 1680–5. Robert Shortis succeeded Furzer at Chatham in 1699. Shortis remained there until his death on 8 February 1705 aged sixty years. He was interred in St Mary's church, Chatham.

A List dated 1 May 1690 showed the *Sovereign* under the flag of the Earl of Torrington as Admiral of the Red Squadron and Commander-in-Chief. On 10 May Captain Johnson of the yacht *Fubbs* conveyed Torrington to the *Sovereign* at the Nore. John Neville, as Flag Captain, received him. John Benbow was her Master. He ordered a twenty-one gun salute in reply to that from the fleet.

Torrington went up to London about 21 May, leaving Sir George Rooke to take twelve vessels from the Nore, in gale force weather, to the Downs. He anchored there on 23 May. Torrington returned to the *Sovereign* at nightfall on 30 May. She was met by a rowdy welcome from the fleet. She replied with a thirty-one gun salute. A Council of War was conducted aboard her on Saturday 31 May.

The French concentrated their Atlantic and Mediterranean Squadrons at Brest, intending to seize control of the English Channel. The French were sighted off the Lizard on 21 June 1690. Their commander was Vice Admiral Comte Anne Hilarion de Tourville, in the *Soleil Royal* of 110 guns.

On 23 June 1690, Torrington in the *Sovereign* weighed anchor, and stood off shore to the south-east. The French were in the Channel. Torrington anchored late in the afternoon, with Culver Cliff bearing south-west by south some six or seven miles. At 5 a.m. the following day, he weighed again, with a fresh gale from the north-east by north. He stood away south-east by east. He anchored at eventide, with Culver Cliff bearing west north-west. He weighed again at 5 a.m. on 25 June and exercised the fleet at tactics until 9 a.m. The wind having veered to south south-east, and thick fog having developed, he anchored. Dunose bore west north-west some fifteen miles. Both fleets were in contact off Dunnose Head on 25 June, as the French proceeded slowly up the Channel intent on blockading the Thames.

The fleet strengths were:

	France	Allies
Warships	68	34 (+ 22 Dutch)
Total Number of Guns	4,624	3,842
Total Crews	28,000	23,000

Each fleet was divided into three squadrons:

French

Van	Centre	Rear
Chateau-Renault	Tourville	d'Estrées (jr)

Allies

White	Red	Blue
C. Evertsen	Torrington	Delaval

Queen Mary II, acting as Regent while King William III was in Ireland, gave orders to Torrington on the evening of 29 June 1690. He was obliged to accept battle commanding a numerically weaker fleet. He held a Council of War with his flag officers aboard his flagship on 29 June 1690 to impart the Queen's orders to engage.

The following day, with a fresh gale from the north-east, and Beachy Head some ten or twelve miles to the north, Torrington, who was to windward, formed his fleet in line of battle and bore down in line abreast upon the French. The action which ensued is known as the Battle of Beachy Head (or Beveziers, a corruption of Pevensey), fought on 30 June 1690.

Tourville waited south of Beachy Head as the Allies approached from the east. Torrington manoeuvred to the windward side of the French, closing up on parallel course. The *Sovereign* had the wind in her favour, but the attack miscarried. Due to faulty dispositions made by Torrington, the Dutch, who were in the van, came into action first at 8.30 a.m., and were severely mauled.

The Blue or rear squadron, under Sir Ralph Delaval in the *Coronation* of 1685, came into action at 9.00 a.m., and the red at 9.30 a.m.

Tourville brought up his squadron, enabling him to attack the Dutch van from both sides.

There was little wind, and Torrington in the *Sovereign* with the *Warspite* and *Lion* were the last into action. Torrington's centre squadron held off from the enemy, leaving the fighting to the Dutch.

Evertsen saved his battered squadron only with great difficulty. Fortunately for the Dutch, the wind dropped completely at around 3 p.m. A heavy pall of smoke lay over the scene of action.

Torrington hesitated from aiding the Dutch. He considered that his priority lay with the English part of his fleet. He decided not to fight. He stood to the south without informing anyone. Under the traditional tactics of line of battle, Torrington should have engaged Tourville. Instead, he held back and engaged the smaller ships of fifty guns under the command of the Marquis d'Amfreville. The *Sovereign* received a bad beating from a much smaller vessel, *Le Fougueux* of fifty-eight guns. The *Sovereign* dropped anchor with sails set.

A calm unfortunately prevented fierce action. Both fleets could move their ships only by towing them with their boats. The action diminished. The Dutch and Blue Squadrons, being close to the French, fought on until 4 and 5 p.m. Only three Dutch ships were capable of further action. The Allies withdrew eastwards with several disabled ships in tow. The French followed slowly.

After a desultory engagement, the Allies withdrew towards the Thames, leaving victory with the French. They did not exploit their mastery of the Channel.

The following day, Torrington was compelled to destroy his damaged ships to prevent them being seized by the enemy.

Tourville lost no ships.

Several of the severely damaged Dutch ships were scuttled or beached, viz. *Wapen van Utrecht* of sixty-four guns, *Maagd van Enkhuizen* of seventy-two guns, *Tholen* of sixty guns, and *Elswout* of fifty guns. The Dutch lost a total of ten ships of the line and around 2,000 dead or wounded seamen. If Tourville had pursued energetically, the Dutch loses may have been heavier.

The English lost two ships and sustained 350 casualties. Aboard the *Sovereign*, nine men were killed and thirty-five wounded. Among the dead was Thomas Mason, a Boatswain's Mate, whose left leg was severed by a great shot.

One English ship to sustain damage was the *Anne*. A third rate of seventy guns and 1,051 tons, she was built by Phineas Pett at Chatham Royal Dockyard in 1677–8. This Phineas (1635–94) was the second son of Peter of Deptford (1592–1652), and grand nephew of Phineas of Chatham (1570–1647). He was Master Shipwright at Chatham 1661–80, and knighted in 1680. The *Anne* was commanded by Captain John Tyrrell, son of Sir Timothy Tyrrell. Severely mauled, she was towed eastwards past Hastings to safety. The French followed in close pursuit. The mainmast, mizen mast and bowsprit were shattered. The foremast was shot away. Some sixty shot had penetrated the hull on the waterline. She was leaking severely. A jury topmast was rigged, but the foresail was too small. She had 100 men killed or wounded. The remainder of the crew remained skilful and gallant. On 3 July Captain Tyrrell beached her at low water close to the shore. The following day he took his crew off and set alight to her to prevent her being taken by the French as a prize. She was burnt to the waterline.

On the plea of growing sickness and shortage of stores aboard his ships, Torrington abandoned the pursuit off Dover and sailed back home. The Allies, still in great confusion, anchored at the Nore on 10 July. Torrington was arrested and imprisoned in the Tower of London.

At a subsequent court martial on board the *Kent* at Chatham on 10 December 1690, presided over by Vice Admiral Sir Ralph Delaval, Torrington was charged with failure to engage the enemy and fight. He was accused of withdrawing and not assisting the Dutch. This indictment was rejected by a partisan jury. Torrington's conduct appeared to be too impulsive, rash and non-committal, suggesting incompetence. He was acquitted. His commission as Vice Admiral of England was revoked by King William III, also a Dutchman. Torrington was allowed to retire to his home near Guildford. He was superseded by Edward Russell.

Considering that Torrington's flagship, the *Sovereign*, was the largest and noblest ship in his fleet, it is unfortunate that Torrington's skills in leadership did not measure up to the demands of the moment. But, perhaps, as some have suggested, he may have been suffering from some illness.

Tourville was dismissed for neglecting to destroy the English fleet.

The *Sovereign* lay at Spithead from 9–13 September 1690.

To secure against a violent wind from the south south-east, the *Sovereign* put into Plymouth Sound on 4 September 1691.

The French were determined to pursue their advantage gained in 1690 off Beachy Head. Another fleet was prepared for an invasion of England intent on restoring James II to the English throne. In 1692 Louis XIV of France concentrated an army of 30,000 men in the Contentin Peninsula in Normandy, poised to invade England. Some 500 transport vessels were assembled to embark the troops.

Admiral Tourville was re-instated as French admiral. He was ordered to gain control of the Channel. The Mediterranean Squadron, intended to reinforce his Atlantic fleet, was delayed. Tourville was obliged to venture out solely with his Brest squadron. His flag was in the *Soleil Royal* of 110 guns.

To counter this menace, a British fleet was prepared and placed under the command of Admiral Edward Russell. By the middle of May 1690, the Anglo-Dutch gathered off Hastings ready to meet the challenge. The French were sighted on 16 May near Cape Barfleur.

The fleet strengths were:

	France	Allies
Warships	44	63 (+ 26 Dutch)
Frigates and Fire Ships	13	38
Total Number of Guns	3,240	6,756
Total Crews	21,000	39,000

Each fleet was divided into three squadrons:

French

Van	Centre	Rear
d'Amfreville	Tourville	de Gabaret

Allies

White	Red	Blue
Van Almonde	Russell	Ashby

The *Britannia* flew the flag of Admiral of the Fleet Edward Russell. She sailed from Portsmouth on 18 May. Her first Captain was David Mitchell, Captain of the Fleet. Her Flag Captain was John Fletcher. The *Britannia*, being the newest and youngest ship in the fleet, was the senior flagship in the Anglo-Dutch operations against the French.

Sir Ralph Delaval, in the *Sovereign*, was Vice Admiral of the Red Squadron with Humphrey Sanders and Joseph Hartnell as Flag Captains. Sir Cloudesley Shovell was Rear-Admiral in the *Royal William*, with Captain Thomas Jennings. The Blue Squadron was commanded by Sir John Ashby in the *Victory*, with Edward Stanley as his captain. George Rooke was Vice Admiral in the *Neptune* with Thomas Gardner as captain. Richard Carter was Rear-Admiral in the *Duke* with Captain William Wright. The remainder of the fleet was Dutch, under the command of van Almonde. Captain John Tyrrell, who had commanded the *Anne* at the Battle of Beachy Head on 30 June 1690, was in command of the *Ossory*. Later in 1692 he died and was interred in Oakley church, Buckinghamshire.

At 10 a.m. on 19 May 1692, the fleets met off the Contentin Peninsula, under a weak south westerly breeze. The action which followed is known as the Battle of Barfleur. In compliance with his orders, Tourville immediately attacked the Allies from windward, and closed up squadron for squadron. The French line of battle was as long as that of the Allies, but much thinner.

Initially, the Allies could gain no advantage. D'Amfreville held the Dutch in check. The *Soleil Royal* laid alongside the *Britannia*, showering her with shot. By 2 p.m., the *Britannia*'s neighbours came to her aid, and the *Soleil Royal* fought all three ships.

The battle lines of the opposing centres and rears gradually dissolved into a pell-mell. By 3 p.m., the *Soleil Royal* fought off five fire ships. The action came to a conclusion at 4 p.m., due to a thick fog and a dead calm. Up to this point the French had fought magnificently. Under cover of fog, the *Soleil Royal* disengaged. She was towed out of action. The *Britannia* attempted to tow after her, but without success in the shroud of fog.

Admiral Carter was killed.

By 5 p.m., with some breeze from the east and a clearing fog, the French line moved, in remarkable order, westwards. By 6 p.m., the up-Channel flood tide set in, and the French, who had anchored, were able to inflict considerable damage on those Allied ships which had not moored and hence passed by on the tide.

Both fleets anchored at nightfall and fighting ceased. The *Britannia* lost her foretopmast in a freshening breeze, having been badly damaged during the heat of the action.

On 20 May at 7 a.m., Tourville gathered forty-four ships together and continued to retire westwards, taking advantage of thick fog and the ebb tide. The remainder of his fleet were wildly scattered and reached Brest independently.

At 8 a.m., Russell sighted the French and ordered a chase. In the almost calm conditions, it was a slow affair. Tourville was obliged to change his flagship. During the night, twenty-one French ships under the command of Pannetier saved themselves by running through the dangerous Race of Alderney and reached St Malo. The remaining fifteen ships of the line were swept eastwards by the flood tide.

Early on 21 May, the *Soleil Royal, Admirable* of ninety guns, and *Triomphant* of seventy-four guns, went aground off Cherbourg. Tourville transferred his flag to the ninety-six gun *Ambitieux*. The *Sovereign* took a terrible mauling from the *Ambitieux*. The *Sovereign*'s gilded upper works were an enticing target for any bold, intrepid enemy intent on risking all to seek glory in the heat of action. Together with twelve other ships, Tourville went to La Hogue, where the ships were hauled close inshore.

The Battle of La Hogue, fought on 22–4 May 1692, was a continuance of Barfleur.

On 22 May the three ships off Cherbourg were destroyed by English fire ships. It fell to the *Sovereign*'s men to burn the famous *Soleil Royal*. The remainder of the French fled into St Malo.

Vice Admiral Rooke mounted a night attack with small boats on the French ships in the Bay of La Hogue. The French troops destined for the invasion of England assisted in the defence. The French cavalry rode down to the boats, but were pulled off their charges by the seamen's boathooks. Six French ships were burnt: *Terrible, Ambitieux, Magnifique, St Philippe, Merveilleux* and *Foudroyant*.

On the following day six more French ships were burnt by boarding parties: *Fier, Tonnant, Gaillard, Bourdon, St Louis* and *Fort*. All the transports and store ships were burnt. The French put up a gallant defence, but were completely defeated at the end of the six day operations. The French lost twelve ships of the line. Four more French vessels rounded Scotland before they reached the safety of France.

The Anglo-Dutch victory at La Hogue, following soon after their defeat at the Battle of Barfleur, was of decisive importance in the War of the English Succession. A British fleet had, once again, kept the sea. It was many years before the French could match the English upon the high seas.

Louis XIV made no further attempts at incursion. But the threat to England remained. Ships of the French navy were leased to privateers. Jean Bart was one such buccaneer. In this manner, great damage was done to the British trade.

On 10 September 1692, the *Sovereign*, together with the *Britannia, Victory* and the *London* of 1670, arrived in the Thames.

W. van de Velde the Elder lived in Sackville Street, London. He was interred in St James church, Piccadilly, on 16 December 1693. His son followed him to the same place of rest on 11 April 1707. The memorial tablet erected there by the Society for Nautical Research, on the initiative of Cecil King in 1929, is a tribute justly deserved by both great artists.

Admiral Russell commanded an English naval squadron in the western Mediterranean during the later part of the seventeenth century to protect English trade from the depravations of Barbary privateers.

During 1693–94, the *Sovereign* bore the flag of Rear-Admiral Aylmer of the Red Squadron. In April 1693, and during 1694, her Master was Edward Whitaker of the *Dover*. She was in good condition on 5 September 1693 while in company with other vessels at St Helens.

Joseph Allin, the Master Carpenter of the *Sovereign*, was appointed Second Assistant Master Carpenter at Portsmouth Royal Dockyard on 20 February 1694. He was promoted to First Assistant there on 14 June 1695. He was transferred to Woolwich in December 1700, and to Sheerness on promotion to Master Carpenter in October 1701. He was again transferred to Woolwich in February 1705, and to Deptford in the following November. He was at Deptford in 1715, when he was dismissed from the service.

By 21 July 1695, due to her un-seaworthy condition, the *Sovereign* was despatched home from Barcelona Road by Admiral Russell, together with the *St Andrew* of 1670, *Duke*, *Sandwich*, *St Michael*, *Grafton* and *Suffolk*.

She was laid up in the Medway throughout the winter. She was moored in Sovereign Reach, above Gillingham Fort. Here, she awaited the spring and extensive repairs and alterations at Chatham Royal Dockyard. Soon after the accession of William III in 1689, fears had developed concerning the possibility of Jacobite supporters' attempts to burn the royal dockyards and ships.

On 27 January 1696 she was burnt. She was in the sixtieth year of her age. Before help could be summoned from the adjacent dockyard, she was completely gutted. The Admiralty were prepared to pay for information which might lead to the detection of the culprit.

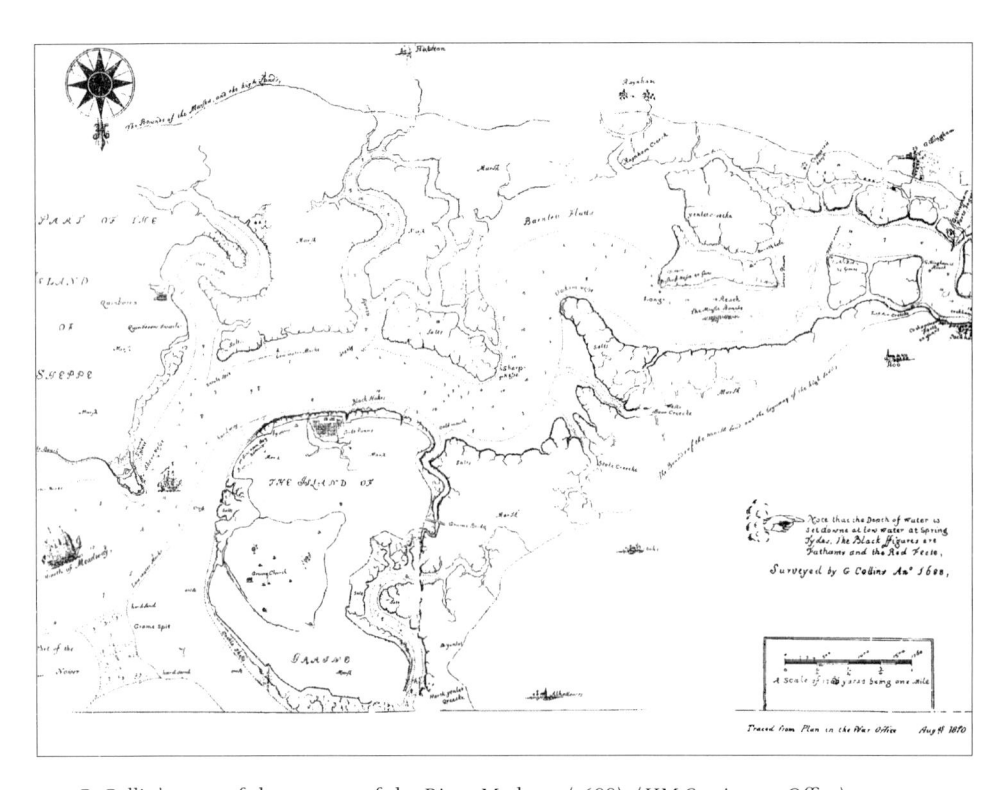

72. G. Collin's map of the estuary of the River Medway (1688). (*HM Stationery Office*)

Mary Poulden, a shipwright's wife living in the Dockyard, listened to those drinking in her house about the lack of care among the ships. The officers were seldom aboard the ships moored near her house. She reported her concern to Mr Taylor and Mr Martin, officials in Chatham Royal Dockyard, who rebuked her. She was the first person ashore to see the fire, and raised the alarm. She proved her claim. An Admiralty order dated 18 February 1696 provided a reward of £50 to be paid to her.

Sir Edward Gregory, returning from Gillingham, witnessed the conflagration.

The burning of the *Sovereign* was carefully investigated. Before an assembly of Lord Berkeley, Admiral of the Blue, as president, Sir Cloudesley Shovell, Vice Admiral of the Red, seventeen captains and nineteen officers, the crew of ship keepers was tried by Court Martial for the loss of the ship. The principal witness was a ship's boy aged fifteen years.

At 4 a.m. on the morning of 27 January 1696, the boy summoned the senior watch keeper, Thomas Couch, who was in his cabin on the middle gun deck, near to the entry port. Couch was a veteran who had served aboard the *Sovereign* for over seventeen years. The boy departed below to attend to the galley fire. Couch went up on deck to keep his watch. He left a lighted candle in his cabin. He returned after some minutes to light his pipe at the candle. He left the candle alight when he resumed the deck aloft.

Some fifteen minutes later the boy saw smoke billowing from the middle gun deck. He ran aft to investigate the cause. He found Couch's cabin on fire. He shouted for help. Two or three sleepy men arrived on the scene, but only one bucket could be found. They tossed a cask of drinking water over the flames, but failed to quench them.

The conflagration quickly spread to the spars and cordage stacked in the waist amidships. By 5 a.m., the vessel was like a roaring furnace, with flames erupting up into the dawn sky.

No warrant officer was aboard the *Sovereign* that night. The Boatswain, John Meacham, who was the senior, had been working all the previous day in Chatham Royal Dockyard. When he departed the Dockyard for the vessel, his boat stuck in the mud. He used this as an excuse for sleeping ashore. The purser, John Steventon, and the gunner, Richard Seale, had not returned from leave. The carpenter, Thomas Everden, was ashore sick, but had not taken the trouble to report his absence. Therefore, his post was abandoned. The acting armourer, who was not a warrant officer, but was next in seniority, was burnt to death in his berth before he could arise.

John Meacham cut the mooring ropes, thereby saving the *Britannia* from a similar fate. The duty boat, lying astern of the *Sovereign*, drifted away. The painter had burnt through. The meagre crew fought the fire unaided. Everyone in the dozen or so adjacent vessels, including the watch, were asleep. No alarm was raised for nearly an hour. The guard boats, ostensibly rowing up and down the Medway every hour from sunset to sunrise, were conspicuous by their absence. A four-oared galley, hastily despatched from the *Britannia* an hour after the outbreak, arrived on the scene and rescued the lives of the men aboard the *Sovereign*.

John Meacham and Thomas Everden were confined aboard the *St Andrew*. Thomas Couch was confined aboard the *Britannia*.

On 28 January, Sir Edward Gregory ordered men and firearms for the yacht *Squirrel* to ride by the *Sovereign* to prevent thieving. The fire was out. Some iron work was saved. Fortunately, the cables, sails and anchors were ashore.

The Court Martial on 4 February 1696 aboard the *St Michael* acquitted all but two. Couch was found guilty of neglect of duty. His conduct was in default of the twenty-seventh Article of War.

With a halter about his neck he was conveyed in a boat on board the hulk against Chatham Royal Dockyard next muster day. There, he received thirty-one lashes on his bare back. He was imprisoned for life. His pay was forfeited to the Chatham Chest. Thomas Everden was found guilty of neglect of duty. He was imprisoned for one year. All pay due to him passed to the Chatham Chest.

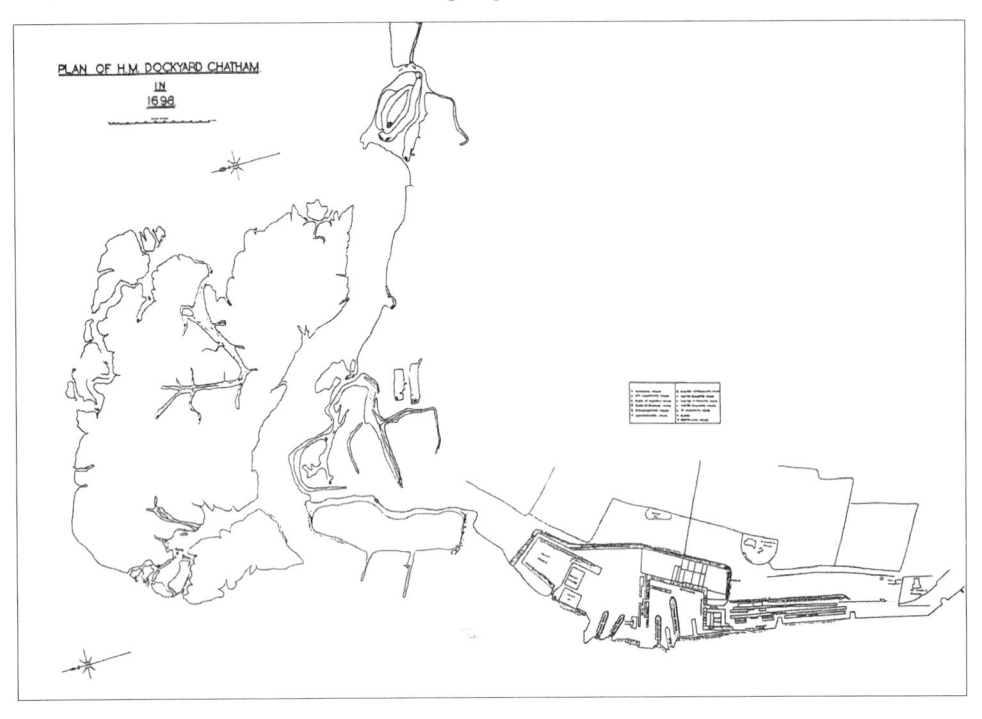

73. Plan of HM Dockyard at Chatham (1698). (*HM Stationery Office*)

On 8 April 1696, Sir Edward Gregory prepared to raise the wreck of the *Sovereign*, using the hulk at Gillingham. On 15 November 1697, Fisher Harding reported that she had been burnt down to the ballast. He could not assess the usefulness of her timbers until she had been taken to pieces. Fisher Harding was promoted to Master Shipwright at Deptford in November 1697.

The Navy Board's report, dated 10 December 1697, attributed the cause to carelessness rather than sabotage. The *Sovereign* was accidentally burnt through the carelessness of a feeble old boatswain, her temporary keeper, who left the lighted end of a candle on a shelf in his cabin. It was a very undignified and ignominious end to such a great and noble ship.

In 1697 peace was signed between the English and French at Rijswijk. Robert Lee, who had supervised the rebuilding of the *Sovereign* at Chatham Royal Dockyard in 1684–85 died on 1 April 1698 and was interred at St Mary's, Chatham. In 1701 King James II died. The threat of French invasion disappeared.

Thomas Everden petitioned the crown on 25 January 1700 for employment as a carpenter. In this capacity he had served for twenty-four years in several of his Majesty's ships. His last vessel had been the *Sovereign of the Seas*.

By order of the Navy Board, she was scrapped. Some of her material parts, including the keel and lower timbers, were allegedly salvaged for use in building at Woolwich Royal Dockyard the *Royal Sovereign* of 1701, a first rate of 112 guns. This work was entrusted to Fisher Harding, who was transferred from Deptford to Woolwich specifically for the purpose. Harding's duties at Deptford were carried out by Samuel Miller, the Master Shipwright of Woolwich, during his absence. After some three years and eight months, she was launched on 25 July 1701. When finished, Fisher Harding requested, and was given, a gift of plate such as was normally reserved for the builders of new ships. Fisher Harding remained at Deptford until his death in 1705.

This *Royal Sovereign* was the flagship of Sir George Rooke when he commanded the unsuccessful Anglo-Dutch fleet at Cadiz in 1702. She was rebuilt in 1728 and repaired in

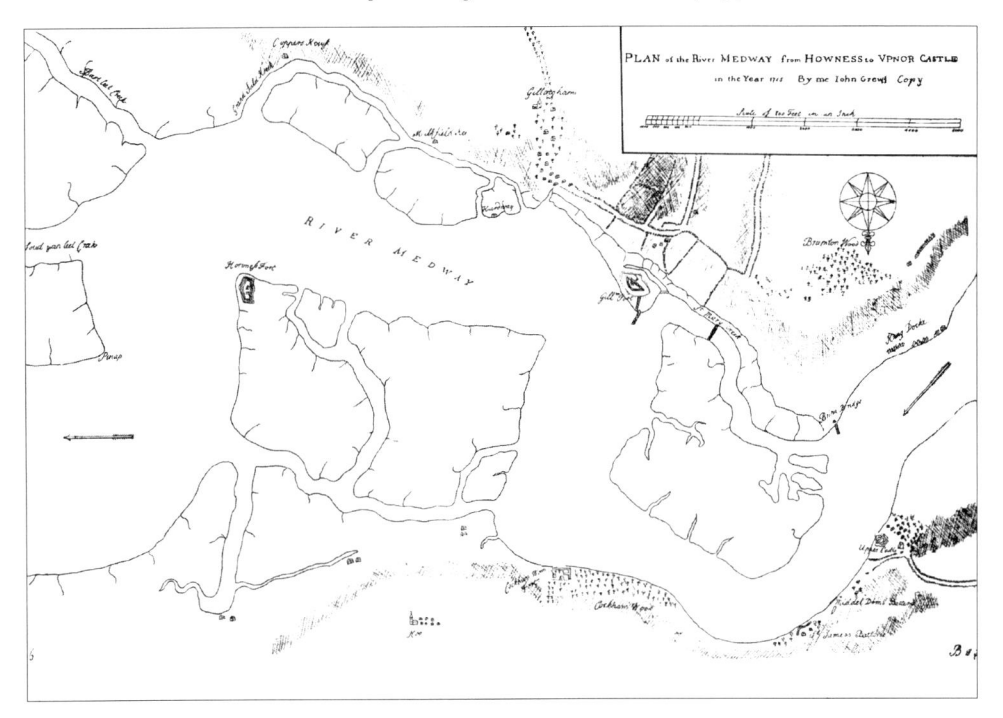

74. J. Grewl's map of the River Medway from Howness to Upnor Castle (1715). (*HM Stationery Office*)

1738. By 1763 she required further major repairs. There was a proposal to cut her down to a eighty-four gun ship. After a survey in dock, it was decided to scrap her. She was broken up in 1768 at Portsmouth Royal Dockyard.

Our historical maritime heritage is personified in the remains of several fine vessels. The remains of the hull of the *Mary Rose* are preserved in No. 3 dry dock workshop in the Naval Base at Portsmouth Royal Dockyard, only a few hundred yards from where she was built in 1509. Over 1,000 artefacts recovered from the wreck are displayed in the *Mary Rose* Exhibition in the same dockyard.

In 1961 the sixty-four gun *Vasa* of 1627 was raised from the mud where she capsized and sank in the Stockholm archipelago in 1628, and preserved in a specially designed museum, Vasamuseet, at Stockholm inaugurated in 1990. Together with artefacts salvaged from her hull, she is displayed to the public. Like the *Mary Rose*, a wax polymer, polyethylene glycol, in a single grade of molecular weight, was used to impregnate the warship's timbers to effect conservation.

The lower part of the hull of the third rate *Anne* survives in the mud on the foreshore at Pett Level, between Hastings and Rye, at position 50° 53/N., 42/E. This site is a designed Historic Wreck under the Protection of Wrecks Act, 1973. The *Anne* is the only surviving substantial part of a warship of our Restoration Navy still in existence. She awaits conservation, restoration and preservation. There are some artifacts and a visual display in the Shipwreck & Coastal Heritage Centre, Hastings.

The *Sovereign of the Seas* was the first great ship to be built in England. It was not until 1759–65, when the *Victory* was built in No. 2 dry dock at Chatham Royal Dockyard, that a warship emerged with greater size, tonnage and fame. The *Sovereign* demonstrated a vital stage in the development of the King's wooden capital ship, which was to manifest its culmination in the *Victory*.

Between 1922–8, the *Victory* was restored, as far as was possible, to the condition in which she fought at Trafalgar on 21 October 1805. Since 1922 she rests serenely and dignified, cradled permanently in the oldest dry dock in the world, viz. No 2. dry dock, the centrepiece of the Naval Heritage Area in the Naval Base at Portsmouth Royal Dockyard, where she is visited daily by throngs of visitors.

Unlike these noble warships, there is no trace of Phineas Pett's workmanship known to have survived. The *Sovereign of the Seas,* an enigma in her time, passed through the twilight zone of legend to immortality in the dim mists of antiquity.

APPENDIX 1

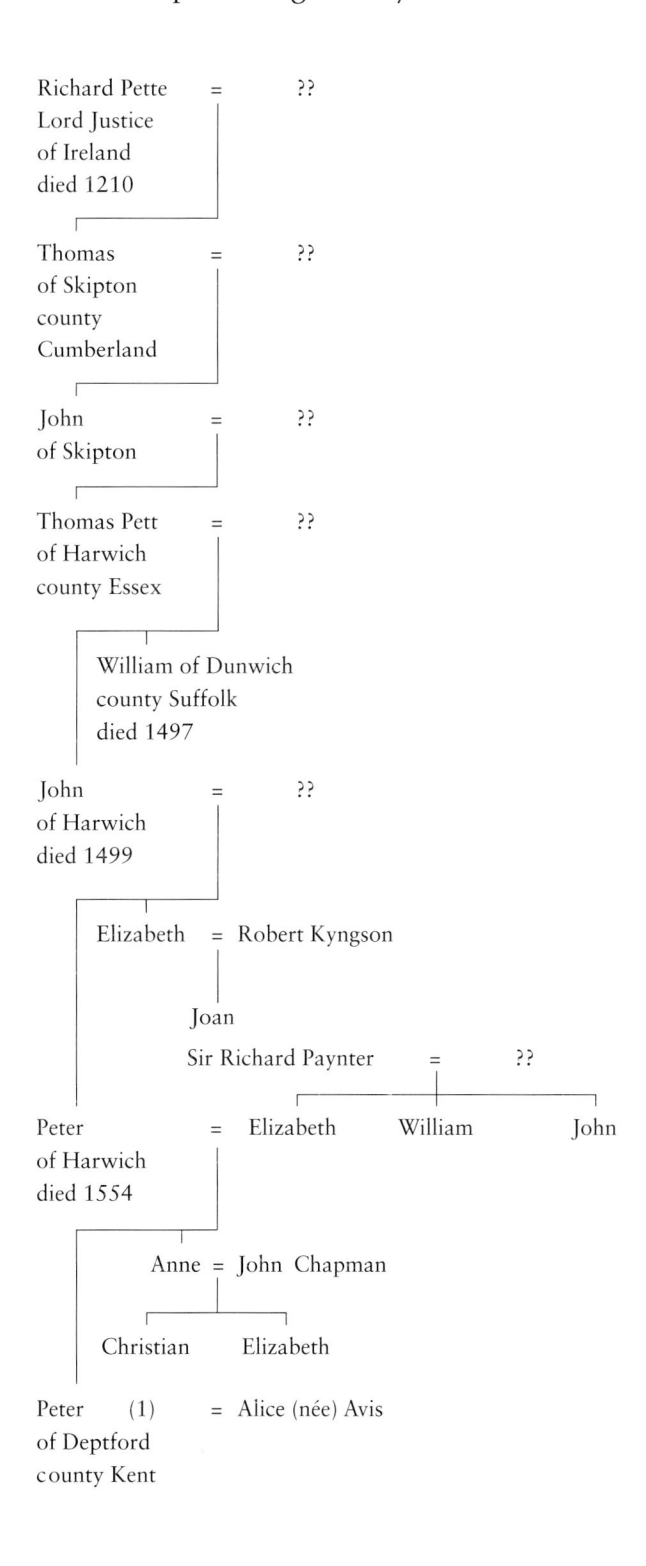

The Shipbuilding Family of Pett

```
Richard Pette      =    ??
Lord Justice
of Ireland
died 1210
    |
Thomas             =    ??
of Skipton
county
Cumberland
    |
John               =    ??
of Skipton
    |
Thomas Pett        =    ??
of Harwich
county Essex
    |
    William of Dunwich
    county Suffolk
    died 1497
    |
John               =    ??
of Harwich
died 1499
    |
    Elizabeth    =   Robert Kyngson
                      |
                     Joan
                     Sir Richard Paynter     =    ??
                                             |
Peter         =   Elizabeth      William          John
of Harwich
died 1554
    |
         Anne  =  John Chapman
                 |
         Christian    Elizabeth
    |
Peter     (1)      =   Alice (née) Avis
of Deptford
county Kent
```

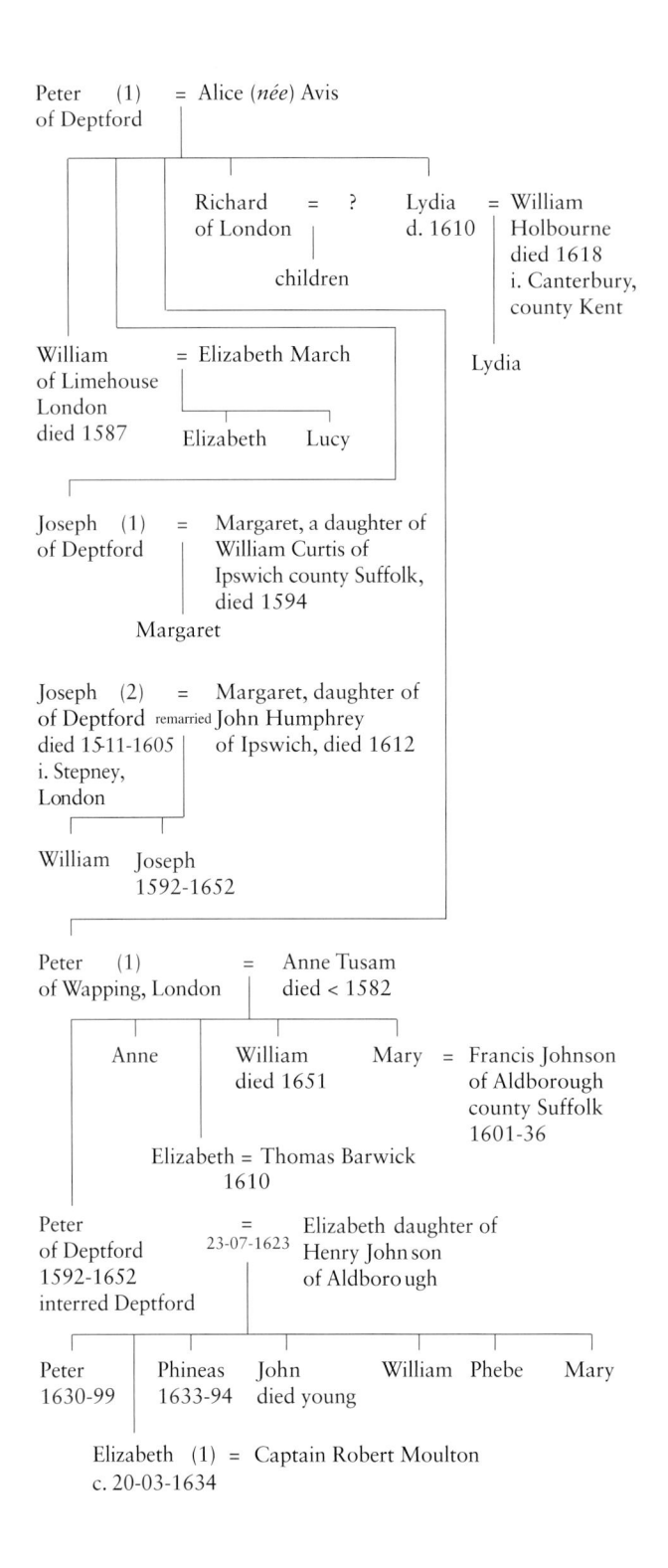

The Shipbuilding Family of Pett (cont.)

```
Peter        (1)      = Alice (née) Avis
of Deptford
 │
 ├─────────────────────┬──────────────┬──────────────────┐
 │                Richard    =  ?     Lydia    =  William
 │                of London           d. 1610    Holbourne
 │                    │                          died 1618
 │                children                       i. Canterbury,
 │                                               county Kent
 │
William       = Elizabeth March              Lydia
of Limehouse        │
London          ┌───┴────┐
died 1587    Elizabeth  Lucy

Joseph    (1)  =  Margaret, a daughter of
of Deptford       William Curtis of
                  Ipswich county Suffolk,
                  died 1594
        │
     Margaret

Joseph    (2)         =  Margaret, daughter of
of Deptford  remarried   John Humphrey
died 15-11-1605          of Ipswich, died 1612
i. Stepney,
London
    │
 ┌──┴────┐
William  Joseph
         1592-1652

Peter       (1)            =  Anne Tusam
of Wapping, London            died < 1582
    │
 ┌──┴────┬─────────┬──────────────────────┐
 Anne   William   Mary  =  Francis Johnson
        died 1651          of Aldborough
                           county Suffolk
                           1601-36
         │
    Elizabeth = Thomas Barwick
                  1610

Peter                =        Elizabeth daughter of
of Deptford      23-07-1623   Henry Johnson
1592-1652                     of Aldborough
interred Deptford
    │
 ┌──┬──────┬──────┬────────┬──────┬──────┐
Peter Phineas John    William Phebe Mary
1630-99 1633-94 died young

     Elizabeth  (1)  = Captain Robert Moulton
     c. 20-03-1634
```

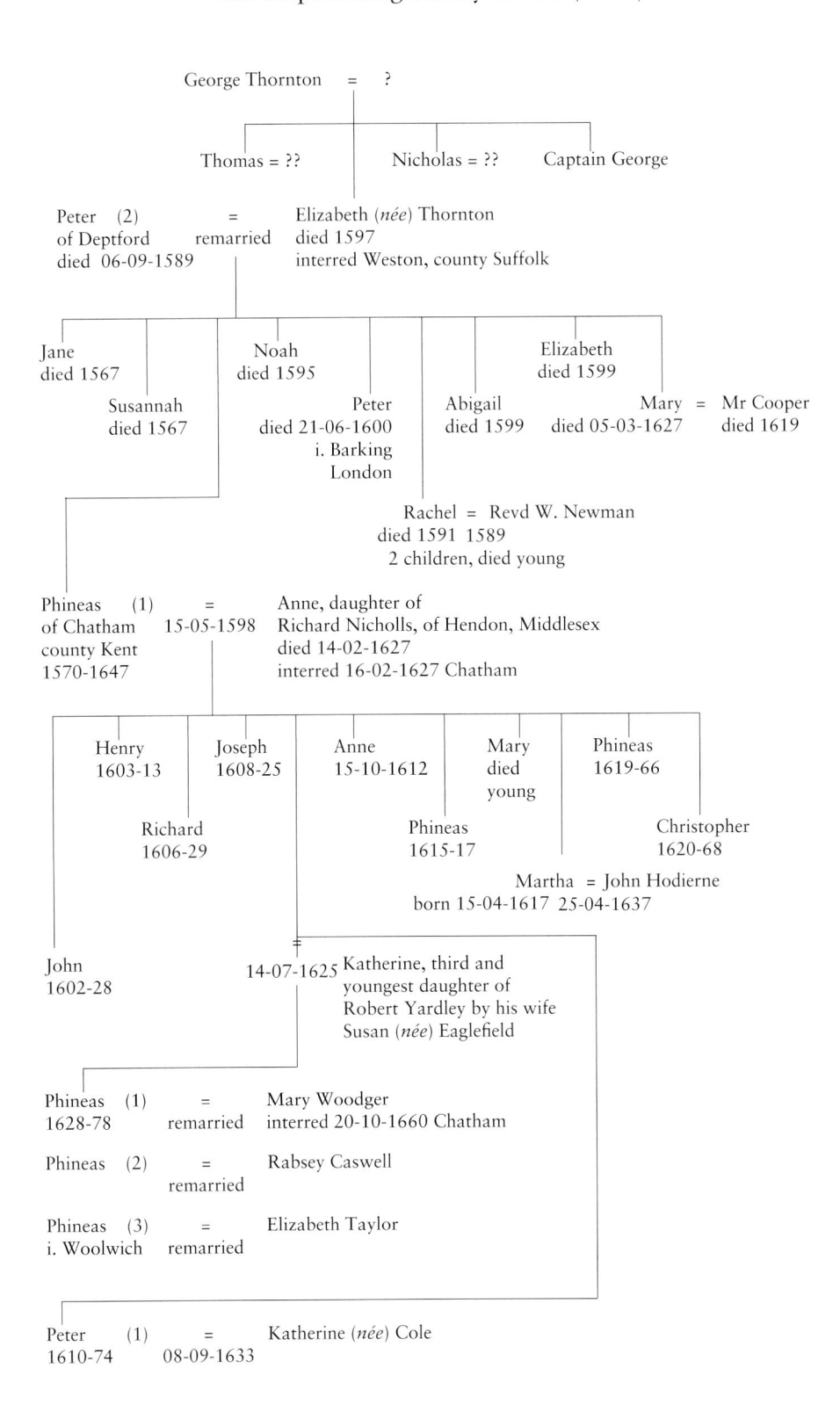

The Shipbuilding Family of Pett (cont.)

```
                    George Thornton  =  ?
                              |
        ┌─────────────────────┼─────────────────────┐
     Thomas = ??          Nicholas = ??      Captain George

Peter    (2)           =        Elizabeth (née) Thornton
of Deptford        remarried    died 1597
died 06-09-1589                 interred Weston, county Suffolk

   ┌──────────┬──────────────┬──────────┬──────────────┬──────────────────┐
  Jane                      Noah                    Elizabeth
  died 1567                 died 1595               died 1599
      |                         |                       |
  Susannah                   Peter        Abigail      Mary    =  Mr Cooper
  died 1567              died 21-06-1600  died 1599  died 05-03-1627  died 1619
                         i. Barking
                         London
                              |
                       Rachel  =  Revd W. Newman
                       died 1591    1589
                       2 children, died young

Phineas     (1)       =       Anne, daughter of
of Chatham       15-05-1598   Richard Nicholls, of Hendon, Middlesex
county Kent                   died 14-02-1627
1570-1647                     interred 16-02-1627 Chatham

      ┌─────────┬──────────┬──────────┬──────────┬──────────┐
    Henry     Joseph     Anne       Mary      Phineas
    1603-13   1608-25   15-10-1612  died       1619-66
                                    young
              Richard              Phineas              Christopher
              1606-29              1615-17              1620-68
                                          |
                                  Martha  =  John Hodierne
                            born 15-04-1617   25-04-1637

John             14-07-1625  Katherine, third and
1602-28                      youngest daughter of
                             Robert Yardley by his wife
                             Susan (née) Eaglefield

Phineas    (1)        =       Mary Woodger
1628-78           remarried   interred 20-10-1660 Chatham

Phineas    (2)        =       Rabsey Caswell
                  remarried

Phineas    (3)        =       Elizabeth Taylor
i. Woolwich       remarried

Peter      (1)        =       Katherine (née) Cole
1610-74         08-09-1633
```

The Shipbuilding Family of Pett (cont.)

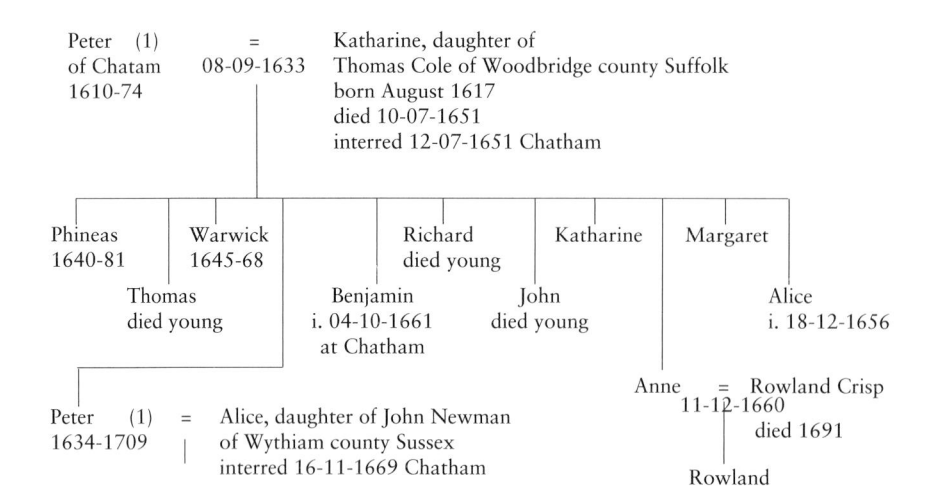

| Peter (1) of Chatam 1610-74 | = 08-09-1633 | Katharine, daughter of Thomas Cole of Woodbridge county Suffolk born August 1617 died 10-07-1651 interred 12-07-1651 Chatham |

Children:
- **Phineas** 1640-81
  - Peter (1) 1634-1709 = Alice, daughter of John Newman of Wythiam county Sussex interred 16-11-1669 Chatham
- **Warwick** 1645-68
  - Thomas died young
- **Richard** died young
  - Benjamin i. 04-10-1661 at Chatham
  - John died young
- **Katharine**
- **Margaret**
  - Alice i. 18-12-1656
    - Anne = Rowland Crisp 11-12-1660 died 1691
    - Rowland

After the death of his wife Anne, on 14 February 1627, Phineas followed the example set by his father Peter, and remarried:

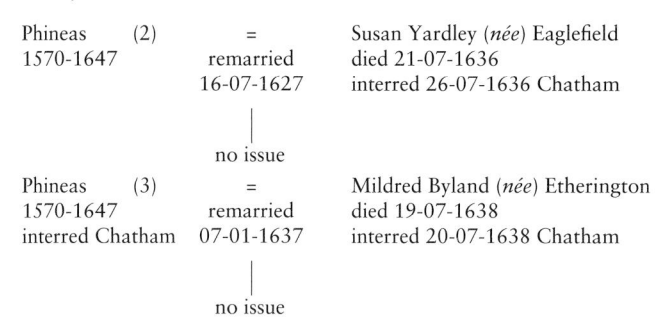

| Phineas (2) 1570-1647 | = remarried 16-07-1627 | Susan Yardley (*née*) Eaglefield died 21-07-1636 interred 26-07-1636 Chatham |

no issue

| Phineas (3) 1570-1647 interred Chatham | = remarried 07-01-1637 | Mildred Byland (*née*) Etherington died 19-07-1638 interred 20-07-1638 Chatham |

no issue

After the death of his wife Katharine, on 10 July 1651, Peter followed the example set by his father Phineas, and remarried:

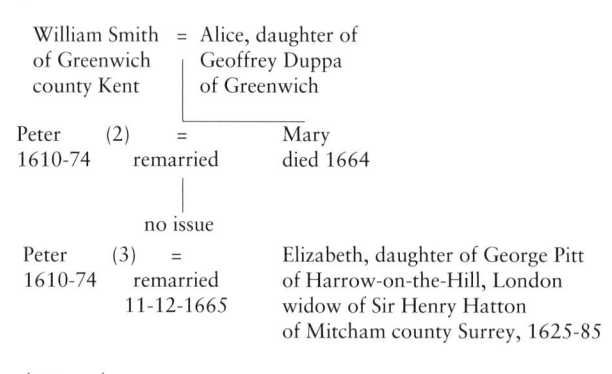

William Smith of Greenwich county Kent = Alice, daughter of Geoffrey Duppa of Greenwich

| Peter (2) 1610-74 | = remarried | Mary died 1664 |

no issue

| Peter (3) 1610-74 | = remarried 11-12-1665 | Elizabeth, daughter of George Pitt of Harrow-on-the-Hill, London widow of Sir Henry Hatton of Mitcham county Surrey, 1625-85 |

NOTES:
c. = christened
d. = died
i. = interred

After: J. H. Sephton, 'The Shipbuilding Family of Pett', *Chatham Dockyard Historical Society Research Paper 2002 No. 24*.

APPENDIX 2

Vessels Built or Rebuilt by Phineas Pett

VESSEL	YEAR BUILT	kfp feet	bm feet	bm inch	h4 feet	h4 inch	BURDEN	GROSS TONNAGE	G
Moon	1602	50	17	0	6	6	55	74	13
Answer	1603–04	65	26	0	12	2	205	274	19
Disdain	1604	25	12	0					
Resistance	1604	140							
Anne Royal	1607–08	107	37	10	15	4	621	828	44
Prince Royal	1608–10	115	43	0	18	0	890	1187	55
Phoenix	1612–13	72	24	0	10	8	185	246	20
Defiance	1613–15	104	36	7	17	3	656	875	38
Merhonour	1613–15	112	38	7	16	5	709	946	40
Destiny (*Convertine*)	1616	96	32	4	15	0	466	621	34
Pinnace	1616	40							
Mercury	1626	300							
Spy	1626	200							
Henrietta	1626–7	52	15	0	6	6	51	68	6
Maria	1626–7	52	15	0	6	6	51	68	6
Charles	1632–3	105	35	7	16	3	607	810	44
Greyhound	1636	60	20	3	7	9	94	126	12
Roebuck	1636	7	18	1	6	7	68	90	10
Sovereign	1635–7	127	46	6	19	4	1141	1522	102

NOTES:

The *Moon*, *Answer*, *Anne Royal*, *Defiance* and *Merhonour* were rebuilds.
The *Moon*, *Answer*, *Disdain*, *Phoenix*, *Henrietta* and *Maria* were built at Chatham Royal Dockyard.
The *Resistance* was built at David Duck's private yard at Gillingham.
The *Anne Royal*, *Prince Royal*, *Defiance*, *Merhonour*, *Destiny*, *Pinnace*, *Charles*, *Greyhound*, *Roebuck* and *Sovereign* were built at Woolwich Royal Dockyard.
The *Mercury* and *Spy* were built at Peter Pett's private yard at Ratcliffe.
The values of tons burden and tons and tonnage were verified using equations (1) & (2) in Chapter 4.

After: R. C. Anderson, 'List of English Men-of-War 1509–1649', *SNR* No.7, 1959.
W. Laird Clowes, *The Royal Navy – A History from the Earliest Times to the Present* Vol. 2, 1996, pp. 10–11.
W. G. Perrin, 'The Autobiography of Phineas Pett', *NRS* 51, 1918, p. 217.

APPENDIX 3

Vessels Built for Charles I

VESSEL	YEAR BUILT	kfp feet	bm feet	inch	h4 feet	inch	d1 feet	inch	BURDEN	GROSS TONNAGE	GUNS	MEN (HARBOUR)	MEN (SEA)
Henrietta	1626–7	52	15	0	6	6			51	68	6	3	25
Maria	1626–7	52	15	0	6	6			51	68	6	3	25
8 Whelps	1627–8	62	25	0	9	0			139	186	12-16	3	60-70
Third Whelp	1627–8	62	25	0	8	2			127	169	12-16	3	60-70
Eighth Whelp	1627–8	62	25	0	7	10			121	162	16	3	60-70
Charles	1632–3	105	35	7	16	3			607	810	44	9	250
Henrietta Maria	1632–3	106	35	9	15	8			594	792	42	9	250
James	1633–4	110	36	10	16	2			656	875	48	9	260
Unicorn	1633–4	107	35	8	15	1			575	767	46	9	250
Leopard	1634–5	95	33	0	12	4	12	9	387	516	34	7	170
Swallow	1634	96	32	2	11	7	12	3	358	478	34	6	150
Greyhound	1636	60	20	3	7	9			94	126	12	3	60
Roebuck	1636	57	18	1	6	7			68	90	10	3	30
Expedition	1636–7	90	26	0	9	8			226	301	30		
Providence	1636–7	90	26	0	9	9			228	304	30		
Sovereign	1635–7	127	46	6	19	4			1,141	1,522	102	60	815

NOTE:
The *Charles, Unicorn, Leopard, Greyhound, Roebuck* and *Sovereign* were built at Woolwich Royal Dockyard.
The *Henrietta Maria, James* and *Swallow* were built at Deptford Royal Dockyard.
The *Henrietta* and *Maria* were built at Chatham Royal Dockyard.

kfp = Length of keel along the rabbet between false posts, viz. the 'touch'
bm = Beam moulded, to inside of planking, at dead-flat ⊖
h4 = Depth in hold, extreme beam, to upper edge of keel at ⊖
d1 = Actual draught, water line to bottom of keel

The values of tons burden and tons and tonnage were verified using equations (1) & (2) in Chapter 4.

After: R. C. Anderson, 'List of English Men-of-War 1509–1649', *SNR* No.7, 1959.
W. Laird Clowes, *The Royal Navy – A History from the Earliest Times to the Present* Vol. 2, 1996 pp. 10–11.
W. G. Perrin, 'The Autobiography of Phineas Pett', *NRS* 51, 1918 p. 217.

APPENDIX 4

Vessels Built for Parliament

VESSEL	YEAR BUILT	kfp feet	bm feet inch	h4 feet inch	BURDEN	GROSS TONNAGE	GUNS
Adventure	1646	94	27 9	14 8	382	510	32
Assurance	1646	89	26 10	14 4	342	456	32
Constant Warwick	1644–46	85	26 5	14 0	315	420	26
Nonsuch	1646	98	28 4	14 2	389	518	34
Dragon	1647	96	28 6	15 2	414	556	32
Elizabeth	1647	101.5	29 8	15 8	471	628	32
Phoenix	1647	96	28 6	15 3	417	556	32
Tiger	1647	99	29 4	15 8	455	608	32

NOTES:

The *Adventure* and *Phoenix* were built at Woolwich Royal Dockyard.
The *Assurance, Nonsuch, Elizabeth* and *Tiger* were built at Deptford Royal Dockyard.
The *Dragon* was built at Chatham Royal Dockyard.
The *Constant Warwick* was built at Peter Pett's private yard at Ratcliffe.

kfp = Length of keel along the rabbet between false posts, viz. the 'touch'
bm = Beam moulded, to inside of planking, at dead-flat Θ
h4 = Depth in hold, extreme beam, to upper edge of keel at Θ

The values of tons burden and tons and tonnage were verified using equations (1) & (2) in Chapter 4.
This table does not include prizes taken in battle.

After: R. C. Anderson, 'List of English Men-of-War 1509–1649', *SNR* No. 7, 1959.
W. Laird Clowes, *The Royal Navy – A History from the Earliest Times to the Present* Vol. 2, 1996 pp. 10–11.

APPENDIX 5

Main Dimensions of the *Prince Royal* (1632)

DIMENSION	SYMBOL	VALUE feet	in
Length of keel between false posts, 'touch'	kfp	115	0
Length of keel, heel to fore-foot, 'tread'	kt	116	0
Length of keel, harping rule	khr	125	9
Length along lower gun deck	gd	159	4
Length between perpendiculars	pp	152	2
Beam moulded, to inside of planking at Θ	bm	43	0
Beam extreme, excluding wales at Θ	bx	45	0
Depth in hold, upper floor of lower gun deck, to upper floor of ceiling at Θ	h1	18	0
Depth in hold, under floor of lower gun deck, to upper floor of ceiling at Θ	h2	17	0
Depth in hold, extreme beam, to upper floor of ceiling at Θ	h3	16	3
Mean beam within ceiling at half of this depth	bs	36	0
Depth in hold, extreme beam to upper edge of keel at Θ	h4	18	0
Draught in water, extreme beam, to bottom of keel at Θ	d3	18	6
Tons burden [equation (1) in Chapter 4]		890	
Gross tonnage [equation (2) in Chapter 4]		1,187	

After: R. C. Anderson, 'The *Prince Royal* and other Ships of James I', *MM* 3, 1913 No. 3, pp. 272–5; 3, 1913 No. 4, 305–7; 3, 1913 No. 4, pp. 341–2.
W. Salisbury, 'A Draught of a Jacobean Three Decker. The *Prince Royal*?' *MM* 47, 1961 No. 3, pp. 170–7.

APPENDIX 6

Main Dimensions of *La Couronne* (1635)

DIMENSION	SYMBOL	VALUE feet	in
Length of the keel, between false posts, 'touch'	kfp	128	0
Length of the keel, from heel to fore-foot, 'tread'	kt	130	0
Rake of stem and stern posts		35	0
Rake of beak		45	0
Length along lower gun deck	gd	165	0
Length between perpendiculars	pp	158	0
Length overall	oa	200	0
Beam moulded, to inside of planking at Θ	bm	44	0
Beam extreme excluding wales at Θ	bx	46	0
Height, from keel to top of taffrail		75	0
Depth in hold, upper floor of lower gun deck to upper floor of ceiling at Θ	h1	17	8
Depth in hold, under floor of lower gun deck to upper floor of ceiling at Θ	h2	17	0
Depth in hold, extreme beam, to upper floor of ceiling at Θ	h3	16	0
Depth in hold, extreme beam, to upper edge of keel at Θ	h4	17	0
Actual draught, waterline to bottom of keel	d1	17	6
Tons burden [equation (1) in Chapter 4]		957	
Gross tonnage [equation (2) in Chapter 4]		1,276	

After: C. H. Hancock, *La Couronne, A French Warship of the Seventeenth Century – A Survey of Ancient and Modern Accounts of This Ship*, The Mariner`s Museum – Newport News, Virginia, 1973.

APPENDIX 7

Proposed Dimensions of the *Sovereign of the Seas* (1635)

DIMENSION	SYMBOL	VALUE feet in
INITIAL PROPOSAL (7 April 1635)		
Length of keel between false posts, 'touch'	kfp	127 0
Beam moulded, to inside of planking at Θ	bm	46 2
Depth in hold, extreme beam, to upper edge of keel at Θ	h4	18 9
Draught in water, extreme beam, to bottom of keel at Θ	d3	21 3
Designed draught, waterline to bottom of keel	d1	18 9
Rake of stem		38 0
Rake of sternpost		8 0
Gun ports of the lower gun deck, square		2 8
Gun ports of the middle gun deck, square		2 6
Gun ports of the upper gun deck, round or square		2 4
Gross tonnage, by the depth in hold		1,466
Gross tonnage, (depth in hold substituted by the draught in water)		1,661
Gross tonnage, by the mean breadth		1,836
FINAL PROPOSAL (17 April 1635)		
Length of keel between false posts, 'touch'	kfp	126 0
Beam moulded, to inside of planking at Θ	bm	46 6
Depth in hold, under side of lower gun deck, to upper floor of ceiling at Θ	h2	17 0
Depth in hold, extreme beam, to upper floor of ceiling at Θ	h3	20 0
Depth in hold, extreme beam, to upper edge of keel at Θ	h4	19 4
Designed draught, waterline to bottom of keel	d1	19 6
Draught in water, extreme beam, to bottom of keel at Θ	d3	21 6
Height between decks, plank to plank		7 6
Height of ports above waterline		5 0
Height of ports above the deck		2 0
Rake of stem		37 6
Rake of sternpost		9 0
Gross tonnage, by the old rule		1,522
Gross tonnage, by the new rule		1,884

After: W. G. Perrin, 'The Autobiography of Phineas Pett', *NRS* 51, 1918, pp. xci-xciv.

APPENDIX 8

Main Dimensions of the *Sovereign of the Seas* (1637)

DIMENSION	SYMBOL	VALUE feet	in
Length of keel between false posts, 'touch'	kfp	127	0
Length of keel, heel to fore-foot, 'tread'	kt	128	0
Length of keel, harping rule	khr	131	0
Length along lower gun deck	gd	167	9
Length between perpendiculars	pp	159	10
Length along deck from fore side of stem to after side of sternpost	ld	159	10
Length of hull along waterline, rabbet to rabbet	wl	166	11
Length overall, forward edge of prow to after edge of stern	oa	232	0
Beam moulded, to inside of planking at Θ	bm	46	6
Beam extreme, excluding wales at Θ	bx	48	0
Depth in hold, upper floor of lower gun deck, to upper floor of ceiling at Θ	h_1	20	2
Depth in hold, under floor of lower gun deck, to upper floor of ceiling at Θ	h_2	19	2
Depth in hold, extreme beam, to upper floor of ceiling at Θ	h_3	17	2
Mean beam within ceiling at half of this depth	bs	42	2
Depth in hold, extreme beam, to upper edge of keel at Θ	h_4	19	4
Actual draught, waterline to bottom of keel	d_1	22	11
Draught in water, waterline to rabbet	d_2	20	8
Draught in water, extreme beam, to bottom of keel at Θ	d_3	21	1
Height of lower gun deck ports above water, at Θ, designed		4	6
Height of lower gun deck ports above water, at Θ, actual		4	0
Height overall, bottom of keel, top of lantern		76	0
Tons burden [verified by equation (1) in Chapter 4]		1,141	
Gross tonnage [verified by equation (2) in Chapter 4]		1,522	

After: J. Charnock, *An History of Marine Architecture* Vol. 2, 1801, pp. 283–4.
G. S. Laird Clowes & E. W. White, *Catalogue of Exhibits with Descriptive Notes*, Part 2, 1952, p. 27.
State Papers, Domestic Series, 22 May 1637 357, 39 p. 142.
State Papers, Domestic Series, 13 June 1637 361, 71.

APPENDIX 9

The Charge in Materials and Workmanship in Building and Launching the *Sovereign of the Seas* (9 January 1638)

The charge was for	£41,642	17s	11d
which included:			
Timber, planks & treenails	£17,548	12s	5d
Deal boards, pitch, tar, rosin & sulphur	£2,216	4s	2d
Iron work about the hull & masts	£2,881	7s	0d
Painting & carving	£6,691	0s	0d
Wages to artisans	£8,554	18s	8d
Hire of farm horses	£149	6s	2d
Travelling expenses	£886	0s	0d
Cleaning the dock	£115	0s	0d
Cordage & materials for the launching	£2,600	9s	6d
We obtain a total of:	£41,642	17s	11d

From this may reasonably be deducted the following register of items, also included in the Certificate of Charge:

Surplus timber & materials in stock	£5,023	12s	8d
Timber & treenails sent to Chatham	£712	10s	0d
Repairs to the *Triumph* at Deptford	£50	10s	0d
Repairs to the *Ann Royal* at Blackwall	£10	4s	8d
Repairs to the ropeyard	£59	11s	6d
Various repairs to the dockyard	£1,064	12s	9d
Building the *Greyhound* & *Roebuck*	£810	0s	0d
Repairs to the *Greyhound*	£65	11s	0d
To produce a total of:	£7,796	12s	7d
From the total of:	£41,642	17s	11d
May be deducted the sum of:	£7,796	12s	7d
To produce a charge of:	£33,846	5s	4d

The actual charge for building and launching was:

	£33,846	5s	4d
From this may reasonably be deducted:			
Cordage & materials for the launching	£2,600	9s	6d
The charge for building the hull:	£31,245	15s	10d

After: J. Bruce, 'Calendar of State Papers, Dom. Ser., of the reign of Charles I 1637, Preserved in HM Public Record Office' 378, 1868, 9 January 1638, No. 32, p. 146.

APPENDIX 10

An Abstract of First Rates from a List (1651)

Vessel		*Triumph*		*Sovereign*		*Resolution*	
Year Built		1623		1637		1641	
Dockyard		Deptford		Woolwich		Woolwich	
		feet	inch	feet	inch	feet	inch
Length of keel between false posts, 'touch'	kfp	110	0	127	0	115	0
Beam moulded, to inside of planking at Θ	bm	36	6	46	6	43	0
Depth in hold, extreme beam, to upper edge of keel at Θ	h4	14	6	19	4	18	0
Draught in water, extreme beam, to bottom of keel at Θ	d3	21	1	18	6		
Tons burden		585		1,141		976	
Men		300		600		500	
Guns		60		100		85	

NOTES:

However, to produce the value of tons burden as recorded in this List, the following value for beam would need to be substituted in equation (1):

Triumph: bm = 36 feet 8 inches

The *Triumph* was built at Deptford as a second rate in 1623. Originally, she was armed with forty-four guns. She was sold in 1688.

The value of 1,141 tons burden for the *Sovereign* was verified using equation (1) in Chapter 4.

These values for the *Resolution* produce 890 tons burden using equation (1) in Chapter 4. It may be coincidence, but if we substitute the values for the *Resolution*, and d3 at 18 feet 6 inches in equation (3), the product is 973.

The *Prince Royal* of 1610 was rebuilt at Woolwich in 1638–41 by Peter Pett. She was rebuilt again in 1652–53. She was known as *Resolution* between 1650 and 1660. She was rebuilt in 1660–63. She was burnt in action against the Dutch 3 June 1666.

After: J. Charnock, *An History of Marine Architecture* Vol. 2, 1801 p. 377.

APPENDIX 11

An Abstract of First Rates from Dering's List (1660)

Vessel		Royal Sovereign		Resolution		Naseby	
Year Built		1637		1641		1655	
Dockyard		Woolwich		Woolwich		Woolwich	
		feet	inch	feet	inch	feet	inch
Length of keel between false posts, 'touch'	kfp	127	0	125	0	131	0
Beam moulded, to inside of planking at Θ	bm	47	0	45	0	42	0
Depth in hold, under floor of lower gun deck, to upper floor of ceiling at Θ	h2	19	0	18	0	18	0
Actual draught, waterline to bottom of keel	d1	21	0	20	0	21	0
Tons burden		1,554		1,295		1,229	
Gross tonnage		2,072		1,726		1,638	
Men		600		500		500	
Guns		100		80		80	

NOTES:

When Dering's dimensions for the *Royal Sovereign* are substituted in equation (8) in Chapter 4, using a divisor of 90 instead of 94, then his tonnage value of 1554 can be verified.

The value of 1295 tons burden for the *Resolution* was verified on a beam of 44 feet 2 inches, using equation (8).

The value of 1229 tons burden for the *Naseby* was verified using equation (8). The *Naseby* of 1655 was re-named *Royal Charles* after 1660. She was captured by the Dutch in the action in the Medway June 1667.

For gross tonnage, one third of the value of tons burden is added, as in equation (2) in Chapter 4.

After: C. S. Perceval, 'On a List (Dering's) of the Royal Navy in 1660', *Arch.* 48, 1885, pp. 167–84.

APPENDIX 12

An Abstract of First Rates from Deane's List (1670)

Vessel		*Sovereign*		*Royal James*		*Charles*		*St Andrew*		*Royal Prince*	
Year Built		1637		1658		1668		1670		1670	
Dockyard		Woolwich		Woolwich		Deptford		Woolwich		Chatham	
		feet	inch	feet	inch	feet	inch	feet	inch	feet	inch
Length of keel between alse posts, 'touch'	kfp	127	0	122	0	128	0	129	0	131	0
Extreme beam, excluding wales at Θ	bx	47	0	42	0	42	6	43	6	44	10
Depth in hold, under floor of lower gun deck, to upper floor of ceiling at Θ	h2	19	0	18	0	18	6	18	8	19	0
Actual draught, waterline to bottom of keel	d1	22	4	21	0	21	0	21	0	20	0
Tons burden		1,492		1,121		1,229		1,298		1,403	
Gross tonnage		1,989		1,480		1,638		1,730		1,870	
Men		800		500		600		600		800	
Guns		100		84		96		96		104	

NOTES:

The value of tons burden was verified using equation (8,) and tons and tonnage from equation (2) in Chapter 4.

The values as listed for the *Royal James* of 1658 produces 1,144 tons burden, and 1,525 gross tons.

If the value for extreme beam for the *Royal James* of 1658 at 41 feet 7 inches were substituted in equation (8), we obtain 1,122 tons burden and 1,496 tons and tonnage by equation (2),

The value of 1,403 tons burden cited in this List for the *Royal Prince* of 1670 may be derived from equation (1), where:

khr = 127 feet 0 inch
bx = 43 feet 3 inches
h2 = 19 feet 2 inches

This product multiplied by 4/3 produces 1,403 tons and tonnage (equation 2). We may presume that anomalies in the values so listed were copied from spurious sources.

The *Royal Prince* of 1670 was built by Phineas Pett (1635–94), who was knighted in 1680.

After: B. Lavery, *Deane's Doctrine of Naval Architecture 1670*, 1986, p. 104.

APPENDIX 13

An Abstract from Deane's List of the *Sovereign of the Seas* (1670)

ITEM	VALUE/NUMBER/WEIGHT
Cost of hull complete from builder	£29,840
Cost/ton of burden	£20
Number of anchors (Appendix 38)	13
Weight of anchors	19 tons 8 cwt
Cost of anchors	£1,423
Number of cables	14
Weight of cables	45 tons 4 cwt
Cost of cables	£2,034
Number of boats	3
Number of brass guns	100
Number of iron guns	NONE
Weight of guns	176 tons
Cost of guns	£26,400
Weight of shot	54 tons
Cost of shot	£728
Weight of powder	400 tons
Cost of powder	£1,200
Cost of gunner's stores	£1,678
Number of blocks and dead-eyes	554
Cost of blocks, tops and pumps	£230
Total weight of cordage	28 tons
Cost of cordage	£1,260
Two complete suits of sails	34
Total area of canvas in 2 suits of sails	11,617 square yards
Cost of canvas	£831 13s 4d
Cost of boatswain's stores and cordage	£800
Cost of carpenter's stores	£92
Cost of rigging and provisioning	£66,506 13s 4d
Cost of provisions for 6 months	£4,853 6s 8d
Crew	800
Cost of seamen's wages for 6 months	£5,598 15s 6d
Cost of officers' pay for 6 months	£869
Total cost	£77,827 15s 6d

NOTE:

It should be emphasised that this List does not include royals on the fore and main nor topgallant on the mizen.

After: B. Lavery, *Deane's Doctrine of Naval Architecture 1670*, 1986, pp. 104–5.

APPENDIX 14

An Abstract of First Rates from Teonge's List (1675–79)

VESSEL	YEAR BUILT	khr feet inch	bx feet inch	h2 feet inch	d1 feet inch	BURDEN	MEN MA MB MC	GUNS GP GB
Royal Sovereign	1637	137 0	47 6	19 0	23 0	1,545	605 815 710	90 100
Charles	1668	128 0	42 6	18 6	21 0	1,257	500 710 605	86 96
St Michael	1669	122 6	40 0	17 5	20 0	1,107	430 600 500	80 90
St Andrew	1670	129 0	43 6	18 8	21 0	1,313	510 730 620	86 96
London	1670	129 0	43 9	19 0	21 0	1,328	510 730 620	86 96
Royal Prince	1670	131 0	44 10	19 0	22 0	1,400	560 780 690	90 100
Royal James	1671	136 0	45 4.5	18 6	20 8	1,421	560 780 670	90 100
Royal Charles	1673	136 0	45 4.5	18 6	20 8	1,441	560 780 670	90 100

NOTES:

The *Royal Sovereign* and *St Andrew* were built at Woolwich Royal Dockyard.
The *Charles* and *London* were built at Deptford Royal Dockyard.
The *Royal Prince* was built at Chatham Royal Dockyard.
The *St Michael, Royal James* and *Royal Charles* were built at Portsmouth Royal Dockyard.

khr = Length of keel from the harping rule
bx = Beam extreme, measured to the outside of the planking, excluding wales at Θ
h2 = Depth in hold, under floor of lower gun deck, to upper floor of ceiling at Θ
d1 = Actual draught, water line to bottom of keel
MA = Crew for peace at home and abroad
MB = Crew for war at home (maximum establishment of guns)
MC = Crew for war abroad
GP = Guns for peace at home and abroad, and war abroad
GB = Guns for war at home (maximum establishment of guns)

The value of 1,400 tons for the *Royal Prince* was verified using equation (8) in Chapter 4. However, to produce the value of tonnage as recorded in this List, the following values would need to be substituted in equation (8):

Royal Sovereign	khr =	127 feet	0 inch	bx =	47 feet 10 inches
Charles	khr =	130 feet	10 inches		
St Michael	khr =	125 feet	0 inch	bx =	40 feet 10 inches
St Andrew	khr =	128 feet	0 inch	bx =	43 feet 11 inches
London				bx =	44 feet 0 inch
Royal James	khr =	132 feet	0 inch	bx =	45 feet 0 inch
Royal Charles				bx =	44 feet 8 inches

The *Royal James* of 1671 was burnt in action against the Dutch at Solebay on 28 May 1672.

After: G. E. Manwaring (ed.), *The Diary of Henry Teonge, Chaplain on Board HM's Ships, Assistance, Bristol, Royal Oak 1675–1679*, 1927, p. 292.

APPENDIX 15

An Abstract of First Rates from Martin's List (1685)

VESSEL	YEAR BUILT	khr feet inch	bx feet inch	h2 feet inch	d1 feet inch	GROSS TONNAGE
Sovereign	1637	127 0	47 6	19 0	23 0	1,545
Charles	1668	128 0	42 6	18 6	21 0	1,257
St Michael	1669	122 6	40 0	17 5	20 0	1,107
Royal Prince	1670	138 0	44 10	19 0	22 0	1,400
London	1670	129 0	43 9	18 8	21 0	1,348
St Andrew	1670	129 0	43 5	18 8	21 0	1,313
Royal Charles	1673	136 0	45 4.5	18 6	20 8	1,441
Royal James	1675	136 0	45 4.5	18 6	20 8	1,441
Britannia	1682	146 0	47 0	19 7.5	22 0	1,739

NOTES:

The *Royal Sovereign* and *St Andrew* were built at Woolwich Royal Dockyard.
The *Charles* and *London* were built at Deptford Royal Dockyard.
The *Royal Prince* and *Britannia* were built at Chatham Royal Dockyard.
The *St Michael*, *Royal Charles* and *Royal James* were built at Portsmouth Royal Dockyard.

khr = Length of keel from the harping rule
bx = Beam extreme, measured to the outside of the planking, excluding wales at Θ
h2 = Depth in hold, under floor of lower gun deck, to upper floor of ceiling at Θ
d1 = Actual draught, water line to bottom of keel

Captain Stephen Martin seems to have copied the dimensions for his first rates from Teonge's List of 1675–79 (Appendix 14).

The value of 1,441 tonnage for the *Royal Charles* and *Royal James* was verified using equation (8) in Chapter 4.

The substitutions necessary to verify equation (8) as recorded in Appendix 12, similarly apply here. However, to produce the value of tonnage as recorded in the List, the following value would need to be substituted in equation (8):

Britannia: bx = 47 feet 4 inches

The keel length of the *Britannia* as recorded in this list is the 'tread' keel length. The *Britannia* was built by Sir Phineas Pett (1635–94) who built the *Royal Prince* of 1670. Martin has succumbed to some additional errors:

		Teonge	Martin
Sovereign	khr	137 feet	127 feet
Royal Prince	khr	131 feet	138 feet
London	h2	19 feet	18 feet 8 inches
	tonnage	1328 tons	1348 tons
St Andrew	bx	43 feet 6 inches	43 feet 5 inches
Royal James	tonnage	1,421 tons	1,441 tons

After: C. R. Markham, 'Life of Captain Stephen Martin 1666–1740', *NRS* 5, 1895, p. 185.

APPENDIX 16

An Abstract of First and Second Rates from Pepys' List (1686)

VESSEL	YEAR BUILT	khr feet inch	bx feet inch	h2 feet inch	d1 feet inch	BURDEN	MEN MA MB MC	GUNS GP GB
Prince Royal	1610	132 0	45 2	18 10	22 0	1,432	500 600 550	90 100
Royal Sovereign	1637	131 0	48 0	19 2	23 6	1,605	605 815 710	90 100
Charles	1655	131 0	42 6	18 0	21 6	1,258	400 650 500	76 86
Royal James	1658	124 0	41 0	18 0	21 0	1,108	350 550 460	72 80
Charles	1668	128 0	42 6	18 6	21 0	1,229	500 710 605	86 96
St Michael	1669	125 0	40 8.5	17 5	19 8	1,101	430 600 520	80 90
St Andrew	1670	128 0	44 0	17 9	21 6	1,338	510 730 620	86 96
London	1670	129 0	44 0	19 0	20 6	1,328	510 730 620	86 96
Royal Prince	1670	131 0	{44 9 {45 10 (girdled)	19 0	21 6	{1,395 {1,463	560 780 670	90 100
Royal James	1671	136 0	45 0	18 5	20 6	1,465	600 800 700	90 102
Royal Charles	1673	136 0	{44 8 {46 0 (girdled)	18 3	20 6	{1,443 {1,531	560 780 670	90 100
Royal James	1675	132 0	45 0	18 4	20 6	1,422	560 780 670	90 100
Britannia	1682	146 0	47 4 {48 8 (girdled)	19 7.5	20 0	1,739	560 780 670	90 100

NOTES:

The *Prince Royal, Royal Sovereign, Charles, Royal James* and *St Andrew* were built at Woolwich Royal Dockyard.

The *Charles* and *London* were built at Deptford Royal Dockyard.

The *Royal Prince* and *Britannia* were built at Chatham Royal Dockyard.

The *St Michael, Royal James* (1671) *Royal Charles* and *Royal James* (1675) were built at Portsmouth Royal Dockyard.

khr = Length of keel from the harping rule
bx = Beam extreme, measured to the outside of the planking, excluding wales at Θ
h2 = Depth in hold, under floor of lower gun deck, to upper floor of ceiling at Θ
d1 = Actual draught, water line to bottom of keel
MA = Crew for peace at home and abroad
MB = Crew for war at home (maximum establishment of guns)
MC = Crew for war abroad
GP = Guns for peace at home and abroad, and war abroad
GB = Guns for war at home (maximum establishment of guns)

The value of tons burden was verified using equation (8) in Chapter 4. However, to produce the value of tons burden as recorded in this List, the following value for beam would need to be substituted in equation (8):

St Andrew: bx = 44 feet 4 inches

The *St Michael* was built at Portsmouth as a ninety-gun second rate in 1669. She was made into a ninety-eight gun first rate in 1672, and reduced again to a second rate in 1689. She was renamed *Marlborough* in 1706 and rebuilt in 1708.

The *Britannia* of 1682 was girdled in 1691. She was rebuilt in 1719.

After: R. C. Anderson, 'English Ships 1649–1702, Lists of Men-of-War 1650–1700', *SNR* 1966, No. 5, Part I, No. 453.
J. R. Tanner, 'A Descriptive Catalogue of The Naval Manuscripts in The Pepysian Library at Magdalene College, Cambridge' *NRS* 26, 1903, Vol. 1, pp. 266–7.

APPENDIX 17

An Abstract of First Rates from a List (1688)

VESSEL	YEAR BUILT	khr feet inch	bx feet inch	h2 feet inch	d1 feet inch	BURDEN	GUNS
Sovereign	1637	131 0	48 0	19 2	23 6	1605	100
St George	1668	128 0	42 6	18 6	21 0	1229	96
St Michael	1669	125 0	40 8.5	17 5	19 8	1101	90
St Andrew	1670	128 0	44 0	17 9	21 6	1338	96
London	1670	129 0	44 0	19 0	20 6	1328	96
Royal Prince	1670	131 0	{44 9 {45 10 (girdled)	19 0	21 6	{1395 {1463	100
Royal Charles	1673	136 0	{44 8 {46 0 (girdled)	18 3	20 6	{1443 {1531	100
Royal James	1675	132 0	45 0	18 4	20 6	1422	100
Britannia	1682	146 0	47 4	19 7.5	20 0	1739	100

NOTES:

The *Royal Sovereign* and *St Andrew* were built at Woolwich Royal Dockyard.
The *St George* and *London* were built at Deptford Royal Dockyard.
The *Royal Prince* and *Britannia* were built at Chatham Royal Dockyard.
The *St Michael, Royal Charles* and *Royal James* were built at Portsmouth Royal Dockyard.

khr = Length of keel from the harping rule
bx = Beam extreme, measured to the outside of the planking, excluding wales at Θ
h2 = Depth in hold, under floor of lower gun deck, to upper floor of ceiling at Θ
d1 = Actual draught, water line to bottom of keel

The value of tons burden was verified using equation (8) in Chapter 4. However, to produce the value of tons burden as recorded in this List, the following value for beam would need to be substituted in equation (8):

St Andrew: bx = 44 feet 4 inches

The *Charles,* a first rate of ninety-six guns, was built at Deptford in 1668. She was renamed *St George* in 1687, and reduced to a second rate in 1691. As a second rate of 96 guns, she was rebuilt at Portsmouth in 1701. She was broken up in 1726.

After: J. Charnock, *An History of Marine Architecture* Vol. 2, 1801, p. 426.

APPENDIX 18

An Abstract of First Rates from Thomas' List (1689)

VESSEL	YEAR BUILT	khr feet inch	bx feet inch	h2 feet inch	d1 feet inc	BURDEN	MEN MA MB MC	GUNS GP GB
Sovereign	1637	131 0	48 0	19 2	23 6	1,605	605 815 710	90 100
Charles	1668	128 0	42 3	18 3	21 0	1,229	500 605 710	86 96
St George	1668	128 0	42 3	18 3	21 0	1,229	500 710 605	86 96
St Michael	1669	125 0	40 8	17 5	19 8	1,101	430 600 520	80 90
St Andrew	1670	128 0	44 4	17 9	21 6	1,338	510 730 620	86 96
London	1670	129 0	44 0	19 0	20 6	1,328	510 730 620	86 96
Royal Prince	1670	131 0	44 4	19 0	21 6	1,463	560 780 670	90 100
Royal Charles	1673	136 0	44 8	18 3	20 6	1,531	560 780 670	90 100
Royal James	1675	132 0	45 0	18 4	20 0	1,422	560 780 670	90 100
Britannia	1682	146 0	47 0	19 0	20 0	1,620	605 815 710	90 100

NOTES:

The *Sovereign* and *St Andrew* were built at Woolwich Royal Dockyard
The *Charles, St George* and *London* were built at Deptford Royal Dockyard
The *Royal Prince* and *Britannia* were built at Chatham Royal Dockyard
The *St Michael, Royal Charles* and *Royal James* were built at Portsmouth Royal Dockyard

khr = Length of keel from the harping rule
bx = Beam extreme, measured to the outside of the planking, excluding wales at Θ
h2 = Depth in hold, under floor of lower gun deck, to upper floor of ceiling at Θ
d1 = Actual draught, water line to bottom of keel
MA = Crew for peace at home and abroad
MB = Crew for war at home (maximum establishment of guns)
MC = Crew for war abroad
GP = Guns for peace at home and abroad, and war abroad
GB = Guns for war at home (maximum establishment of guns)

The value of tons burden was verified using equation (8) in Chapter 4. However, to produce the value of tons burden as recorded in this List, the following values for beam would need to be substituted in equation (8):
St George: bx = 42 feet 6 inches
Royal Prince: bx = 45 feet 10 inches
Royal Charles: bx = 46 feet 0 inch

The *Britannia*'s keel length by the harping rule was 135 feet 8 inches, while her beam extreme was 47 feet 4 inches. These values produce a tonnage of 1,616 when substituted in equation (8).

After: E. H. H. Archibald, *The Fighting Ship in the Royal Navy AD 897–1984*, 1984, p. 341
C. Derrick, *Memoirs of the Rise and Progress of the Royal Navy*, 1806.

APPENDIX 19

Cross-Sectional Areas for the Immersed Hull of the *Sovereign of the Seas*

STATION	AREA of CROSS SECTION (square feet)	STATION	AREA of CROSS SECTION (square feet)
30	259	Θ	778
26	397	B	773
22	506	F	768
18	595	K	758
14	653	O	710
10	717	S	621
6	755	X	429
2	768	b	182

NOTES:
These values have been calculated by the author, from a study of the reconstruction draught of the *Sovereign of the Seas* (1800) (Plate 38). The mean area of cross section of the immersed hull, at a draught in water of 20 feet 8 inches = 604 square feet.

APPENDIX 20

Height Between Decks of the *Sovereign of the Seas* from the Draughts

DIMENSION	RECONSTRUCTION DRAUGHT around 1800 feet / inch	EDYE'S DRAUGHT 1817 feet / inch	SEPPINGS' DRAUGHT 1827 feet / inch
Lower gun deck to middle gun deck			
a) Forwards	8 / 10	9 / 4	12 / 3
b) Midships	8 / 8	9 / 0	11 / 5
c) Stern	8 / 6	8 / 9	8 / 9
Middle gun deck to upper gun deck;			
a) Forwards	7 / 3	7 / 7	7 / 6
b) Midships	7 / 7	7 / 7	7 / 11
c) Stern	8 / 6	6 / 7	8 / 6
Upper gun deck to forecastle;	7 / 5	8 / 7	7 / 8
Upper gun deck to quarterdeck;			
a) Forwards	9 / 0	—	9 / 0
b) Stern	9 / 3	—	9 / 5
Quarterdeck to half-deck;	6 / 10	—	6 / 11
Half-deck to poop;	5 / 6	—	5 / 4

NOTES:
These measurements were taken from the upper side of one deck, to upper side of the adjacent higher deck. No allowance has been made for the thickness of deck timbers. This is not, therefore, an indication of the head room between decks. The values published by R. C. Anderson are compatible with those taken from the reconstruction draught of 1800. It will be seen from an examination of Appendix 7 that these values are exaggerated.

After: R. C. Anderson, 'The *Royal Sovereign* of 1637' MM 3, 1913, No. 3, p. 210.

APPENDIX 21

Main Dimensions of the *Sovereign of the Seas* from the Table on the Draughts

DIMENSION	SYMBOL	RECON. DRAUGHT around 1800 feet inch	EDYE'S DRAUGHT 1817 feet inch	SEPPINGS' DRAUGHT 1827 feet inch	FINCHAM'S DRAUGHT 1851 feet inch
Keel length	khr	139 11.75	139 0	139 11.75	139 11.75
Length along lower gun deck	gd	173 0	173 0	173 0	173 0
Beam extreme	bx	50 0	50 0	50 0	50 0
Depth in hold	h2	20 0	20 0	20 0	20 0
Tons burden		1861 53/94	1861 53/94	1861 53/94	1861 23/94

NOTES:

Fincham's values were published in his text with the draughts. The value of tons burden for the reconstruction draught, Seppings' draught and Fincham's draught was verified on a keel length of 139 feet 11.75 inches using equation (8) in Chapter 4. The remainder is more precisely 40/94.

After: R. C. Anderson, 'The *Royal Sovereign* of 1637', *MM* 3, 1913, No. 3, p. 210
J. Fincham, *A History of Naval Architecture*, 1851, p. 54.

APPENDIX 22

Main Dimensions of the *Sovereign of the Seas* from the Draughts

DIMENSION	SYMBOL	RECONSTRUCTION DRAUGHT around 1800 feet inch	EDYE'S DRAUGHT 1817 feet inch	SEPPINGS' DRAUGHT 1827 feet inch
Keel length	kfp	126 0	126 0	130 0
Keel length	kt	142 0	147 0	148 0
Keel length	khr	145 6	143 0	143 9
Length along lower gun deck	gd	169 9	172 0	171 9
Length between perpendiculars	pp	174 6	173 0	173 0
Length of hull	wl	165 6	171 0	170 0
Length overall	oa	230 0	238 0	238 0
Beam extreme	bx	48 0	49 0	48 9
Depth in hold	h1	20 0	21 6	20 9
Depth in hold	h2	19 0	20 6	19 9
Depth in hold	h3	19 0	19 6	19 0
Beam within ceiling	bs	43 0	42 0	43 0
Depth in hold	h4	19 4	19 0	20 0
Draught in water	d1	23 0	23 0	22 9
Draught in water	d2	21 0	21 0	21 0
Draught in water	d3	23 0	23 0	23 0
Lower deck ports above water		4 0	4 0	4 0
Height overall		> 72 0	79 0	79 0
Coefficient of fineness	cf	0.609		
Area cross section	A	604 square feet		

NOTES:

These values have been derived by the author. There is a remarkable resemblance between the dimensions scaled up from Edye's draught and those similarly produced from Seppings' draught. There is the suggestion that one was copied from the other.

APPENDIX 23

Principal Guns of the Sixteenth Century

PIECE	BORE inches	LENGTH feet	WEIGHT lb	WEIGHT of SHOT lb	POWDER CHARGE lb
Basilisk	8.75	11.5	9,000	60	60
Cannon royal	8.5	12.0	8,000	66–74	30
Cannon of VII	8.0	8.5–10.0	6,000–8,000	60	27
Cannon serpentine	7.0		5,500	42–53.5	25
Bastard cannon	7.0	9.5	4,500	41–42	20
Demi-cannon	6.4–6.75	10–12	4,000–6,000	32–33.5	18
Cannon petro	6.0		3,800–4,000	24.5–26	14
Culverin	5.2–5.5	11–13	4,000–4,840	18–24	12
Basilisk	5.0		4,000	14–15	9–10
Demi-culverin	4.0–4.5	9–12	3,000–3,400	8–9.5	6–8.5
Culverin bastard	4.0–4.56	8.5	3,000	5–11	5.7
Saker	3.5–3.65	7–9	1,400–1,500	6–8	4–5.5
Minion	3.25–3.5	6.5–8	1,000–1,200	4–6	3–4
Falcon	2.5–2.75	6.0	660–800	2–4	1.2–3.5
Falconet	2.0	3.75–6	500	1–1.5	0.4–3
Serpentine	1.5		400	0.5–0.75	0.3–1.5
Rabinet	1.0	5.5	300	0.3–0.5	0.18–0.75

NOTES:
This List does not include the weight of the gun-carriages.
The powder charge for a drake was 75 per cent of the service charge.

After: W. Laird Clowes, *The Royal Navy – A History from the Earliest Times to the Present* Vol. 1, 1996, pp. 410–1.
W. Congreve, *An Elementary Treatise on the Mounting of Naval Ordnance*, 1811.
H. B. Culver & G. Grant, *The Book of Old Ships and Something of Their Evolution and Romance*, 1936, p. 295.
J. S. Hodgkinson, 'Gunfounding in the Weald', *Jour. of the Ordnance Society* 12, 2000, pp. 31–47.
W. James, *The Naval History of Great Britain* Vol. 1, 1837, pp. 7–9 & 376.
B. H. St. J. O'Neil, *Castles and Cannon – A Study of Early Artillery Fortifications in England*, 1960, p. xix.
M. Oppenheim, 'The Naval Tracts of Sir William Monson in Six Books' *NRS* 45, 1913, Vol. 4, pp. 36–45.
E. Straker, *Wealden Iron*, 1969, p. 159.
J. Topham, 'A Description of an ancient Picture in Windsor Castle', *Arch.* 6, 1782, p. 189.

APPENDIX 24

Principal Guns of the Seventeenth Century

PIECE	BORE inch	DIAM. of SHOT inch	WEIGHT of SHOT lb	WEIGHT of SHOT oz	GUN WEIGHT BRASS lb	GUN WEIGHT IRON lb	POWDER CHARGE BRASS lb	POWDER CHARGE BRASS oz	POWDER CHARGE IRON lb	POWDER CHARGE IRON oz
Cannon	8	7.5	58		8,000	7,100	32	8	24	
Demi-cannon	6.75	6.63	36		6,000	5,340	18		13	8
Cannon	6.5	6.17	32		5,600		17	8	13	2
Cannon	6.25	6.0	30		5,400		14		10	8
Culverin	5.5	5.25	20		4,800	4,300	12	8	9	6
Culverin	5.25	5	17	5	4,500		11	6	8	10
Culverin	5.0	4.75	15		4,000		10		7	8
Demi-culverin	4.75	4.5	12	11	3,000	2,700	8	8	6	6
Culverin	4.5	4.25	10	10.5	2,700		7	4	5	7
Culverin	4.25	4.0	9		2,000		6	4	4	11
Sakers-old	4	3.75	7	5	1,800		5		3	12
Sakers	3.75	3.5	6		1,500	1,340	4		3	
Sakers	3.5	3.25	4	12	1,400		3	6	2	10
Minions	3.25	3	3	12	1,000		3	4	2	7
Minions	3	2.88	3	4	750		2	8	1	14
Falcons	2.75	2.63	2	8	750		2	4	1	11
Falconets	2.25	2.13	1	5	400		1	4	0	15
Robinet	1.5	1.38	0	8	300		0	12	0	9
Base	1.25	1.13	0	5	200					

NOTE:
Nye does not record whether the smaller charge of powder used in the iron gun produced the same effective range as that of the bronze gun.

After: N. Nye, *A Treatise of Artificial Fire-Works for War and Recreation*, 1647.

APPENDIX 25

Dimensions of English Culverins

DATE	BORE inch	LENGTH feet	WEIGHT lb	WEIGHT of SHOT lb	DIAM. of SHOT inch	POWDER CHARGE lb
1574	5.5	12.8	4,000	18	5.25	18
1590	5.5		4,500	17.3		12
1599	5.5					
1600	5.5		4,500	17.5		12
1628	5.5	13.25	4,600	19	5.25	15
1643	5.5	12.8	4,500			15
1646	5.0	11.0	4,000	15		
1646	5.0	11.0	4,600	15		12
1692	5.25	12.0	4,500	17.31	5.0	11.37
1753		9.0	5,400	18		
1753		9.0	4,628	18		
1753	5.292	7.5	3,100	18	5.04	6
1753	5.292	9.0	4,030	18	5.04	8
1753	5.292	9.0	2,270	18	5.04	6
1760		9.0	5,040	18		
1760			5,600	18		

NOTES:
This list does not include the weight of the gun-carriages.
The powder charge for a drake was 75 per cent of the service charge.

After: E. H. H. Archibald, *The Wooden Fighting Ship in the Royal Navy AD 897–1860*, 1968 p. 159.
O. F. G. Hogg, *Artillery – Its Origin, Heyday and Decline*, 1970, pp. 268–75.
W. James, *The Naval History of Great Britain*, Vol. 1, 1837, p. 376.
D. Macintyre & B. W. Bathe, *The Man-of-War*, 1968, p. 38.
J. Smith, *A Sea Grammar*, 1627, p. 86.
State Papers, Domestic Series, 242, pp. 64–5.

APPENDIX 26

Bore of Piece, Diameter of Round Shot and Windage

PIECE	WEIGHT of SHOT lb	BORE of PIECE inch	DIAM. of SHOT inch	WINDAGE inch
Cannon of VII	60	7.92	7.54	0.38
42-pounder	42	7.03	6.69	0.34
32-pounder	32	6.42	6.11	0.31
24-pounder	26	5.99	5.71	0.28
18-pounder	18	5.30	5.05	0.25
12-pounder	14	4.87	4.64	0.23
9-pounder	8	4.04	3.85	0.19
6-pounder	6	3.68	3.50	0.17
Falcon	2	2.55	2.43	0.12

NOTE:
These values have been calculated by the author.

APPENDIX 27

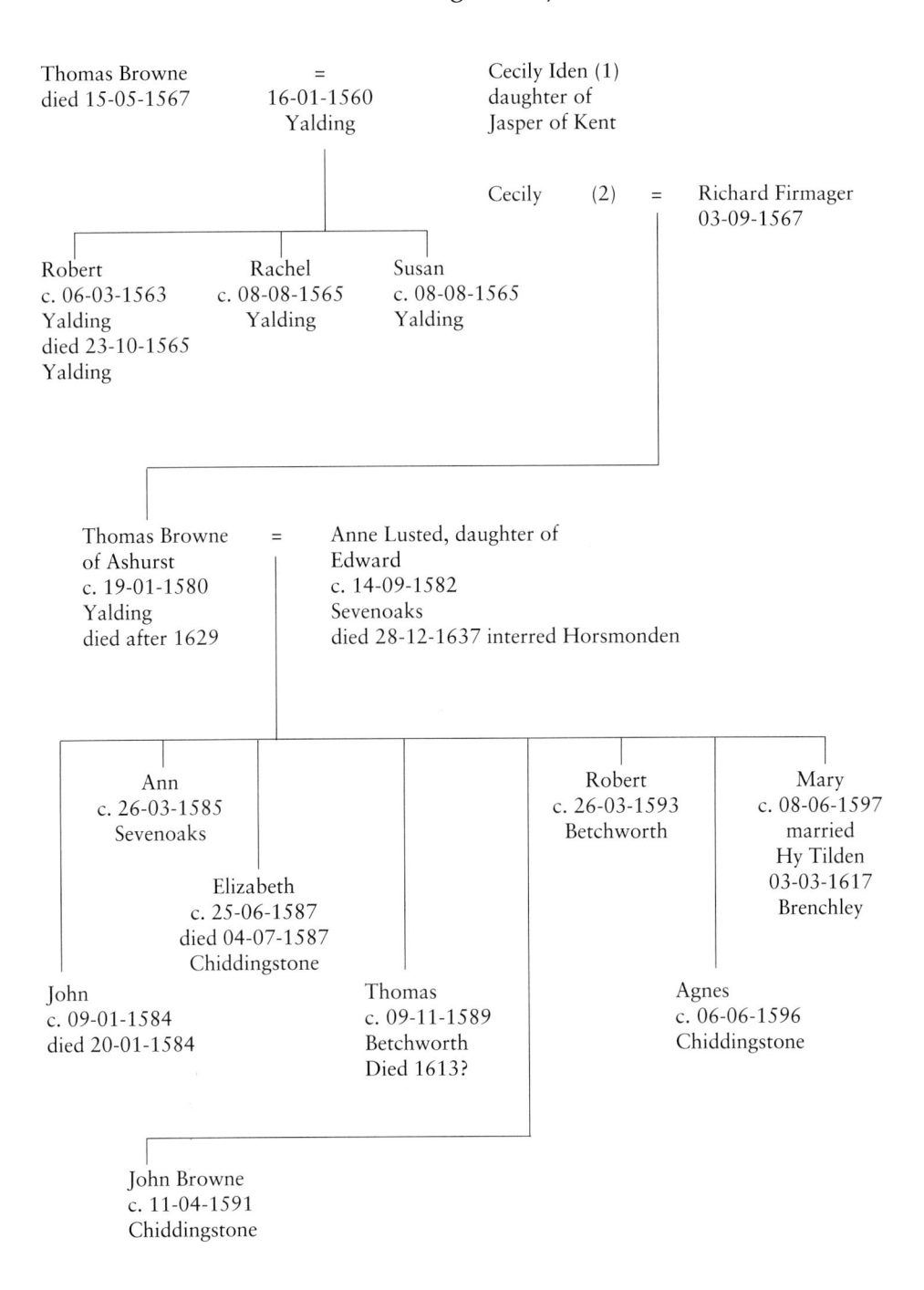

The Gunfounding Family of Browne

```
Thomas Browne            =              Cecily Iden (1)
died 15-05-1567      16-01-1560         daughter of
                      Yalding           Jasper of Kent

                                 Cecily      (2)    =    Richard Firmager
                                                         03-09-1567

   Robert           Rachel          Susan
   c. 06-03-1563    c. 08-08-1565   c. 08-08-1565
   Yalding          Yalding         Yalding
   died 23-10-1565
   Yalding


   Thomas Browne       =    Anne Lusted, daughter of
   of Ashurst               Edward
   c. 19-01-1580            c. 14-09-1582
   Yalding                  Sevenoaks
   died after 1629          died 28-12-1637 interred Horsmonden


        Ann                                          Robert              Mary
        c. 26-03-1585                                c. 26-03-1593       c. 08-06-1597
        Sevenoaks                                    Betchworth          married
                                                                         Hy Tilden
                     Elizabeth                                           03-03-1617
                     c. 25-06-1587                                       Brenchley
                     died 04-07-1587
                     Chiddingstone
   John                           Thomas                    Agnes
   c. 09-01-1584                  c. 09-11-1589             c. 06-06-1596
   died 20-01-1584                Betchworth                Chiddingstone
                                  Died 1613?

        John Browne
        c. 11-04-1591
        Chiddingstone
```

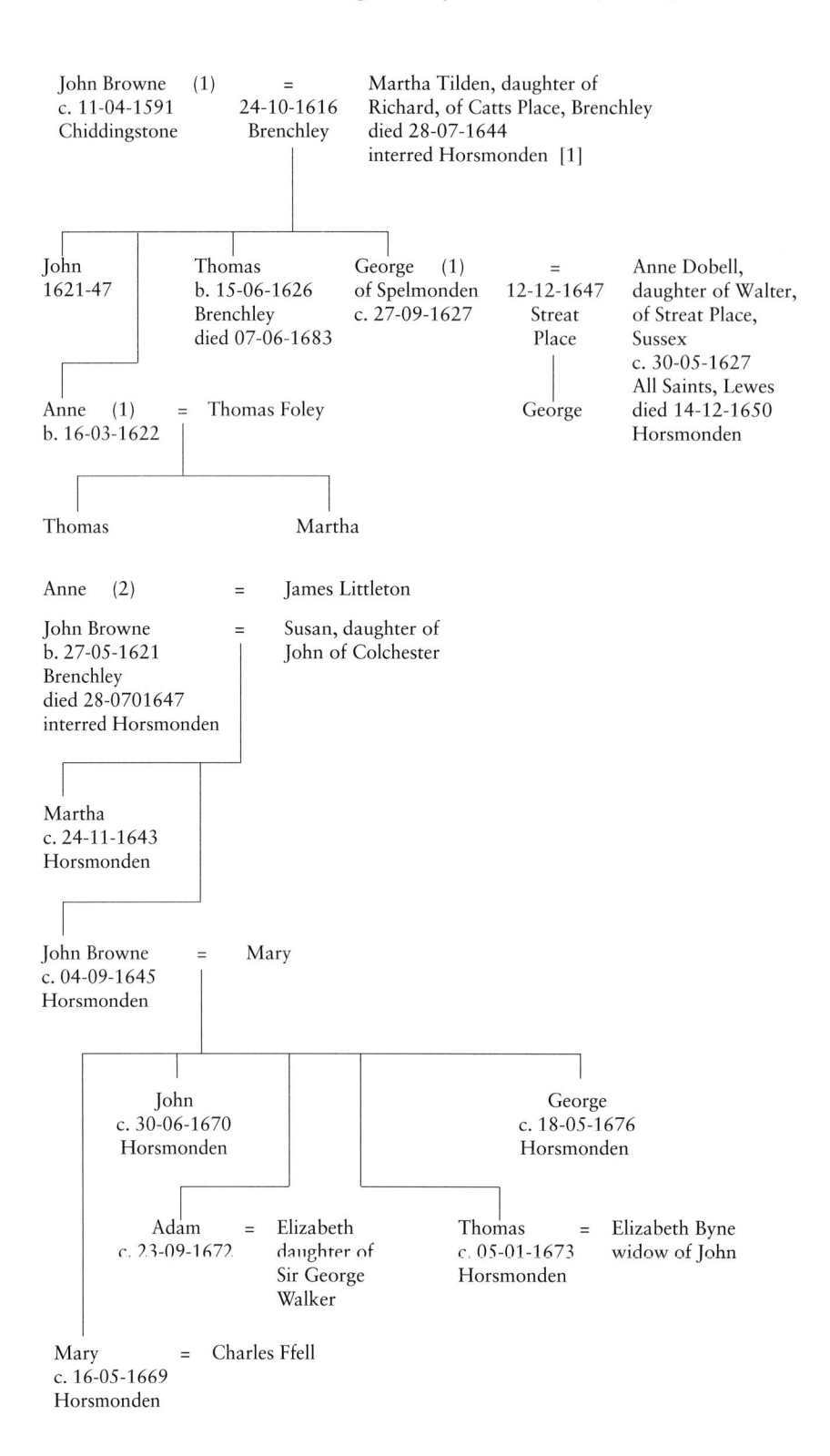

The Gunfounding Family of Browne (Cont.)

```
John Browne      (1)    =    Martha Tilden, daughter of
c. 11-04-1591    24-10-1616   Richard, of Catts Place, Brenchley
Chiddingstone    Brenchley    died 28-07-1644
                              interred Horsmonden [1]
```

```
John         Thomas              George      (1)    =    Anne Dobell,
1621-47      b. 15-06-1626       of Spelmonden  12-12-1647   daughter of Walter,
             Brenchley           c. 27-09-1627   Streat       of Streat Place,
             died 07-06-1683                      Place       Sussex
                                                              c. 30-05-1627
                                                              All Saints, Lewes
Anne   (1)   =  Thomas Foley                      George     died 14-12-1650
b. 16-03-1622                                                 Horsmonden
```

```
Thomas              Martha
```

Anne   (2)   =   James Littleton
John Browne =   Susan, daughter of
b. 27-05-1621   John of Colchester
Brenchley
died 28-0701647
interred Horsmonden

Martha
c. 24-11-1643
Horsmonden

John Browne   =   Mary
c. 04-09-1645
Horsmonden

```
         John                          George
         c. 30-06-1670                 c. 18-05-1676
         Horsmonden                    Horsmonden

    Adam     =  Elizabeth        Thomas     =  Elizabeth Byne
    c. 23-09-1672  daughter of   c. 05-01-1673  widow of John
                Sir George       Horsmonden
                Walker
```

Mary   =   Charles Ffell
c. 16-05-1669
Horsmonden

The Gunfounding Family of Browne (Cont.)

After the death of his wife Martha, on 28 July 1644, John Browne remarried:

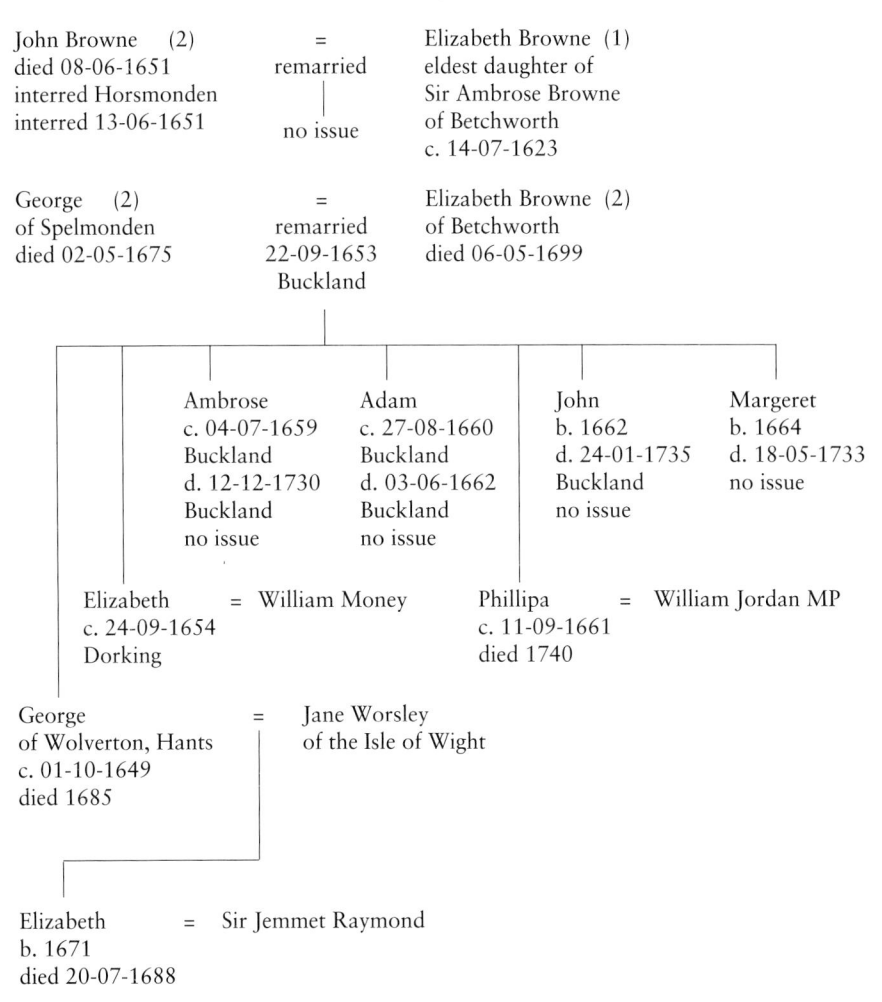

John Browne (2) = Elizabeth Browne (1)
died 08-06-1651   remarried   eldest daughter of
interred Horsmonden   Sir Ambrose Browne
interred 13-06-1651   no issue   of Betchworth
                              c. 14-07-1623

George (2) = Elizabeth Browne (2)
of Spelmonden   remarried   of Betchworth
died 02-05-1675   22-09-1653   died 06-05-1699
               Buckland

Children:

- Ambrose c. 04-07-1659 Buckland, d. 12-12-1730 Buckland, no issue
- Adam c. 27-08-1660 Buckland, d. 03-06-1662 Buckland, no issue
- John b. 1662, d. 24-01-1735 Buckland, no issue
- Margeret b. 1664, d. 18-05-1733, no issue

Elizabeth c. 24-09-1654 Dorking = William Money

Phillipa c. 11-09-1661 died 1740 = William Jordan MP

George of Wolverton, Hants c. 01-10-1649 died 1685 = Jane Worsley of the Isle of Wight

Elizabeth b. 1671 died 20-07-1688 = Sir Jemmet Raymond

NOTES:
[1] Below the chancel arch of St Margaret's church, Horsmonden, is a brass plaque 15 inch 6 inches set in an iron grave slab and inscribed; 'Martha, wife of John Browne Esquire, 164

- b. = born
- c. = christened
- d. = died
- i. = interred

After;
S. Edwards, *Children of the Weald – A Fascinating Account of Kent Life in a Bygone Age*, 1997, pp 129-53.

APPENDIX 28

Original Armament of the *Sovereign of the Seas* from the Record of Production of John Browne and Thomas Pitt

No.	WEIGHT cwt	qr	lb	LENGTH feet	No.	WEIGHT cwt	qr	lb	LENGTH feet
	Cannon of VII Drakes					Culverins Fortified			
1	45	1	18	9.0	1	48	2	24	11.5
2	45	1	18	9.0	2	48	3	24	11.5
3	44	1	8	8.5	3	50	2	11	11.5
4	44	2	24	8.5	4	51	2	27	11.0
5	45	1	14	9.0	5	48	2	23	11.5
6	47	0	6	9.5	6	51	3	9	11.0
7	46	2	2	9.0					
8	46	3	14	9.0		Culverin Drakes			
9	47	0	4	9.5	1	27	2	7	9.5
10	44	2	16	8.5	2	27	0	4	9.5
11	46	1	14	9.0	3	26	3	18	9.5
12	44	1	22	8.5	4	27	1	0	9.5
13	45	2	12	9.0	5	27	1	6	9.5
14	43	3	18	8.5	6	27	3	2	9.5
15	46	3	26	9.0	7	27	1	17	9.5
16	46	0	6	9.0	8	27	0	22	9.5
17	45	3	22	9.0	9	27	3	2	9.5
18	45	2	24	9.0	10	27	3	19	9.5
19	45	0	6	9.0	11	28	1	16	9.5
20	46	2	27	9.0	12	27	3	8	9.5
					13	27	3	6	9.5
	Demi-Cannon Drakes				14	27	3	18	9.5
1	43	0	23	11.0	15	27	1	10	9.5
2	43	0	6	11.0	16	27	2	15	9.5
3	55	2	7	11.5	17	27	3	0	9.5
4	48	3	1	11.0	18	28	0	9	9.5
5	56	0	11	10.0	19	27	2	6	9.5
6	53	2	23	11.5	20	28	1	7	9.5
7	57	0	1	10.0	21	27	2	26	9.5
8	57	0	23	10.0	22	26	3	25	9.5
	Culverin Cutts					Demi-Culverins Fortified			
1	12	3	2	6.0	1	28	0	5	10.0
2	12	3	2	6.0	2	28	0	12	10.0
					3	28	1	2	10.0
	Demi-culverin drake cutts				4	28	0	4	10.0
1	8	1	4	6.0					
2	8	1	16	6.0					

	WEIGHT			LENGTH		WEIGHT			LENGTH
No.	cwt	qr	lb	feet	No.	cwt	qr	lb	feet
	Demi-Culverin Drakes					Demi-Culverin Drakes (cont.)			
1	18	2	14	8.0	20	17	3	3	8.0
2	17	2	14	8.0	21	19	0	2	8.6
3	18	2	6	8.0	22	18	2	20	8.0
4	19	0	8	8.6	23	17	3	1	8.0
5	18	2	18	8.0	24	17	2	22	8.0
6	19	0	0	8.6	25	19	1	27	8.6
7	18	3	4	8.0	26	17	2	22	8.0
8	19	1	10	8.6	27	17	1	18	8.0
9	18	0	24	8.0	28	20	3	14	9.0
10	19	0	0	8.6	29	20	1	7	9.0
11	17	3	24	8.0	30	20	2	25	9.0
12	19	0	5	8.6	31*	20	0	23	9.0
13	20	0	10	9.0	32	21	1	0	9.0
14	21	0	11	9.0	33	20	0	21	9.0
15	17	3	14	8.0	34	21	0	12	9.0
16	19	3	14	8.6	35	20	2	6	9.0
17	20	1	26	9.0	36	18	1	0	8.0
18	20	1	1	9.0	37	18	0	18	8.0
19	20	0	13	9.0	38	17	1	14	8.0

SUMMARY	No.	Weight			Length
		tons	cwt	qr	lb	feet
Cannon of VII drakes	20	45	14	0	21	0
Demi-cannon drakes	8	20	14	2	11	11.0
Culverins fortified	6	15	0	2	6	11.5
Culverin drakes	22	30	7	1	19	9.5
Culverin cutts	2	1	5	2	4	6.0
Demi-culverins fortified	4	5	12	1	23	10.0
Demi-culverin drakes	38	36	8	0	23	8–9
Demi-culverin drake cutts	2	0	16	2	20	6.0
TOTALS:	102	155	19	2	15	

NOTES:

These were all brass pieces.
This List does not include the weight of the gun-carriages.
* Demi-culverin drake No. 31 is displayed in the Royal Artillery Museum at Woolwich (Plates 81, 82 & 83.)

After: A. B. Caruana, *The History of English Sea Ordnance 1523–1875 Vol. 1 The Age of Evolution 1523–1715*, 1994, pp. 62–4.
Public Record Office WO 49–78.

APPENDIX 29

Original Armament of the *Sovereign of the Seas* (1637)

LOCATION	PIECE	No.	feet	WEIGHT EACH cwt	TOTAL tons
LOWER GUN DECK					
Luffs, quarters, sides	Cannon of VII drakes	20	8.5–9.0	43–47	45.7
Fore chase	Demi-cannon drakes	2	11.5	48–52	5.0
Bows abaft the chase	Demi-cannon drakes	2	11.0	43	4.3
Stern chase	Demi-cannon drakes	4	10.5	55–57	11.4
MIDDLE GUN DECK					
Luffs, quarters, sides	Culverin drakes	22	9.5	26–28	30.4
Fore chase	Culverins fortified	2	11.5	48–51	4.8
Bows abaft the chase	Demi-culverin drakes	2	8–9	17–20	1.9
Stern chase	Culverins fortified	4	11.5	48–51	10.2
UPPER GUN DECK					
Quarters, sides	Demi-culverin drakes	22	8–9	17–20	21.1
Fore chase	Demi-culverins fortified	2	10.0	30	2.8
Stern chase	Demi-culverins fortified	2	10.0	30	2.8
Forecastle	Demi-culverin drakes	8	9	17–20	7.7
Half-deck	Demi-culverin drakes	6	9	17–20	5.7
Quarterdeck	Demi-culverin drake cutts	2	6	8	0.8
Forecastle bulkhead aft	Culverin cutts	2	6	11	1.3
	TOTALS:	102			155.9

NOTE:
This list does not include the weight of the gun-carriages.

After: A. B. Caruana, *The History of English Sea Ordnance 1523–1875 Vol. 1 The Age of Evolution 1523–1715*, 1994, pp. 62–4.

APPENDIX 30

Gunners' Stores of the *Sovereign of the Seas* for 1654–55

PIECE	NUMBER
Cannon of VII drakes	19
Demi-cannon	9
Culverin	28
Demi-culverin	30
Saker drakes	5
12-pounder bullet	4
TOTAL:	95
Round shot for cannon of VII drakes	540
Round shot for demi-cannon	240
Round shot for culverin	900
Round shot for demi-culverin	900
Round shot for saker drakes	150
Round shot for 12-pounder bullet	120
Double headed hammered shot for culverin	360
Double headed hammered shot for demi-culverin	360
Tin cases for demi-culverin	180
Tin cases for saker drakes	30
Ladles and sponges for cannon of VII drakes	6
Ladles and sponges for demi-cannon	4
Ladles and sponges for culverin	8
Ladles and sponges for demi-culverin	8
Ladles and sponges for saker drakes	2

NOTE:

This list dated 22 January 1654–55, seems to have been a proposal for selected ships rather than an actual state of affairs. The ordnance was to be composed of iron and brass pieces.

After: B. Lavery, *The Arming and Fitting of English Ships of War 1600–1815*, 1987, pp. 279–82.
Public Record Office WO 47/3.

APPENDIX 31

Analysis of Armament of First Rates from a List (1664)

PIECE	*Sovereign*	*Prince Royal*	*Charles*	*Royal James*
Cannon of VII	20	20	20	12
Demi-cannon	8	8	6	14
Culverin	28	28	28	28
Demi-culverin	26	24	22	22
Demi-culverin cutts	8	6	4	4
TOTALS:	90	86	78	78

NOTES:

This List, dated 18 May 1664, seems to have been a proposal rather than an actual state of affairs. The totals for the *Charles* and *Royal James* do not correspond to the sum of the constituents. The proposal was based on the availability of ordnance in store for use in the event of war.

The establishment was to be made up of iron and brass pieces.

There was insufficient cannon of VII in store for the fore chase for first rates. The proposal was to use demi-cannon.

After: B. Lavery, *The Arming and Fitting of English Ships of War 1600–1815*, 1987, p. 270.

APPENDIX 32

Armament of the *Sovereign of the Seas* from the Ordnance Establishments

PIECE	1666	1666 (Actual)	1677	1685
Cannon of VII	22	13	26	26
Demi-cannon	6	13	0	0
24-pounders	0	0	28	26
Culverin fortified	28	36	0	0
12-pounders	0	0	0	28
Demi-culverin fortified	36	18	28	0
Saker fortified	0	22	14	20
3-pounders	0	0	4	0
TOTALS:	92	102	100	100

After: F. Fox, *Great Ships – The Battlefleet of King Charles II*, 1980, pp. 183–91
F. L. Fox, *A Distant Storm – The Four Days' Battle of 1666 – The Greatest Sea Fight of the Age of Sail*, 1996, pp. 389–90.

APPENDIX 33

Analysis of Armament of First Rates from Teonge's List (1675–9)

VESSEL	YEAR BUILT	Cannon of VII	Demi-cannon	24-pdrs	Culverin	Demi-culverin	Sakers	3-pdrs	TOTAL
Royal Sovereign	1637	26	0	28	0	28	14	4	100
St Michael	1669	0	26	0	26	26	10	2	90
Charles	1668	26	0	0	28	26	12	4	96
St Andrew	1670	26	0	0	28	26	12	4	96
London	1670	26	0	0	28	26	12	4	96
Royal Prince	1670	26	0	0	28	28	14	4	100
Royal James	1671	26	0	0	28	28	14	4	100
Royal Charles	1673	26	0	0	28	28	14	4	100

NOTES:
The *Royal Sovereign* and *St Andrew* were built at Woolwich Royal Dockyard.
The *St Michael*, *Royal James* and *Royal Charles* were built at Portsmouth Royal Dockyard.
The *Charles* and *London* were built at Deptford Royal Dockyard.
The *Royal Prince* was built at Chatham Royal Dockyard.

After: G. E. Manwaring (ed.), *The Diary of Henry Teonge, Chaplain on Board HM's Ships, Assistance Bristol Royal Oak 1675–1679*, 1927 p. 292.

APPENDIX 34

Principal Guns on the Establishment of 1677

		WEIGHT (cwt)	
PIECE	MIN	MEAN	MAX
Cannon of VII	51	57	63
Demi-cannon	40	45	50
24-pounder	32	38.5	43
Culverin	30	35	40
12-pounder	27	30.5	34
Demi-culverin	22	26	30
6-pounder	15	22	30
Saker	14	20	26
Demi-culverin cutts	10	13	16
Saker cutts	8	10	12
Minion	7	9	11
3-pounder	3.5	4.25	5

NOTE:
This List does not include the weight of the gun-carriage.

After: W. James, *The Naval History of Great Britain*, Vol. 1, 1837, p. 375.

APPENDIX 35

An Abstract of First Rates from James' List on the Establishment of 1677

VESSEL	YEAR	GUNS	GW	GT	LG	MG	UG	FC	QD	Poop
Sovereign	1637	100	177	1,543	26 C-VII	28 x 24-lb	28 D-Cn	4 x S	10 x S	4 x 3-lb
Charles	1668	96	157	1,229	26 C-VII	28 Cn	26 C-Cn	2 x S	10 x S	4 x 3-lb
St Michael	1669	90	138.25	1,079	26 D-C	26 Cn	26 D-Cn	None	10 x S	2 x 3-lb
St Andrew	1670	96	165	1,318	26 C-VII	28 Cn	26 D-Cn	2 x S	10 x S	4 x 3-lb
London	1670	96	165	1,328	26 C-VII	28 Cn	26 D-Cn	2 x S	10 x S	4 x 3-lb
Royal Prince	1570	100	173	1,395	26 C-VII	28 Cn	28 D-Cn	4 x S	10 x S	4 x 3-lb
Royal James	1671	100	173	1,426	26 C-VII	28 Cn	28 D-Cn	4 x S	10 x S	4 x 3-lb
Royal Charles	1573	100	173	1,443	26 C-VII	28 Cn	28 D-Cn	4 x S	10 x S	4 x 3-lb
Royal James	1675	100	187.75	1,485	26 C-VII	28 Cn	28 x s	4 x S	12 x S	2 x 3-lb

NOTES:

The *Sovereign* and *St Andrew* were built at Woolwich Royal Dockyard.
The *Charles* and *London* were built at Deptford Royal Dockyard.
The *Royal Prince* was built at Chatham Royal Dockyard.
The *St Michael*, *Royal James* (1671) *Royal Charles* and *Royal James* (1675) were built at Portsmouth Royal Dockyard.
GW = Gross Weight; GT = Gross Tons; LG = Lower Gun-deck; MG = Middle Gun-deck; UG = Upper Gun-deck; FC = Forecastle;
QD = Quarter Deck
C-VII = Cannon of VII; 24-lb = 24-pounder; D-Cn = Demi-Culverin; S = Saker; Cn = Culverin; D-C = Demi-Cannon
After: R. C. Ancerson, 'English Ships 1649-1702, Lists of Men-of-War 1650-1700', *SNR* 1966, No. 5, Part 1.
W. James, *The Naval History of Great Britain* Vol. 1, 1837, p. 375.

APPENDIX 36

Analysis of Armament of First Rates from a List (1687–88)

PIECE	Royal Sovereign	St Michael	St Andrew	London	Royal Prince	Britannia
Cannon of VII	26	0	26	24	24	22
Demi-cannon	0	26	0	4	0	0
24-pounders	17	0	0	0	0	0
Culverins fortified	0	26	24	26	30	32
12-pounder	19	0	0	30	0	0
Demi-culverins fortified	0	26	25	0	31	0
Demi-culverin cutt	0	10	0	0	9	0
6-pounders	0	2 brass	0	12	0	0
Sakers fortified	20	0	13	0	0	44
Saker cutt	0	0	2	0	0	0
3-pounder	0	4 brass	0	0	0	2
TOTALS:	82	94	90	96	94	100

NOTES:

The *Royal Sovereign, London, Royal Prince* were listed with brass ordnance, while the *St Michael, St Andrew* and the *Britannia* were listed with iron ordnance. The *Royal Sovereign*'s brass ordnance was subsequently consigned to the *Britannia*.

After: A. B. Caruana, *The History of English Sea Ordnance 1523–1875, Vol. 1: The Age of Evolution 1523–1715*, 1994, p. 102.
Public Record Office SRO D(W) 1778–V–1371.

APPENDIX 37

Armament of the *Sovereign of the Seas* from the Survey of 1696

No.	WEIGHT cwt	qr	lb	LENGTH feet	DIAMETER of TRUNNION inch	DIAMETER at TRUNNION inch
				Cannon of VII		
6864	60	2	27	9.5	7	18.5
6865	60	1	26	9.5	7	18.5
6866	54	1	14	9.5	7.5	18.25
6867	59	1	26	9.5	7.25	18.5
6868	61	3	27	9.5	7.25	18.5
6869	60	3	27	9.5	7	18.5
6870	61	0	2	9.5	7	18.5
6871	59	2	19	9.5	7	18.5
6872	54	1	25	9.5	7	18.5
6873	61	0	22	9.5	7.5	18.5
6874	62	0	5	9.5	7.5	19
6875	60	0	20	9.5	7	18.5
6876	62	2	4	9.5	7.5	19
6877	64	0	10	9.5	7.5	19.5
6878	62	0	11	9.5	7.5	19
6879	61	1	13	9.5	7	19
6880	62	1	3	9.5	7.5	19
6881	62	1	26	9.5	7.5	19
6882	62	0	26	9.5	7.5	19
6883	61	3	17	9.5	7.5	18.75
6884	61	3	27	9.5	7.5	18.75
6885	59	3	26	9.5	7	18.5
				Culverins		
6886	38	0	12	9.5	6	15.25
6887	40	2	26	9.5	6	15.25
6888	42	0	11	9.5	5.5	15.25
6889	42	1	18	9.5	6	15.5
6890	43	2	9	9.5	6	15.5
6891	40	3	3	9.5	5.75	15.25
6892	42	0	3	9.5	5.5	15.75
6893	41	1	7	9.5	5.75	15.75
6894	40	1	3	9.5	5.5	15
6895	42	0	15	9.5	5.75	15.5
6896	43	0	20	9.5	6	15.75
6897	42	0	21	9.5	5.75	15.5
6898	40	0	11	9.5	5.75	15
6899	40	2	5	9.5	5.5	15
6900	38	3	26	9.5	6	15.25
6901	40	2	24	9.5	5.25	15.25
6902	40	0	0	9.5	5.75	15
6903	37	2	12	9	5.75	15.25
6904	51	0	17	11	5.75	15.5

| | WEIGHT | | | LENGTH | DIAMETER | DIAMETER |
No.	cwt	qr	lb	feet	of TRUNNION inch	at TRUNNION inch
6905	49	3	3	11	6	15.25
6906	50	2	9	11	5.75	15.75
6907	49	2	15	11	5.5	15.25
6908	49	2	23	11	5.75	15
6909	50	0	15	11	5.75	15.5
6910	48	1	7	11	6.75	15.25
6911	49	3	13	11	5.5	15.25
				Demi-Culverins		
6912	27	2	10	9	4.75	13
6913	26	3	13	9	4.5	13
				Demi-Culverins		
6914	31	0	26	10	4.5	13.25
6915	26	2	9	9	4.75	12.75
6916	28	1	13	9	4.75	13
6917	25	3	10	9	4.5	12.5
6918	30	2	8	9.5	4.75	13.25
6919	26	2	10	9	4.75	12.5
6920	26	3	17	9	4.5	12.75
6921	28	3	2	9	4.75	13.5
6922	27	3	9	9	4.75	13
6923 $	31	0	13	10	5.25	13.5
6924	25	1	3	9	4.5	12.25
6925	30	0	0	9	4.5	12.75
6926	27	0	6	9	4.5	13
6927	26	0	20	9	4.75	12.5
6928	27	3	13	9	4.75	13
6929	26	2	7	9	4.75	13
6930	25	2	14	9	4.5	12.5
6931	29	0	27	9	5	13.25
6932	27	2	14	9	4.5	13
6933	27	1	4	9	4.5	13
6934	13	1	0	6	4.5	11
6935	13	1	4	6	4.5	11
6936	17	1	10	7	4	12
6937	16	1	14	6	4.5	12.5
6938	16	0	10	6	4.75	12
6939	12	3	7	6	4.5	11.25
6940	16	2	12	7	4.25	11.5
6941	15	2	0	7	4	10.75
6942	18	0	0	6.5	4.5	12.5
6943	17	3	14	6.5	4.5	12.5
6944	16	2	21	7	3.75	11.25
6945	15	3	4	6	4.5	12.25
6946	13	0	14	6	4.5	11
6947	16	1	0	7	4	11.5
6948	16	3	14	6	4.5	12.75
6949	17	2	12	6.5	4.25	12.25
6950	15	3	21	7	4.5	11.5

	WEIGHT			LENGTH	DIAMETER	DIAMETER
No.	cwt	qr	lb	feet	of TRUNNION inch	at TRUNNION inch
6951	15	3	4	6	3.75	12.25
6952	16	1	25	6	4.5	12.25
6953 *	16	2	2	7	4.25	11.5

SUMMARY	No.	WEIGHT		
		tons	cwt	qr	lb
Cannon of VII	22	66	17	2	11
Culverins	26	56	15	3	20
Demi-culverins	42	46	9	2	16
TOTALS:	90	170	3	0	19

NOTES:

These were all iron pieces. None were tapered bored. None required venting. None were required to be cut at the muzzle.

Two demi-culverins are known to have survived:

$ Demi-culverin 6923 is in Barbados.
* Demi-culverin 6953 is in Chatham Dockyard Historical Society Museum.

After: A. B. Caruana, *The History of English Sea Ordnance 1523–1875 Vol. 1: The Age of Evolution 1523–1715*, 1994, pp. 118 & 126–7.

APPENDIX 38

Ground Tackle of the *Sovereign of the Seas*

	1640				1660			
ANCHORS	tons	cwt	qr	lb	tons	cwt	qr	lb
Sheet anchor	2	15			3	0		
First bower anchor	2	4			2	15		
Second bower anchor	2	0			2	14		
Third bower anchor	1	16			2	5		
					2	5		
Fourth bower anchor	1	3			2	4		
Anchor					2	3		
Stream anchor		16			1	4		
Kedge		8				8		
Kedge		4				5		
Long boat's anchor		1	2			3	2	
Barge's grapnel		1	2					
Pinnace grapnel		3				1		
Skiff's grapnel		2					3	
TOTALS:	12	0	1		19	8	1	
7 x 21 inch cables					31	10		
4 x 20 inch cables	16	0						
2 x 20 inch cables					8	0		
4 x 19 inch cables	16	0						
2 x 14 inch cables	4	1						
1 x 14 inch cable					2	0	2	
2 x 10 inch cables	2	1	2	8	2	1	2	8
2 x 9 inch cables	1	15	2	26	1	15	2	26
3 x 8.5 inch cables	1	13	2	23				
2 x 5 inch cables	1	0	3	4		11	2	24
TOTALS:	42	12	3	5	45	19	2	2

NOTES:

A cable is measured around its circumference.
A cable's length is 78 fathom, which is equal to 468 feet.

After: G. S. Laird Clowes (ed.), 'The Lengths of Masts & Yards, etc. 1640 (Containing also Sizes of Cables, Anchors, Standing Rigging, Boats and Sails) – From a Manuscript formerly at Petworth House & now in the Science Museum' *SNR* 1931, No. 3, pp. 17 & 19.
E. Hayward, *The Sizes and Lengths of Riggings*, 1967, pp. 31, 49 & 51.
G. Robinson, *Ships that Have Made History*, 1936, p. 99.
R. Willett, 'Memoir on British Naval Architecture' *Arch.* 11, 1794, p. 167.

APPENDIX 39

Weight of Stores and Equipment of the *Sovereign of the Seas* (1637)

ITEM	WEIGHT tons
Displacement tonnage, un-laden (draught in water of 19 feet 6 inches)	2,721
Ballast (removed when vessel was laden)	??
Guns x 102 (Appendix 29)	151.2
Gun carriages x 102	??
Shot, assorted	54
Powder, 200 kegs	10
12 anchors (Appendix 38)	12
19 cables (Appendix 38)	42.6
Rigging, sails, boats and stores	33
Full crew of 815 men (mean 140 lb/man)	50.9
Food, water and beer for 815 men for 180 days (mean consumption 3.8 lb/man/day)	249
TOTAL:	3,279
Displacement tonnage, laden (draught in water of 23 feet 6 in)	3,279

NOTE:
These values have been deduced by the author.

APPENDIX 40

Dimensions of Boats of the *Sovereign of the Seas*

BOAT	KEEL feet inch	BEAM feet inch	DEPTH feet inch	BURDEN	GROSS TONNAGE
Long boat	50 10	12 6	4 3	27.0	36.0
Pinnace	36 0	9 6	3 3	11.1	14.8
Skiff	27 0	7 0	3 0	5.67	7.56

NOTE:
The values of tons burden and tons and tonnage were verified using equations (1) & (2) in Chapter 4.

After: E. Keble Chatterton, *Sailing Ships*, 1909, p. 242.
G. S. Laird Clowes (ed.), 'The Lengths of Masts & Yards, etc. 1640 (Containing also Sizes of Cables, Anchors, Standing Rigging, Boats and Sails) – From a Manuscript formerly at Petworth House & now in the Science Museum' *SNR* 1931, No. 3, p. 30.
E. Hayward, *The Sizes and Lengths of Riggings*, 1967, p. 53.

APPENDIX 41

Mast and Spar Dimensions of the *Sovereign of the Seas*

MAST	1640 LENGTH feet inch	1640 MAX DIAM inch	1670 LENGTH feet inch	1670 MAX DIAM inch	1685 LENGTH feet inch	1685 MAX DIAM inch
Bowsprit	93 0	31	66 8	20.8	87 0	34
Spritsail topmast	27 0	8	22 6	7.0	27 0	8.5
Fore mast	95 6	32	87 0	27.2	97 6	34
Fore topmast	51 0	16	55 6	17.3	54 0	17.5
Fore topgallant mast	28 0	9	25 6	8.0	28 0	9
Fore royal mast	19 6	4	11 6	3.6	19 6	4.9
Mainmast	113 0	38	109 0	36.5	115 6	40.5
Main topmast	58 6	18	64 6	20.2	61 0	20.5
Main topgallant mast	31 6	10	28 0	8.8	37 6	10
Main royal mast	22 0	5	12 0	3.8	22 0	5.5
Mizen mast	87 6	29	79 0	24.7	100 6	32.5
Mizen topmast	39 0	12	33 0	10.3	39 0	11.5
Mizen topgallant mast	24 6	8	19 6	6.1	24 3	7.6

SPAR						
Spritsail yard	63 0	13.1	58 9	12.2	63 0	17.3
Spritsail topsail yard	30 0	6.3	26 5	5.5	30 0	7
Fore yard	86 0	21.5	89 0	18.5	56 0	21.5
Fore topsail yard	43 0	9	49 0	10.2	43 0	12
Fore topgallant yard	21 6	4.5	22 6	4.7	21 6	5.4
Fore royal yard	11 0	1.8	11 3	2.3	11 0	1.8
Main yard	113 6	28.4	100 6	20.9	102 0	33
Main topsail yard	51 9	10.8	55 10	11.6	55 6	15.3
Main topgallant yard	25 6	5.3	26 5	5.5	24 0	6
Main royal yard	11 0	1.8	13 2	2.7	11 0	1.8
Mizen yard	81 0	13.5	80 0	16.7	81 0	15
Mizen topsail yard	25 10.5	5.4	26 5	5.5	25 10.5	6.9
Mizen topgallant yard	13 9	2.8	13 2	2.7	13 9	3
Crossjack yard	51 9	10.8	52 9	11.0	42 9	8.5

After: G. S. Laird Clowes (ed.), 'The Lengths of Masts & Yards, etc. 1640 (Containing also Sizes of Cables, Anchors, Standing Rigging, Boats and Sails) – From a Manuscript formerly at Petworth House & now in the Science Museum, *SNR* 1931, No. 3, p. 9.
B. Lavery, *Deane's Doctrine of Naval Architecture 1670*, 1986, p. 82.
J. Lees, *The Masting and Rigging of English Ships of War 1625–1860*, 1984, pp. 192, 194.

APPENDIX 42

Standing Rigging of the *Sovereign of the Seas* (1640)

ROPE	FOREMAST			FORETOPMAST		
	No.	cir.	long	No.	cir.	long
Stay	1	15	17	1	5	17
Shrouds	18	8	234	10	4.5	75
Standing backstays	2	8	26	2	5	40
Laniard of the stay	1	5	12			
Laniard of shrouds	18	4	90	10	2	30
Laniard of standing backstays	2	4	10	2	2.5	12

ROPE	MAIN MAST			MAIN TOPMAST		
	No.	cir.	long	No.	cir.	long
Stay	1	17	25	1	8	20
Shrouds	20	8.5	280	12	5	108
Standing backstays	2	8.5	28	2	5	44
Collar of the stay	1	16	12			
Laniard of the stay	1	6	16	1	4	12
Laniard of shrouds	20	4.5	100	12	2.5	48
Laniard of standing backstays	2	4.5	10	2	3	14

ROPE	MIZEN MAST		
	No.	cir.	long
Stay	1	6	15
Shrouds	12	5.5	144
Laniard of the stay	1	3	6
Laniard of shrouds	12	3	48

NOTE:

cir. = circumference.

After: G. S. Laird Clowes (ed.), 'The Lengths of Masts & Yards, etc. 1640 (Containing also Sizes of Cables, Anchors, Standing Rigging, Boats and Sails) – From a Manuscript formerly at Petworth House & now in the Science Museum' SNR 1931, No. 3, p. 21.

APPENDIX 43

Standing Rigging of a First Rate from Hayward's List (1660)

ROPE	BOWSPRIT cir.	BOWSPRIT long	SPRITSAIL TOPMAST cir.	SPRITSAIL TOPMAST long
Gammoning	7.5	100		
Gammoning	6	30		
Horse	6	10		
Shrouds			3	28
Futtock shrouds			3	14
Pendants for tackles			3	3
Pendants for back stays			3	6
Pendants and falls of crane-lines			2.5	50
Falls for tackles			2	18
Falls for back stays			2	30
Laniards of shrouds			2	15

ROPE	FORE MAST cir.	FORE MAST long	FORE TOPMAST cir.	FORE TOPMAST long	FORE TOPGALLANT cir.	FORE TOPGALLANT long
Stay	15	17	5	17	2.75	30
Collar of the stay	10	5				
Shrouds	8	234	4.5	75	2.5	30
Standing back stays	8	26	5	40		
Futtock shrouds			5	60	3	20
Pendants of tackles	8	24	4.5	5	2.5	6
Runners of tackles	5.5	100				
Laniard of the stay	5	12	4	12	1.75	9
Laniards of back stays	4	10	2.5	12		
Pendant of the laniard			4	6		
Pendant of running back stays			4	12	2.5	8
Fall of the laniard			3.5	24		
Falls of running back stays			3	52	2	74
Laniards of shrouds	4	90	2	30	1.5	18
Falls of tackles	4	200	2.5	30	2	30
Legs of catharpins	2.5	16				
Falls of catharpins	2	18				

ROPE	MAINMAST cir.	MAINMAST long	MAIN TOPMAST cir.	MAIN TOPMAST long	MAIN TOPGALLANT cir.	MAIN TOPGALLANT long
Stay	17	25	8	20	3	20
Collar of the stay	16	12				
Shrouds	8.5	280	5	96	3	46
Pendants of tackles	8.5	40	5	12	3	8
Standing back stays	8.5	28	5	44		

Rope						
Runners of tackles	6	132				
Guy	6	18				
Laniard of the stay	6	16	4	12	2.5	6
Laniards of shrouds	4.5	100	2.5	42	1.75	24
Falls of tackles	4	260	2.5	70	2.5	32
Laniards of back stays	4.5	10	3	14		
Legs of catharpins	2.5	18				
Falls of catharpins	2	20				
Futtock shrouds			5	88	3.5	36
Pendant of running back stays			5	17	3	9
Pendant of the laniard			4	6		
Falls of running back stays			4	60	2	88
Fall of the laniard			3.5	24		

ROPE	MIZEN MAST		MIZEN TOPMAST	
	cir.	long	cir.	long
Stay	6	15	3	20
Collar of the stay		none		
Pendants of tackles	5.5	16	3.5	8
Futtock shrouds			3.5	30
Shrouds	5.5	144	3	55
Standing back stays			3	12
Runners of tackles	4	50		
Laniard of the stay	3.5	6		
Laniards of shrouds	3	48	2	25
Falls of tackles	3	80	2.5	36
Laniards of standing back stays			2.5	40
Pendant of the laniard				none
Fall of the laniard				none
Pendant of running back stays			2.5	15
Falls of running back stays			2	60

NOTE:

cir. = circumference.

It should be emphasised that this List does not include royals on the fore and main nor topgallant on the mizen.

After: E. Hayward, *The Sizes and Lengths of Riggings*, 1967, pp. 1–13.
B. Lavery, *Deane's Doctrine of Naval Architecture 1670*, 1986, pp. 101–3.

APPENDIX 44

Running Rigging of a First Rate from Hayward's List (1660)

ROPE	BOWSPRIT cir.	long	SPRITSAIL TOPMAST cir.	long
Tie	7	14	3	5
Pendants for sheets	6	24		
Slings for spritsail yard	6	6		
Halliards	4.5	40	2	15
Parrel ropes			2	6
Falls for sheets	4.5	60		
Lifts	4	60	2	30
Pendants for braces	4	6	2.5	4
Garnets	3.5	60		
Buntlines	3	60		
Clue-lines	3	50	2.5	36
Falls for braces	2.5	60	2	48
Laniards			2	15

ROPE	FORE MAST cir.	long	FORE TOPMAST cir.	long	FORE TOPGALLANT cir.	long
Tacks	8.5	60				
Runner of top rope			8	16		
Tie	8	26	6	10	3	6
Breast ropes	8	8				
Jeers	6.5	100				
Sheets	6	100	7	68		
Halliards	6	65	2	42		
Runner of the halliards			5.5	20		
Fall of top rope			5.5	50		
Parrel ropes	5	18	4	10	2	5
Bowlines	4.5	70	2.75	84	2	75
Bridles	4.5	18	2.5	14	2	75
Lifts	4	80	2.5	72	2	30
Falls of the halliards			4	66		
Pendants of braces	4	8	3	6	2	4
Clue-garnets	3.5	80				
Falls of braces	3	70	2.5	80	1.5	70
Runners of martnets	3	48				
Buntlines	3	150	3.5	40		
Falls of martnets	2.5	100				
Clue-lines			3.5	80	2	65
Top rope			3.5	36		

			MAIN		MAIN	
ROPE	MAINMAST		TOPMAST		TOPGALLANT	
	cir.	long	cir.	long	cir.	long
Tacks	9.5	60				
Tie	9	29	8.5	12	3	7
Jeers	8.5	100				
Pendant of the garnet	8.5	14.5				
Breast ropes	8	12				
Sheets	6.5	100	8	90		
Halliards	6.5	90	3	65		
Runner of the halliards			6	24		
Falls of the halliards			4	60		
Parrel ropes	6	35	4	12	2.5	8
Bowlines	5.5	80	4.5	80	2.5	80
Lifts	4.5	94	3.5	64	2.5	30
Bridles	4.5	24	4	22	2	12
Fall of the garnet	4.5	45				
Clue-garnets	4	90				
Pendants of braces	4	12	3	7	2.5	5
Buntlines	3.5	230	4	100		
Falls of braces	3	88	2.5	85	2	80
Falls of martnets	3	110				
Runners of martnets	2.5	110				
Runner of top rope			8.5	20		
Fall of top rope			6	65		
Clue-lines			4.5	100	2	80
Top rope					4.5	43
Flagstaff stay					2.5	25

ROPE	MIZEN MAST		MIZEN TOPMAST	
	cir.	long	cir.	long
Top rope			4	35
Tie	7	11	3	7
Jeers	5.5	42		
Parrel ropes	5.5	7	3	6
Halliards	5	50	2.5	36
Sheets	4	30		
Bowlines	4	20	2.5	50
Truss	3.5	40		
Lifts			2.5	38
Pendants of braces			2.5	4
Falls of braces			2	45
Bridles			2	12
Clue-lines			2	80
Tacks	3	15		
Brails	2.5	210		
Crossjack lifts	4	66		
Crossjack halliards	4	40		
Crossjack pendants	3.5	6		
Crossjack braces	2.5	60		

NOTE:

cir. = circumference.

It should be emphasised that this List does not include royals on the fore and main nor topgallant on the mizen.

After: E. Hayward, *The Sizes and Lengths of Riggings*, 1967, pp. 1–13.
B. Lavery, *Deane's Doctrine of Naval Architecture 1670*, 1986, pp. 101–3.

APPENDIX 45

Tackles of a First Rate from Hayward's List (1660)

TACKLE	SIZE cir.	long
Pendant of the winding tackle	12	12
Fall of the winding tackle	12	11
Viol cable	10	40
Stoppers at bitts	10	20
Boat rope and slings	9	60
4 buoy-ropes cable	8.5	100
Ordnance slings	8	7
Pendant of the fish hook rope	8	16
Woolding for the bowsprit	7.5	100
Stoppers at the bow	7.5	52
Shank-painters	7.5	48
Pendants of cat-ropes	7	36
Pinnace rope and slings	6.5	50
Passing rope	6	30
Woolding for the stem	6	30
Buoy rope for the stream anchor cable	5.5	16
Buoy rope for the kedge anchor cable	5.5	16
Stopper of the stream anchor	5.5	13
Shank-painter	5.5	12
Guest rope to boat rope	5.5	50
Falls of cat-ropes	5	90
Fall of the fish hook rope	5	35
2 pair of butt slings	5	10
Guest rope to pinnace rope	4.5	40
2 pair of hogshead slings	4	8
Laniards	4	20
Ratlines	1.8	1100
For robins, earings, and clue seizings	3	600
	2.5	260
For one complete suit of sails	2	300
	1.5	300

NOTE:
cir. = circumference

After: E. Hayward, *The Sizes and Lengths of Riggings*, 1967, p. 13.
B. Lavery, *Deane's Doctrine of Naval Architecture 1670*, 1986, p. 103.

APPENDIX 46

Sails of the *Sovereign of the Seas*

SAIL	CLOTHS	1640 DEPTH yards	TYPE OF CANVAS	1660 AREA square yards
Spritsail course	28 square	8.75	}Noyans canvas	308
Spritsail bonnet	28 square	2.5	}	
Spritsail topsail	20.5 square	13	Ipswich warped	192
Fore course	40 double	11.75	}Ipswich double	1230
Fore bonnet	40 double	3.125	}	
Fore topsail	28 square	16.5	Noyans canvas	482
Fore topgallant	14.5 square	9	Vittory	130
Fore royal	6			
Main course	49 double	13.75	}Ipswich double	1640
Main bonnet	49 double	3.75	}	
Main topsail	33 square	19	Noyans canvas	721
Main topgallant	17.5 square	10.25	Ipswich warped	180
Main royal	7			
Mizen course	14.5 square	18	}Noyans canvas	430
Mizen bonnet	32 square	2.5	}	
Mizen topsail	17.5 square	12.5	Ipswich warped	200
Mizen topgallant	7			
			Total area	5,513 sq yards

After; G. S. Laird Clowes (ed.), 'The Lengths of Masts & Yards, etc. 1640 (Containing also Sizes of Cables, Anchors, Standing Rigging, Boats and Sails) – From a Manuscript formerly at Petworth House & now in the Science Museum', *SNR* 1931, No. 3, p. 32.
E. Hayward, The Sizes and Lengths of Riggings, 1967, p. 55.

Bibliography

PRIMARY SOURCES (PAINTINGS, DRAWINGS AND MODELS)

J. Payne's engraving of the *Sovereign of the Seas* (1636)
W. Marshall's frontispiece in T. Heywood's *A True Description of His Majesty's Royall Ship, ...* (1637)
W. van de Velde the Elder's broadside drawing of the *Sovereign of the Seas* (1660)
Van de Veldes' *The Portrait of Peter Pett and the* Sovereign of the Seas (1660)
W. van de Velde the Elder's unfinished drawing of the *Sovereign of the Seas* (1661)
W. van de Velde the Younger's unfinished drawing of the *Sovereign of the Seas* (1675)
Reconstruction draught of the *Sovereign of the Seas* (c. 1800)
W. Edye's draught of the *Sovereign of the Seas* (1817)
Sir R. Seppings' draught of the *Sovereign of the Seas* (1827)
Sir R. Seppings' model of the *Sovereign of the Seas* (1827)
J. Fincham's draught of the *Sovereign of the Seas* (1851)
G. Robinson's draught of the *Sovereign of the Seas* (1936)
H. B. Culver's model of the *Sovereign of the Seas* (1921)
A. C. Jackson's model of the *Sovereign of the Seas* (1943)

PRIMARY SOURCES (STATE PAPERS)

F. H. Blackburne Daniell & F. Bickley, *Calendar of State Papers, Domestic Series, of Charles II 1660–73*.
J. Bruce, *Calendar of State Papers, Dom. Ser., of the reign of Charles I 1634–8, Preserved in the State Paper Department of HM Public Record Office*, 1864–9, 5 volumes.
M. A. E. Green, *Calendar of State Papers, Dom. Ser., Interregnum 1649–54*.
State Papers, Dom. Ser., 22 May 1637 357, 39 p. 142.
State Papers, Dom. Ser., 13 June 1637 361, 71.
State Papers, Dom. Ser., 242, pp. 64–5.
Public Record Office WO 47/3.
Public Record Office WO 49–78.
Public Record Office SRO D(W) 1778-V–1371.
ADM. 106/488/3 & 4.

ADM. 106/483//70.
ADM. 106/488/56.
ADM. 1/5256.

SECONDARY OR PRINTED SOURCES (ABBREVIATIONS)

Arch.	*Archaeologia*
Arch. Cant.	*Archaeologia Cantiana* – The Kent Archaeological Society
DNB	*Dictionary of National Biography*
MM	*The Mariner's Mirror – The International Journal of the Society for Nautical Research*
NRS	*Navy Records Society*
Neptune	*American Neptune, A Quarterly Journal of Maritime History*
SNR	*Society for Nautical Research, Occasional Publications*
SSM	*Ships and Ship Models*

SECONDARY OR PRINTED SOURCES (PUBLISHED BOOKS)

H. F. Abell, *Kent and the Great Civil War*, 1901.
R. G. Albion, 'The Timber Problem of the Royal Navy 1652–1862', *Maritime Miscellany Series*, 1952, No. 5.
R. C. Anderson, 'The *Royal Sovereign* of 1637', *MM* 3, 1913, No. 2, pp. 109–12; 3, 1913, No. 2 pp. 168–70; 3, 1913, No. 3, pp. 208–11.
R. C. Anderson, 'Seventeenth Century Rigging, Payne's Engraving', *MM* 3, 1913 No. 2 p. 152.
R. C. Anderson, 'The Bowsprit beside the Stem Head', *MM* 3, 1913, No. 3, p. 221.
R. C. Anderson, 'The *Prince Royal* and other Ships of James I', *MM* 3, 1913, No. 3, pp. 272–5; 3, 1913, No. 4, pp. 305–7; 3, 1913, No. 4, pp. 341–2.
R. C. Anderson, 'Castro's Painting of the *Sovereign*', *MM* 6, 1920, No. 4, p. 346.
R. C. Anderson, 'The *Prince Royal* of 1610', *MM* 6, 1920 No. 4, pp. 365–8.
R. C. Anderson, 'Naval Operations in the Latter Part of the Year 1666' in W. G. Perrin (ed.), 'The Naval Miscellany', *NRS* 63, 1928, Vol. 3.
R. C. Anderson, 'The Journal of Edward Montagu, First Earl of Sandwich, Admiral and General at Sea, 1659–1665', *NRS* 64, 1929.
R. C. Anderson, 'The Journals of Sir Thomas Allin, 1660–1666' *NRS* 79, 1939, Vol. 1, '1667–1678', *NRS* 80, 1940, Vol. 2.
R. C. Anderson, 'Journals and Narratives of the Third Dutch War' *NRS* 86, 1946.
R. C. Anderson, *Catalogue of Ship-Models (Scale-Models) National Maritime Museum*, 1952, p. 2.
R. C. Anderson, 'The Framing of Models', *MM* 39, 1953, No. 2, p. 139.
R. C. Anderson, 'The Framing of Models – and of Actual Ships', *MM* 40, 1954, No. 2, pp. 155–6.
R. C. Anderson, 'A Treatise on Rigging Written about the Year 1625, from a Manuscript formerly at Petworth House', *SNR* 1958, No. 6, pp. 46–64.
R. C. Anderson, 'The Story of the Woolwich Ship', *MM* 45, 1959, No. 2, pp. 94–9.
R. C. Anderson, 'List of English Men-of-War 1509–1649', *SNR* 1959, No. 7.
R. C. Anderson, 'English Ships 1649–1702, Lists of Men-of-War 1650–1700', *SNR* 1966, No. 5, Part 1.
R. C. Anderson, *The Rigging of Ships in the Days of the Spritsail Topmast 1600–1720*, 1984.
Romola & R. C. Anderson, *The Sailing Ship, Six Thousand Years of History*, 1980, Plate XVI.
E. H. H. Archibald, *The Wooden Fighting Ship in the Royal Navy AD 897–1860*, 1968.

Bibliography

E. H. H. Archibald, *Dictionary of Sea Painters*, 1980, p. 91.

E. H. H. Archibald, *The Fighting Ship in the Royal Navy AD 897–1984*, 1984.

C. T. Atkinson, 'Letters and Papers Relating to the First Dutch War 1652–1654' NRS 37, 1910, Vol. 4; 41, 1912 Vol. 5; 66, 1930 Vol. 6.

Capt. E. E. Eglinton-Bailey, 'Carved Work on Elizabethan Ships', SSM 1, 1932, No. 8, p. 249.

W. A. Baker, 'Early Seventeenth Century Ship Design', Neptune 14, 1954, No. 4, pp. 262–77.

W. A. Baker, 'More on the Framing of Models', MM 40, 1954, pp. 80–1.

P. Banbury, *Shipbuilders of the Thames and Medway*, 1971, p. 139.

E. S. de Beer (ed.), *The Diary of John Evelyn*, 1959, p. 358.

H. L. Blackmore, *The Armouries of the Tower of London Vol. 1: Ordnance*, 1976, pp. 64–6 & 409, Plates 17 & 74.

E. W. Blocksidge, *Hints on the Register Tonnage of Merchant Ships*, 1942.

Sir J. Borough, *Sovereignty of the Seas of England ...*, 1633.

F. C. Bowen, 'The Romance of the Figurehead', SSM 1, 1931, No. 1, pp. 9–12.

F. C. Bowen, *From Carrack to Clipper: A Book of Sailing-Ship Models*, 1948 p. 23, Plates 10 & 11.

E. Bradford, *The Story of the* Mary Rose, 1982.

H. Farnham Burke & O. Barton, 'The Builders of the Navy: a Genealogy of the Family of Pett', Ancestor 10, 1904, pp. 147–78.

Sir G. A. R. Callender, *The Portrait of Peter Pett and the* Sovereign of the Seas, 1930.

W. V. Cannenburg, 'The Van de Veldes' MM 36, 1950, No. 3, pp. 185–204.

W. Y. Carman, 'Odd Numbers for Gun Salutes', Jour. Soc. Army Historical Research 36, 1958, No. 1228, p. 40.

C. Carter, *Handbook and Guide to the Shipping Gallery in the Public Museums, Liverpool*, 1932.

A. B. Caruana, *The History of English Sea Ordnance 1523–1875, Vol. 1: 1523–1715, The Age of Evolution*, 1994.

R. F. Channon & J. Fisher, 'The portraits of Phineas Pett' MM 90, 2004, No. 2, pp. 234–6.

J. Charnock, *An History of Marine Architecture*, Vol. 2, 1801, pp. 281–7.

E. Keble Chatterton, *Sailing Ships – The Story of their Development from the Earliest Times to the Present Day*, 1909, pp. 229–30 & 242.

E. Keble Chatterton, *Ship-Models*, 1923, Plates 19, 20 & 21.

E. Keble Chatterton, *Sailing Models Ancient & Modern*, 1934, Figs. 29 & 30.

A. M. Clark, *Thomas Heywood, Playwright and Miscellanist*, 1931.

J. S. Clark, S. Jones & J. Jones, 'The *Sovereign of the Seas*', Naval Chronicle for 1807 17, 1807, pp. 308–9.

S. Clark, 'Kent welcomes back a King in 1660', Bygone Kent 13, 1992, No. 1, pp. 21–4.

G. S. Laird Clowes (ed.), 'The Lengths of Masts & Yards, etc. 1640 (Containing also Sizes of Cables, Anchors, Standing Rigging, Boats and Sails) – From a Manuscript formerly at Petworth House & now in the Science Museum', SNR 1931, No. 3.

G. S. Laird Clowes & E. W. White, *Catalogue of Exhibits with Descriptive Notes, Sailing Ships, Their History and Development, As Illustrated by the Collection of Ship Models in the Science Museum*, 1952, Part 2.

W. Laird Clowes, *The Royal Navy – A History from the Earliest Times to the Present* Vols. 1 & 2, 1996.

J. J. Colledge, *Ships of the Royal Navy – The Complete Record of all Fighting Ships of the Royal Navy*, 2003.

W. Congreve, *An Elementary Treatise on the Mounting of Naval Ordnance*, 1811.

J. Copland, *The Taking of Sheerness by the Dutch*, 1895.

J. D. Crawshaw, *The history of Chatham Dockyard*, 1999, 2 Volumes.

F. B. Crockett, *Early Sea Painters – 1660–1730 – The group who worked in England under the shadow of the Van de Veldes*, 1995.

S. Cronk, *St Margaret's Church, Horsmonden*, 1967.

F. Cull, 'Chatham Dockyard; Early Leases and Conveyances for its Building during the 16th and 17th Centuries', *Arch. Cant.* 73, 1959, pp. 75–96 & Fig 1.

F. Cull, 'Chatham, The Hill House 1567–1805', *Arch. Cant.* 77, 1962, pp. 95–110.

H. B. Culver, 'A Scale Model of the *Sovereign of the Seas* of 1637', *MM* 8, 1922, No. 4 pp. 367–72.

H. B. Culver, *Contemporary Scale Models of Vessels of the Seventeenth Century*, 1926, No. 4, pp. 49–50.

H. B. Culver & G. Grant, *The Book of Old Ships and Something of their Evolution and Romance*, 1936.

J. D. Davies, *Gentlemen and Tarpaulins – The Officers and Men of the Restoration Navy*, 1991.

J. Day, *Bristol Brass, A History of the Industry*, 1973.

Rev. S. Denne, 'Extracts from a MSS Entitled "The Life of Mr Phineas Pett, One of the Master Shipwrights to King James the First, Drawn up by Himself"', *Arch.* 12, 1796, pp. 217–96.

C. Derrick, *Memoirs of the Rise and Progress of the Royal Navy*, 1806, pp. 62–4.

N. Dews, 'Phineas Pett' in *The History of Deptford, in the Counties of Kent and Surrey*, 1884, pp. 217–20.

M. B. Donald, Elizabethan Copper, *The History of the Company of Mines Royal 1568–1605*, 1955.

P. Downton, *The Dutch Raid – Samuel Pepys' account of the Dutch raid on the Medway 1667*, 1998.

A. Dudszus & E. Henriot, *Dictionary of Ship Types*, 1986, p. 104.

F. E. Dyer, 'Captain John Narbrough and the Battle of Solebay', *MM* 15, 1929, No. 3, pp. 222–32.

S. Edwards, *Children of the Weald – A Fascinating Account of Kent Life in a Bygone Age*, 1997, pp. 129–53.

J. Ehrman, *The Navy in the War of William III*, 1953.

R. P. Evershed, K. Jerman & G. Eglinton, 'Pine wood origin for pitch from the *Mary Rose*', *Nature* 314, 1985, No. 6011, pp. 528–30.

P. Le Fevre, 'Arthur Herbert, Earl of Torrington 1648–1716', in P. Le Fevre & R. Harding (ed.), *Precursors of Nelson – British Admirals of the Eighteenth Century*, 2000, pp. 33, 36 & 40.

P. Le Fevre, 'Portraits of Phineas Pett', *MM* 89, 2003 No. 3 pp. 362–3.

W. Falconer, *An Universal Dictionary of the Marine*, 1780.

C. Ffoulkes, *The Gunfounders of England, with a List of English and Continental Gunfounders from the 14th to the 19th Centuries*, 1937.

J. Fincham, *A History of Naval Architecture*, 1851, p. 54 Plates 16, 16A.

F. Fox, *Great Ships – The Battlefleet of King Charles II*, 1980.

F. L. Fox, *A Distant Storm – The Four Days' Battle of 1666 – The Greatest Sea Fight of the Age of Sail*, 1996.

J. Franklin, *Navy Board Ship Models 1650–1750*, 1989.

A. Franzen, *The Warship* Vasa, *Deep Diving and Marine Archaeology in Stockholm*, 1961.

E. Fraser, *In the Fighting Days at Sea*, pp. 26–7.

S. R. Gardiner, 'Letters and Papers Relating to the First Dutch War 1652–1654', *NRS* 13, 1899, Vol. 1; 17, 1900, Vol. 2.

S. R. Gardiner & C. T. Atkinson, 'Letters and Papers Relating to the First Dutch War 1652–1654', *NRS* 30, 1906, Vol. 3.

W. A. Green, 'The Builders of the Navy', *Ancestor* 12, 1904, pp. 194–5.

J. G. G., 'The Building-Place of the *Victory*' *MM* 30, 1944, No. 3, p. 161.

H. Hamilton, *The English Brass and Copper Industries to 1800*, 1967.

C. H. Hancock, La Couronne, *A French Warship of the Seventeenth Century – A Survey of Ancient and Modern Accounts of This Ship*, 1973.

E. Harris, *Restoration House, or, Rochester in the Time of the Commonwealth*, 1904.

S. Hasell, 'Anglo-Saxon Kings Crowned at Kingston', in 'Anglo-Saxon Local Antiquities', *Gentleman's Magazine Library, Archaeology*, 1886, Part 2, pp. 203–4.

E. Hayward, *The Sizes and Lengths of Riggings*, 1967.
E. S. Hedges & W. R. Lewis, 'Bronze' in 'Tin' in *Thorpe's Dictionary of Applied Chemistry*, 11, 1954, pp. 609–29.
T. Heywood, *A True Description of His Majesty's Royall Ship, Built this Yeare 1637. at Wooll- witch in KENT. To the great glory of our English Nation, and not paraleld in the whole Christian World*, 1637.
T. Heywood, *A true Discription of His Majesties royall and most stately Ship called the Soveraign of the Seas, built at Wolwitch in Kent 1637. With the names of all the prime Officers in Her, who were appointed by his Majesty since the time of her launching at Wolwitch.*, 1638.
J. S. Hodgkinson, 'Gunfounding in the Weald', *Jour. of the Ordnance Society* 12, 2000, pp. 31–47.
O. F. G. Hogg, *Artillery – Its Origin, Heyday and Decline*, 1970, pp. 268–75.
Sir G. C. V. Holmes, *Wooden Sailing Ships, Part 1: Ancient and Modern Ships*, 1900, pp. 153–6.
F. Howard, *Sailing Ships of War 1400–1860*, 1987, p. 152.
R. Humble, *The Saxon Kings*, 1980.
B. Isherwood-Kay, *Catalogue of the National Portrait Gallery 1856–1947*, 1949.
H. A. James, *The Dutch in the Medway 1667*, 1967.
W. James, *The Naval History of Great Britain* Vol. 1, 1837.
T. Jenner & M. Simmons, *The Common-Wealths Great Ship Commonly called the Sovereign of the Seas, built in the yeare, 1637, etc.*, 1653.
A. W. Johns, 'The Stability of the Sailing Warship', *Engineer* 134, 1922, pp. 133–4.
A. W. Johns, 'Phineas Pett' *MM* 12, 1926, No. 4, pp. 431–42.
E. R. Johnson, *Measurement of Vessels for the Panama Canal*, 1913.
P. Kemp & R Ormond, *The Great Age of Sail – Maritime Art and Photography*, 1986, p. 34.
A. & H. Kriegstein, 'The Kriegstein Ship Model Collection', *Nautical Research Jour.* (USA) 27, 1981, No. 2, pp. 82–3.
B. Landström, *The Ship – A Survey of the History of the Ship from the Primitive Raft to the Nuclear-Powered Submarine with Reconstructions in Words and Pictures*, 1961, pp. 150–1.
R. & B. Larn, *Shipwreck Index of the British Isles*, 1995.
Sir J. K. Laughton, 'Peter Pett 1610–1670?' in *DNB* 15, 1950, pp. 989–90.
Sir J. K. Laughton, 'Phineas Pett 1570–1647' in *DNB* 15, 1950, pp. 990–2.
L. G. Carr Laughton, 'The Ship Models of Phineas Pett', *MM* 3, 1913, No. 4, pp. 308–9.
L. G. Carr Laughton, 'The Study of Ship Models' *MM* 11, 1925, No. 1, pp. 4–28.
L. G. Carr Laughton, *Old Ship Figureheads and Sterns*, 1925.
B. Lavery, *Deane's Doctrine of Naval Architecture 1670*, 1986.
B. Lavery, *The Arming and Fitting of English Ships of War 1600–1815*, 1987.
S. Lee, *Dictionary of National Biography* 44, 1895, p. 110.
J. Lees, *The Masting and Rigging of English Ships of War 1625–1860*, 1984.
J. Lyman, 'Register Tonnage and its Measurement', *Neptune* 5, 1945, No. 3, pp. 223–34.
J. Lyman, 'Tonnage, Weight and Measurement', *Neptune* 8, 1948, No. 2, pp. 99–113.
D. Lyon, *The Sailing Navy List – 1688–1860*, 1993, pp. 13 & 17.
P. MacDougall, 'Malaria: Its Influence on a north Kent Community' *Arch. Cant.* 95, 1980, pp. 255–64.
C. MacFarlane, *The Dutch in the Medway*, 1897.
D. Macintyre & B.W. Bathe, *The Man-of-War*, 1968.
L. Magalotti, *Travels of Cosimo III, Grand Duke of Tuscany, through England, during the reign of King Charles II 1669*, 1821.
S. F. Manning, 'New England Masts and the King's Broad Arrow', *Maritime Monographs and Reports*, 1979.
A. R. Mansir, *The Art of Ship Modelling*, 1982, pp. 80, 135, 138, 146, 148, 180, 187 & 238.
G. E. Manwaring, 'Naval Relics', *MM* 5, 1915, No. 3, p. 61.
G. E. Manwaring, 'An Unknown Painting of the *Sovereign of the Seas*', *MM* 6, 1920 No. 4,

pp. 290–2.

G. E. Manwaring, 'The Life and Works of Sir Henry Mainwaring', NRS 54, 1920.

G. E. Manwaring, 'The Seaman's Dictionary' in 'The Life and Works of Sir Henry Mainwaring', NRS 56, 1922, Vol. 2.

G. E. Manwaring (ed.), *Diary of Henry Teonge, Chaplain on Board HM's Ships,* Assistance, Bristol, Royal Oak *1675–1679*, 1927.

C. R. Markham, 'Life of Captain Stephen Martin 1666–1740', NRS 5, 1895, p. 185.

P. Marsden, *The Historic Shipwrecks of South-East England*, 1987, pp. 20–2.

P. Marsden, *Ships and Shipwrecks*, 1997, pp. 15–6, & 80–2.

L. C. Martin, 'John Crane (1576–1660) of Loughton, Bucks.' MM 70, 1984, No. 2 pp. 143–8.

O. Millar, *Sir Peter Lely (1618–80)*, 1978, pp. 43–4.

F. Moll, 'The History of Wood preserving in Shipbuilding', MM 12, 1926, No. 4, pp. 357–74.

G. Moorsom, 'On the New Tonnage-Law, as Established in the Merchant-Shipping Act of 1854', *Trans. Inst. Naval Architects* 1, 1860, pp. 128–44.

R. Morton Nance, 'Seventeenth Century Rigging', MM 3, 1913, No. 2, p. 151.

R. Morton Nance, 'The *St Louis* of Hondius', MM 4, 1914, No. 1, p. 52.

R. Morton Nance, 'Castro's Painting of the *Sovereign*', MM 6, 1920, No. 4, pp. 344–6.

R. Morton Nance, *Sailing-Ship Models – A Selection from European and American Collections with Introductory Text*, 1949, Plates 14, 15, 52 & 53.

R. Norton, *The Gunner, Showing the Whole Practice of Artillery*, 1628.

N. Nye, *A Treatise of Artificial Fire-Works for War and Recreation*, 1647.

B. Ohrelius, Vasa, *The King's Ship*, 1962.

B. H. St. J. O'Neil & S. Evans, 'Upnor Castle, Kent', *Arch. Cant.* 65, 1952, pp. 1–11.

B. H. St. J. O'Neil, *Castles and Cannon – A Study of Early Artillery Fortifications in England*, 1960.

M. Oppenheim, *A History of the Administration of the Royal Navy and of Merchant Shipping in Relation to the Navy*, Vol. 1, 1896.

M. Oppenheim, 'Naval Accounts and Inventories of the Reign of Henry VII', NRS 1, 1896, Vol. 8.

M. Oppenheim, 'The Naval Tracts of Sir William Monson in Six Books', NRS 23, 1902; 43, 1913; 45, 1913; 47, 1914.

G. Dyfnallt Owen, 'Report on the Manuscripts of the Right Hon. Viscount de L`Isle, VC., Preserved at Penshurst Place, Kent', 'Sydney Papers 1626–1698', *Historical Mss Commission* 6, 1966, No. 77.

S. Pepys, *Memoirs Relating to the State of the Royal Navy of England*, 1690.

C. S. Perceval, 'On a List (Dering's) of the Royal Navy in 1660', *Arch.* 48, 1885, pp. 167–84.

W. G. Perrin, 'The Autobiography of Phineas Pett', NRS 51, 1918.

B. Philp & D. Garrod, 'The Woolwich Ship', *Kent Archaeological Review* 1983 No. 74, pp. 87–91.

D. Piper, *Catalogue of Seventeenth-century Portraits in the National Portrait Gallery 1625–1714*, 1963, pp. 273–5.

O. Pipping, 'Whipstaff and Helmsman: An Account of the Steering-Gear of the *Vasa*', MM 86, 2000, No. 1, pp. 19–36.

J. R. Powell & E. K. Timings, 'Documents Relating to the Civil War 1642–1648', NRS 105, 1963, pp. 350–1.

J. Presnail, *Chatham – The Story of a Dockyard Town*, 1952.

Col. R. Preston, *The Seventeenth Century Marine Painters of the Netherlands*, 1974.

H. P. Richard, 'Discovery of Two Portraits of Phineas Pett', MM 89, 2003, No. 2, pp. 203–7.

H. P. Richard, 'The Portraits of Phineas Pett', MM 90, 2004, No. 4, pp. 477–8.

G. Robinson & R. C. Anderson, 'The Identification of Models of Men of War', MM 2, 1912, No. 2, pp. 142–6; 4, 1914 No. 1 pp. 69–72.

G. Robinson, *Ships that Have Made History*, 1936, pp. 99–101.

M. S. Robinson, *A Catalogue of Drawings in the National Maritime Museum made by the*

Elder and the Younger Willem Van de Velde, Vol. 1, 1958; 2, 1974.

M. S. Robinson, *A Catalogue of the Paintings of the Elder and the Younger Willem van de Velde*, 1990, Vols. 1–2.

G. Rogachev, 'Two coats of arms. The history of model from collection of Peter I' in *Maritime History – Scientific Historical Journal – Russia*, 1999, Issue 1, pp. 11–5.

P. G. Rogers, *The Dutch in the Medway*, 1970.

M. Rule, *The* Mary Rose, *the Excavation and Raising of Henry VIII's Flagship*, 1983.

W. B. Rye, 'Visits to Rochester and Chatham made by Royal, Noble and distinguished personages, English and Foreign, from the year 1300 to 1783', *Arch Cant* 6, 1865, pp. 43–82.

W. Salisbury, 'A Treatise on Shipbuilding written about 1620', *SNR* 1958, No. 6, pp. 1–45.

W. Salisbury, 'The Framing of Models', *MM* 40, 1954, No. 2, pp. 156–9.

W. Salisbury, 'The Woolwich Ship', *MM* 47, 1961, No. 2, pp. 81–90.

W. Salisbury, 'A Draught of a Jacobean Three Decker – The *Prince Royal*?' *MM* 47, 1961, No. 3, pp. 170–7.

A. D. Saunders, *Upnor Castle Kent*, 1990.

A. J. Scarth, *The Ship Models Collection of Merseyside Maritime Museum: A Concise Catalogue*, 1995, p. 88, No. 720.

J. H. Sephton, 'The *Sovereign of the Seas* A Unique English Warship of the Seventeenth Century', *Journal of Kent History* 1995, No. 40, p. 11.

J. H. Sephton, '*Sovereign of the Seas* An Epigram', *Shipwreck Heritage Association, Newsletter* 2000, No. 12, p. 6.

J. H. Sephton, 'The Shipbuilding Family of Pett', *Chatham Dockyard Historical Soc. Research Paper*, 2002, No. 24.

J. H. Sephton, 'Firepower at Woolwich', *Nautical Heritage Association – Newsletter*, 2002, No. 17, p. 5.

J. Smith, *A Sea Grammar*, 1627.

V. T. C. Smith, 'Cockham Wood Fort', *Arch. Cant.* 112, 1994, pp. 55–75.

A. T. Stewart, 'The *Prince Royal* of 1610–1666', *The Blue Peter* 1931, May, pp. 226–32.

E. Straker, *Wealden Iron*, 1969 pp. 159, 162–5 & 280–1.

W. Sutherland, *The Ship-Builders Assistant*, 1711, p. 87.

J. R. Tanner, 'A Descriptive Catalogue of The Naval Manuscripts in The Pepysian Library at Magdalene College, Cambridge', *NRS* 26, 1903 Vol. 1 pp. 89 & 266–7; 27, 1904 Vol. 2; 36, 1909 Vols. 3 & 57; 1923 Vol. 4.

Sir R. C. Temple, 'The Travels of Peter Mundy in Europe and Asia, 1608–1667', *Hakluyt Society* 45, 1925, pp. 35–6.

J. Topham, 'A Description of an ancient Picture in Windsor Castle', *Arch.* 6, 1782, pp. 179–210

J. Thorpe, *Registrum Roffense: or a Collection of Ancient Records, Charters, and Instruments of Divers Kinds, necessary for Illustrating the Ecclesiastical History and Antiquities of the Diocese and Cathedral Church of Rochester, together with Monumental Inscriptions*, 1769, p. 939.

T. Callender Wade, *Sir John Borough's 'The Sovereignty of the Seas of England'*, 1920.

F. Whyler, 'The Petts and Petts Wood', *Jour. North West Kent Family History Soc.* 1, 1979, No. 4, pp. 100–2.

R. Willett, 'Memoir on British Naval Architecture', *Arch.* 11, 1794, pp. 154–99

G. C. Williamson, 'John Payne' in *Bryan's Dictionary of Painters and Engravers* 4, 1926, pp. 82–3.

A. R. Young, *His Majesty's Royal Ship, A Critical Edition of Thomas Heywood's 'A True Description of His Majesty's Royal Ship'*, 1990.

Index

Aeolus 53, 55, 57, 61, 91 & 94–5
Allin, Joseph 182
Allin, Sir Thomas 153–4, & 156–7
Anchor 29, 41, 46, 55, 60, 65, 102, 105, 107, 150 & 154
Angel 29, 87, 93 & 96
area of cross section 83
Archimedes Principle 83
Arkinstall, Thomas 143 & 147
Arms 18, 25, 55, 61, 63, 68, 86–7, 93, 95, 99 & 177
Ayscue, Sir George 145 & 154–5
Aylesford 99

back stay; running 127
standing 121
barnacle 35 & 147
Battles; Kentish Knock (28/9/1652) 145–7
Four Day's Fight (1–4/6/1666) 153–5
St James's Day Fight (25/7/1666) 156–7
Dutch in the Medway (7/6/1667) 158–9
Solebay (28/5/1672) 165–7
First Battle of Schooneveld (28/5/1673) 168–9
Second Battle of Schooneveld (4/6/1673) 169
Texel Fight (11/8/1673) 170–1
Beachy Head (30/6/1690) 178–9
Barfleur (19/5/1692) 180–1
La Hogue (22–4/5/1692) 181
Beach, Sir Richard 167–168
beak 21, 28, 33, 141 & 148
beakhead 21, 23, 27, 36, 55, 58–9, 63–5, 86–8, 96, 103–4, 121, 125 & 141
beam; extreme 173
moulded 173
beech 34 & 37
Berkeley, Lord 150 & 183
Berkeley, Sir William 154
Bertie, Robert 17
bittacle 38
bitts 36 & 120
block 38, 122, 125, 127–130, 132–5 & 137
boatswain 22, 38, 44, 144, 147, 151, 153, 156, 172, 179 & 183–4
bolster 87 & 122
bonnet 130 & 132–3
bore 99, 100, 103 & 110
Borough, Sir John 39
Bourne, John 145–6
Bowline 130, 132–3 & 135
bowsprit 46, 58–9, 68, 87, 118, 120–2, 124–5, 127, 129, 132, 137
brace 130, 133–4 & 137
brass 97–8 & 105
breast-hook 33–4
breast-rope 129
Breda 148 & 158
breech loading 100
Brenchley 99
Bridle 132–3
Bristol 98
bronze 97
Browne; family 142
John 97–9, 104–5, 107 & 142
Bunt 130 & 135
Buntline 131 & 133–5

cable 29, 38, 41, 87, 89, 102, 105 & 107
cannon 21, 102, 105 & 111–2
canvas 118, 121, 127 & 130
capstan 68
careening 147
carpenter 19, 22, 28, 32, 38, 44, 141, 144, 150, 175 & 182–4
carvel 21, 24, 34–5 & 39
Castro, L. A. 50 & 56
Catharpin 127
cat-head 21, 46, 55, 63, 65 & 89
chain-wales 63, 89, 123–4 & 132
chalice 22 & 39
charcoal 98–9 & 109
Charles I 17–8, 24–8, 30, 32, 34, 36–9, 41, 43, 45–6, 71, 85–7, 92, 95–6, 99–100, 104–5, 107, 109, 135, 139–40, 141 & 176
Charles II 56, 61, 97–8, 148, 164–5, 169–70, 172 & 176
Chase 96, 100 & 102–5
Chatham 18–9, 22–5, 28, 32, 36–7, 42, 44, 51, 54–5, 60, 88, 105, 113, 121, 138–142, 143–4, 147–9, 150–2, 156, 158–9, 160, 163–4, 166–7, 171–5, 177, 179, 182–4 & 186
Chatham Chest 41, 177,139, 177 & 184
Cheek 122, 129 & 138
Chilworth 109
Christening 22
Christmas; Gerard 37 & 148
John 37 & 88
Matthias 37, 88, 148 & 175
Clinker 39

Index

Clue 132–3 & 135
clue garnet 132–3 & 135
Cockham Wood 160
coefficient of fineness 82–3
collar 125 & 135
comb 132
Company of Mines Royal 98
Cooke, William 41 & 148
Coolidge, J. Templeman 56
Core 64, 99 & 109
Cosimo III 160
Cost 21, 23, 26, 31–2, 41–2, 63, 85, 99, 105, 107, 111, 130, 137–8, 139, 143, 160 & 171–2
Couch, Thomas 183
counter 38, 94 & 96
Cox, Capt. John 151, 153, 155–9 & 164–6
Crane, John 41
crane-line 46–7
de Critz, John 23 & 25
Cromwell, Oliver 146 & 148
cross-tree 122–3 & 133–4
crowsfeet 47 & 137
culverin 17, 21, 103, 105, 111, 113 & 160
cupid 53, 87 & 93
Cuttance, Capt. Roger 150
cutts 100
cypher 98–9 & 104–107

dead-eye 120, 123–7, 129 & 132–3
dead-flat 71
deal 28 & 34
Deane, Sir Anthony 111, 121, 136–7, 160 & 174
deck; forecastle 21, 27–8, 35–6, 89 & 104
   half 21, 27, 35, 43, 104 & 141
   lower gun-deck 21, 27–8, 30, 35–6, 73, 81–2, 100–2, 105, 144 & 147
   main (middle) gun-deck 27, 35, 38 & 101–3
   orlop 27
   poop 22 & 28–9
   quarter 21, 27, 36 & 86
   spar 21, 27, 46, 104 & 141
   upper gun-deck 28, 35, 94, 101 & 103–4
Delaval, Sir Ralph 176, 178–9 & 180
demi-cannon 21, 102, 105, 107 & 111
demi-culverin 17, 21, 103–5, 111–3, 144 & 160
Deptford 18–20, 22–5, 28, 32, 50, 71, 107, 119, 141, 147, 150, 159, 172, 174, 179, 182 & 184–5
depth in hold 71, 73, 77, 81 & 84

d' Estrées, Count 171 & 178
Dirkin 141
Displacement 82–4
Dock 18, 21–4, 32–3, 35, 38–40, 42, 51–3, 55, 93, 101, 103–4, 138, 140, 147–8, 150–1, 163, 167, 172 & 185–6
drake 100
draught in water 83–4
Dufnall 86
Durkin, Richard 37

Eadwig 85
Earing 132
Edgar, King 85
Edmund, King 85
Edye, William 61–5, 68, 81, 86–8, 91–3, 95, 120–1 & 125
Elm 33–34
England, New 136
entry port 21, 46, 55, 57–9, 61, 92–3, 103, 173–4 & 183
Everden, Thomas 183
Evelyn, John 86 & 152
falcon 112
farthel 46, 65 & 135
Faversham 109
Figurehead 21, 29, 45, 58–9, 61, 63, 81, 85–7, 94, 124, 148 & 173
Fincham, John 63
Flags 23, 44, 47–8, 54, 58, 60, 65, 92, 135, 143, 148, 152, 157–8, 164–6, 169, 170–1, 176–8, & 180–2
flagstaff 36
Fletcher, Thomas 148 & 175
Forecastle 21, 24, 27–8, 35–6, 39, 56, 58, 63, 65, 89, 91, 100, 104, 107, 112, 132–3 & 141
forefoot 33 & 72
fore-stay 125, 127, 129–30, 132 & 134
fortified 103–4, 105 & 113
frontispiece 46, 53, 55, 61–4, 68 & 94–6
Furzer, Daniel 177
futtock rib 32–3
futtock-shroud 126–7

gammoning 121
garnet 130, 132–3 & 135
Gibbons, Col. 148
Gillingham 148, 158 & 160
Greenwich 18, 24, 32, 37, 39, 41, 63, 105 & 140
Gregory, Sir Edward 183
Grenville, Sir Richard 27
Griffith 86
gun-carriage 27, 65, 99, 107, 109, 113, 117, 144, 160 & 176

gunner 22, 43–4, 102, 105, 111, 116–7, 141, 144, 146–7, 150, 156–7, 160 & 183
gunpowder 109 & 160
gunwale 29, 45, 55, 123, 129, 130 & 132
guy 135

Haddock, Sir Richard 169
Halliard 129, 133–4 & 137
Hampton Court 23, 28 & 39
Harman, Sir John 154 & 165–6
harping rule 79, 81 & 82
Hartnell, Joseph 176
Hastings 179
Hawse 63, 87, 102, 167 & 173
Hawthorne, Edward 141
Hayward, E. 150
Hayward, Capt. John 167
Heart 125
height – ports above water 30–1
hemp 121 & 138
Hercules 29, 53 & 94–5
Heywood, Thomas 36–7, 45–7, 50, 61, 63–4, 68, 77, 86–8, 91, 94–6 & 139
Hondius, Henry 48 & 50
Hooper, William Harvey 56
horse 137
Horsmonden 98–9
hounds 120, 122 & 136
House; Athlone Castle 105
   Banqueting 141
   Block 149
   Chatham 18–9 & 24
   Commissioner's 138
   Commons 150
   Deptford 18
   Dublin 105
   Grand Store 98
   Harwich 18
   Hill 18–9, 149, 150–1 & 160
   Lords 159
   Mansion 55
   mast 118–9
   Master Gunner`s 105
   Petworth 50 & 64
   President`s 56
   Queen`s 18, 37, 50–1 & 63
   Restoration 149
   Round 36, 45, 65 & 141
   Somerset 63
   Trinity 24, 30, 39, 55–6, 71, 77, 143, 148 & 153
Howard, Charles Edward 19 & 20
Huval 86

Jackson, A. C. 68
Jacob 86
James I 20–4 & 73

James II 138, 150, 153, 164, 169, 174–5, 176, 179 & 184
Jason 53, 55, 57, 61 & 94–5
Jeer 129 & 137
Jenner, Thomas 50
Jordan, Sir Joseph 164 & 166
Judithil 86
Jupiter 61 & 91

Keel 21–2, 23–4, 27, 31–6, 38–40, 64, 71–4, 77, 79, 81–2, 84, 119–20, 128, 130, 138, 140–1, 172–4 & 184
kevel 36 & 132
knights 36, 126 & 129
Kriegstein 67
Kynadus 86

Ladle 116
Laniard 53, 123, 125–6 & 167
Lantern 21, 29, 36, 46, 55, 58, 93, 95, 150 & 177
launch 18–20, 22–5, 28–9, 34–5, 38, 42, 45, 47, 57, 60, 77, 81, 85, 88, 102, 138–40, 150–1, 167–8, 172–3 & 185
Lee, Robert 172, 174, 177 & 184
Lely, Sir Peter 51 & 53
length between perpendiculars 72, 79, 82 & 83
lift 130, 133–5 & 137
lion 47, 56 & 59

Mainwaring, Sir Henry 119 & 128
Malcolm 86
Mansell, Sir Robert 39
Manwaring, G. E. 50
Maria, Henrietta 24, 37–8, 43, 87 & 91
Mars 61
Marshall, William 45–6
martnets 133–4
mast; bonaventure 21, 41 & 46
 fore 22, 29, 35–6, 47, 58–9, 60, 118, 120–1, 123–4 & 138
 fore topmast 125
 fore topgallant 127
 fore royal 127
 mainmast 17, 29, 36, 47, 51, 53, 58–9, 118–9, 120–1, 123–4 & 136–8
 main topmast 125
 main topgallant 127
 main royal 127
 mizen 29, 35, 41, 47, 53, 58–9, 120 & 123–4
 mizen topmast 125
 mizen topgallant 127
 spritsail topmast 47, 58, 125 & 127

step 34, 40 & 120
Meacham, John 183
model by; Clyde Chaffin 68
 H. B. Culver 63–7
 John Dupray 68
 V. H. Green 67
 A. C. Jackson 68
 Mantua Model 68
 Navy Board 61, 86, 88, 93, 95 & 104
 Peter Pett 28
 Theodore Pugh 68
 Sir Robert Seppings 62–3
 Sergal 68
Monck, George, First Duke of Albemarle 147–8 & 153
Monson, Sir William 25, 119 & 128
Montagu, Sir Edward 148, 153 & 164
Morgan, Junius S. (jnr.) 55
Mundy, Peter 86
Museums & Galleries: Central Naval Museum, Saint Petersburg, Russia 81, 86, 88, 95 & 173
 Chatham Dockyard Historical Society Museum 36–7, 105 & 113
 Franz Hals Museum, Haarlem 23
 Maidstone Museum & Art Gallery 110
 Merseyside Maritime Museum, Liverpool 23, 93, 104 & 174
 Musee Naval, Palais du Louvre, Paris 30
 Museum of Fine Arts Museum, Boston, Mass., USA 56
 National Maritime, Greenwich 22–3, 25, 36, 41, 50–1, 53–5, 58–9, 60–1, 63, 81, 93, 102, 136, 150 & 173
 National Portrait Gallery, London 23, 25 & 53–4
 Naval Academy Museum, Annapolis, Maryland, USA 67 & 173
 Parham Park, Storrington 50
 Royal Armouries Museum, Leeds 97 & 107
 Royal Artillery Museum, Woolwich 105
 Royal Canterbury Museum & Art Gallery 57
 Science Museum, London 41, 50, 61, 68 & 93
 Shipwreck & Coastal Heritage Centre, Hastings 185
 Vasamuseet, Stockholm 185
 Weald & Downland Open Air

Museum, Chichester 32
 'Wooden Walls' Chatham Historic Dockyard 32 & 37

Narbrough, Sir John 164–6, 169–70 & 174
Navy Board 39, 61, 81, 86, 88, 93, 95, 104, 112–3, 150, 171–4, 177 & 184
Neptune 55, 57, 91 & 94
Neville, John 177
Newberry, Mr 147

Parrel 129 & 133–4
Partners 120, 125 & 136
pay 20, 26, 42, 85, 99, 143–4, 150, 160 & 183–4
Payne, John 45–8, 50, 55–7, 62–5, 68, 86–8, 91–3, 95, 100, 102–3, 120–2, 124, 127, 129, 130, 132–5, 137 & 140
Penn, William 145
Penn, Sir William 150 & 152
Penshurst Place 45
Pepys, Samuel 138, 148, 150–3, 170–2, 174 & 177
Petro 112
Pett; Christopher 50
 Peter 18–9, 23–5, 28, 32, 34, 38–9, 42, 44–8, 51, 53–6, 61, 63–4, 68, 101, 122, 128, 130, 134–5, 139–43, 147, 149–52 & 158–9
 Phineas 17–26, 27–46, 50, 64, 68, 71, 74, 100, 122, 139–40, 151 & 186
 Sir Phineas 88, 138, 151 & 173–4
 pinnace 17, 19, 23–4, 34 & 41
 pitch 35, 37 & 39
Pitt, Thomas 104
Plymouth 145 & 179
Poop 22, 28–9, 36, 46, 55, 58, 95, 112, 130, 141 & 166
Portsmouth 39
Poulden, Mary 183
powder 109 & 160
powder charge 146
Prince of Wales 19, 21–3, 85–7, 93, 95 & 98
Pump 36

Quaker 152

Rabinett, Thomas 38, 44, 144 & 147
rake; masts 120
stem post 27, 33 & 77
sternpost 27, 33 & 77
ratline 65, 125 & 127
reconstruction draught 60, 63, 68, 81, 93, 95, 100 & 102–4

Index

Reed, Capt. Nicholas 144–5
Reeves, Sir William 169 & 171
rigging; standing 121–8
running 128–35
Robinson, Gregory 68
Rochelle 17
Rochester 18, 140, 147 & 160
Rogers, Col. H. H. 173
Rooke, Sir George 177, 180–1 & 185
rope 37, 41, 55, 99, 113–4, 116–7, 120–1, 123, 125, 127–9, 132 & 137
Royal Naval Hospital 56
Rudder 38, 96 & 138
Rupert, Prince 165, 168–9 & 170–1
de Ruyter, Michiel Adriaenszoom 145–6, 154–8, 164–9 & 170–1

sail; fore course 132
   fore topgallant 127 & 134
   fore topsail 133–4
   main royal 133
   main topgallant 134
   main topsail 128, 133–4 & 137
   mizen topgallant 127, 133, 135 & 137
   mizen topsail 128, 133–4 & 137
   spritsail topsail 128, 130, 134–5 & 137
Sailmaker, Isaac 51, 53 & 55–6
Saint; Dunstan 85
   John 85
Saker 112
Saltpetre 109
Sanders, Humphrey 176
Sandwich, First Earl 148, 153 & 164–6
Seale, Richard 183
Seppings, Sir Robert 61–5, 68, 81, 86–8, 91–3, 95, 100, 120–1 & 124
Serpentine 100, 110 & 116
Sheerness 160
Sheets 132–3 & 135
ships; *Adventure* (1646) 44 & 74
   Anne Royal 43–4
   Anne 179–80 & 185
   Answer (1603/4) 19
   Antelope 144–5 & 157
   Ark (Anne) Royal 20
   Barbabella 169
   Bear (1618) 119 & 128
   Bendish 153
   Bonaventure 44
   Brederode 145
   Britannia (1682) 88, 173, 180–1 & 183
   Charles 17, 24, 166, 168–9, & 170
   Cleveland 170
   Constant Warwick (1644/6) 140
   Convertine (1616) 24
   Coronation (1685) 155 & 178
   Defiance (1613/5) 23 & 156
   Destiny (1616) 24
   Diamond 153 & 168
   Discovery 23
   Disdain (1604) 19
   Drake 147
   Duke 180 & 182
   Edgar 170
   Fairfax 155 & 157
   Fellowship 140–1
   Foresight 111
   Fubbs 177
   Garland 44 & 155
   George 104, 164 & 171
   Golden Hind 168
   Grafton 182
   Greyhound (1636) 34 & 38
   Henri Grace a Dieu (1512/4) 73 & 100
   Henrietta (1626/7) 24 & 144
   Henrietta Maria (1632/3) 17 & 24
   Henry 154
   James (1633/4) 17, 143, 145–8 & 153
   Kent 179
   Kitchen 170
   La Couronne (1635) 28–48, 50, 74 & 119
   Laurel 111
   Leopard (1634/5) 17 & 164
   Lion 145, 155, 157 & 178
   Little President 145
   London 145, 151, 158, 166, 169, 172 & 181
   Maria (1626/7) 24
   Marston Moor 147
   Martin 147
   Mary Rose (1509/10) 21, 30, 73, 100 & 185
   Mercury (1626) 24
   Merhonour (1613/5) 23
   Merlin 147
   Montagu 158
   Moon (1602) 19
   Naseby (1655) 111 & 148
   Neptune (1683) 93, 104 & 180
   Nonsuch (1646) 147
   Ossory 180
   Phoenix 23
   Philip 27
   Prince Royal (1610) 21–5, 36, 40–1, 43, 73–4, 86, 89, 93, 102, 120, 123, 125 139, 141, 147, 152 & 154–5
   Providence (1636/7)
   Rainbow (1586) 18
   Renown 145
   Repulse (1596) 19
   Resistance (1604) 20
   Resolution 23, 111, 129, 143, 145–6, 151 & 156–7
   Revenge (1577) 18 & 27
   Roebuck (1636) 34
   Royal Charles 102, 148, 154–8 & 171
   Royal James 155–8, 164–7 & 173
   Royal Katherine 153 & 155–6
   Royal Oak 156–8
   Royal Prince (1670) 61, 88, 121, 163, 165–6, 169, 171 & 175
   Royal Sovereign (1701) 81, 86, 88, 95, 173 & 184
   Royal William (1719) 102 & 180
   Sandwich 182
   Sovereign (1488) 39–40
   Spy (1626) 24
   Squirrel 183
   St Andrew 23, 41, 44, 146–7, 166, 168–70 & 182–3
   St George 156 & 173–4
   St Michael 61, 93, 166–7 & 182–3
   Sun (1586) 23
   Suffolk 182
   Swallow (1634) 17
   Swiftsure 23, 111 & 147
   Triumph 19, 155 & 157
   Unicorn (1633/4) 17
   Vanguard 143
   Vasa (1627/8) 31, 35–6, 38, 61, 89, 94, 100 & 185
   Victory 20, 167–8 & 180–1
   Victory (1765) 28 & 186
   Warspite 178
   Whelps (1627/8) 17
   White Bear (1598/9) 92
   Zeven Provincien 154 & 156–7
Shortis, Robert 177
Shot 28, 43, 86, 96–7, 99, 100, 102–4, 107, 109, 110–2, 116, 140, 142, 144, 146 & 151
Shrouds 29, 46, 48, 50, 53, 65, 121, 123–7, 129–30 & 132–5
Simmons, Matthew 50
Skelton, Francis 37
slings 129
Smith, J. 64
sponge 114
stay; collar 47 & 125
   Fore 125, 127, 129, 130, 132 & 134
   Main 88, 125, 133 & 135
   Mizen 125
steeving 46 & 121
stem 27, 33, 64, 73, 77, 120 & 172
steps of the side 57–8 & 93
stern-post 27, 33, 35, 38, 64, 72–3, 77, 83, 120 & 172

Steventon, Mr 183
Stockholm 31, 37, 41, 121 & 185
Stokes Bay 147
Strakes 34–5, 62, 82, 87 & 102
Sulphur 35 & 109
Swabber 44

tackle; 22, 26, 30, 38–9, 40–1, 53, 74, 104, 117, 121, 125, 127, 129 130, 136 & 147
  bowline 130
  breeching 113 & 117
  burton 122–3, 125 & 127
  cat 46 & 89
  jeers 129
  relieving 38
  train 113
  truss 130
  winding 135
tacks 50, 65 & 132–3
tar 35, 37, 41, 121, 128 & 138
Teddiman, Sir Thomas 156–7
Teredo navalis 35
Thompson, William 142
Tie 54, 129–30, 133–5 & 137
Tiller 38
tonnage; displacement 82–4
  register 73
  Thames Yacht 83–4
tons and tonnage 73–4
tons burden 73
top 122, 126–7, 130, 133–5 & 137
top rope 127
Torrington, Earl 176–9

Touch 72
Tourville, Comte de 177–9 & 180–1
Tower of London 39, 98–9, 105 & 107
Transom 35, 45–6, 94, 114 & 117
Tread 72
treenail 32, 34–5 & 39
trestle-tree 122, 125, 127, 129 & 133–4
Tromp, Cornelis 154–7 & 168–71
Tromp, Maarten 143 & 145
Truss 129–30
tuck 21, 35, 46, 52, 55, 57–8, 62, 64 & 68
Tudor portcullis 87
tumblehome 28 & 55
Tuscany, Grand Duke 160
Tyrrell, Capt. John 179

Unicorn 86, 93 & 95–6
Upnor 22, 110, 139–40, 149–50, 153, 158–9 & 160

Velde, van de; Adriaen 60
  Willem, the Elder 51, 53–5, 57, 59–61, 64, 68, 88, 93, 100–2, 120–1, 124–5, 127, 150, 170, 174 & 182
  Willem, the Younger 51, 58, 86 & 182
Victory 53, 55, 88 & 94–5
Vincent, Francis 109

Wales 29, 31, 35, 46, 57–8, 63, 65, 73–4, 82, 89, 92, 119, 123–4, 132, 147 & 172
Wetwang, Sir John 169 & 171
Wharf 19, 40 & 98–9
Whitehall 28, 36, 38 & 141
Wigram, C. H. 55
Windage 110–1
windlass 36, 41 & 167
window 18, 34, 36, 55, 65, 91, 93, 95–6, 141 & 149
de Witt, Cornelis 145–6
woolding 58–9 & 120
Woolwich 17, 19–21, 23–4, 32, 34, 36, 38–40, 42, 48, 50, 81, 98, 105, 107, 139, 174, 176, 182 & 184–5

yard; crossjack 129, 133 & 137
fore royal 137
main royal 137
main topgallant 128
main topsail 137
main 128, 134 & 137
mizen topgallant 137
mizen 129–130, 133 & 138
spritsail 129–30
spritsail topsail 134
Young, Anthony 169–70

Zodiac 89 & 91